Automotive Software Engineering

Principles, Processes, Methods, and Tools

Other SAE titles of interest:

Vehicle Multiplex Communication:
Serial Data Networking Applied to Vehicular Engineering
By Christopher A. Lupini
(Order No. R-340)

Finite Element Analysis for Design Engineers
By Paul M. Kurowski
(Order No. R-349)

Automobile Electrical and Electronic Systems, Third Edition
By Thomas H. Denton
(Order No. R-363)

Electronic Control Systems
By Ross Bannatyne
(Order No. T-107)

For more information or to order a book, contact SAE at
400 Commonwealth Drive, Warrendale, PA 15096-0001;
phone (724) 776-4970; fax (724) 776-0790;
e-mail CustomerService@sae.org;
website http://store.sae.org.

AUTOMOTIVE SOFTWARE ENGINEERING

PRINCIPLES, PROCESSES, METHODS, AND TOOLS

Jörg Schäuffele
Thomas Zurawka

Translated by Roger Carey

Warrendale, Pa.

For permission and licensing requests, contact:
SAE Permissions
400 Commonwealth Drive
Warrendale, PA 15096-0001 USA
E-mail: permissions@sae.org
Tel: 724-772-4028
Fax: 724-772-4891

Library of Congress Cataloging-in-Publication Data

Schäuffele, Jörg.
    [Automotive software engineering. English]
    Automotive software engineering: principles, processes, methods, and tools / Jörg Schäuffele, Thomas Zurawka ; translated by Roger Carey.
      p. cm.
    Translation from the German language ed.
    Includes bibliographical references and index.
    ISBN 0-7680-1490-5
    1. Automotive computers. 2. Software engineering. I. Zurawka, Thomas.
II. Title.

TL272.53.S33 2005
629.2'7--dc22   2005045902

Translated from the German language edition:
Automotive Software Engineering: Grundlagen, Prozesse, Methoden und Werkzeuge
by Jörg Schäuffele and Thomas Zurawka
Copyright © Friedr. Vieweg & Sohn Verlag/GWV Fachverlage GmbH, Wiesbaden, Germany, 2003
ISBN 3-528-01040-1

SAE International
400 Commonwealth Drive
Warrendale, PA 15096-0001 USA
E-mail: CustomerService@sae.org
Tel: 877-606-7323 (inside USA and Canada)
       724-776-4970 (outside USA)
Fax: 724-776-1615

THE ROLE OF SOFTWARE
IN THE AUTOMOBILE

Managing complexity is possible only through new approaches to development.

No other technology offers developers as high a degree of design freedom as software technology does. The almost exponential growth of software in the vehicle is driven by an increase in vehicle functions and networks of functions, stringent reliability and safety requirements, as well as an increasing number of vehicle variants. Managing the resulting complexity poses a great challenge to both vehicle manufacturers and their suppliers: They must reduce software complexity to a minimum by using methodology in development that ensures the safe functioning of software and systems. This book proffers a host of ideas for the design of development processes and for the effective application of methods and tools.

Dr. Siegfried Dais, Deputy Chairman, Board of Management, Robert Bosch GmbH, Stuttgart, Germany

Software in the vehicle is becoming a strategic product.

For vehicle manufacturers, software in the vehicle is evolving into a product of increased strategic value. Electronics and software in the vehicle have become an essential impetus for innovation—about 90% of innovations in the vehicle today are driven by electronics. On the one hand, more and more of the classic vehicle functions are being realized by means of software; on the other hand, entirely new opportunities are created by networking functions that formerly used to be independent of each other. Consistent application of systems engineering methods is a crucial factor for success in managing the vehicle as a complete system. This book addresses this extensive topic with special emphasis on the major vehicle subsystems of powertrain, chassis, and body.

Hans-Georg Frischkorn, Senior Vice President System Architecture and Integration, BMW Group, Munich, Germany

From cost driver to competitive advantage.

Only a pioneer in software technology will gain technological advantage in the automotive industry. Successful cooperation between engineers from various disciplines in systems engineering, however, will be possible only if everyone shares the same background knowledge, the same terminology, and an appropriate process model. This book uses real-life examples in an impressive demonstration of software engineering essentials and applicable methods.

Dr.-Ing. Wolfgang Runge, Member, Board of Management, ZF Lenksysteme GmbH, Schwäbisch Gmünd, Germany

Embedded systems are an automotive asset.

Embedded computer systems provide opportunities to distinguish transportation products and services in the increasingly competitive automotive business. To interpret Moore's Law, electronics continue to become more powerful while prices keep dropping. The resulting systems complexity can be managed only with an in-depth understanding of the principles, practices, methods, and tools discussed in this essential text.

I applaud Dr. Zurawka and Mr. Schäuffele of ETAS GmbH on their comprehensive work on very important topics. This material must be understood by any organization wishing to participate in the automotive business. As we continue to evolve our engineering processes, I look forward to more assistance from the leaders in this field.

Craig A. Brown, GM Powertrain Engineering, General Motors Corp., Detroit, MI

Advanced education—an opportunity and a challenge.

In the greater Stuttgart area, vehicle manufacturing is the preeminent industry, with development centers of major vehicle manufacturers and suppliers offering a great many job opportunities. At the University of Stuttgart, courses in software technology are part and parcel of the engineering program. This book offers students who are pursuing an academic degree in engineering the opportunity to familiarize themselves with practical automotive industry applications. In fact, the methods introduced in this book may even serve as models for applications in other industries.

Prof. Dr.-Ing. Dr. h.c. Peter Göhner, Institute for Automation and Software Technology, University of Stuttgart, Germany

Vehicle development needs perspective based on integrated model.

As a natural consequence of ongoing advances in vehicle development, customer expectations must be satisfied while ensuring compliance with government regulations. Increasingly, these and related areas are the special domain of automotive electronic systems.

In fact, most of the competitive advantage in vehicles today tends to lie in the electronic content of the vehicle, the software component being a major part of these systems. The safe, reliable, cost effective, and rapid development of automotive software-based systems are major issues for vehicle and component manufacturers. Authors Schäuffele and Zurawka address the complex issues of automotive electronic systems development from a perspective based on an integrated model, offering students a paradigm for an integrated systems solution to vehicle embedded software engineering. The book will serve as a foundation for integrated vehicle software development practices as this technology continues to emerge and expand.

Prof. Mark Thompson, Electrical and Computer Engineering, Kettering University, Flint, MI

A new system science is needed.

As hardware development costs and manufacturing fixed costs have been increasing dramatically and as product requirements change faster and faster over a short period of time, embedded system, subsystem and even IC designers have turned to software as a way of coping with these problems. Yet this shift has caused an entire new set of challenges. Software programs have not been born equal. Software for transportation systems for example has to satisfy hard constraints that depend on the implementation platform thus making the very base of the traditional software abstraction invalid. It is no wonder that more than 30% of severe malfunctions in automobiles are originated by faulty software. We need a new system science to deal with the digital abstraction and the physical world in a unified way. This book is the documentation of pioneering work carried out by the authors in developing *methodologies* and tools for automotive software. The importance of methodologies cannot be overemphasized as tool power can only be unleashed by appropriate methodologies as I have learned over the years in my work in EDA. The unique value of this book is in documenting the effort of conjugating methodologies and tools, a very successful one indeed as the prosperity of ETAS witnesses.

Prof. Alberto Sangiovanni Vincentelli, The Edgar L. and Harold H. Buttner Chair of EECS, University of California at Berkeley; Co-founder, Chief Technology Advisor and Member of the Board of Directors, Cadence Design Systems, Berkeley, CA

PREFACE

After a history of more than 100 years, the automobile as a product continues to evolve at a very fast pace. Since the early 1970s, its evolution has strongly been influenced by a steady increase in onboard electronic systems and software in the vehicle—a trend that continues unabated. As a consequence of this trend, vehicle development, production, and service are changing in fundamental ways. Using software to implement functions in the vehicle provides developers with new degrees of freedom and solutions to existing conflicts of objectives. The resulting complexity can be managed only by using processes, methods, and tools that are appropriate for vehicle-specific applications.

In the last few years, various methods and standards have been devised for the development of software for in-vehicle electronic systems. These methods and standards are best described by the collective term *automotive software engineering*.

Over time, a complex terminology has evolved in automotive software engineering. All of us working in this field are confronting these terms on a daily basis. However, it is no overstatement to say that many of us are no longer sure of a clear or shared definition of many of these terms. In fact, some of the terms are used in very different contexts where they clearly do not mean one and the same thing. For example, the term "process" occurs not only in the context of control engineering but is also used (to designate a very specific thing) in conjunction with real-time systems—to say nothing of its general meaning in development, where it describes development methods in a wider context. In this book, we define essential terms and then use them consistently as defined.

The chapters of this book focus on the processes, methods, and tools for the development of software for electronic systems in the vehicle. The book also places emphasis on the interaction between software development (as a professional discipline limiting itself to certain vehicle components) and the all-embracing systems engineering (a field that considers all vehicle components). The development methods introduced—the so-called *processes*—take the form of models, that is, they comprise an abstract and idealized reflection of daily practice. Although they may serve as guidelines for a variety of development projects, they will need to be evaluated and adapted before they are applied to specific projects. We have taken great pains to provide clear and unambiguous descriptions of processes and supporting methods and tools.

The wealth of information available on many aspects of our topic forced us to forgo detailed discussion of some of them. Generally speaking, we have limited our discussion to aspects that are relevant and specific to the automotive industry.

We certainly make no claim of having provided here the only proper or even a complete methodological approach. As employees of ETAS, we are convinced, however, that tools and software components by ETAS are ideally suited to support the processes and methods introduced in this book.

Practical Cases in Point

To a development team, a process serves only as a supporting structure. The introduction of any given process will be successful only if every team member sees it as a benefit. When extensive practical tasks and their solutions can be made transparent to everyone in the team because every activity associated with any given task can be traced, this is a benefit. In this sense, this book is not a theoretical textbook, far removed from the practical world. On the contrary, all of its ideas, concepts, and suggestions are based on practical use cases that we present by means of appropriate examples. Of course, these aspects are derived from the experience we gained over the years while working closely with vehicle manufacturers and suppliers. Examples come from production projects, including associated service considerations, as well as from research and advanced development projects.

Readership of This Book

We would like to offer this book to all who work for manufacturers and suppliers in vehicle development, production, and service and who encounter software in the vehicle during their daily activities. We hope to be able to pass on some useful suggestions.

In addition, we hope this book will serve as a basic tool for the instruction of engineering students and for the introduction of new employees to their respective workplaces. Basic familiarity with open-loop and closed-loop control engineering, system theory, and software engineering, although helpful, is not a prerequisite for being able to understand the topic of this book.

Readers may feel in some places that they could benefit from more detailed discussion of one topic or another. If you are one of these readers, please let us know. We welcome any and all feedback and especially any suggestions for improvement, which we will carefully consider for inclusion in subsequent reprintings.

ACKNOWLEDGMENTS

We would like to take this opportunity to express to all of our customers our appreciation for the many years of successful and trusting cooperation. This book would not have been possible without this valuable exchange of experiences.

We also wish to thank the BMW Group for its kind permission to include experiences gathered while working on proprietary BMW projects—in the case of one author (Jörg Schäuffele), also in his capacity as an employee at BMW. This includes the consideration of process definitions, as well as recommendations for production projects at BMW. We are indebted to Hans-Georg Frischkorn for his foreword to this book, and special thanks go to Heinz Merkle, Dr. Helmut Hochschwarzer, Dr. Maximilian Fuchs, Prof. Dr. Dieter Nazareth, and all of their staff.

Many of the processes and methods presented in this book evolved over many years of trusting cooperation with Robert Bosch GmbH. These processes and methods are now widely accepted, and they keep recurring here and there throughout this book. We gratefully acknowledge the valuable input from the capable staff in the Chassis Systems, Diesel Systems, and Gasoline Systems Divisions, and the Research and Advanced Development Department of Robert Bosch GmbH.

Sincere thanks also go to Dr. Siegfried Dais, Dr. Wolfgang Runge, Craig A. Brown, Prof. Dr. Peter Göhner, Prof. Mark Thompson, and Prof. Alberto Sangiovanni Vincentelli for their words in the foreword section titled "The Role of Software in the Automobile."

We also are indebted to our many colleagues who, over these past years, have contributed to this book in many different ways.

For the careful and critical task of copy-editing the manuscript, we express our sincere appreciation to Roland Jeutter, Dr. Michael Nicolaou, Dr. Oliver Schlüter, Dr. Kai Werther, and Hans-Jörg Wolff.

Finally, for the careful English translation of the manuscript, sincere thanks go to Roger Carey.

Jörg Schäuffele
Thomas Zurawka
Stuttgart, Germany
June 2005

TABLE OF CONTENTS

CHAPTER ONE

INTRODUCTION AND OVERVIEW

The fulfillment of increasing customer demands and stringent legal requirements with regard to reducing fuel consumption and harmful emissions, and increasing driving safety and driver/ passenger comfort, is inextricably linked to the advancement of electronics in modern vehicles.

As a result, the automobile has become today's most technically complex consumer article. However, note that the requirements for automotive electronics differ substantially from those for other areas of consumer goods electronics. The most prominent requirements for automotive electronics are as follows:

- Deployment under frequently harsh environmental conditions (e.g., temperature range, humidity, vibration) or stringent demands on electromagnetic compatibility (EMC)

- Stringent reliability and availability requirements

- Stringent operational safety demands

- Comparatively long product life cycles

Although the requirements for electronic components for vehicles are stringent, developers still face high pressure for low cost, shortened development cycles, and a great number of model variants. Regardless, these requirements must be fulfilled for products that can be manufactured in high volume.

To bring a development project in onboard automotive electronics to a successful conclusion, project leaders must manage the increasing complexity of their products while maintaining a consistent quality and managing both risk and cost.

A basic understanding of the requirements for and trends in vehicle engineering is essential for anyone who wants to develop suitable methods for development, production, and service of electronic systems for vehicles and who wants to support these by praxis-oriented standards and tools. This introductory chapter provides an analysis of the current state of the art, as background for a description of future perspectives and the associated challenges.

Following an overview of automotive electronic systems and their functions, this chapter introduces the methods used to develop electronic systems and software for automotive applications. The chapter concludes with an introduction to model-based engineering methods.

The remaining chapters of this book feature detailed discussions of essential system basics (Chapter 2), processes (Chapters 3 and 4), and methods and tools (Chapter 5) for the development of software for automotive electronics, as well as the production and service of software for automotive electronics (Chapter 6). Throughout the book, special emphasis is given to vehicle subsystems such as powertrain, chassis, and vehicle body. The book introduces the field of multimedia systems but does not cover it in detail. Chapter 7 provides a summary review of the topics discussed throughout the book. It also outlines the future prospects and challenges for the development of automotive electronics.

1.1 The Driver–Vehicle–Environment System

The objective of any development project is the completion of a new, or the improvement of an existing, function for the vehicle. In the context of this book, the term *function* denotes all of the functional features of the vehicle. These functions ultimately provide a value or benefit to the user (i.e., the operator of the vehicle) that the latter is able to experience directly or that he or she can perceive only indirectly.

The question whether the technical implementation of a given functional feature involves a mechanical, hydraulic, electrical, or electronic system onboard the vehicle is of minor importance from the user's point of view.

However, from the point of view of the engineer who is implementing the functions, the use of electronic components combined with mechanical, electrical, or hydraulic systems provides numerous benefits, especially with regard to attainable reliability, weight, required installation space, and cost. For all of these reasons, electronics has become the key technology in the implementation of many innovations in automotive construction. In fact, nearly all functions of the vehicle today are electronically controlled or monitored.

1.1.1 Design and Method of Operation of Vehicle Electronic Systems

The following provides a closer look at the design and method of operation of electronic systems in the vehicle, using an electrohydraulic braking system as an example.

Example: Configuration of Sensotronic brake control [1]

Figure 1-1 shows the system configuration of the Bosch Sensotronic brake control (SBC) [1]. The electrohydraulic braking system combines the functions of brake booster, antilock braking system (ABS), and electronic stability program (ESP).

The driver's mechanical actuation of the brake pedal is registered in the brake pedal unit and is transmitted electrically to the so-called *electronic control unit* (ECU). The ECU uses this setpoint and additional signals from various sensors, such as the steering angle signal or wheel rotational speed signal, to calculate output variables that again are electronically transmitted to the hydraulic modulator. There they are converted by means of brake-pressure modulation to variables for the wheel brakes. The wheel brakes influence the vehicle drivability, the so-called *controlled system* or *plant*. Thus, the wheel brakes are referred to as actuators.

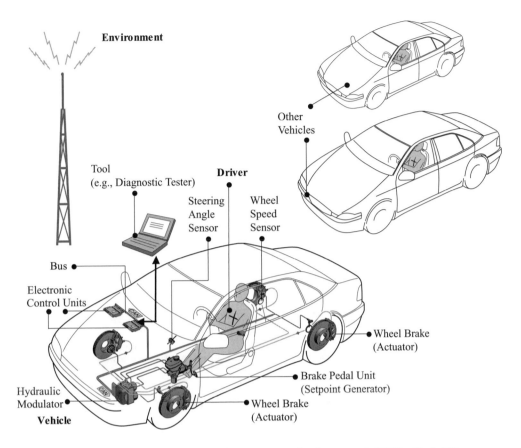

Fig. 1-1. *Diagram of the Bosch Sensotronic brake control (SBC). (Ref. [1])*

Because the ECU communicates with other ECUs onboard the vehicle via a data bus (e.g., the CAN bus [2]), functions that go beyond those mentioned so far and that involve more than a single ECU also can be implemented. One example of this kind of function is the *traction control system* (TCS), which represents a mediating function between engine management and the braking system.

The system configuration of the electrohydraulic braking system exemplifies the typical configuration of all electronic control (open-loop/closed-loop) and monitoring systems of the vehicle. Generally, the following components are involved in such a system: setpoint generators, sensors, actuators, ECUs, and the controlled system, the so-called *plant*. The networked interconnection of the involved ECUs facilitates the exchange of data.

The driver and the environment—considered components of the higher-level driver–vehicle–environment system—are able to influence the way the vehicle behaves.

Seen alone, an ECU merely represents a means to an end, because it is—as an isolated component—of no apparent value to the vehicle user. Only a complete system comprising ECUs, setpoint generators, sensors, and actuators will influence and monitor the plant (i.e., respond to the actions or requests of the user). However, in many situations, and especially when, as is frequently the case, so-called *embedded systems* are at work, the electronic implementation of functions is not even visible to the vehicle user.

As shown in Fig. 1-2, control and monitoring systems onboard the vehicle can be represented as a structured block diagram. Components are shown as blocks, with arrows depicting the signal flow between the blocks. For an introduction to the fundamentals and terminology of control and monitoring technology, see Sections 2.1 and 2.6 in Chapter 2.

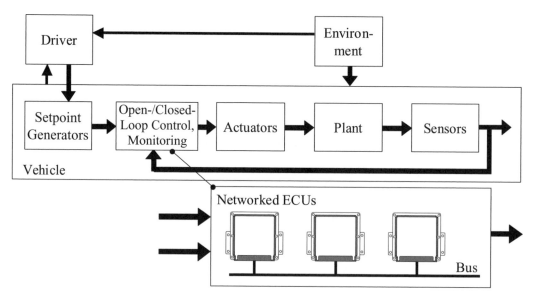

Fig. 1-2. *Block diagram of control and monitoring systems.*

As shown in Fig. 1-2, signal flow may exist among a number of the components (i.e., the driver, vehicle, and environment). In this figure, the driver serves as a placeholder for all users of a particular vehicle function (i.e., for driver and passengers).

The environment also encompasses other vehicles, as well as electronic systems located in proximity to the vehicle. These include tools, such as diagnostic test equipment in the service shop, that are connected to the electronic systems onboard the vehicle (Fig. 1-1).

New technologies aiding the exchange of information between driver and vehicle, driver and environment, and vehicle and environment facilitate a plethora of innovative functions—an example would be networking beyond the physical periphery of the vehicle by means of wireless communication systems. The idea of networking beyond the physical periphery of the vehicle enables a new class of systems (e.g., driver assistance systems). During the past few years, the area of multimedia systems in particular has seen the introduction of many functions that became feasible only through vehicle–environment networking. One example is the dynamic navigation feature, which considers environment-specific information (e.g., traffic gridlock reports) in the process of route computation.

Another area that has benefitted from many recent innovations is the area of interfaces (i.e., the interaction—through so-called *user interfaces*—between the driver and/or passengers and the vehicle). For example, operating and display systems today may be based on voice control concepts.

In light of the foregoing, discussions of the term *networking* throughout this book will not be limited to only the electronic functions of the vehicle, but will include electronic functions or systems that interact with the driver and vehicle from outside the physical boundaries of that vehicle. Therefore, it is helpful at this point of the discussion to introduce and define the terms *onboard* and *offboard*, and *online* and *offline*.

1.1.2 Electronic Systems of the Vehicle and the Environment

Throughout subsequent chapters, communications among electronic systems in the vehicle is termed *onboard communications*. By contrast, communications linking the onboard systems of the vehicle and systems in the environment is called *offboard communications*. A similar differentiation between *onboard* and *offboard interfaces* is made when referring to the interfaces of the electronic systems in the vehicle. Figure 1-3 provides an overview.

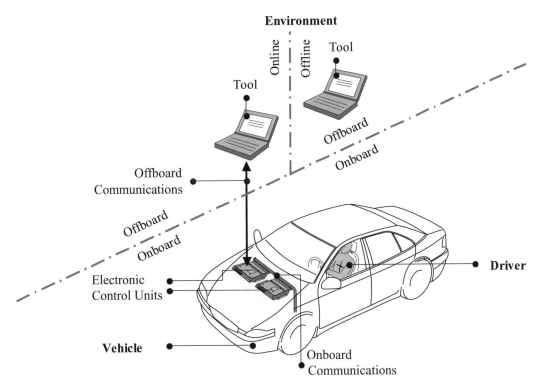

Fig. 1-3. *Electronic systems of the vehicle and the environment.*

With regard to the functions performed by the electronic systems of the vehicle and those handled by systems in the environment, a differentiation is made between *onboard functions* and *offboard functions*, respectively. The division of functions into subfunctions and the distributed implementation of subfunctions by means of both onboard and offboard systems are also conceivable.

Another differentiation characteristic is the point in time at which a given function is executed by an offboard system, relative to the point in time at which a function is executed by an onboard system. In this case, a differentiation is made between the synchronized execution (also referred to as *online* execution) and the unsynchronized execution of functions (*offline* execution).

For several years, the onboard/offboard and online/offline differentiation criteria have been used in the context of diagnostic systems for vehicle functions, giving rise to the distinction between onboard and offboard diagnostics, a term that by now surely is familiar to many readers. Design methods and tools dedicated to the development of automotive electronic systems are designated in a similar fashion.

1.2 Overview of Vehicle Electronic Systems

By way of introduction, the various electronic systems onboard a vehicle are presented in an overview. Vehicles typically contain more than one ECU for the controlling and monitoring of various subsystems. In the early days of the deployment of electronics in the vehicle, the operation of these ECUs was largely autonomous. With no interaction among ECUs, it was relatively easy to assign functions associated with a specific vehicle subsystem, such as powertrain, chassis, body, and multimedia, to the ECU responsible for controlling and monitoring that subsystem (Fig. 1-4).

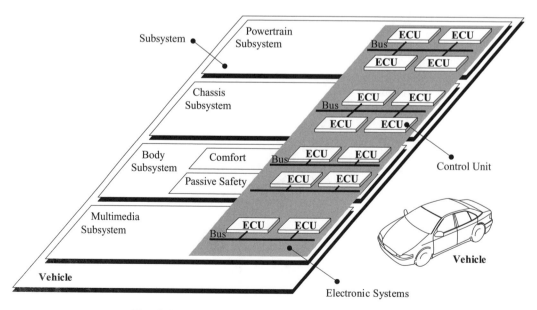

Fig. 1-4. *Assignment of ECUs to vehicle subsystems.*

Thus, the classic systems of engine management and transmission control are assigned to the powertrain, and the antilock braking system (ABS) to the chassis subsystem, whereas the heating and air conditioning system, central locking system, and seat and mirror adjustment are part of the comfort and convenience subsystem belonging to the body subsystem. Contributing to increased vehicle occupant safety in the event of an accident, the airbag and restraint systems belong to the passive safety system, whereas radio and telephone are part of the multimedia system.

The continuing quantum leaps in hardware technology and performance facilitate the implementation of many increasingly powerful vehicle functions by means of software. These functions are referred to as *software functions*.

The introduction of powerful bus systems, such as the CAN (Controller Area Network) bus [2] in the early1990s, initiated the second phase of ECU technology. Networking of electronic systems was now possible and with it, the implementation of new higher-level software functions, as well as the associated cost savings. For example, multiple systems could use signals from individual sensors without the need for costly wiring connections.

Whenever higher-level software functions influence any functions of a single subsystem, this implementation approach is also known as an integrated powertrain, integrated chassis, integrated body, or integrated safety management. In distributed and networked systems, however, it is often no longer possible to assign software functions to a single ECU. As a result, software functions are divided into subfunctions for implementation in several ECUs.

Whenever higher-level software functions influence functions of several subsystems, they can no longer be assigned to one specific subsystem. As discussed in the context of the introductory example, the traction control system (TCS) comprises a set of functions that affects both powertrain and chassis. Many other driver assistance systems, such as distance-sensing adaptive cruise control, also belong to this category. Functions working across subsystem boundaries exist in the areas of comfort systems and passive safety systems. One example of such a set of functions is the vehicle access system that includes the locking and theft deterrent systems. These examples underscore the fact that transitions among subsystems are at best fluid if seen from a functional standpoint.

Multiple access to and use of *sensor* signals by various ECUs can be handled in most instances without difficulty. As soon as various ECUs (or better, several software functions) *compete* for access to the same *actuators*, however, the developer is presented with serious challenges, one of which is that of finding a suitable method of specification. Another challenge is the definition of interfaces for accurate data and request exchange among the various functions and systems, so that, for example, commands sent to various actuators can be clearly coordinated. For a more detailed discussion of this and related topics, please consult CARTRONIC [3].

Following an overview of the electronic systems assisting the powertrain, chassis, and body groups, this section also describes multimedia systems. Although these systems are not given wide exposure within the context of this book, an overview is nevertheless helpful for the purposes of identifying multimedia boundaries *vis-à-vis* those of the other application areas. Finally, several examples of functions are discussed, whose implementation is possible only after the electronic systems are communicating within a network.

In this section, systems are classified according to typical features, such as the following:

- User interfaces and setpoint generators
- Sensors and actuators
- Software functions
- Installation space
- Model variants and scalability

Current and foreseeable trends are considered and referenced in the discussion.

In many cases, the technical implementation of functions must consider a number of legal regulations. For example, any development in powertrain—in particular, the development of software functions for engine ECUs—often is driven by guidelines and laws concerning fuel economy and exhaust emissions. By contrast, the development of chassis and body group functions is driven mostly by safety and comfort requirements.

This section limits the discussion to an overview of automotive electronic systems and their functions. Individual aspects of electronic function and system development will be examined more closely in subsequent chapters, using appropriate examples. For a comprehensive treatment of these topics, please refer to the extensive specialist literature (e.g., [4]).

1.2.1 Electronic Systems of the Powertrain

The powertrain of a vehicle encompasses the following units and components:

- Drive group (i.e., internal combustion engine, electric motor, hybrid drive, or fuel cell)
- Clutch and manual transmission, or automatic transmission
- Transfer case, front- and/or rear-axle drive
- Driveshafts and propshafts
- Engine auxiliary systems, such as the starter and alternator

The electronic systems of the driveshaft include the following:

- Engine ECUs
- Transmission ECUs

A variety of control and monitoring functions for engine, transmission, and auxiliary units use as input variables driver requests and a number of sensor signals and thus are able to control the actuators in the powertrain.

1.2.1.1 User Interfaces and Setpoint Generators

The electronic powertrain control functions have a relatively small number of user interfaces. Other than by starting the engine and shutting it off, the driver can directly transmit his or her requests only by changing the position of the accelerator pedal. A manual transmission provides two additional user interfaces, the clutch pedal and the shift lever; an automatic transmission merely offers one, the drive selector. Additional user interfaces may be required to meet special needs, such as mode selector switches for automatic transmissions.

1.2.1.2 Sensors and Actuators

A relatively large contingent of sensors is required, for example, to capture attitude and position, rotational speeds, pressures, temperatures, lambda values, or engine-knock intensity. This is complemented by a similarly large number of actuators handling ignition, injection, throttle valve, clutches, or valves. This results in a large number of ECU interfaces. Figure 1-5 shows the interfaces of an engine ECU. Onboard communications are handled primarily via the CAN bus [2]. For dedicated offboard communication with the diagnostic tester, the K-Line [5] is being progressively replaced by the CAN bus [2].

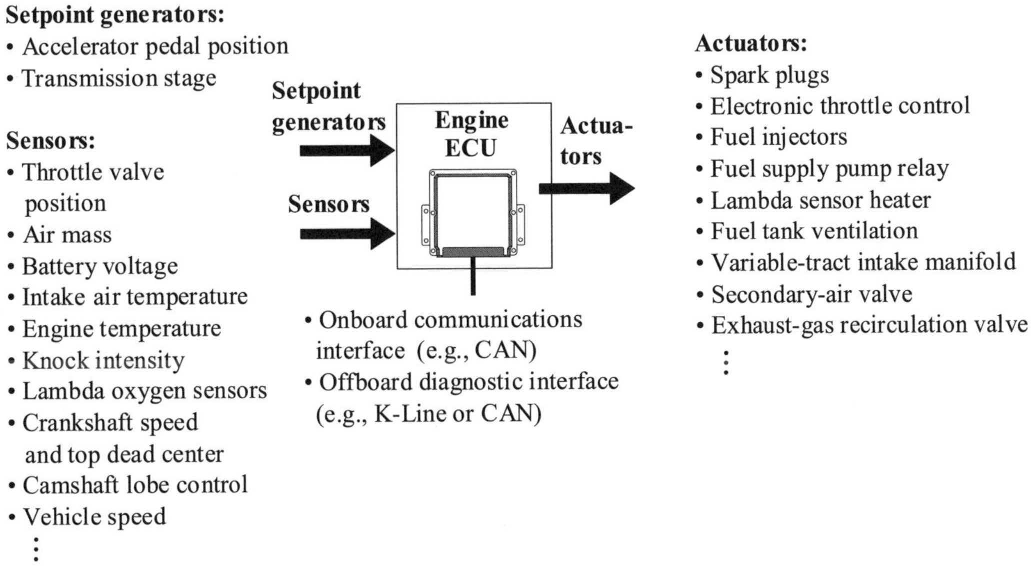

Setpoint generators:
- Accelerator pedal position
- Transmission stage

Sensors:
- Throttle valve position
- Air mass
- Battery voltage
- Intake air temperature
- Engine temperature
- Knock intensity
- Lambda oxygen sensors
- Crankshaft speed and top dead center
- Camshaft lobe control
- Vehicle speed
  :

Setpoint generators

Engine ECU

Sensors

Actuators

- Onboard communications interface (e.g., CAN)
- Offboard diagnostic interface (e.g., K-Line or CAN)

Actuators:
- Spark plugs
- Electronic throttle control
- Fuel injectors
- Fuel supply pump relay
- Lambda sensor heater
- Fuel tank ventilation
- Variable-tract intake manifold
- Secondary-air valve
- Exhaust-gas recirculation valve
  :

Fig. 1-5. *Interfaces of a gasoline-engine ECU. (Ref. [6])*

1.2.1.3 Software Functions

An engine ECU handles a considerable number of software functions; advancing technology has pushed the envelope into the three-digit range. The objective is to develop powerful software functions that work together internally but also feature numerous interfaces to functions in the chassis or body groups (e.g., to the traction control system or the air conditioning system).

Many software functions typically feature a large number of parameters, such as characteristic values, characteristic curves, and characteristic maps. Developers need these parameters to adapt the software functions not only to the respective engine, transmission, or vehicle variant but to the various operating points.

1.2.1.4 Installation Space

Because of the numerous interfaces with sensors and actuators that are located primarily on the engine or transmission, these ECUs often are installed close to the components they control, and the operating conditions for these ECUs tend to be harsh. In many cases, these units are exposed to an extended temperature range, humidity, and vibration.

1.2.1.5 Variants and Scalability

There are hardly any scalability requirements to be met. However, the automotive customer can normally select from engine and transmission variants.

For the preceding reasons, the powertrain typically features a small number of powerful ECUs that handle a great number of software functions. One mandatory component is always the engine ECU and, in the presence of an automatic transmission, an additional transmission ECU [4, 6–8].

1.2.2 Electronic Systems of the Chassis

The chassis encompasses the following vehicle components:

- Axles and wheels
- Brakes
- Suspension and shock absorbers
- Steering systems

As a result, the electronic chassis systems include, for example:

- Antilock braking system (ABS)
- Electronic braking-force distribution
- Electronic stability program (ESP)
- Parking brake
- Tire pressure monitoring system
- Pneumatic suspension
- Roll stabilization
- Power steering
- Active steering
- Electrohydraulic or electromechanical brake
- Brake-by-wire and steer-by-wire systems

For a driver, a functional failure of the braking system means either that there is no response when he or she steps on the brake pedal, or that the car will brake without the application of the brake pedal. If a functional steering system failure occurs, either a driver will experience this as no response to his or her turning the steering wheel, or the car will swerve without the driver turning the steering wheel. Depending on the circumstance in which any of these four failures occurs, a driver may completely lose control of the vehicle. In other words, the risk of accidents with casualties and personal injuries is very high when either of the two systems fails. For these reasons, the safety requirements for these systems are very stringent. To meet the requirements for safety-relevant systems, developers follow stringent design principles, such as applying monitoring and safety concepts, finding ways to keep the number of interfaces to other systems low, and modularization. In fact, the overall design of the electronics in modern vehicles is often very much influenced by the design of these safety-relevant systems.

1.2.2.1 User Interfaces and Setpoint Generators

Similar to the electronic functions in the powertrain, those in the chassis group also have few user interfaces. Drivers generate setpoints via three user interfaces: the brake pedal, the steering wheel, and the parking brake. Confirmation that the driver has activated the parking brake is provided by means of another user interface, the indicator lamp in the instrument cluster. Some chassis systems, such as the air suspension, have additional user interfaces (control elements) for activation/deactivation.

1.2.2.2 Sensors and Actuators

The wheel rotational speeds are among the major input variables for the ABS ECU. The wheel brakes comprise the actuators. The ESP ECU uses additional input variables, such as the steering-angle and yaw-angle sensor signals [1].

Compared with the electronic powertrain systems or the engine ECU, there are fewer sensors and actuators. Figure 1-6 shows the interfaces of an ABS ECU [1].

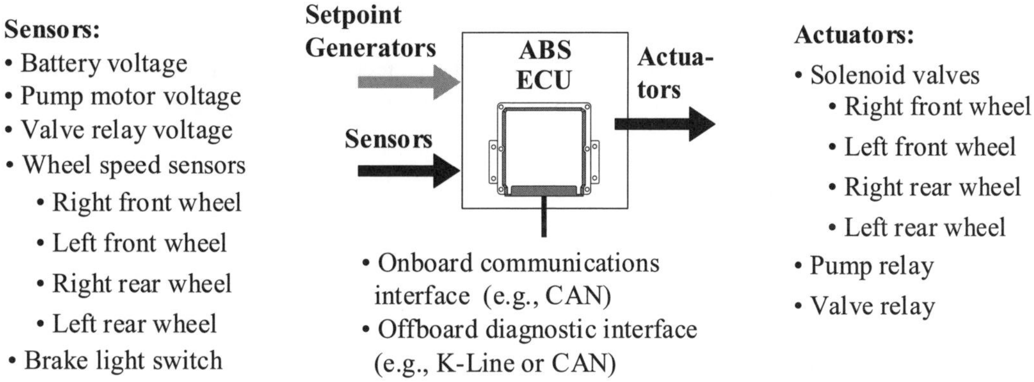

Sensors:
- Battery voltage
- Pump motor voltage
- Valve relay voltage
- Wheel speed sensors
  - Right front wheel
  - Left front wheel
  - Right rear wheel
  - Left rear wheel
- Brake light switch

Setpoint Generators

ABS ECU

Actuators

Sensors

- Onboard communications interface (e.g., CAN)
- Offboard diagnostic interface (e.g., K-Line or CAN)

Actuators:
- Solenoid valves
  - Right front wheel
  - Left front wheel
  - Right rear wheel
  - Left rear wheel
- Pump relay
- Valve relay

Fig. 1-6. Interfaces of an ABS ECU. (Ref. [1])

1.2.2.3 Software Functions

The chassis group features a number of ECUs for which an extensive array of functions must be implemented. These functions cooperate internally but feature numerous interfaces with miscellaneous software functions in the chassis, powertrain, or body groups. It is foreseeable that some of the current hydraulic or mechanical implementations of certain functions will be complemented by means of software functions.

1.2.2.4 Installation Space

Due to the required high degree of safety and because of the wide spatial distribution throughout the chassis of the sensor and actuator interfaces, the number of ECUs is higher in the chassis group than it is in the powertrain.

Electronic control units in the chassis group include an ABS ECU, an ABS/TCS ECU, or an ESP ECU, as well as the mostly optional ECUs for steering, suspension, and damping functions or tire pressure monitoring. These ECUs are exposed to similar rough conditions as those of the powertrain [1].

1.2.2.5 Variants and Scalability

The standard equipment of the chassis components varies, depending on the markets in which vehicles are to be sold. In addition, a number of functions are offered as special options or optional packages. Therefore, scalability requirements frequently must be met. In many markets, vehicle buyers can select and combine various optional extras.

1.2.3 Body Electronics

Electronic body systems frequently are divided into the *passive safety* group and the *comfort/convenience* group.

The comfort and convenience group includes the vehicle access system, including the central locking system, radio-controlled key, and theft alarm system, as well as systems for control of the following:

- Power window units and tailgate
- Sliding/pop-up roof
- Convertible top
- Wipers and rain sensor
- Mirror adjuster, dimmer, and heater
- Seat adjustment and heater
- Steering column adjustment
- Interior heating and air conditioning
- Interior lighting
- Vehicle headlamp control and headlamp cleaning system
- Parking aid features

The phrase *passive safety systems* applies to all onboard systems that contribute to increased safety and accident protection for the occupants of the vehicle. These include the following:

- Restraint systems with functions such as seat belt tighteners
- Airbag ECU, including seat-occupant detection
- Extendable rollover bars

By contrast, the phrase *active safety systems* applies to all onboard systems that increase the safety of the occupants of the vehicle during travel and that contribute to the control of critical driving situations and thus to accident prevention. The ABS and ESP belong to this system group.

1.2.3.1 User Interfaces and Setpoint Generators

Comfort and convenience systems feature a multitude of user interfaces. Driver and passengers can use a large complement of control elements, such as switches, pushbuttons, sliders, or rotary controls to adjust to their liking the temperature of their seat heater, the height of their seat, the angle of the steering wheel, and so forth. In other words, users frequently control setpoint generators that send a request to a system (and thus are somewhat aware of interfacing with that system) and directly experience the response of the system to this request. Consequently, user awareness of convenience functions is very high.

By contrast, there are practically no user interfaces for the passive safety systems. Therefore, a user will perceive and appreciate the existence of these functions only if a high level of vehicle safety is important to him or her.

1.2.3.2 Sensors and Actuators

The inputs for the various body group functions comprise specified nominal values and a variety of sensor signals. In many instances, the actuators are implemented by means of electrical drives.

1.2.3.3 Software Functions

The largest number of independent software functions exists in the body of the vehicle. In a manner typical of autonomous applications, ECUs are equipped with microcontrollers featuring limited computing power and a relatively small number of input/output interfaces. In this way, independent software functions can be implemented in separate ECUs. As a natural consequence of this type of implementation, the required number of ECUs is relatively large.

Here, too, networking the various ECUs facilitates the implementation of software functions that transcend the limits of ECUs and subsystems. The centralized access and locking system is a typical example.

The number of calibration parameters is smaller for body electronics functions than that of the software functions assisting the powertrain or chassis.

1.2.3.4 Installation Space

The various ECUs are widely distributed throughout the vehicle; in many cases, they perform a function directly at their installed locations. Actuators and sensors in vehicle doors, exterior mirrors, and roof, rear, and front-end areas, as well as in the vehicle interior, must be connected to their respective ECUs. In many cases, the installation space for ECUs and wiring harnesses is limited (e.g., inside doors or seats). In some vehicle models, several sensors, actuators, and ECUs compete for the same installation space. For example, sensors and actuators that service airbag and convenience functions must be accommodated in doors, seats, or the roof. Obviously, these "geometric" constraints exert a great influence on electronic systems architecture. Intelligent sensors and actuators combined with ECUs with limited functionality often are used to address problems of limited space.

1.2.3.5 Variants and Scalability

The electronic systems architecture also is influenced by the different body variants of a given vehicle series.

Example: Influence of body variants on electronic systems architecture

Some equipment options are mutually exclusive. A convertible does not require a sliding roof and thus does not need an ECU for that function. Likewise, there is no convertible top on a sedan and at least no need for an ECU controlling an automatic roof up/down function. Similar associations exist between station wagons and coupes. This is another reason for the existence of many ECUs providing a limited complement of functions (modularization).

In addition to the demands arising from different vehicle variants, scalability requirements also must be satisfied. The vehicle buyer has the option to select from a large number of body function extras.

1.2.4 Multimedia Systems

The group of multimedia systems includes the following:

- Tuners and antennas
- CD changers
- Amplifiers and audio systems
- Video systems
- Navigation systems
- Telephone
- Voice control
- Internet access

The added value provided by many functions of these identified systems is created only through suitable networking with the remaining electronic systems (e.g., through voice control or visualization concepts for comfort and convenience functions).

1.2.5 Distributed and Networked Electronic Systems

The networking of ECUs facilitates the implementation of comprehensive software functions. The following two examples will underscore this fact.

Example: Adaptive cruise control system

The adaptive cruise control (ACC) system is an advanced development of the classic cruise control. The host vehicle is equipped with a forward-looking sensor (e.g., a radar sensor) that captures the distance, relative speed, and relative position of any vehicle directly ahead of it. The ACC ECU uses this sensor input to calculate and maintain a constant safe distance from the vehicle ahead of it. To achieve and maintain a safe distance, the ECU controls the longitudinal dynamics of the host vehicle by deliberate acceleration and deceleration, intervening with the engine ECU to influence engine torque, with the transmission ECU to influence the transmission, and with the ESP ECU to act on the braking torque. For all of these reasons, ACC comprises a function affecting both powertrain and chassis components (Fig. 1-7).

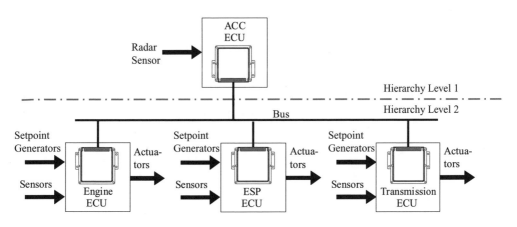

Fig. 1-7. *The ACC ECU and ACC system.*

Example: Display system for information, warnings, and fault messages

The display of information, warnings, and fault messages in the instrument cluster is the result of data sent by various ECUs. For example, the task of the instrument cluster unit software is not only to display information, warnings, and fault messages inbound from all ECUs onboard the vehicle, but to assign the required priorities. In this process, it evaluates the messages received from all ECUs before the information, warnings, and fault messages are displayed in accordance with a defined strategy (Fig. 1-8).

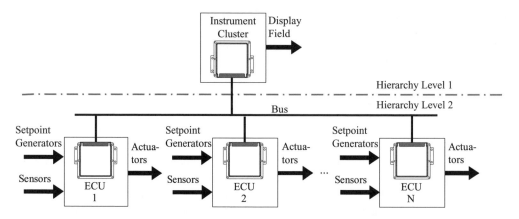

Fig. 1-8. *Display system for information, warnings, and fault messages.*

1.2.6 Summary and Outlook

The technical implementation of electronic systems continues to be influenced to a large degree by the steadily improving performance of microcontrollers and by the fact that they are frequently networked.

During the past decades, not only the per-vehicle count of ECUs has increased, but the number of functions per ECU has also increased at a steady rate (Fig. 1-9).

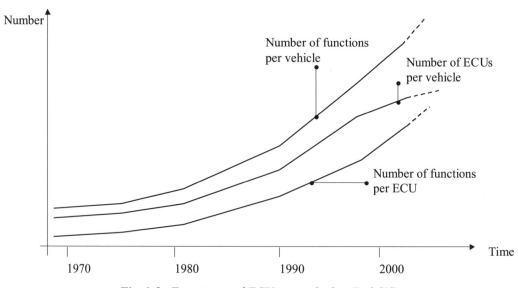

Fig. 1-9. *Functions and ECUs per vehicle. (Ref. [9])*

A steady rise in the number of functions per vehicle also is anticipated in the future. As mentioned, many new functions become possible only through the networking of the vehicle and environment. To a large degree, traditional functions of the vehicle that heretofore were handled by mechanical or hydraulic systems will at least be implemented partially by means of software functions.

It also is foreseeable that the trend toward further additions to the standard equipment across all vehicle classes will continue, with luxury-class vehicles providing the impetus. However, the attendant rise in cost, as well as limitations to installation space in smaller vehicles, will require a reduction in the number of ECUs. For this reason, the number of ECUs may be expected to drop, or at least there will be no further increase in that number. For example, a variety of software functions currently implemented in separate ECUs may be implemented in the future in a single ECU, if available installation space is limited. This is another reason for the continuing increase in the number of software functions per ECU.

1.3 Overview of the Logical System Architecture

When electronic components were first used in vehicles, the typical ECU schematic resembled the one shown in Fig. 1-4. This representation was not problematic, because the individual systems largely worked autonomously, and function assignments therefore were unambiguous. Under those circumstances, the ECU view was identical to the function view.

1.3.1 ECU and Function Networks of the Vehicle

The adaptive cruise control (ACC) system introduced as an example in the preceding section, however, underscores that the approach to design and development of such networked systems must be different. The development of distributed and networked software functions requires two distinct levels of representation or views of the system. The networked and distributed functions are represented as an abstract view of the system. The various networked ECUs in the vehicle are represented as a concrete view of the system (Fig. 1-10) [10].

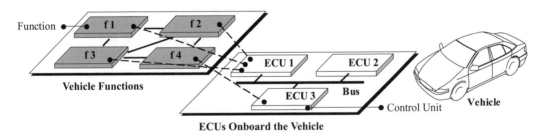

Fig. 1-10. *Function and ECU networks of the vehicle. (Ref. [10])*

Based on the preceding information, it is feasible to assign the functions to specific subsystems throughout the vehicle, as shown in Fig. 1-11.

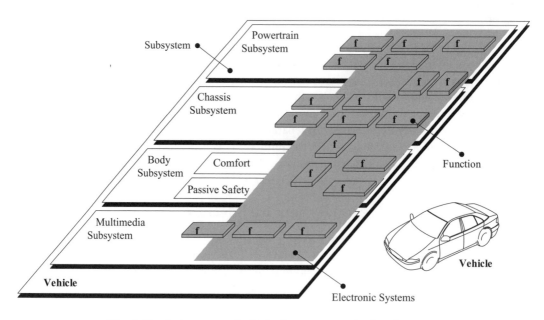

Fig. 1-11. *Assignment of vehicle functions to vehicle subsystems.*

1.3.2 Logical System Architecture for Open-Loop/Closed-Loop Control and Monitoring Systems

The differentiation between abstract and concrete views can be expanded to include all components of the vehicle, as well as the driver and the environment. In the following discussion, the abstract view is termed *logical system architecture*, whereas the concrete view of a given implementation is called *technical system architecture*. To facilitate identification throughout this book, the logical system architecture is represented with gray background, and the technical system architecture is represented with white background. For example, the logical system architecture for open-loop/closed-loop control and monitoring systems is depicted in Fig. 1-12; a diagram of the technical system architecture appears in Fig. 1-2.

1.4 Processes in Vehicle Development

The increasing number of functions in a given vehicle, their networking, and high and steadily rising requirements for reliability, availability, and safety, together with variant and scalability requirements, all result in a level of complexity that can hardly be managed without a defined development process.

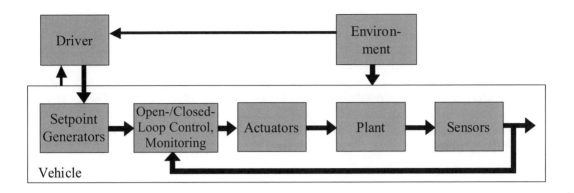

Fig. 1-12. *Logical system architecture for control and monitoring systems.*

One procedural approach to the mastery of complexity that has been in use in the automotive industry for a long time reads as follows:

Divide et Impera!
(Divide and Conquer!)

1.4.1 Overview of Vehicle Development

In vehicle development, the expression "*Divide et Impera!*" refers to the method of partitioning the vehicle into the powertrain, chassis, body, and multimedia subsystems (Fig. 1-11). Following a step-by-step procedure, these subsystems are then further divided into secondary subsystems and components. Components are developed separately but in parallel and are tested at the end of this step. The components are subsequently evaluated and integrated into subsystems across the various system levels. In the final step, the powertrain, chassis, body, and multimedia subsystems are integrated to create the vehicle.

This approach not only requires a clear-cut division of labor in the development of subsystems and components, it also mandates that development teams cooperate when decisions must be made about how to partition and later integrate the systems in terms of installation space, vehicle functions, and production technology.

In addition, the development of vehicle subsystems and components is usually accomplished through close cooperation between vehicle manufacturers and suppliers. For this reason, a clear definition of task assignment is also a basic requirement for successful development.

Another dimension is added by the simultaneous development of different vehicles or vehicle variants. For vehicle manufacturers and their suppliers alike, this means a daily routine of working on multiple projects on all system levels.

The cooperation among different engineering disciplines and various companies requires a common familiarity with the overriding issues, a shared understanding of problem-solving processes, and an equal appreciation of the effects and implications that solutions will have on the overall system. Further, the responsibilities and accountabilities for a given project must be defined. Mechatronics [11] on the technical side or systems engineering methods [12] on the organizational side of a development project may serve as examples of proven, harmonized approaches.

In the context of cross-corporate teamwork between vehicle manufacturers and suppliers, all aspects of the business model, as well as legal issues such as product liability or patent rights, also must be addressed and settled. However, this book limits its discussion to technical and organizational aspects.

1.4.2 Overview of the Development of Electronic Systems

The development process of electronic systems in the vehicle follows similar steps as those of vehicle development. Therefore, electronic systems in the vehicle are first partitioned into subsystems, such as ECUs (hardware and software), setpoint generators, sensors, and actuators (Fig. 1-2), and are developed based on the principle of division of labor. The subsystems are then tested and validated, and subsequently integrated step by step into an electronic system (Fig. 1-13). Here, too, partitioning and integration require teamwork reaching beyond subsystem boundaries.

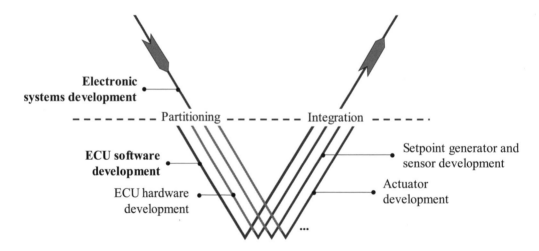

Fig. 1-13. *Overview of the development of electronic systems.*

Electronic system development should be thoroughly planned and prepared by applying sound and proven methods, such as the Capability Maturity Model Integration® (CMMI®) [13], Software Process Improvement and Capability Determination (SPICE) [14], or the V-Model [15].

Further, electronic systems and components intended for vehicles should support automotive standards such as OSEK [16] and ASAM [17]. OSEK is a German acronym for "open systems and the corresponding interfaces for automotive electronics." ASAM is an acronym for Association for Standardization of Automation and Measuring Systems."

In addition, proven test procedures, such as simulation or rapid prototyping, should be considered when defining a development process.

This approach to electronic system development as recommended here requires, of course, a great measure of interaction between engineers engaged in vehicle development and those involved in electronic systems development. These interactions will carry over into software development as well.

1.4.2.1 Trend from Hardware to Software

Electronic systems development as a whole exhibits a general trend going from hardware- to software-based solutions.

Software solutions are ideally suited to the implementation of the functional aspects of electronic systems. For example, the software-based implementation of open-loop/closed-loop control functions and monitoring functions provides the highest degree of freedom (e.g., in the design of linearizations, adaptive or learning algorithms, and safety and diagnostic concepts). In other words, anyone taking this approach to implementation can largely disregard consideration of installation space and manufacturing constraints.

For all of these reasons, the software-based implementation of vehicle functions provides vehicle manufacturers and suppliers with a great differentiation potential *vis-à-vis* the competition. This is also the case in other industries.

Therefore, the focus of this book is on the current, widely used approach to the development of software functions and their functional integration with other components of an electronic vehicle system.

Particular emphasis will be placed on the description of the requirements and constraints applicable to the development of software for ECUs intended for vehicles. These differ markedly from the requirements for the development of software for other industrial applications. To help readers appreciate this difference, such requirements will be introduced by way of comparison.

For example, it will be strictly differentiated between the specification of software functions of ECUs and their actual design and implementation. Specification means the development of a given software function and includes its early, broad-based functional validation in the real vehicle. Design and implementation mean adapting a software function to a specific target ECU (with consideration of all technical aspects) and then verifying the result against the specification. Additional requirements, imposed by vehicle production and service, also must be fulfilled by software intended for in-vehicle ECUs. These requirements include diagnostics and software updates for ECUs.

1.4.2.2 Cost

In the automotive industry, proportional production cost frequently dictates unit cost because enormous pressure for low cost in combination with high production volume characterize that industry in general. Low unit cost for ECUs translates into restricted memory space and limited computing capacity. Software developers are consequently challenged to optimize wherever possible (e.g., by implementing functions in integer arithmetic whenever feasible).

1.4.2.3 Long Product Life Cycles

At the current state of the art, vehicles are estimated to have the following life cycle:

- A development phase of three years
- A production phase of approximately seven years
- A subsequent operation and service phase of up to fifteen years

This adds up to a total product life cycle of about twenty-five years (Fig. 1-14).

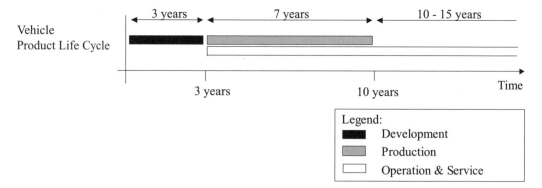

Fig. 1-14. *Product life cycle of a vehicle.*

For electronic components, however, these phases are dramatically shorter due to the continuing advancements in hardware technology. As one consequence, supplying the market with electronic spare parts over the long term represents a considerable challenge. Clearly, challenges such as these must be taken into consideration during the development phase of a vehicle.

The fact that electronic hardware has a decidedly short life cycle has an impact on software architecture as well. In development, the trend toward standardization of software architecture is one example of this impact. Another example is the trend toward a hardware-independent specification of software functions that ensures simplified porting of software functions to new generations of hardware in the future.

For vehicles already in the field, updates to the software running in the ECUs are beneficial; in other words, the life cycles of the ECU software are shorter than that of the ECU hardware. The deployment of Flash technology supporting easy reprogramming of ECUs—in conjunction with the networking of all ECUs onboard the vehicle—facilitates cost-efficient software updates in the field. This often is done via the central offboard diagnostic interface of the vehicle, without the need for costly removal or exchange of the ECUs in the vehicle. Therefore, the extremely long vehicle life cycles must be taken into consideration during development.

1.4.2.4 Safety Requirements—High and Still Rising

Safety requirements for vehicle functions are very stringent compared to safety requirements in other industries, such as manufacturing systems engineering or telecommunication. This is due to a 100% probability of a person—the driver—being in the proximity of the vehicle in the event of an accident. Therefore, the respective functions usually are classified for a high safety integrity level. This is generally not the case in the machine-building industry, as the probability of persons being in the vicinity of any machine can be lowered considerably, reduced by appropriate access restrictions to workers.

Basic safety regulations are defined in standards, such as DIN 19250 [18] or IEC 61508 [19], and in ECE Directives (e.g., [20, 21]). The prerequisite for awarding road-use and registration permits to vehicles consists of the "simple" procedure of providing verification of functional safety.

In the past few years, the safe and reliable operation of electronic systems in the vehicle is becoming crucial, because they do important safety-related work. Such functions range from providing a situation analysis (e.g., speedometer display) to giving a situation assessment (e.g., black-ice warning), or from recommending an action (e.g., navigation system) to executing it (e.g., accelerating or braking intervention), or even to correcting a driver's action, such as in active steering intervention (in a vehicle equipped with active front steering, or AFS) [22].

For this reason, operational safety analysis strongly influences function development and, as a consequence, software development. Stringent reliability requirements force the implementation of fault detection and fault handling procedures, with redundant system design being one of the most powerful of these procedures. In fact, stringent operational safety requirements have reinforced the trend toward distributed and networked systems in the vehicle.

These considerations and constraints force special requirements on development processes and tools as well. Examples are the certification of tools, as well as standardized software components such as the OSEK operating systems.

1.4.3 Core Process for Electronic Systems and Software Development

The many demonstrated interactions among vehicle, electronic, and software development necessitate an integrated development process that covers all steps—from the analysis of user requirements to acceptance tests of electronic systems.

This book focuses on the integrated development of electronic systems and software, using a procedural approach suggested by the V-Model [15]. The V-Model integrates quality inspection and test procedures by differentiating between a system view and a component view. Therefore, it is widely used in the automotive industry.

The referenced development process model may be visualized in the form of the letter "V." An adapted V-Model provides for the representation of the project phases and interfaces between system and software development. The same is true for the specific steps of vehicle development. Figure 1-15 shows an overview of this so-called *core process*, which is discussed in detail in Chapter 4 of this book. The methods and tools supporting this core process are introduced in Chapter 5.

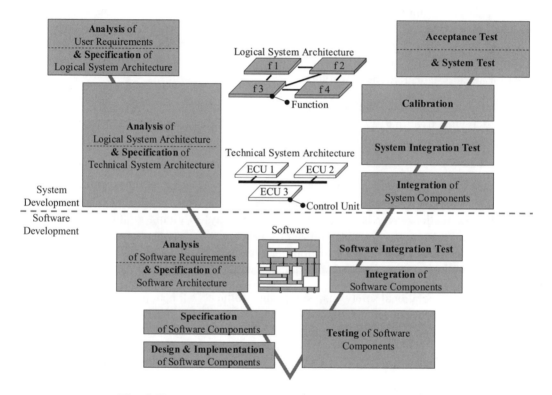

Fig. 1-15. *Overview of the core process for the development of electronic systems and software.*

The core process comprises a number of distinct development steps:

- **Analysis of user requirements and specification of logical system architecture**

  The objective of this process step is to define the logical system architecture based on the project-relevant user requirements. Logical system architecture includes definition of the function network, the function interfaces, and the communication among the functions across the entire vehicle or, as the case may be, for a single subsystem. This process step does not yet produce any decisions with regard to technical implementation.

- **Analysis of the logical system architecture and specification of technical system architecture**

  The logical system architecture is the basis for the specification of the actual technical system architecture. The analysis of technical implementation alternatives is based on a unified logical system architecture and is supported by a variety of methods of the participating engineering disciplines. The technical system architecture also includes a definition of all functions or subfunctions that will be implemented by means of software. This definition is also called software requirements.

- **Analysis of software requirements and specification of software architecture**

  The software requirements thus defined are analyzed in the next step, and the software architecture is specified. That is, the software system boundaries and interfaces are defined, with software components, software layers, and operating modes.

- **Specification of software components**

  This step is followed by the specification of software components. The procedure initially assumes an "ideal-world" environment. This means that this step ignores any implementation details, such as the implementation in integer arithmetic.

- **Design, implementation, and tests of software components**

  In the design phase, the previously ignored real-world aspects are subject to scrutiny. At this point, all details affecting the implementation must be defined. The resulting design decisions govern the implementation of software components. At the end of this step, software components are tested.

- **Integration of software components and software integration tests**

  When the development of the software components is completed—frequently done by applying the principle of division of labor—and components have passed the subsequent tests, integration can begin. After integration of the components into a software system, a software integration test concludes this step.

- **Integration of system components and system integration tests**

  In the next step, the software must be installed on the ECU hardware to provide the respective ECU with functional capabilities. The ECUs then must be integrated with the other electronic system components such as setpoint generators, sensors, and actuators. In a subsequent system integration test, the interaction of all systems with the plant is evaluated.

- **Calibration**

  The calibration of the ECU software functions comprises their parameterization; the setting of parameter values must frequently be carried out individually for each type or variant of a given vehicle. Parameter settings may be supplied by the software in the form of characteristic values, characteristic curves, and characteristic maps.

- **System test and acceptance test**

  Finally, a system test focusing on the logical system architecture can be performed, with an acceptance test that concentrates on user requirements.

1.4.4 Support Processes for Electronic Systems and Software Development

The core process must be complemented by a number of additional processes, ranging from the systematic identification and documentation of requirements, fault messages, and modification requests through planning and implementation tracking, to the archiving of variant data. These so-called *support processes* include requirements management, configuration management, and project and supplier management, as well as quality assurance (Fig. 1-16). For a detailed discussion of the referenced support processes, see Chapter 3.

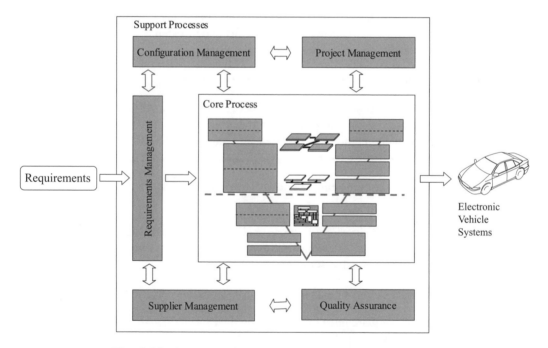

Fig. 1-16. *Overview of support processes for the development of electronic systems and software.*

To ensure continuous progress in the development of electronic systems and software, a number of widely disparate groups and tasks must be managed, supported, and integrated. These include all development steps, the customer/supplier relationship between companies and within companies, intermediate development results, development happening parallel in time, and transition/synchronization points between development steps. Similar to what is general practice in the representation of business processes, development processes also can be clearly represented in graphical form.

1.4.4.1 Customer/Supplier Relationships

Figure 1-17 [23] shows a graphical process structure of customer/suppplier relationships. Efficient teamwork, of course, presupposes a close integration of methods and tools as well.

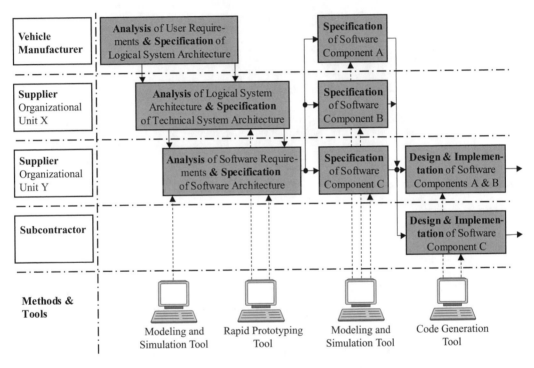

Fig. 1-17. *Diagram of customer/supplier relationships. (Ref. [23])*

1.4.4.2 Simultaneous Engineering and Different Development Environments

In many cases, the mandate of shortening the development time calls for the concurrent handling of development tasks (i.e., simultaneous engineering). In software development, simultaneous engineering means that typical development activities, such as analysis, specification, design, implementation, and integration of a given software function, followed by testing and calibration, are all being performed for that function, while all of these activities are performed for any number of software functions in development at the same time. In addition, various different development environments must be coordinated or ideally integrated; that is, simulation procedures and development steps in the laboratory, on the test bench, and in the vehicle must be designed with the highest possible degree of standardization and then synchronized with each other. Figure 1-18 shows a sample structure for simultaneous engineering within various development environments.

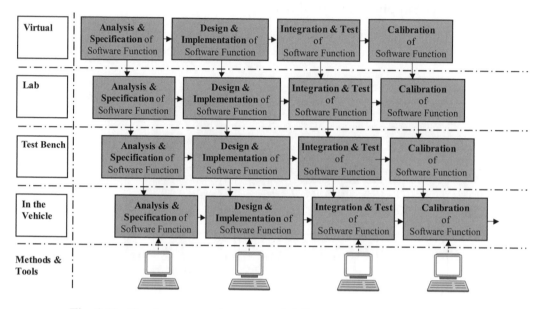

Fig. 1-18. *Simultaneous engineering and different development environments.*

1.4.5 Production and Service of Electronic Systems and Software

Quite often, the fact that software variants lend themselves, in terms of production and service, to easier handling than their hardware counterparts, results in the call for the software implementation of variant-specific portions of a given electronic system.

In those cases, vehicle variants give rise to the software variants of ECUs. For this reason, both production and service must provide a procedure for programming the ECUs with software variants or updates, or for inputting the parameter values for software functions at the end of the manufacturing process.

Service is faced with the additional demand for the support of troubleshooting in electronic systems through suitable diagnostic procedures and with the relevant interfaces and tools. The long product life cycles, high volume production, and worldwide distribution of vehicles comprise the framework conditions to be taken into account in the development of suitable service concepts.

Methods and tools for production and service are discussed in Chapter 6.

1.5 Methods and Tools for the Development of Software for Electronic Systems

Virtually every development step can benefit from suitable tool-assisted methods that contribute to the improvement of quality while providing risk and cost reductions. Accordingly, the integration of the various tools gains special significance. The following sections discuss possible approaches to tools integration and their effect on the three critical success factors of quality, risk, and cost.

The V-Model is implicit in its assertion that the user requirements initially are almost completely identified and analyzed, and that a sufficiently accurate specification for the technical system architecture may be derived from those findings. Tool integration is based on a series of subsequent steps that are closely defined.

However, experience shows that these prerequisites are not fulfilled in many cases. Often at the start of development, user requirements are not fully understood and are updated as development work progresses. For this reason, specifications initially tend to reflect merely a rough idea of the system; the definition of details occurs gradually. During system integration, component-related delays result in delays of the integration process and of all subsequent steps. Whenever software development tasks are handled by different companies, the execution of integration and test steps for a given component frequently is limited by the unavailability of related components or by outdated versions of related components.

For these reasons, the reality of development is characterized by incremental and iterative procedures, forcing developers to repeat some steps or even all steps of the entire V-Model many times.

However, a number of methods or tools are available to support a process-oriented approach to software function development. Applying such methods and tools will help to ensure the timely validation of requirements, specifications, and implemented components, in the laboratory and on the test bench, as well as in the vehicle.

1.5.1 Model-Based Development

In software development, interdisciplinary cooperation (e.g., among powertrain, chassis, and electronics development) presupposes a common, integrated understanding of problems and solutions. When designing control engineering functions for a vehicle, for example, reliability and safety aspects also must be considered, as well as the implementation of these control functions by means of software in embedded systems.

A graphical function model that includes all system components frequently serves as the basis for gaining a common understanding of functions. Therefore, customized model-based software development methods with notations such as block diagrams and finite state machines are increasingly replacing software specifications in plain text form.

Aside from a common appreciation of issues and solutions, software function *modeling* offers additional benefits.

Provided the specification model is formal, that is, unambiguous and without leeway for interpretation, the specification can be executed on the computer in a *simulation*. It then can be experienced in the vehicle at an early point in time with the aid of *rapid prototyping*. All of these benefits have contributed to a wide acceptance of "digital specification."

Using automated *code generation* methods, specified function models can be implemented in software components for ECUs. To accomplish this, function models must be enhanced by adding design information that also includes required nonfunctional product properties such as optimization measures.

The operating environment of ECUs can be simulated by means of so-called *laboratory vehicles*, or *lab cars*. Lab cars facilitate early testing of ECUs in a laboratory setting. Using lab cars for testing facilitates the reproduction of test cases and offers greater flexibility than test bench and in-vehicle tests can provide.

The *calibration* of software functions often can be finalized only at some point toward the end of the development process. In many cases, this procedure is carried out in the vehicle with all systems running and requires support by means of suitable methods and tools.

To summarize, a model-based approach to software function development comprises a number of well-defined, clearly separated development steps, as shown in Fig. 1-19 [24].

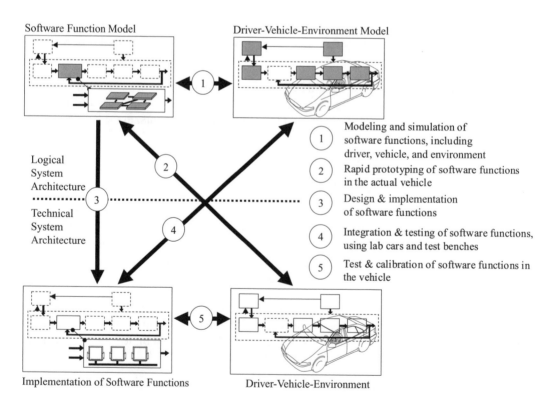

Fig. 1-19. Overview of the model-based development process.

A model-based approach is also suitable for the development of function networks and networked ECUs. In those contexts, however, the process gains additional degrees of freedom, such as the following:

- Combinations of modeled, virtual, and implemented functions
- Combinations of modeled, virtual, and implemented technical components

1.5.2 Integrated Quality Management

Creating high-quality software is the objective of any systematic approach to software design. Software quality characteristics include adequate functional range, reliability, usability, efficiency, adaptability, and portability.

Quality management covers all measures that will ensure that a given product meets its requirements. Quality can be "built into" a product, as long as guidelines for quality assurance, plus measures for quality control and testing, have been established and are followed.

1.5.2.1 Quality Assurance Guidelines

Quality assurance includes a complement of "preventive" measures, such as the following:

- Employment of appropriately educated, experienced, and trained developers
- Use of a suitable, specified development process
- Use of guidelines, measures, and standards supporting the process
- Use of a suitable tool environment supporting the process
- Automation of manual, error-prone work procedures

1.5.2.2 Quality Control, Validation, and Verification Measures

The aim of quality control measures is fault detection. Quality control should be carried out after as many individual tasks within the function development process as possible. Therefore, quality control means performing a series of scheduled tasks throughout the entire development cycle.

Software quality control differentiates between controlling for specification errors and the design and implementation errors. Research has shown that specification errors predominate in most development projects. Therefore, the V-Model differentiates between validation and verification in quality control and testing.

Validation Versus Verification

- *Validation* is defined as the process of evaluating a system or a component of the system to establish that it is satisfactory for its intended application and that it meets customer expectations. Accordingly, *function validation* as a process has the aim of establishing that the *specification* meets customer expectations and that it will have customer acceptance.

- The term *verification* describes the process of evaluating a system or a component of a system to establish that the results of a given development phase meet the requirements for that phase. Accordingly, *software verification* establishes that an *implementation* adequately meets the specifications defined for the respective development step.

Quite often, traditional development, integration, and quality control methods for software do not allow for a clear separation of verification and validation. Modern development tools, however, offer a clear advantage over traditional tools. With modern development tools, function validation in the vehicle without the actual ECU present is possible because the tools support rapid prototyping with an experimental system.

Figure 1-20 shows the validation and verification steps available through the application of simulation, rapid prototyping, and code generation tools.

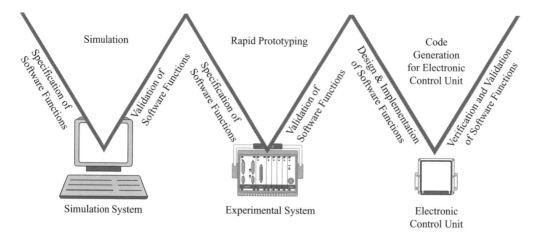

Fig. 1-20. *Function validation and software verification, including simulation, rapid prototyping, and code generation for the ECU.*

1.5.3 Reducing the Development Risk

A risk is defined as an event whose occurrence may seriously interfere with the scheduled flow of a project. Several different measures for intervention to minimize risk are available for function development. Two of these warrant closer examination.

1.5.3.1 Early Validation of Software Functions

Early function validation with rapid prototyping greatly contributes to curbing risk, as the more costly implementation of ECU software can be done after the function has been successfully validated in the vehicle. Unnecessary iteration within the software development process thus can be avoided. The validated function model can be used as the specification for the design and implementation by the automated and tool-supported code generation for a specific ECU. It also may serve as a reference for the subsequent software verification.

To enable early validation, the following methods may be considered:

- Formal specification and modeling
- Simulation and rapid prototyping

Integration and test systems for laboratory application support the early validation of ECUs without requiring an actual vehicle. One such method is the previously discussed simulation of an ECU environment by means of lab cars.

This process must accommodate the special requirements of the frequently cross-corporate development, integration, and test tasks. For example, prototype vehicles are available only in limited numbers. Frequently, the manufacturer of a component that he is required to supply does not have a complete or updated environment for that unit at his disposal. There is a good likelihood that the strictures imposed by the test environment also limit the scope of available test procedures.

The component integration comprises a synchronization point for all participating component developments. The testing of integration, system, and acceptance can be carried out only when all components are physically present and have been integrated. Delays related to individual components will result in delays in the integration process and will delay the execution of all subsequent test steps.

Therefore, a software function test for ECUs can be carried out only when all of the components making up the overall vehicle system (i.e., ECUs, setpoint generators, sensors, actuators, and plant) are available. The use of lab cars facilitates early tests of ECUs without the need for real-world environment components. This approach also prevents the possible exposure of test drivers or vehicle prototypes to a range of hazards.

Virtual validation methods of this kind will continue to gain in significance. However, even in the future, the final validation of a given function, that is, the test of whether or not the user requirements are being met, can be carried out only from the user perspective, meaning acceptance testing in the actual vehicle.

1.5.3.2 Reuse of Software Functions

A second way to check risk is reuse. The prerequisite for successful reuse is a clear modularization of the system as a whole. If operationally proven software at the source code level is targeted for reuse today, new software and system architecture often cannot be introduced easily, and portability to future generations of microcontroller models often is limited.

However, distinct advantages with respect to reuse may be realized at the model level. Here, risk can be minimized through the reuse of proven specification models of functions and environment, and through the reuse of test cases, as well as calibration data from simulation to the laboratory and test bench down to the vehicle.

1.5.4 Standardization and Automation

Standardization and automation efforts may be employed as major contributors to cost savings and quality improvement in function development.

1.5.4.1 Standardization

The major documentation on the standardization of processes and description formats for measuring, calibration, Flash programming, and diagnostic tools appears in ASAM [17] and ISO [25, 26]. These standards are widely used in the automotive industry. Figure 1-21 shows an overview of the approved software architecture for tools, and for the ASAM-MCD 1b, 2, and 3 interface standards.

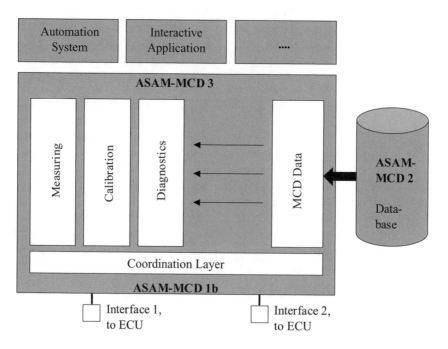

Fig. 1-21. Software architecture for tools and ASAM standards. (Ref. [17])

Meanwhile, the introduction of approaches to the standardization of the software architecture for the microcontrollers used in ECUs has also been successful. For example, a differentiation is made between the "actual" software functions (i.e., the control and monitoring functions of the so-called *application software*) and the *platform software* that is partially hardware dependent.

The platform software category also includes the software components required for onboard and offboard communication. The distinction between platform and application software enables developers to specify application software functions that are largely hardware independent, which in turn facilitates porting to a variety of microcontrollers.

Those software components that cover the hardware-related aspects of microcontroller input/output (I/O) units are grouped together in the so-called *hardware abstraction layer* (HAL) of the platform software. As shown in Fig. 1-22, the I/O units required for the communication with other systems via data bus are excluded from the HAL; the required bus drivers are viewed separately. Platform software also includes the software components of higher-level layers required for communication with other ECUs on the network, or with tools such as diagnostic testing devices.

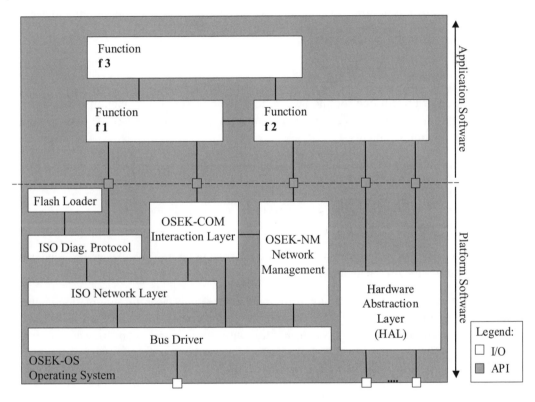

Fig. 1-22. *Software architecture for microcontrollers and OSEK/ISO standards. (Ref. [16])*

Examples of standardized software components are real-time operating systems and communication and network management based on the OSEK [16] standard, as well as diagnostic protocols based on ISO [25, 26].

So far, standardization has concentrated mainly on the components belonging to the platform software category, as vehicle manufacturers and automotive suppliers perceive them to be without competitive significance (Fig. 1-22) [27, 28]. These software components provide standardized application programming interfaces (APIs). In this way, the platform software can be standardized for a variety of applications. Application software functions can be developed largely independently of the hardware. Chapter 2 provides a detailed discussion of the software architecture and standardized components for microcontrollers.

The complete standardization of all platform software components provides further potential with regard to cost savings and quality control. For the application software functions that often carry competitive value, however, the introduction of open standards is not in the interest of vehicle manufacturers and their suppliers. Still, when the aspects of liability and copyright protection have been settled, both sides can benefit from an enterprise-wide standardization (e.g., through the assembly of function libraries). Vehicle manufacturers then could deploy software functions across the domains of different suppliers. Suppliers would have the opportunity to deploy standardized software functions to all of their customers.

1.5.4.2 Automation

The automation of error-prone routine tasks offers great potential for function development. The higher reproducibility achieved by automation permits cost and time-related benefits and, above all, quality improvements.

More and more automotive manufacturers and suppliers are automating the following development steps:

- Production of function prototypes by means of rapid prototyping tools
- C-code generation for ECUs (Fig. 1-20).

With the use of lab cars, test procedures previously carried out in the vehicle can be transferred to the laboratory for subsequent automation.

Measurement and calibration tools support remote control interfaces for automating calibration, measuring, and test tasks [29]. Via this interface, time-consuming calibration tasks can be automatically performed on the test bench. For this purpose, a separate standard was developed (e.g., ASAM-MCD 3).

Automation of some process steps in the right branch of the V-Model presupposes, however, that automation as an option is already integrated into the design phase (i.e., in the left branch of the V-Model). The relevant keywords are "design for testability" or "design of experiments." These design methods promise great benefit but remain currently in development [30, 31].

Routine tasks performed by developers in the course of version, configuration, and variant management tend to allow the introduction of errors. However, these routine tasks can be automated via suitable interfaces from the development tools to configuration-, version-, and variant-management systems.

1.5.5 Development Steps in the Vehicle

Compared to other industries, in-vehicle development constitutes a unique feature of the automotive industry. For many development steps that must be carried out in the vehicle, it is often not possible to connect the development tools to the infrastructure (i.e., to the corporate data network). Thus, software development that includes both simultaneous engineering and in-vehicle development requires not only robust but sophisticated tools for in-vehicle use, but a very clear methodological approach to the management of development results and consistent data management.

The measuring technology required for in-vehicle testing and calibration must be designed to withstand applications in the most harsh environmental conditions, characterized by extreme temperature ranges, humidity, electromagnetic compatibility issues, fluctuating supply voltages, vibration, and cramped installation spaces. In addition, the user interface to the in-vehicle measuring technology must be suitable for in-vehicle use.

The in-vehicle measuring technology used in development for the validation of a vehicle function—comprising the interaction of a system of ECUs, setpoint generators, sensors, and actuators—must belong to a higher performance class than that selected for the sensor systems of the ECUs onboard a production vehicle. In particular, the data interface connecting the ECUs and measuring tools must be able to transfer data at a high transmission rate to enable the capture of internal ECU signals.

CHAPTER TWO

ESSENTIAL SYSTEM BASICS

An important prerequisite for the development of automotive software is the smooth interaction of a variety of engineering disciplines. Examples that come to mind are mechanical engineering, electrical engineering, and software technology, to name only a few. It would be safe to say that several players representing a variety of disciplines often work simultaneously toward the completion of a diversity of tasks. The successful and efficient completion of the tasks at hand is predicated on a shared appreciation of issues and solutions.

This chapter provides an introduction to the various contributing disciplines exerting significant influence on software in its application as a subsystem. This chiefly concerns the development of open-loop and closed-loop control systems, discrete embedded real-time systems, and distributed and networked systems providing reliability and safety functions.

The information in this book is intended to provide readers with a basic understanding of both the functional principles and the interaction of the various software components of a microcontroller, as shown in Fig. 1-22 of Chapter 1. For the purposes of this book, it stands to reason that this objective cannot be to consider a full treatment and in-depth investigation into the various related disciplines. Instead, the text focuses on providing explanations of basic principles and terms, to the extent that such information shall be relevant and required throughout subsequent chapters.

The terminology used throughout this book, although based on the technical engineering language used in the original German manuscript, has been carefully translated.

The order in which the various engineering disciplines are examined should not be construed to represent any kind of order of importance. However, because the respective disciplines are interdependent at various levels, their order of discussion results from the stipulation that, taken by itself, this introduction should be effective enough without requiring the reader to look up information in subsequent sections of this book.

2.1 Open-Loop and Closed-Loop Control Systems

Most vehicle functions in the areas of powertrain, chassis, and body perform some kind of control task. For this reason, in-depth familiarity with the methods and technical terms related to the technologies involved comprises a necessary foundation for the design of many of these functions.

2.1.1 Modeling

In the initial phase of the design procedures related to controlling and monitoring functions, these may be regarded as an abstraction of the technical implementation. The task of abstracting (i.e., *modeling)* produces a *model.* A distinction is made between the task of modeling for the controlling or monitoring device (the so-called *open-loop control model* or *closed-loop control model*) and that of modeling for the system to be controlled or monitored (the so-called *open-loop plant model* or *closed-loop plant model*).

The approach chosen to find solutions to controlling tasks is largely independent of the characteristic aspects of physical construction of the respective technical system to be controlled. A major decisive factor influencing the design of open-loop and closed-loop control devices is the operating characteristic, both static and dynamic, of the technical system to be controlled. In an effort to simplify this somewhat complex matter, this book takes a cue from automotive industry jargon in referring to *control units* throughout the text. This term describes devices that perform—in addition to other functions—both open-loop and closed-loop control tasks.

Of secondary importance is the type of physical variable—be it temperature, voltage, pressure, torque, output power, or rotational speed—to be controlled, with the technical implementation of a given device.

This abstraction potential enabled the technology governing open-loop and closed-loop control systems to develop into a separate engineering discipline. In fact, this branch of engineering science is trying to identify common properties in systems characterized by great technical diversity. With the relevant findings laying the foundation for the development of commonly applicable design methods for control systems, this discipline has matured into a connecting element for a diversity of engineering branches.

2.1.2 Block Diagrams

In many cases, modeling is done by means of graphic visualization, with preference given to so-called *block diagrams*. These depict the response characteristics of individual components, as well as the signal flow occurring between the components of a system. Figure 2-1 shows the block diagram representing the logical system architecture for open-loop and closed-loop vehicle functions.

Figure 2-1 facilitates the explanation and definition of the essential terms of closed-loop and open-loop control technology.

The term *closed-loop control task* defines a procedure during which a variable X to be controlled (i.e., regulated) is subjected to continuous capture. It is then compared with reference variable W on a similar ongoing basis. Depending on the result of this compare operation, variable X is influenced with a view to attaining an approximation of reference variable W. The resulting sequence of actions occurs within a closed circuit, the so-called *control loop*. The purpose of the closed-loop control procedure is to approximate the value of controlled variable X to that of reference variable W, irrespective of the disturbance values introduced by interference variable Z [32].

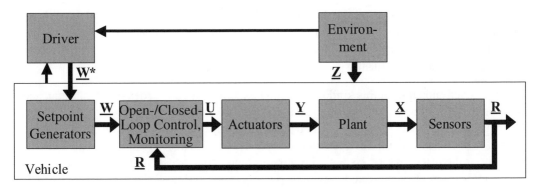

Fig. 2-1. *Function model using a block diagram of open-loop and closed-loop vehicle control systems.*

By contrast, the term *open-loop control task* defines a procedure within a system during which one or more input variables influence specific output variables in conformity with the design characteristics of that system. The distinguishing feature of the controlling action is the open-loop sequence of actions involving either a single transfer element or an entire open control loop [32].

Open-loop and closed-loop control models describe the components of a system in the form of block diagrams, with visual blocks depicting transfer elements, and arrows connecting the blocks, representing signal flows. More often than not, control systems for automotive applications belong to the category of multi-input/multi-output systems. For this reason, the signals being processed are vector shaped (Fig. 2-1). A number of signal types are differentiated:

Measured or feedback variables	$\underline{R}$
Output variables of open-loop/closed-loop control	$\underline{U}$
Reference variables or setpoint values	$\underline{W}$
Driver-specific setpoint values	$\underline{W}^*$
Open-loop/closed-loop controlled variables	$\underline{X}$
Manipulated variables	$\underline{Y}$
Interference variables	$\underline{Z}$

In terms of the blocks making up the function model, a distinction is made between the open-loop/closed-loop controller model, the actuator models, the plant model, the models covering setpoint generators and sensors, the driver model, and the environment model. The driver is able to influence the functions of one or the other control system by introducing setpoint values. The components engaged in the acquisition of these driver-specific setpoint values—such as switches or pedals—are also termed *setpoint generators*. By contrast, sensors capture the signals occurring in the control section, or plant.

It follows that, in standard operation, the reference variables or setpoint variables $\underline{W}$ can normally be introduced by the users of a system by means of a setpoint generator, or transferred in the form of default parameter values from a higher-level system. More often than not, the systems involved are of the hierarchical type.

Another benefit inherent in this kind of modeling encompasses a broader set of consequences. Because the open-loop and closed-loop control models are abstractions based on the technical implementation, they also are ideally suited to the modeling of the various software control functions of ECUs. This, in turn, facilitates an accurate description not only of the interaction of the software of the respective ECUs with the setpoint generators, sensors, and actuators, but with the components of the vehicle and miscellaneous electronic systems. For the reasons given, the open-loop/closed-loop control modeling approach on the basis of block diagrams is also widely used in conjunction with the development of software-implemented vehicle functions. Thus, it serves as a connecting element for a consistent development process, despite the fact that it tends to neglect essential software aspects.

Example: Block diagram for a PI controller

Block diagrams also are used to describe individual blocks within the closed-loop control circuit, as in the example of the controller block. Figure 2-2 represents the block diagram of a controller featuring two components. One of these features *proportional* response characteristics, while the other provides *integral* signal-handling characteristics. Thus, this type of controller is termed *PI controller* (proportional-plus-integral control).

External View:

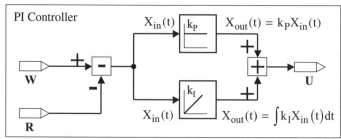

Internal View:

Fig. 2-2. Block diagram of a PI controller.

A characteristic feature of any controller is the comparison of controller input variables W and R. As is the case with the PI controller shown in Fig. 2-2, this comparison often is accomplished by calculating the difference between the two input variables, that is, reference variable W and feedback variable R. The difference thus obtained—the so-called *system deviation*—becomes the input variable for both controller sections:

the proportional component, with response characteristic

$$X_{out}(t) = k_P X_{in}(t) \tag{2.1}$$

and the integral component, with response characteristic

$$X_{out}(t) = \int k_I X_{in}(t) dt \tag{2.2}$$

with their assigned magnification factors or controller parameters k_P and k_I. Adding the outputs of both controller components produces the PI controller output variable U.

Therefore, the so-called *transfer function* of the PI controller is expressed as

$$U(t) = k_P(W(t) - R(t)) + \int k_I(W(t) - R(t)) dt \tag{2.3}$$

For each block within the block diagram, there exists an external and internal view (Fig. 2-2).

Models of this type, applied to all blocks of the control loop, form the basis for the analysis and specification of open-loop/closed-loop controllers, down to systems design, implementation, and testing.

Because it is neither practical nor intended to make reference to the numerous modeling, analysis, and design methods for open-loop and closed-loop control systems, reference is made to the relevant specialized literature [33–36].

The decisive factor determining the characteristics of a control function is the transfer function—the so-called *control algorithm*—on one hand, and the settings of the relevant *control parameters*, on the other hand. Taken as a group, the various control parameters attached to a given controller function are termed *parameter set*. The control parameters used in many vehicle functions utilize, in addition to scalar quantities such as k_P and k_I in the preceding example, characteristic curves and three-dimensional characteristics maps in lieu of control parameters.

Example: Ignition map

One such example is the ignition map required onboard by engine ECUs (Fig. 2-3). Depending on the current working point of the engine (i.e., the input parameters of engine speed and

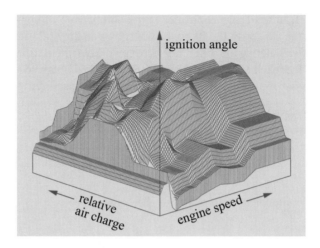

Fig. 2-3. *Ignition map stored onboard by engine ECUs. (Ref. [4]).*

load and/or relative air charge), the ignition map provides the most suitable ignition angles with respect to the fuel consumption and emission characteristics of the engine [4].

Because the parameter values contained in the ignition map are engine-specific, they must be determined and fine-tuned during the development phase for a vehicle.

As already noted in the discussion of control devices, from the vantage point of controller technology, it is of secondary importance whether, in the final analysis, the implementation of a control function is effected with the use of a mechanical, hydraulic, or electronic system. For example, arriving at the implementation of the PI controller shown in Fig. 2-2 may involve a variety of different approaches that are totally divergent in terms of applied technologies. However, it is critical to observe that the area of vehicle manufacture is one field of endeavor in which the implementation of control functions by means of ECUs in conjunction with mechanical, electrical, or hydraulic components provides a number of benefits in terms of attainable reliability, vehicle weight, required installation space, and costs. For a number of reasons, this form of implementation is most often preferred. Accordingly, the following sections will discuss the applicable functional principles and the configuration of ECUs in greater detail (Fig. 2-4).

As perceived from the development standpoint of software to be used by the microcontrollers powering ECUs, the open-loop/closed-loop controller models also are known as *function models*, whereas the models describing setpoint generators, sensors, actuators, plant, driver, and environment are termed *surrounding models*.

2.2 Discrete Systems

In contrast to the analog signal processing occurring in mechanical, electrical, or hydraulic components, the input variables of ECUs are discretely processed by the digital microprocessors

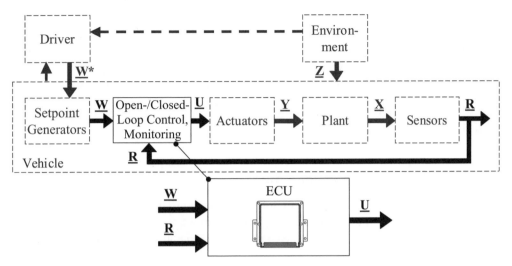

Fig. 2-4. *Open-loop/closed-loop control functions implemented in an ECU.*

typically found in such devices. In consequence, this also calls for the discrete implementation of open-loop/closed-loop control functions.

This section presents several terms and basic information relevant to discrete systems [37, 38]. Figure 2-5 shows the simplified block diagram of an electronic control unit.

Once acquired by the setpoint generators and sensors, the external input signals $\underline{W}$ and $\underline{R}$ first are preprocessed in the input module of the ECU to a point where they become suitable for further processing by the microcontroller as internal input variables $\underline{W}_{int}$ and $\underline{R}_{int}$. Similarly, the output

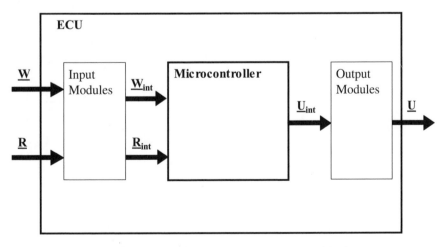

Fig. 2-5. *Model of an ECU comprising a block of an open-loop/closed-loop control system.*

modules convert the internal output variables $\underline{U}_{int}$ of the microprocessor into the external output signal $\underline{U}$ required by the actuators. More often than not, input and output modules comprise signal conditioning or gain circuits. The software development for the microprocessor of a microcontroller concerns itself with the internal signals. Therefore, to simplify the discussion that follows, the text will no longer differentiate between internal and external signals.

Unless explicitly stated otherwise, the internal signals discussed in the following text will be termed $\underline{W}$, $\underline{R}$, and $\underline{U}$.

2.2.1 Time-Discrete Systems and Signals

In analog systems, all occurring signals comprise continuous functions of time. Therefore, when observing signal X for the duration of interval (time) t, the unambiguous state X(t) may be assigned to the signal (Fig. 2-6(a)). Signals of this type are termed *continuous time and value signals.*

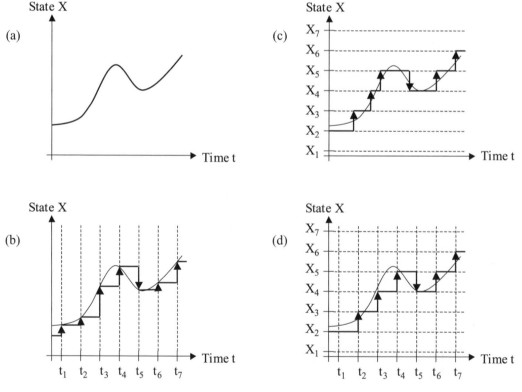

Fig. 2-6. *Sampling modes for continuous signal. (a) Continuous time and value. (b) Discrete time and continuous value. (c) Continuous time and discrete value. (d) Discrete time and value.*

If a signal of the type X(t), as shown in Fig. 2-6(b), is measured or "sampled" only at specific discrete instants t_1, t_2, t_3, and so forth, the result is a *discrete time and continuous value signal* or a *sampled signal*. It is defined by the expression

$$X(t_k) = \{X(t_1), X(t_2), X(t_3),...\} \qquad (2.4)$$

with k = 1, 2, 3, and so forth.

The interval $dT_k = T_k - t_{k-1}$ is termed *sampling rate*. The sampling rate may be constant for all sampling instances, or it may vary.

Example: Sampling rates in the engine ECU

The engine ECU performs a number of individual functions. Using sensors to acquire engine status and driver command, it controls the engine-specific actuators.

The two basic functions of ignition and injection must enable the actuators of the engine at instants that are synchronized with specific crankshaft positions. A change in engine speed also changes the sampling rate of these functions.

However, other functions, such as the acquisition of the driver command via the drive pedal position by means of the pedal travel sensor, can be executed at constant timeline intervals (i.e., at a constant sampling rate).

The sampling rate dT represents an essential design parameter for time-discrete systems. The required sampling rate is determined by the dynamics inherent in the closed-loop or open-loop control section (or plant). A rule of thumb for determining the sampling rate for controlling continuous-time systems by means of time-discrete controllers states that the sampling rate dT should be selected to be somewhere within the range of a minimum of one-tenth and a maximum of one-sixth of the essential time constants of the controlled system [34]. The behavior of time-discrete control functions is decidedly dependent on the selected sampling rate dT. It is quite normal for a control unit to process several controller functions at once, each having a different sampling rate, as shown in the preceding example.

If at least one time-discrete signal occurs in a given system, this is known as a time-discrete system. In the case of microcontrollers, for example, such time discretization characteristic arises from the time-discrete sampling of input signals.

2.2.2 Value-Discrete Systems and Signals

The analog-digital converters (*A/D converters*, for short) customarily used in the acquisition of input signals are also termed *sampling elements* [34]. A consequence of the limited word size of these devices is the occurrence of amplitude quantization (i.e., the formation of a *value-discrete signal* (Fig. 2-6(c)).

The described amplitude quantization comprises a nonlinear effect. In the case of analog-digital conversion, for example, the nonlinearity is manifested by the limitation of the value range by X_{min} and X_{max}, where each state $X(t)$ is unambiguously assigned exactly one discrete value X_i of the quantity

$$\{X_1, X_2, X_3, ... X_n\} \tag{2.5}$$

where $X_{min} \leq X_i \leq X_{max}$.

The difference $X(t) - X_i(t)$ is referred to as the *quantizing* error.

A similar effect occurs in the output of control unit signals, the so-called *digital-analog conversion*. Here, a pulse width modulated signal is output in many cases. For the purpose of this text, all methods employed for the purpose of outputting discrete signals will be collectively referred to as *digital-analog conversion* (*D/A conversion*, for short). In D/A conversion, the assigned value X_i is held constant until the subsequent sampling cycle. Accordingly, D/A converters are also termed *holding elements* [34].

2.2.3 Time- and Value-Discrete Systems and Signals

If both discretization effects occur together, the result is a *time- and value-discrete signal* (Fig. 2-6(d)).

If at least one time- and value-discrete signal occurs in a given system, the same is termed a *time- and value-discrete system* or *digital system*.

Any variables being processed as input variables for a program being executed on the microcontroller of an ECU represent time- and value-discrete signals. The microprocessor may be drawn as a block in the closed control loop or open control loop, as shown in Fig. 2-7.

Here, the normally time- and value-continuous input signals $\underline{W}$ and $\underline{R}$ are mapped onto the time- and value-discrete signals $\underline{W}_k$ and $\underline{R}_k$. From these, a program calculates the time- and value-discrete output signals $\underline{U}_k$ which, in turn, are mapped onto the time- and value-continuous signals $\underline{U}$. The response characteristics of open-loop and closed-loop control functions, as well as the respective control parameters, must be implemented by software components running on the microcontroller.

2.2.4 State Machines

Whereas physical variables normally comprise continuous time and value signals, and the response characteristics of continuous time and value systems may be described in terms of physics by differential equations, the response characteristics of discrete systems may be described by means of difference equations.

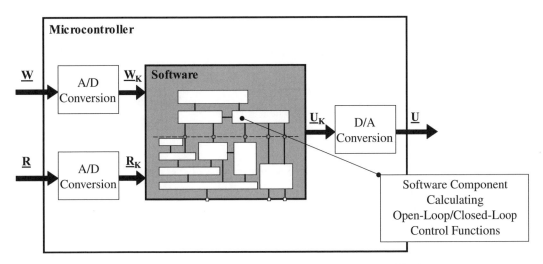

Fig. 2-7. *Model of a microcontroller comprising a block of an open-loop/closed-loop control system.*

The process of time and value discretization causes the transition from one discrete state $X(t_k)$ to a subsequent state $X(t_k + 1)$ to be reduced to an event. The number of possible or relevant states, as well as the number of possible or relevant events, often are limited in the majority of discrete technical systems. This fact is exploited through the use of state machines for modeling.

Example: Controlling the low-fuel indicator lamp

The fuel level sensor measures the level inside the fuel tank of a vehicle and produces an analog signal (i.e., a signal proportional to the measured fuel level) within the range of 0 and 10 V. This analog signal is used as the input for controlling the low-fuel indicator lamp. It is then subjected to time- and value-discrete sampling in the instrument cluster.

In this process, an analog signal value of 8.5 V is the reading produced by the spare fuel quantity of 5 liters remaining in the fuel tank. A signal value of 10 V corresponds to an empty tank, and a signal value of 0 V a full tank. It follows that the low-fuel indicator lamp must be energized in the presence of a signal value greater than 8.5 V.

To prevent a flickering of the lamp by virtue of it being switched on and off in rapid succession by minute movements of the fuel volume in the tank, a hysteresis function must be implemented. It is desirable that the low-fuel indicator lamp be switched off only at the point where a fuel volume exceeding 6 liters, corresponding to a signal value of less than 8.0 V, has been reached. Figure 2-8 shows the relevant switching operations.

Based on the foregoing, the only factors of interest in the control of the low-fuel indicator lamp are the instants—or *events*—of overshooting the "signal value less than 8.0 V" and "signal value greater than 8.5 V" thresholds, and the previous "off" or "on" state of the lamp.

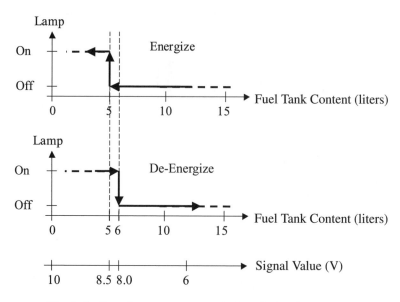

Fig. 2-8. Switching operations of a low-fuel indicator lamp.

Figure 2-9 shows a diagram of the discrete "Lamp off" and "Lamp on" states, with the possible transitions between these states, to which the corresponding events have been assigned.

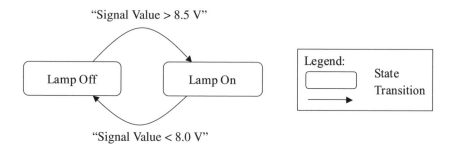

Fig. 2-9. State/transition graph of a low-fuel indicator lamp.

This type of state transition graph, also termed *state machine*, serves as a graphical notation for the representation of discrete systems. It frequently is used to model discrete vehicle functions, too.

For a detailed discussion of the representation of continuous and discrete signals and systems, reference is made to suggested reading and advanced literature [37, 38].

2.3 Embedded Systems

Electronic control units, setpoint generators, sensors, and actuators form an electronic system that influences the status of the plant, or control section. In most cases, the ECU, comprising a component of the overall driver–vehicle–environment system, remains entirely "out of sight." For example, if the ECU is dedicated exclusively to controller functions, it will not be equipped with a direct *user interface* of any kind. Usually, this is a characteristic common to ECUs deployed in powertrain, chassis, and body applications. The driver and the vehicle occupants exercise a degree of influence on the ECUs that may be described as indirect in many cases, negligible on many occasions, and nonexistent in some instances. The user interfaces acquiring the reference variables are almost always indirectly implemented and often are restricted (Fig. 2-10). Systems exhibiting the described features are also termed *embedded systems*.

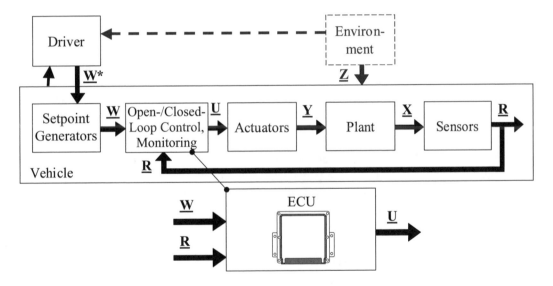

Fig. 2-10. *Identifiers of embedded systems.*

As perceived by the ECU, setpoint generators can be handled in the same way as sensors (i.e., with a view to acquiring user instructions). For this reason, the discussion throughout the following sections, in instances where this will foster an easier understanding of the subject matter, will consider setpoint generators as a special type of sensor. In a similar fashion, all components engaged in delivering a driver feedback of some kind will be regarded as special types of actuators. This feedback may cover events or states and may take the form of visual displays or acoustic signals.

It follows that the function development of ECUs also must account for the response character-istics of the control unit interfaces, with that of the setpoint generators, sensors, and actuators.

In turn, the actuators and sensors often compose systems incorporating electrical, hydraulic, pneumatic, or mechanical, and, to an increasing measure, electronic components. In cases where signal conditioning or post-processing occurs in conjunction with actuators and/or sensors featur-ing electronic components, the term *intelligent actuators* or *sensors* often is used.

The response characteristics encompass the dynamic response along a given timeline, on one hand, and the static behavior, such as the range of physical values or the physical resolution of the transmitted signals, on the other.

There always exist direct interfaces between an embedded system and its immediate environment (i.e., between an ECU and its closed-loop or open-loop plant). By contrast, in most cases, there are only indirect interfaces between the system and its user (i.e., the driver or passengers).

For this reason, software development for the microcontrollers of an ECU must accommodate an essential difference. It often is possible to make certain assumptions with regard to the dynamic behavior of an open-loop or closed-loop control system. Such assumptions may facilitate the acquisition of the plant's current state variables by means of cyclical sampling using a fixed or variable sampling rate. However, when it comes to acquiring driver commands, assumptions of a different nature provide more advantages in many cases. For example, in the context of switches acting as operating elements, a driver command should rather be seen as an event that recurs as a single event now and then but that calls for immediate response as soon as it occurs.

Generally speaking, the microcontroller therefore is required to process both *periodic* and *ape-riodic events*. For this reason, a basic understanding of the construction, operating principles, interfaces, and programming of microcontrollers of the type used in ECUs is an essential pre-requisite for all developers participating in function development.

2.3.1 *Microcontroller Construction*

A microcontroller incorporates the following components, all of which function interactively (Fig. 2-11) [39–41]:

* *Microprocessor.* This functions as the central processing unit (CPU). The microprocessor contains its own control unit and arithmetic and logic unit (ALU). The latter unit handles arithmetic and logical operations, whereas the former unit ensures the execution of instruc-tions received from the program memory. This division of labor facilitates adaptation to a variety of practical applications through appropriate programming.

* *Input and output modules (I/O modules).* These handle the data transfer with the periphery. This includes input/output devices, circuits for controlling interrupts of a program, and bus systems carrying communications with other control devices, such as CAN [2].

* *Program and data memory.* This is nonvolatile, permanent storage holding the program, such as the open-loop and closed-loop control algorithm, and the constant parameter sets,

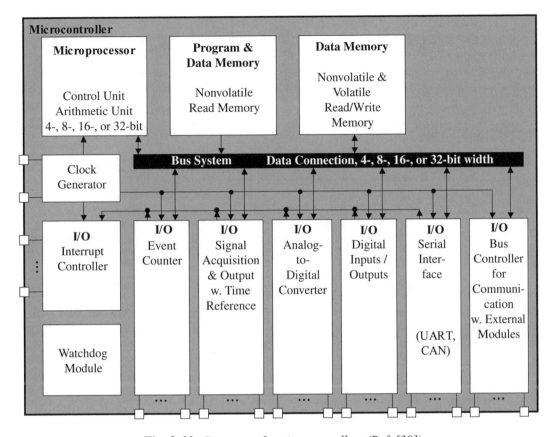

Fig. 2-11. *Diagram of a microcontroller. (Ref. [39])*

such as open-loop and closed-loop control parameters. Ideally suited to this task are the nonvolatile memory technologies. This memory often is organized in such a fashion that the program and the associated parameter sets are stored in separate memory segments. Accordingly, the term *program and data memory* is used.

- *Data memory.* This stores the data that are changed as a consequence of program execution. Because of its special characteristics, this memory segment is also termed *random access memory* (RAM). Ideally suited to this task are read/write memory technologies. Depending on the requirements of the application, volatile or nonvolatile read/write memory is used.

- *Bus system.* This system interconnects the individual microcontroller components.

- *Clock generator.* Also known as an oscillator, this device ensures that all operations taking place within the microcontroller adhere to the same clock frequency.

- *Watchdog module.* This is a number of monitoring functions that closely observe program execution.

With advancing technology, the various microcontroller components shown here are increasingly integrated on a single processor chip. This makes the microcontroller capable of operating as a standalone unit. To meet the requirements of a given application, additional external modules may be connected. One example would be external memory extensions. For this reason, a distinction often is made between *internal* and *external memory*.

2.3.2 Memory Technologies

Having discussed the differing demands on program memory versus data memory, this section will take a closer look at the various semiconductor memory technologies.

Semiconductor memory is used to store the following:

- Data, such as I/O data, states, and intermediate results that often require rapid read and write access

- The executable program, which, in most cases, requires permanent storage

- Constant parameter sets, which also require permanent storage in many cases

Memory storage encompasses the following activities:

- Writing
- Short-term or permanent storage
- Retrieval and reading of information

Semiconductor memory exploits physical effects that allow the easy generation and recognition of two different states. The benefit of semiconductor memory lies in its technological compatibility with the components deployed in other sections of the microcontroller, and in the manifold integration options offered by this combination.

To store information, the state pairs "conductive/nonconductive" or "charged/noncharged" are exploited. The following sections discuss the major technologies, either in accordance with their standardization or with a view to their most common applications (Fig. 2-12).

Depending on their individual application, semiconductor memory uses either bit or word-oriented organization, where "word" describes the logical collection of bits suitable for parallel processing by the microcontroller. Thus, the *word length* is equal to the number of bits being processed in parallel. Microcontrollers customarily accommodate word lengths of 4, 8, 16, 32, or 64 bits. A group of 8 bits is termed a *byte* (1 byte = 8 bits).

2.3.2.1 Read/Write Memory

- **RAM**

   The random access memory (RAM) provides direct access to any main memory location. Information can be read from and written to RAM as often as desired. Main memory uses volatile RAM, meaning that the memory contents will be lost in the event of operating power.

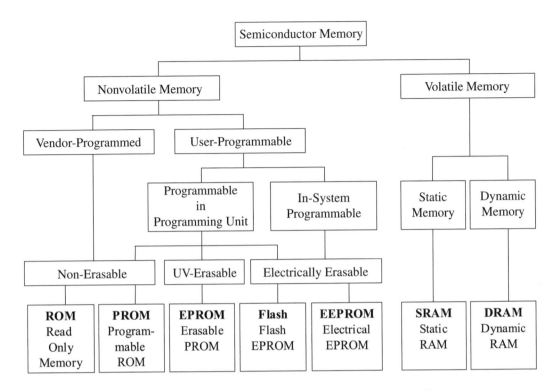

Fig. 2-12. *Overview of memory technologies. (Ref. [39])*

In random access memory, a differentiation is made between static RAM (abbreviated as SRAM) and dynamic RAM (abbreviated as DRAM) [39].

Static RAM is written to only once and retains its memory contents as long as there is a working voltage present. Because leakage currents would cause the memory contents of dynamic RAM to be lost over time, these must be periodically refreshed.

Also, the integration of an additional backup battery in the power supply maintaining the RAM facilitates nonvolatile data storage. The designation for this nonvolatile RAM is NV-RAM.

2.3.2.2 Non-Erasable Read-Only Memory

The read-only memory (ROM) provides direct access to any main memory location. However, as the name implies, its contents can only be read but not changed by means of write access.

- **ROM/PROM**

  ROM is nonvolatile memory. The memory contents are retained even in the absence of a working voltage. ROM customarily accommodates program code, such as the algorithms for open-loop and closed-loop control functions, and constant data, such as the associated parameter sets. This information can be accessed at any time and either may be programmed into memory by the manufacturer—as one of the final steps of production—or may be programmed by the user onto specially prepared memory modules by means of dedicated procedures. These programmable read-only memory modules are also termed *programmable ROM* (PROM).

2.3.2.3 Reprogrammable Nonvolatile Memory

On some types of read-only memory, the contents can be erased and reprogrammed with different contents. This group includes the following:

- **Erasable PROM (EPROM)**

  This rewritable read-only memory can be fully erased through exposure to ultraviolet (UV) radiation and then newly programmed. However, note that this procedure requires relatively high expenditures in terms of special equipment.

- **Electrical EPROM (EEPROM)**

  The electrical EPROM (EEPROM) is also termed E^2PROM. This rewritable read-only storage can be electrically erased and reprogrammed. The erasure and rewriting procedure can be accomplished either at a separate station or in the ECU. The EEPROM makes it possible to rewrite each individual line of memory.

  For these reasons, this storage technology is also employed as a nonvolatile data memory. One example application, in engine management, would be the storing of adaptive control parameters once the engine has been shut off. Another example would be the storing of detected faults in the so-called fault memory. A detailed discussion of fault memory configuration appears in Section 2.6. The EEPROM also can be used to store software parameters required by variant control in production, as well as in automotive service procedures. A detailed discussion of available procedures appears in Chapter 6.

- **Flash EPROM**

  The Flash EPROM (sometimes simply termed Flash) comprises the next development level of the EPROM and EEPROM. This memory allows the erasure, or flashing, of entire memory areas or complete memory contents through the application of electrical pulses. Once erased, the affected areas can be reprogrammed.

  Flash memory programming can be accomplished with the use of a programming unit. However, the decisive advantage of Flash technology lies in the fact that the Flash memory allows in-system reprogramming with the use of a reprogramming tool, even while contained in an ECU installed onboard a vehicle. For this reason, Flash technology is applied in situations where relatively large volumes of data must be committed to nonvolatile storage but possibly require modification in the course of the product life cycle (e.g., serving as program or data memory in ECUs). The procedures used in Flash programming are discussed in Chapter 6.

2.3.3 Microcontroller Programming

The program executed by the microprocessor onboard a microcontroller normally is stored permanently in nonvolatile memory. It is not exchanged or modified to handle different applications. An exception to this generalization occurs whenever a new software version is downloaded and Flash programmed as part of a software update.

This section examines microcontroller programming in some detail. Here, the term *software* encompasses the entirety of programs and data stored in the memory of a microcontroller-driven system. The programs are executed by microprocessors.

This means that in software engineering, specifications such as those arising from the descriptions of control functions must be implemented both in the form of program code suitable for execution by the microprocessor, and a parameter and data set to be stored in the data memory of the microprocessor.

2.3.3.1 Program Version and Data Version

In the following discussion, the *program code* will be termed *program version*; it must be downloaded into the *program memory* of the microprocessor.

The *parameter set* will be designated *data version*; its download destination is the *data memory* of the microprocessor.

By way of simplification, mention often is made of the terms *control unit software* or *ECU program*. However, note that the physical configuration of a given ECU may integrate several microcontrollers (i.e., function computer and monitoring computer). Therefore, the term *microcontroller software* provides greater accuracy, as does the distinction between the *program version* and *data version* of microcontroller software.

2.3.3.2 Functional Principles of Microcontrollers

With regard to programming, it would be feasible to start with the simplified model of the microcontroller shown in Fig. 2-13. As depicted in the figure, the microcontroller consists of the microprocessor, the memory area holding the instructions—also termed *program memory*—and the input/output modules [39]. All of these components exchange data and control information via buses.

The *microprocessor* comprises the programmable entity handling the addressing and manipulation of data, as well as the control of the time-specific and logical execution of a program.

The various memory areas provide storage for data and program instructions. A read/write access type of memory (e.g., RAM) is required to provide storage for variable data. The memory type suited to the tasks of storing program instructions and permanent data is read-only memory (e.g., ROM). Most microprocessors also contain a small, integrated memory module holding the so-called *registers*. Their purpose is to provide rapid read and write access.

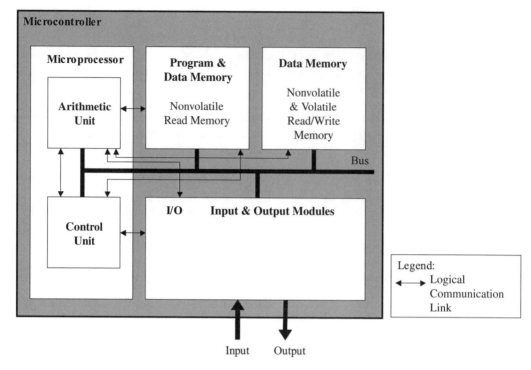

Fig. 2-13. *Simplified diagram of a microcontroller.*

The *input and output modules* (I/O modules) provide the means for accepting external information and passing data to peripheral devices. To facilitate adaptation of their functionalities to the application they are serving, I/O modules provide limited programming options. Typical examples of I/O modules are analog-digital converters used for data input, as well as pulse width modulation modules and digital-analog converters to handle data output. Timers are employed for counting external pulses or measuring intervals between events. Communications with external components and/or other microcontrollers can be implemented by means of serial and parallel interfaces. One example is digital data communications with extraneous microcontrollers by means of the CAN bus [2]. Depending on the requirements of a given application, additional functions may be integrated in a microcontroller.

2.3.3.3 Principal Microcontroller Operations

The blocks shown in Fig. 2-13 provide for the principal operating tasks of the microcontroller:

- Data processing
- Data storage
- Data exchange with peripherals

With these principal functions, the microcontroller can be used for the purposes of data transfer, storage, and processing. The following sections provide a closer look at the individual microcontroller building blocks facilitating these operations.

2.3.3.4 Microprocessor Architecture and Instruction Set

The microprocessor processes the inbound data entering via the input modules and controls the flow of data. Its registers provide storage for operands, results, and addresses. Figure 2-14 shows an example of microprocessor architecture [39].

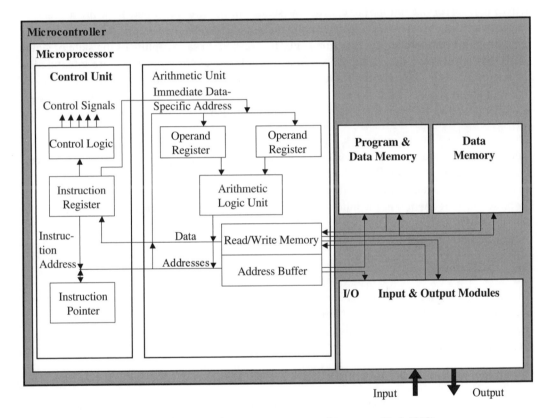

Fig. 2-14. *Typical microprocessor architecture. (Ref. [39])*

In this simplified diagram, optional extensions that would increase computing speed were omitted for the sake of clarity.

The architecture may be described in terms of the quantity of all registers available to the programmer.

Certain configurations requiring merely infrequent changes are set by specific control registers. As a result, the control registers represent a quasi-static instruction set extension. For example, the interrupt control register defines which interruptions, or so-called *interrupts*, are permitted and which are disabled. Additional control registers may be used to define the functionality of the arithmetic and logic unit (ALU) and of the I/O modules.

Some operations may influence program processing onboard the microprocessor. For example, if an interrupt request is received from the periphery, this may generate program branching to a defined memory address. While the so-called *interrupt service routine* stored at that location is being processed, only interrupts having higher priority may interrupt this routine.

All other interrupt requests are stored in memory and are processed only after the currently active interrupt service routine has ended. The status information generated in the process can be committed to intermediate storage in program memory. However, in certain circumstances, this may result in extremely long instructions. For this reason, to save capture of the state or status of the microprocessor, special registers—in addition to the control registers—are integrated in the microprocessor. This group of status registers also includes the program status register, the interrupt status register, and the multiplier status word. Whenever this type of interrupt logic is implemented in the form of a hardware solution, it also is known as a *hardware interrupt system*.

Often, to reduce the number of read/write operations of the microprocessor memory, several special computing registers, so-called *accumulators*, are integrated in the microprocessor. In this way, intermediate results and frequently needed variables can be held onboard the microprocessor. The reduction in the number of read/write memory operations accomplished in this way facilitates an increase in clock frequency and, at the same time, reduces the current draw of the microprocessor.

Operand Memory

The information linking arithmetical or logical operations is known as *operands*. To ensure rapid operand loading prior to and after an arithmetical operation, several options are available. With the memory location of the operands being the determining factor, the following microprocessor architectures are distinguished:

- **Memory/memory architecture**

   The memory/memory architecture provides rapid operand loading by means of the main read/write memory (i.e., the RAM). This is accomplished by explicitly linking the operand memory addresses and the result of an arithmetical operation at the instruction level. Using this method, for example, two operands stored in RAM can be added together with the use of a single instruction. The result is then immediately available for write-back to RAM. The designation "memory/memory architecture" is derived from the operand storage location.

- **Accumulator architecture**

   The accumulator architecture utilizes a memory cell that is integrated in the microprocessor. This cell, termed *accumulator*, is permanently designated as both source and sink for any arithmetical operation. Only the address of the second operand is part of the instruction code. Prior to each arithmetical operation, the first operand must be copied from memory to the accumulator by means of a load instruction. Subsequent to the operation, the result is again copied from the accumulator to the memory location.

- **Memory/register architecture**

   The memory/register architecture integrates a series of registers in the microprocessor. Both operands are explicitly encoded in the instruction. However, only one of the operands can be addressed directly through its memory address. The second operand and the result are addressed in one of the registers. In a manner similar to the accumulator architecture, one of the operands must be copied from memory to a register prior to the arithmetic operation. With the operation completed, the result must be written back to memory. However, if the number of registers is sufficiently large, intermediate results may be held in registers, dispensing with the need to constantly copy this data back and forth. Again, the designation "memory/register architecture" is derived from the operand storage location.

- **Load/store architecture**

   The load/store architecture explicitly addresses both operands of an operation in the registers. For this reason, each operation must be preceded by loading the operands into the registers. The result is then copied back to memory again.

Operand Addresses

An additional distinguishing feature is the available number of implicitly and explicitly encoded addresses. A simple example will facilitate an explanation. The operation $C = A + B$ requires an address for each of the three operands:

- Operand A

- Operand B

- Result operand C

- **Explicit addressing**

   Instruction set architectures permitting the random selection of the preceding three addresses (i.e., providing the option of explicit encoding of three addresses) are known as *nondestructive instruction set architectures*.

- **Implicit addressing**

   Because three addresses often occupy an excessively large number of bits in an encoded instruction, implicit addressing is used in many architectures. In implicit addressing, one of the addresses of the two source operands also serves as the destination address. Therefore, the result of the operation is stored at the address of one of the source operands, which causes that operand to be overwritten (i.e., it is thus destroyed). This destructive procedure gave rise to the designation *destructive instruction set architecture*.

The full complement of instructions for a given microprocessor is termed *instruction set*. Aside from differentiations in operand memory and operand addresses, the architectures governing instruction sets for microprocessors differ in many aspects, among them the instruction size and/or the manner in which instructions are executed [39].

In hardware-oriented programming, many additional details of the deployed microcontroller—some of them quite specific—must be considered. This includes, for example, additional special requirements related to interrupt processing, memory organization, and Flash programming, as well as a variety of possible microcontroller operating states with regard to current draw (power reduction modes). Because it is beyond the scope of this book to discuss these issues in detail, reference is made to the documentation supplied with the respective microcontroller.

2.3.3.5 I/O Module Architecture

The input/output modules provide for the input of external signals and the influencing of manipulated variables by means of output signals. In this way, the I/O modules comprise a link between the microprocessor and its environment. In addition to a connection to the internal data bus of the microcontroller, each I/O module features external connections termed *pins*, which are suitable for connecting sensors and actuators, for example.

Figure 2-15 shows the schematic diagram of an I/O module [39]. Its principal tasks may be divided as follows:

- Communications with the internal data bus of the microcontroller
- Communications with the environment
- Data storage
- Watchdog functions and timer control
- Fault recognition

Addressing

Input/output module types are differentiated as follows:

- **Isolated I/O**

    Two separate address areas accommodate the microprocessor memory and the memory designated for the I/O modules. Because only special instructions can be used for I/O modules, their programming is subject to severe limitations.

- **Memory mapped I/O**

    Microprocessor and I/O modules share a memory area with a common address range. This arrangement has the advantage of allowing the large number of instructions dedicated to addressing microprocessor memory to be used for the I/O modules. One drawback—the occupation of address space—does exist, especially affecting microprocessors utilizing a word length of 4 or 8 bits. By contrast, state-of-the-art microprocessors handling word lengths of 16 or 32 bits operate only in conjunction with memory mapped I/O architectures.

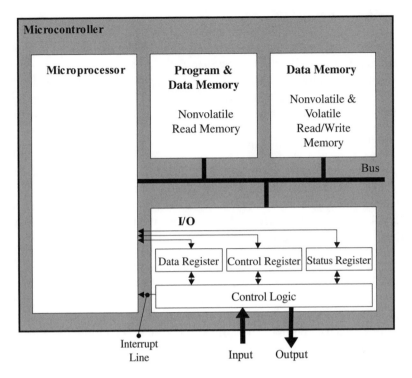

Fig. 2-15. *Typical architecture of an input/output module. (Ref. [39])*

Operating Mode

Another distinguishing characteristic of I/O modules consists of the supported operating modes. Four different operating modes can be identified:

- **Programmed I/O**

  The I/O module is directly controlled by the microprocessor, which handles its entire set of functions by means of a single program. The microprocessor is thus forced to wait while an I/O module is performing an operation. Therefore, this operating mode is used exclusively with microprocessors handling only input/output tasks (e.g., controlling intelligent sensors and actuators).

- **Polled I/O**

  The I/O module is capable of performing independent operations, during which the input/output data are committed to intermediate storage in special buffers. The microprocessor periodically checks the status of the I/O module and transfers new data if required. This operating mode is suitable mainly for those microprocessors that feature only a software-based interrupt system, a so-called *software interrupt system*.

- **Interrupt-driven I/O**

  The I/O module independently processes all input/output operations. Using a so-called *interrupt line*, it informs the microprocessor of the presence of new data or of a required microprocessor operation. As an essential advantage of this operating mode, the microprocessor and I/O modules are able to operate in parallel. The microprocessor program must be interrupted only in situations where the I/O module requires microprocessor assistance.

- **Direct-memory I/O access (DMA)**

  In this operating mode, the I/O modules are capable of a direct data exchange with the memory area without the need for microprocessor participation. This operating mode is supported mainly by microprocessors belonging to the top-end performance category. As is the case with the interrupt-driven I/O, this operating mode requires hardware that prioritizes all waiting requests and even blocks these if required.

More often than not, the software components covering the described hardware-oriented aspects of the I/O modules of a microcontroller are grouped together in a layer of the platform software, the so-called *hardware abstraction layer*. As depicted in Fig. 1-22 in Chapter 1, this book omits from the hardware extraction layer those I/O units that are required for communicating with other systems (e.g., via data buses). The software components required for communication are considered separately. Their construction is discussed in Sections 2.5 and 2.6. Also, to evaluate the influences on the real-time behavior of the microcontroller, a basic understanding of the interrupt system of the microcontroller is an essential prerequisite.

2.4 Real-Time Systems

It has already been noted that the execution of control functions by the microprocessor—referred to as *processor* in the sections to follow—is also subject to requirements based on time. This is where the term real-time system has its origin. This section discusses the required terms, basic principles, and configuration of real-time systems in general, and of real-time operating systems in particular.

2.4.1 Defining Tasks

Before attempting a description of the various methods used in the management and allotment of resources for a single processor or an entire processor network, it makes good sense to provide a balanced but general overview of all of the tasks to be handled and/or processed.

A network of processors is capable of handling several tasks simultaneously. In the following discussion, the term *task* will be used to describe each unit of work that may be scheduled or executed by one processor or a processor network, and that is slated for potential or actual parallel processing. In this context, it is of secondary importance whether the various tasks are actually handled by a network of processors, or whether they are executed in a quasi-parallel fashion by a single processor.

The definitions used in this book closely follow the OSEK standard [16]. Therefore, rather than applying the term *process*—although widely used in literature—to describe a unit of work to be processed in a parallel fashion, the term *task* will be used—again, in adherence to OSEK. This section discusses the definition and organization of task processing in relation to time.

Example: Various engine management tasks

In engine management, it may be logical, for example, to perceive the individual functions of *ignition, injection,* or *pedal value acquisition* to be tasks that must be executed by the microcontroller of the engine ECU on the basis of defined, time-specific requirements. In the following section, tasks are represented by horizontal bars in relation to a timeline, as shown in Fig. 2-16.

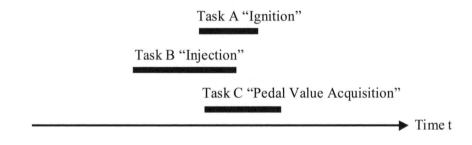

Fig. 2-16. *Miscellaneous tasks handled by the engine ECU.*

To dispense with the necessity of applying a variety of different designations in conjunction with the processing of a given task—such as *ignition, injection,* or *acquisition*—summary reference is made to *task execution.*

Task execution by a processor occurs sequentially. That is, the processor executes one instruction after another. In the diagrams to follow, the order in which the instructions of a task are executed is represented by a time axis, or timeline, that follows a left-to-right progression.

In the event that several tasks are to be executed by a processor in a quasi-parallel fashion, the processor must be allotted specific intervals for the individual tasks. At specific points along the timeline, switchovers between the various tasks are required. The resulting time-based graph assigning specific processor intervals to the various tasks is termed *arbitration diagram* (Fig. 2-17).

Note that the term *arbitration*, denoting either the portioning-out of snippets of time to the processor or the assignment of bus access permissions, may be used interchangeably with the term *scheduling* introduced in Section 2.4.4, albeit with the caution that the application of the latter is more OSEK-specific and relates explicitly to the allotment of processor time.

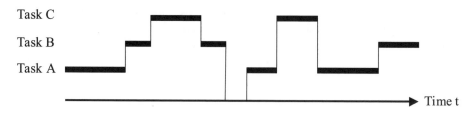

Fig. 2-17. *A processor arbitration diagram for Tasks A, B, and C.*

Example: Allotting processor time to three tasks

Figure 2-17 shows the processor arbitration diagram for the three Tasks A, B, and C. In this figure, a single task may be characterized by different states. The figure shows the respective time slot during which the task is being executed by the processor. In adherence to OSEK, this *task state* is labeled *Running* throughout this book.

Accordingly, Task A is initially in the Running state. When the processor has switched to another task—Task B in Fig. 2-17—that task assumes the Running state, and so forth.

However, because the processor is capable of processing only one task at a time, it stands to reason that only one task may assume the Running state at any time. In consequence, the task executed prior to the switchover—Task A in our example—is required to enter into another state.

The following section discusses the various defined task states, with the events triggering *task switching*, and different strategies for task switching in real-time systems.

2.4.2 Defining Real-Time Requirements

At this point, with a view to planning and controlling tasks in real-time systems, it makes good sense to formulate exact definitions for a suitable description of the time-specific task requirements. To this end, a clear-cut differentiation between a point in time (*instant*) and a time period (*interval*) is needed.

2.4.2.1 Instants of Task Activation and Task Deadline

Two important parameters distinguishing a given task in a real-time system from that in a non-real-time system are the instants of *task activation* and *task deadline* (Fig. 2-18) [42].

- In a real-time system, the *activation point* of a task is the instant at which task execution is triggered or enabled.

- The task *deadline point* is the latest point in time at which task execution must be concluded.

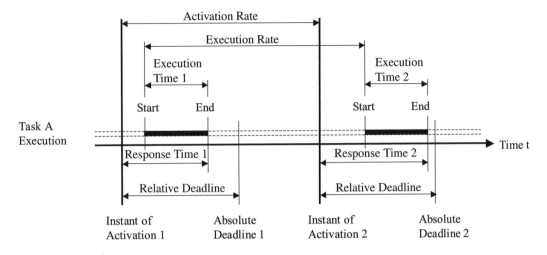

Fig. 2-18. *Definition of real-time requirements. (Ref. [42])*

- The *response time* is the interval between the activation point and the conclusion of task execution.

- The maximum permitted response time for a given task is also termed *relative deadline*. The task deadline, also termed *absolute deadline*, can be calculated by adding, on the timeline, the relative deadline to the activation point.

- The interval between two activations of a given task is termed *activation rate*. The activation rate must not be confused with the interval between two task executions, the so-called *execution rate*.

This type of task-limiting condition, which is imposed on task execution in the form of a specified time window, is termed *real-time requirement*. In the simplest case, a real-time requirement for a task can be described by its activation points and the associated relative or absolute deadlines. Task real-time requirements are frequently defined by the activation rate or an activating event and a relative deadline.

It is important to differentiate between the real-time requirements imposed on a task—effectively a time window for task execution—and the *time interval* required for task execution, which is also termed task *execution time*. As shown in Fig. 2-18, whenever the execution of a task is not interrupted, the term *execution time* describes the interval between the start and end of task execution. If task execution is interrupted, the task execution time is equal to the sum of those intervals between the start and end of task execution during which the processor is handling that task.

2.4.2.2 Hard and Soft Real-Time Requirements

The discussion thus far has established that real-time systems must complement specific input values by providing correct output values within a specified time interval.

Real-time requirements often are divided into two categories, that is, *hard* and *soft* real-time requirements. The relevant literature mentions many different definitions of hard and soft real-time requirements. This book takes its orientation from the following definition, which adheres to the specifications in [42].

A real-time requirement for a given task may be said to be *hard*, and the task termed a *hard real-time task* if there is a request for a validation confirming that specified real-time requirements for that task are always fulfilled. The validation in this case would be proof obtained by means of a procedure that is both accurate and verifiable. On the other end of the scale, if a verification of this type is not requested, all real-time requirements for a given task are deemed to be *soft*, and the task is termed a *soft real-time task*.

Thus, hard real-time requirements for tasks may not be confused with, let alone equated to, the safety relevance or "speed" of task execution.

Example: Real-time requirements for the functions of an engine ECU

The dynamics of the numerous engine subsystems to be controlled vary widely. The real-time requirements for the functions of the engine ECU vary accordingly.

Those functions that must be executed in synchronization with specific crankshaft positions, and thus require variable sampling rates, exhibit the highest, or fastest, sampling rates in conjunction with high engine speeds. Depending on the number of cylinders and the maximum engine speed, the fastest sampling rates for the calculation of injection and ignition are in the range of approximately one to two milliseconds.

Very high sampling rates are also used for intake and exhaust valve positioning functions, or for engine management functions referenced to combustion pressure. Typical sampling rates are in the range of 50 microseconds for valve positioning, and approximately 5 microseconds in the area of combustion pressure acquisition.

By contrast, other subsystems exhibit significantly lower dynamics. Thus, the respective functions, such as those controlling engine cooling, can be handled with significantly lower sampling rates.

Therefore, it is safe to say that a typical real-time system for engine ECUs is characterized by a large number of tasks. These are subject to a variety of real-time requirements—some of them very demanding—specifying both constant and variable activation rates.

2.4.2.3 Defining Processes

A collection of different individual tasks featuring identical real-time requirements may be processed either as a set of tasks or combined to one single task. The term *process* is used in this context throughout this book. A succession of processes with identical real-time requirements can be grouped together into a single task (Fig. 2-19). Here, the real-time requirements are not specified for the various processes but instead for the resulting task. The *processes* of a given task are consecutively executed in the specified order.

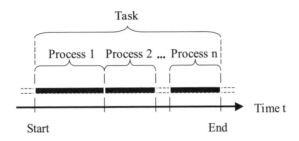

Fig. 2-19. *Definition of processes and tasks.*

2.4.3 Task States

2.4.3.1 Basic Task State Model (per OSEK-OS)

As demonstrated in Fig. 2-18, compliance with a task real-time requirement does not make it mandatory for the activation point to be congruent with the commencement of the actual execution (i.e., the starting point). During the interval between activation point and execution, the task enters a special intermediate state, which may be assumed, for example, at a point where the processor is busy handling the execution of another task. In adherence to OSEK, this state is termed *Ready* throughout this book. By contrast, the state assumed by the task prior to activation and after execution is termed *Suspended*. These states and the transitions between them can be visualized with the aid of a *state machine*. Based on OSEK-OS, the so-called *basic task state model* is shown in Fig. 2-20. (The abbreviation OS stands for *operating system*.)

The task transitions are designated *Activate*, *Start*, *Preempt*, and *Terminate*. As applied to Fig. 2-18, the state transition Activate occurs at the activation point, the transition Start marks the starting point, and the transition Terminate occurs at the end point of task execution. The task transition Preempt is designated for situations in which several tasks compete for the processor. Depending on the selected processor arbitration strategy, it is conceivable that one task, although in Running state, is displaced—or preempted—by a competing task before its execution can run its course. In this case, the task being preempted undergoes the Preempt task transition. A detailed discussion of several arbitration or scheduling strategies appears later in Section 2.4.4.

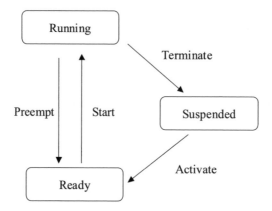

Fig. 2-20. *The basic task state model (per OSEK-OS V2.2.1).*
(Ref. [16])

2.4.3.2 Extended Task State Model (per OSEK-OS)

In addition to the basic task state model, OSEK-OS defines an *extended task state model*. As shown in Fig. 2-21, it defines an additional task state, that is, *Waiting*.

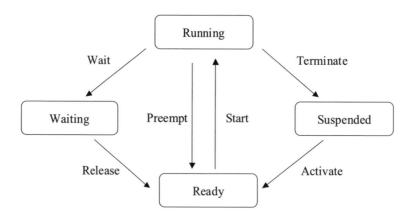

Fig. 2-21. *The extended task state model (per OSEK-OS V2.2.1).*
(Ref. [16])

In certain circumstances, a task may need to interrupt its execution in order to wait for an event that will allow it to continue processing. It then enters the task state Waiting until it may resume its execution. The transition into this Waiting state is triggered by the task itself. During the Waiting state, the processor can be assigned to another task. The additional state transitions necessary for this strategy are designated *Wait* and *Release*.

2.4.3.3 Task State Model (per OSEK-TIME)

To assist time-controlled arbitration strategies, the time-triggered *task state model* was defined per OSEK-TIME and is shown in Fig. 2-22. (The abbreviation *TIME* stands for Time-Triggered Operating System.) A detailed discussion of time-triggered arbitration strategies appears later in this chapter in Section 2.4.4.6. This task state model differentiates among the three states *Suspended*, *Running*, and *Preempted*. The direct transition from the Suspended to the Running state is designated *Activate*. The absence of the Ready state denotes that the activation point and starting point for the execution of a task always coincide.

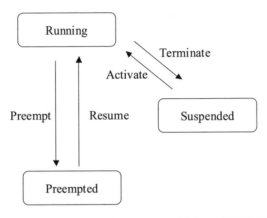

Fig. 2-22. *The time-triggered task state model (per OSEK-TIME V1.0).*
(Ref. [16])

As is the case with the task state models conforming to OSEK-OS, tasks in the Running state can have their execution interrupted by other tasks. If this occurs, the interrupted task undergoes the Preempt task state transition.

2.4.4 Strategies for Processor Scheduling

This section discusses several strategies for processor *scheduling*. The first order of business for a strategy of this type is to make a selection in situations where several tasks compete for processor time. Using the example of the OSEK-OS extended task state model, a similar situation is depicted in Fig. 2-23. Five tasks in the Ready state compete for the processor.

Generally speaking, this situation may be said to exist as soon as a certain number of tasks have entered each of the possible states. It is possible to discern between the set of inactive tasks in the Suspended state, the set of ready tasks in the Ready state, the set of waiting tasks in the Waiting state, and the set of executed tasks in the Running state. Of course, in the case of a single processor, the latter set encompasses only one element [43].

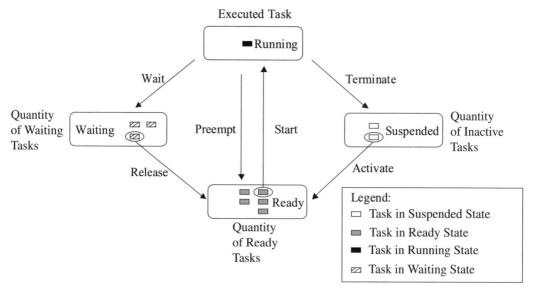

Fig. 2-23. *Task management by means of state sets. (Ref. [43])*

In addition to the various task state models discussed in this section, OSEK-based real-time operating systems also support several strategies for processor scheduling. The operating system component required for the implementation of the scheduling strategy is termed *scheduler*. The component required to start execution is designated *dispatcher*. The structure of real-time operating systems is discussed later in this chapter in Section 2.4.5.

2.4.4.1 Processor Scheduling—In Sequential Order

One available strategy enabling processor scheduling for the set of Ready tasks is the processor allocation based on the sequential order of task activations. This is accomplished by arranging the set of Ready tasks in a queue organized according to the FIFO (First In, First Out) principle.

In plain terms, this means that tasks that were activated at a later time need to wait until the execution of their counterparts with earlier activation is concluded. It stands to reason that this may take some time in some circumstances.

2.4.4.2 Processor Scheduling—By Priority

A strategy that is not based on the order of task activation may be implemented, for example, by mapping scheduling rules on a scale of priorities, and by sorting the set of Ready tasks in accordance with that priority scale.

2.4.4.3 Processor Scheduling—Combined Sequential and Priority Strategy

OSEK allows for the allocation of such a priority rating to any task, where a higher number corresponds to a higher priority. Tasks possessing the same priority rating are managed on the basis of the FIFO principle. The overall management of the set of Ready tasks follows the combined strategy depicted in Fig. 2-24. As a consequence, the respective next task to be executed is the "oldest" one with the highest priority, shown in the upper left portion of the figure.

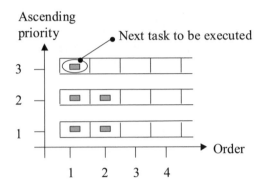

Fig. 2-24. *Managing the set of Ready tasks (per OSEK-OS). (Ref. [16])*

For this reason, the X-axis of the arbitration diagram frequently arranges the tasks in ascending order of priority, as shown in Fig. 2-25.

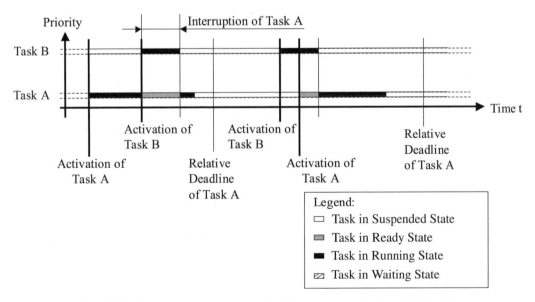

Fig. 2-25. *Preemptive processor scheduling—two tasks (per OSEK-OS).*

Another differentiation criterion of priority-controlled arbitration strategies is the issue of whether the scheduling of a higher-priority task occurs with or without preemption of the task being executed at the time and which is in the Running state. Accordingly, a differentiation is made between *preemptive* and *nonpreemptive scheduling*.

2.4.4.4 Processor Scheduling—Preemptive Strategy

The preemptive processor scheduling strategy allows for the interruption of the execution of a low-priority task by a task that has a higher priority. If this interruption may occur at any point of the execution, this is termed *fully preemptive scheduling*. A scenario of this kind is depicted in Fig. 2-25. The execution of Task A is interrupted by the higher-priority Task B, as soon as Task B has entered the Ready state. Processing of Task A continues only after Task B has been executed.

2.4.4.5 Processor Scheduling—Nonpreemptive Strategy

The nonpreemptive processor scheduling strategy dictates that the switchover from a low-priority task to a higher-priority task may occur only at specific points in time. This would be the case, for example, after the conclusion of the currently active process of the low-priority task. Alternatively, the switchover may occur after all processes associated with the low-priority tasks have been executed. This results in a situation where a non-interruptible process or task with low priority can delay the execution of a task with higher priority. A scenario of this kind, with Task A and Task B, is depicted in Fig. 2-26.

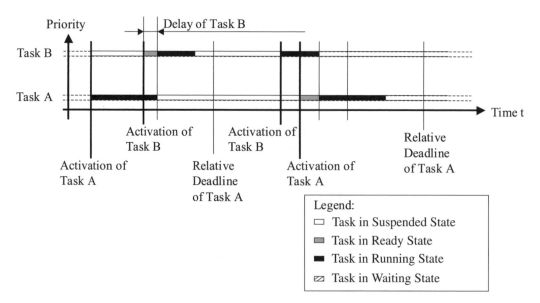

Fig. 2-26. *Nonpreemptive processor scheduling—two tasks (per OSEK-OS).*

As is the case with the real-time requirement and the task state, the priority is a so-called *attribute* that is assigned to each task.

However, the differentiation between preemptive and nonpreemptive scheduling is not a task attribute but instead an attribute of the scheduling strategy. This strategy is applied to the entire set of Ready tasks that must be scheduled.

For example, it also would be possible to divide the collection of Ready tasks into a first subset for preemptive scheduling, and into a second complementary subset slated for nonpreemptive scheduling. In the event that both subsets compete for the same processor, an appropriate scheduling strategy again must be defined at the subset level—possibly in the form of a priority for each subset.

2.4.4.6 Processor Scheduling—Event-Driven and Time-Controlled Strategies

Under the auspices of a dynamic processor scheduling strategy, scheduling decisions are made only in the course program execution during the so-called *runtime*, or *online*. This means that flexible responses to events are possible during execution, which in turn may cause the processing sequence of the Ready tasks to be rearranged. If this is the case, the term *event-driven strategy* often is used. The time expended in the calculation of scheduling decisions, that is, the execution time of the scheduler itself, may well influence the real-time characteristics of the entire system. This effect contributes to an increase of the execution time required by the real-time system itself, the so-called *runtime overhead*. Because of the possible response to random events, an accurate prediction of the runtime characteristics of an event-driven system is not possible.

By contrast, a static processor scheduling strategy allows for all scheduling decisions to be finalized prior to program execution, or *offline*. Because this strategy requires that all events must be known beforehand, it stands to reason that the nature of this approach introduces restrictions in terms of responses to events. Thus, the only possible responses are related to predefined and therefore time-dependent events. Hence the term *time-driven strategy* is often used. The effect on the real-time characteristics of the overall system of the time expended in the calculation of scheduling decisions is negligible because—if a scheduler is needed at all—only a very simple function is needed. The runtime overhead of the real-time operating system is correspondingly lower.

The arbitration diagram can be calculated prior to the actual execution and stored in the form of a *dispatcher table*. In this way, a specific point in time is defined for the activation of each task. This dispatcher table is evaluated by the dispatcher function, which starts the task execution at the predetermined point instants.

Figure 2-27 shows an example of a dispatcher table. The associated arbitration diagram appears in Fig. 2-28. The situation depicted here defines a fixed time window for the execution of each task. When the table has been processed in a procedure termed *dispatcher round*, the activation of the task succession is repeated, beginning with the first—or top—table entry. In this example, this occurs after a *dispatcher cycle interval* of 40 time units has elapsed.

Time	Action	
0	Start of Task A	
8	Start of Task B	
11	Start of Task C	Dispatcher Round
20	Start of Task A	
31	Start of Task D	
35	Start of Task E	

Fig. 2-27. *Static dispatcher table.*

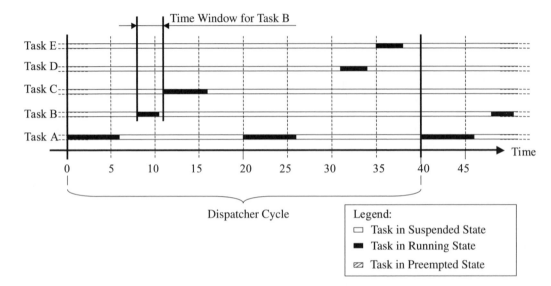

Fig. 2-28. *Static scheduling diagram.*

The runtime characteristics of a system of this type may be accurately predicted, provided the time window allotted for a given task is sufficiently large for the execution of that task. Because the execution time required for a task can vary, depending on the program path being processed, an estimation of the maximum required execution time—a kind of worst-case estimate—is necessary. This so-called *worst-case execution time* (WCET) for a given task becomes a determining variable for the definition of the lower threshold for the time windows, which also affects time control. Appropriate methods for determining the WCET are discussed in Section 5.2 of Chapter 5.

2.4.5 Organization of Real-Time Operating Systems

Generally speaking, real-time operating systems distinguish three essential components. The components shown in Fig. 2-29 follow the organization of a real-time operating system as described in OSEK-OS.

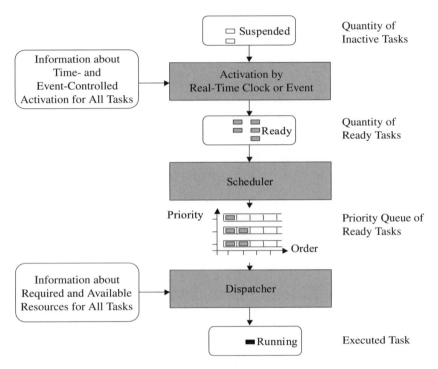

Fig. 2-29. *Simplified organization of real-time operating systems.*

- One component handles the activation of tasks and manages the set of Ready tasks. Task activation may be time dependent (based on a real-time clock) or event driven (e.g., an interrupt). To accomplish this, this component requires all information regarding the activation points or activating events for all tasks.

- The *scheduler* evaluates the set of Ready tasks and prioritizes their execution in accordance with the processor scheduling strategy.

- The *dispatcher* manages the resources for all tasks. For example, provided that resources are available, it starts the execution of the task with the highest priority rating.

2.4.6 Interaction Among Tasks

It was already noted that tasks were introduced as working units—or individual tasks—for possible or actual parallel processing, all of which carry an individually defined real-time requirement. This assertion notwithstanding, different tasks work together to provide a primary function. For example, the three tasks shown in Fig. 2-16 represent a basic function of the engine ECU.

Thus results the necessity of interaction among the tasks, that is, the exchange of information across individual task boundaries [43]. The discussion throughout the following sections touches on available mechanisms for inter-task interaction, such as event-based synchronization, cooperation using global variables, and message-based communication.

2.4.6.1 Synchronization

Figure 2-30 shows the processing sequences of two tasks engaged in event-based interaction. This type of diagram is also termed *message sequence chart* [44]. It is used repeatedly in depicting task interaction throughout the following sections. The time axis t in the message sequence chart is characterized by a top-to-bottom progression.

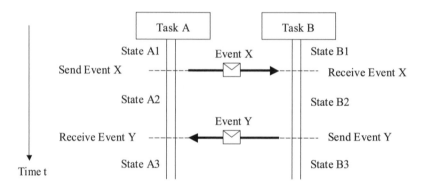

Fig. 2-30. *Message sequence chart describing the synchronization between quasi-concurrent Tasks A and B.*

In this example, receiving Event X in Task B causes a state transition from B1 to B2 in Task B. Further, the feedback about Event Y sent to Task A causes the recipient to enter a corresponding state transition. In this way, the synchronization of so-called *quasi-concurrent tasks*—or quasi-parallel tasks—can be accomplished, ensuring a logical processing sequence. Section B2 or, more precisely, State B2 in Task B, will be entered only after receiving Event X and thus after State A1. State A3 in Task A will be entered only after receiving Event Y and thus after State B2.

Because the task execution is quasi-parallel, conflicts may arise (e.g., when several tasks attempt to access shared resources). Examples of some of the typical conflict situations are depicted here (e.g., Figs. 2-33 and 2-35). Any mechanisms designed to facilitate inter-task interaction must consider conflicts of this nature, with a view to resolving them by way of synchronization.

The set of all states and the set of all events causing state transitions in a distributed system can be depicted by state machines (Fig. 2-31).

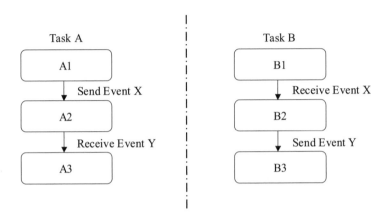

Fig. 2-31. *The state machine for Task A and Task B*

Interactions of this type among tasks for which only one event is of relevance and there is no content information (i.e., data are transferred) are termed *synchronization*. Real-time operating systems generally support a number of mechanisms for inter-task synchronization.

2.4.6.2 Cooperation

If payload data are to be transferred during an interaction, additional mechanisms will be required. The simplest option consists of the interaction of different tasks by means of shared data areas, so-called *global data areas* [43]. This procedure is also known as *cooperation*. By way of example, Fig. 2-32 shows a global Variable X that is used for the purpose of cooperation between Tasks A and B. Task A writes a value x onto Variable X, and this value is read by Task B.

Note that this approach of utilizing global variables may, in certain circumstances, result in data inconsistencies in real-time systems. Figure 2-33 depicts a critical situation of this type. Task A, engaged in the process of writing to global Variable X, is interrupted by Task B. Because the write access is not yet concluded, Variable X now contains an invalid or inconsistent data fragment, which, at this instant, is being read by Task B. Thus, further processing of this piece of inconsistent data may be expected to produce wholly unpredictable consequences.

Therefore, it is logical to require an assurance of data consistency of any cooperation mechanism. Because of its importance, this demand bears formulating in most certain terms: It must be warranted that the following will be true for the time interval framed by the start and end points of

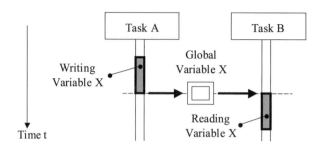

Fig. 2-32. *Cooperation using global variables.*

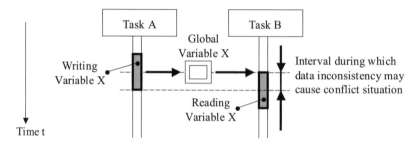

Fig. 2-33. *Inconsistent data and global variables.*

a Task T_i. All data being accessed by the Task T_i shall change their value if—and only if—that value is changed by the Task T_i itself!

There are two methods by which this requirement may be met:

- Method 1 guarantees the data consistency during a write access. All interrupts are locked for the duration of a write access to the global Variable X (Fig. 2-34). This is not required in the case of so-called *atomic operations*, that is, operations being handled by the processor

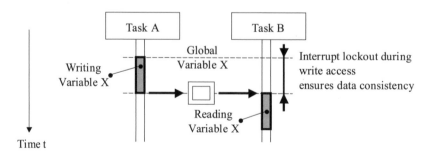

Fig. 2-34. *Interrupt lock during write access, ensuring data consistency.*

in a continuous fashion. For example, for a processor with a word length of 16 bits, write operations to 8-bit and 16-bit variables are termed *atomic*, whereas this is not the case with write operations to 32-bit variables. Accordingly, the interrupt inhibit for a 16-bit processor must be activated only while writing to variables greater than 16 bits (e.g., for 32-bit variables).

- Method 2 concerns data consistency during read access. If a global variable is read repeatedly while a task is being processed, the consequence may be inconsistent values of the variable during task execution. Figure 2-35 shows an example of this. Task A initially writes the value x_1 to Variable X. This value x_1 is then read and processed by Task B. In the course of events, Task B is interrupted by Task A, and Task A again writes a value to Variable X—only this time, the value is x_2. As processing continues, if Task B were to use value x_2 for its calculations, the consistency of its output variables could not be guaranteed. Again, there may be unpredictable consequences.

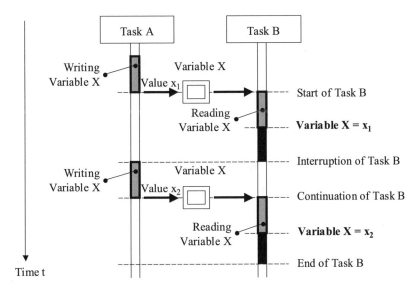

Fig. 2-35. *Inconsistent values resulting from interruption of Task B by Task A.*

One such example is the further processing of Variable X in Task B in a division $Z = \dfrac{Y}{X}$. Although the division is carried out only if $X \neq 0$, a division by 0 may occur. This will happen, for example, if, prior to carrying out the division, x_1 was used to verify whether $x_1 \neq 0$, and if, during the actual division, the value $x_2 = 0$ is used because Task B is interrupted in the interval between the verification and division operations.

The data consistency during read access must be ensured by way of synchronization based on a defined event.

2.4.6.3 Communication

Any inter-task interaction across separate local data areas requires data transport. A mechanism for handling data transport is termed a *communication* [43].

A communications method of this kind also may be employed to resolve the synchronization issue described in Fig. 2-35. In this way, the consistency of the value of global variables subject to read and write access during task execution may be preserved through additional copy mechanisms.

With respect to read-accessed variables, this means that local copies of the input variables are made each time a task execution is started—regardless of the point in time at which these input variables may be needed. Expressed differently, the starting point of task execution becomes the defined synchronization point. The values that were valid at the synchronization point are then used for the duration of task execution. Given the circumstances, this copy mechanism also may require that the interrupts be locked.

Relative to the example in Fig. 2-35, this means that a local copy of Variable X is stored at the time the execution of Task B is started. In the subsequent diagram in Fig. 2-36, this copy carries the value x_1. Accordingly, Task B uses the value x_1 contained in this copy for the entire duration of task execution.

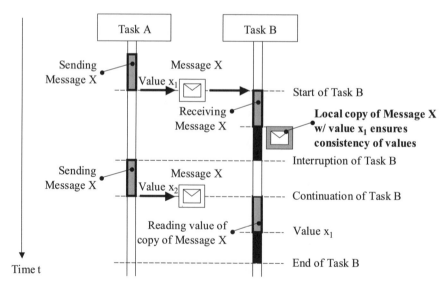

Fig. 2-36. *Consistent values resulting from local message copies.*

The mechanism providing tasks with repeated write access to variables is similarly structured. Again, the procedure starts with an internal copy that is written to the global variable only at the end of task execution. In other words, it is also the end point of task execution that may be defined as a synchronization point.

It stands to reason that the described mechanisms must be applied to all input and output variables for a given task. Thus, it must be ensured that the entire collection of input and output variables is consistent within itself, and that a given Variable X may not be permitted to adopt an older value, while Variable Y uses a more recent value.

This book—as does OSEK—refers to any mechanism facilitating inter-task communications as a *message mechanism*. Therefore, instead of referring to a write access—with the aforementioned protective measures—to a global variable, the term *sending a message* is used. Conversely, the action of reading—with the described protective measures—from a global variable is referred to as *receiving a message*.

Additional variants of the message mechanism are discussed in Section 2.5.5.1.

At this point, note that in certain circumstances, and with the application of the nonpreemptive scheduling strategy, there may not even be a chance for the critical situations discussed here to occur. The simple reason is that this scheduling strategy does not normally permit the interruption of a write operation to a global variable. Also, the interruption of the execution of a low-priority task by a higher-priority task—if possible at all—may occur only at predefined points. These points can be defined in such a way that they become noncritical. In such cases, the behavior of both global variables and messages in inter-task interaction is identical. This characteristic may be exploited with a view toward achieving offline optimization of the required memory and runtime resources by reducing the volume of unnecessary copies. To this end, Section 5.4 in Chapter 5 presents a more detailed discussion of suitable methods.

2.4.6.4 Interaction Among Tasks in the Logical System Architecture

The simple examples presented in the preceding sections clearly indicate that a *logical view of the interaction* among tasks, comprising an abstraction of the real-world technical implementation on the basis of events, global variables, or messages, provides advantages in many cases. This being the case, the following sections also utilize message sequence charts at the level of logical system architecture, as shown in Fig. 2-37, in the depiction of the interaction among tasks being executed on a single processor or on multiple processors. In this context, instead of referring to mechanisms such as events, global variables, and messages, the collective term is *signal*. Therefore, in Fig. 2-37, Task A sends a Signal X to Task B, which may be implemented by way of several mechanisms.

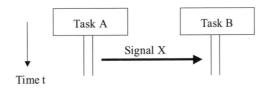

Fig. 2-37. *Logical view of the interactive relation between Task A and Task B.*

For detailed information on real-time systems and real-time operating systems, reference is made to the relevant specialized literature [42, 43, 45] and to the OSEK specifications [16].

2.5 Distributed and Networked Systems

Until this point, the discussions and observations were limited to information germane to the topic of electronic systems with autonomous operation (Fig. 2-38).

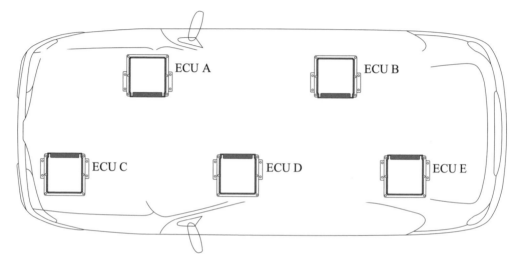

Fig. 2-38. *Electronic systems with autonomous operation.*

Early in the course of development, rising expectations concerning the functions provided by electronic systems led to demands for a new concept, that is, the transition from separate individual systems with autonomous operation to a fully integrated system. A multifunctional system of this kind requires the knowledge of all essential functions and signals onboard the vehicle. This integrated system is a result of the networking of the various ECUs of the vehicle, as well as the implementation of comprehensive general functions (Fig. 2-39). One example of this is the traction control system—a high-level function implemented by the concerted action of both the engine and ABS ECUs. As a consequence, rather than requiring individual optimizations, this approach also facilitates a general optimization.

However, as may be expected, the design and implementation of these so-called *distributed and networked systems* present a variety of additional challenges. In addition to the implementation of various quasi-concurrent tasks on a single processor, the development now has reached a point where the interaction of many interdependent tasks with spatial distribution and truly parallel execution, termed *truly concurrent tasks,* is taking center stage. The respective task interaction is handled by a communications network (Fig. 2-40).

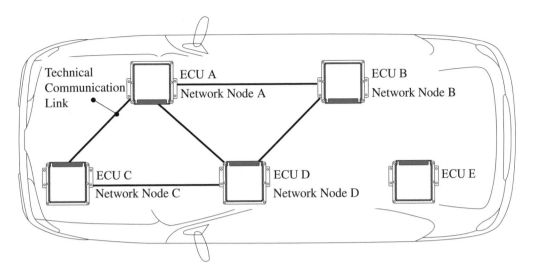

Fig. 2-39. *Networked ECUs forming a distributed and networked system.*

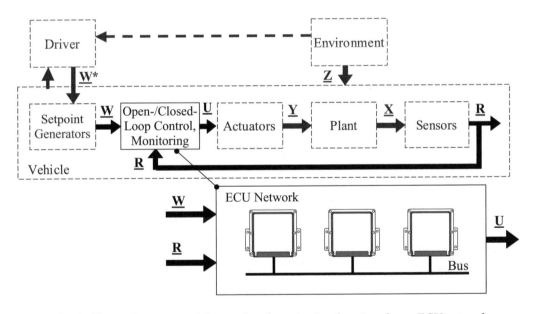

Fig. 2-40. *Implementation of control and monitoring functions by an ECU network.*

Some of the features, properties, and mechanisms of distributed systems were first mentioned in Section 2.4. To the extent that additional terms will be required for better understanding of subsequent sections, these are introduced next.

Throughout this book, the definition of distributed and networked systems follows the definition in [38]:

> *A distributed and networked system comprises several sub-systems engaged in communication. In this process, data control, hardware and the data itself are—at least in part—decentrally organized.*

A distributed and networked system often represents an integration of several processors featuring individual onboard memory. The processors are interconnected by a communications network. The system control occurs in parallel in the various local areas and handles the control of quasi-concurrent tasks. The data to be processed are distributed among the various memory areas.

Thus, a network of electronic control units—or an ECU network—of the type deployed in vehicles may be called a *distributed and networked system*.

Compared with centralized systems, distributed and networked systems provide a large array of benefits in the automobile.

- They provide for the spatial distribution of individual systems that work together to provide a coherent function. For example, the body systems, such as the vehicle access system, are characterized by extreme spatial distribution. The various individual systems in the doors (e.g., locking system, power window unit, and mirror adjustment), in the roof area (e.g., sliding sunroof control or soft top controller), the tailgate controller in the trunk, and cabin interior systems (e.g., such as seat adjustment and steering column adjustment) must work together. Compared with a centralized system, distributed or networked systems provide a significant reduction of wiring expense.

- Quite often, distributed and networked systems also provide benefits in terms of simple expandability and scalability. The automotive customer is able to assemble his or her own vehicle from a portfolio of optional extras. Given the modular implementation of these optional functions by means of distributed and networked systems, expandability is simple and cost effective, and scalability is particularly great. Even vehicle variants such as sedan, convertible, coupe, or station wagon—or engine or transmission variants—can be implemented with distributed and networked systems. An added value is the reuse or multiple use of components in the manner contemplated by a modular or building block strategy.

- Compared with individual systems with autonomous operation, distributed and networked systems frequently exhibit a higher level of functionality. A case in point is the adaptive cruise control system (i.e., a driver-assistance system with distance-sensing radar). In controlling vehicle speed to harmonize with traffic flow, the system also provides "high-level functions" for engine control and the braking system (see Fig. 1-7 in Chapter 1).

- Distributed and networked systems also provide advantages in terms of fail-safe or failure-tolerant design. This plays an important role in system reliability and safety. A detailed discussion of reliability and safety aspects appears later in this chapter in Section 2.6.

2.5.1 Logical and Technical System Architecture

If the communications between ECUs are handled, as depicted in Fig. 2-39, by assigned hard-wired communication links between two ECUs in each case, the result is a rapid rise in the number of peer-to-peer connections. However, considering the aspects of cost, reliability, weight, and maintenance, this approach cannot be implemented onboard a vehicle. It stands to reason that the technical connectivity between the network participants, the so-called *network nodes*, calls for a decidedly simpler implementation. In actual practice, the approach of mapping individual communication links onto a shared communications medium, the so-called *bus*, has been very successful (Fig. 2-40).

Thus, the difference between the view of logical communication links and that of technical communication links is beneficial for the development of distributed and networked systems.

To illustrate this assertion, the following sections make use of the notation featured in Fig. 2-41. *Logical communication links* are drawn as connecting arrows, whereas *technical communication links* are represented by solid lines. To emphasize this differentiation, the network nodes in the logical system architecture are shaded grey, and those in the technical system architecture remain white.

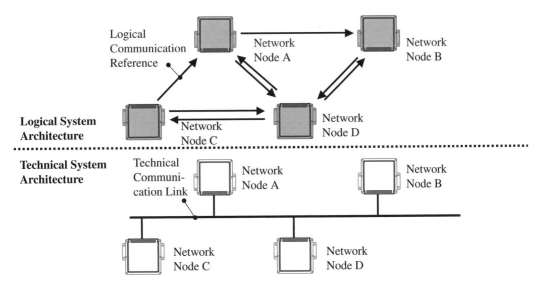

Fig. 2-41. *The logical and technical system architecture of distributed and networked systems.*

The challenge inherent in designing, commissioning, and testing distributed and networked systems consists of mapping the logical communication links among network nodes onto the technical communication links, that is, the shared communication medium, the bus.

Characteristic issues arise from situations where several network nodes compete for send access to the bus. For this reason, the *communication system* must ensure that only one network node is sending on the bus at any time. Various strategies for bus arbitration—the so-called *bus access*—are discussed later in this chapter in Section 2.5.6.

2.5.2 *Defining Logical Communication Links*

As shown in Fig. 2-37, message sequence charts can be used as a logical notation for descriptions of communication links among tasks being executed by different processors. The client/server model and the producer/consumer model comprise essential models for the description of communication links.

2.5.2.1 Client/Server Model

Figure 2-42 shows the sequential progression of a communication procedure in the form of a *client/server model*. Task A—the *client*—calls for the *service* from the communication system by issuing a *request*. The communication system informs Task B—the server—of this request by sending an *indication*. The server reports the execution of the service by sending *a response* to the communication system. The latter informs the requesting party—Task A—of the execution of the requested service by sending a *confirmation*. In the case of services for which there is no confirmation, response and confirmation are dropped.

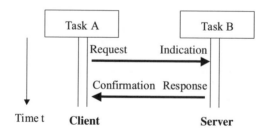

Fig. 2-42. *Message sequence chart for confirmed service in a client/server model.*

The client/server model always describes a peer-to-peer relation between client and server, even in situations where several clients or several servers may exist.

Example: Communications between an ECU and diagnostic tester

Onboard the vehicle, the client/server model is ideally suited to the task of defining the off-board communications between the diagnostic tester and the ECUs. The diagnostic tester converts the instruction of the user into event-driven communications with an ECU. To accomplish this, the diagnostic tester, acting as a temporary network node, assumes the role of client and issues its standard request for a service on a server—the ECU. Figure 2-43 shows an example of the logical and technical system architecture.

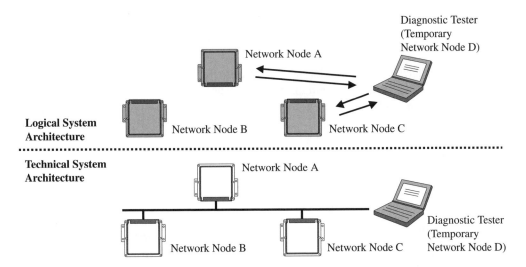

Fig. 2-43. *Offboard communications between a diagnostic tester and ECUs.*

2.5.2.2 Producer/Consumer Model

Figure 2-44 shows the sequential progression of a communications procedure according to the producer/consumer model. This type of logical notation is suited to the description of services in which one task (the *producer*) furnishes, without prior request, several other tasks (the consumers) with information.

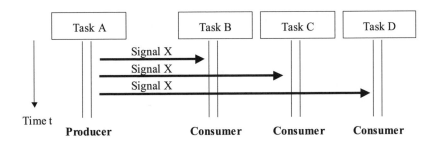

Fig. 2-44. *Message sequence chart for a service in the producer/consumer model.*

The producer/consumer model describes a relation between a producer and several consumers. Thus, it is suitable for sending signals to a group of network nodes or to all network nodes (broadcast relation).

Example: Onboard communications among ECUs

The producer/consumer model is suited to the implementation of control and monitoring functions that are distributed across several network nodes and that require periodic exchanges of signals. Therefore, the predominant application of the model is the definition of onboard communications, that is, communications among several networked ECUs onboard the vehicle. Figure 2-45 shows an example of the logical and technical system architecture.

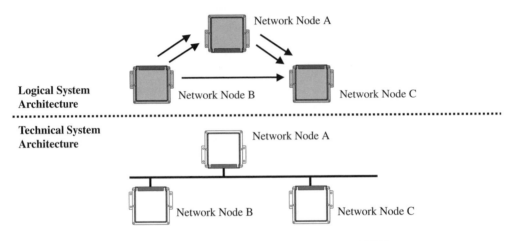

Fig. 2-45. *Onboard communications among ECUs.*

2.5.3 Defining the Technical Network Topology

The architecture determining the organization of technical communication links is termed *network topology*. Figure 2-46 presents schematic diagrams of the three important basic configurations (i.e., the star, ring, and linear topologies).

More sophisticated network topologies can be assembled on the basis of these three basic configurations. Individual network segments can be interconnected by so-called *gateways*.

2.5.3.1 Star Topology

In the star topology, the network nodes are interconnected via peer-to-peer connections with a central network node Z. All communications are handled via the central network node Z. Thus, the node Z requires $(n - 1)$ interfaces in the presence of n network nodes. A failure of the central node Z curtails all communications.

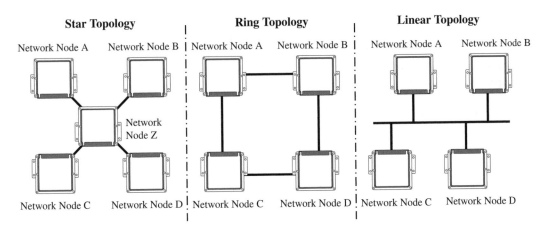

Fig. 2-46. *Network topologies.*

2.5.3.2 Ring Topology

The ring topology comprises a closed daisy-chain of peer-to-peer connections. All network nodes are designed to function as active elements, capable of regenerating and forwarding inbound information. This topology permits the implementation of networks of great spatial expanse. It is instructive to note, however, that unless suitable measures (e.g., for the detection and bridging of failed nodes) are introduced, the failure of a single network node may disable the entire network.

2.5.3.3 Linear Topology

The characteristic feature of the linear topology is the passive connection of all network nodes to a common communication medium. A unit of information sent by one network node is available to all other nodes. The linear topology facilitates easy cabling and network node connection and allows for simple expandability. The failure of one network node will not necessarily cause the entire network to fail. A random number of logical communications relations can be implemented without great effort.

Because of the benefits discussed, the linear topology is frequently found in vehicles. The most well-known representative of linear topologies is the controller area network (CAN) [2]. It has been deployed in vehicles since the beginning of the 1990s.

2.5.4 Defining Messages

In most automotive applications, serial communication systems are employed. This requires that signals among tasks being executed on different processors must be transferred serially. This is accomplished by embedding the signals to be transferred in standardized *message frames*, whose size is defined in most cases. A message frame that is filled with information is termed *message*.

The serial transfer procedure may produce situations where one signal is divided into several messages; conversely, it is also possible that one message transports several signals. The messages are conveyed via a communications medium (e.g., an electrical or optical medium). To aid the synchronization of tasks being executed on different processors, blank messages devoid of signals may be used.

The information conveyed by means of a message is termed *payload data*. Figure 2-47 shows a typical message structure.

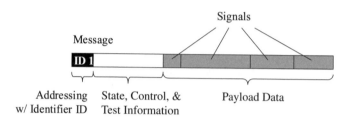

Fig. 2-47. *Message, payload data, and signals.*

In addition to the payload data, the message frame contains information about the message itself, such as an identifier for addressing purposes, as well as status, control, and CHECKSUM information required, for example, for the recognition and handling of transmission errors.

2.5.4.1 Addressing

Addressing is used to map the relations between the sender and recipient of a message. Here, a differentiation is made between *node addressing* and *message addressing*.

For example, if a message is to be transferred from network node A to network node B, node addressing causes the address of network node B to be entered in the identifier of that message. Upon receiving the message, each network node compares the identifier of the incoming message with its own address and processes only those messages carrying identifiers that produce a match.

However, if each message is unambiguously marked with a message address, an incoming message can be easily received and evaluated by several network nodes. In this process, each network node employs frame filtering to determine whether or not the incoming message is of interest to the respective node. The benefit of this addressing method lies in the fact that a given message needed by several network nodes must be transmitted only once, and that it becomes available to all receiving network nodes at the same time.

2.5.4.2 Communications Matrix

All communications relations within a network may be collected in the form of sender/recipient relations in a table termed a *communications matrix*, or *C-matrix*, for short. As a result, the C-matrix will contain all network information bearing relevance to communications.

A sectional excerpt of a C-matrix appears in Fig. 2-48. The left-hand column lists all network nodes (i.e., all networked ECUs). The next columns to the right present the messages and the payload data in the form of signals being sent by the respective network node. The remaining columns again indicate the network nodes. Here, the senders and recipients of messages are identified by the respective code letters. The letter "R" stands for Recipient, denoting those network nodes that receive and evaluate messages. Correspondingly, the letter "S" identifies a message sender.

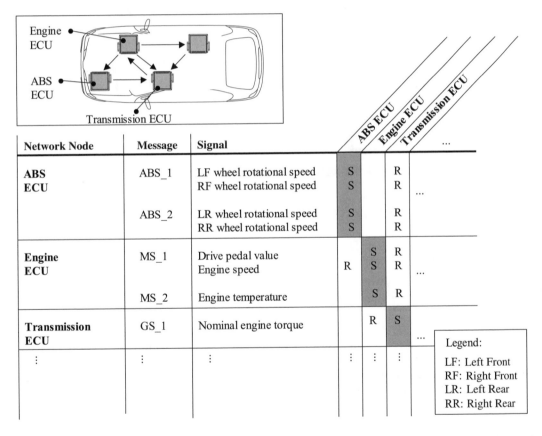

Fig. 2-48. Communications matrix.

2.5.5 Organization of Communications and Network Management

To recap, although messages must be sent and received at the technical network level, in many cases the item of interest at the logical network level is the payload data (i.e., the transferred signals). Thus, each network node requires a component that handles the mapping of signals onto messages, and vice versa. This component of the communication system is also termed *transport layer*. Figure 2-49 shows an overview of a communications model.

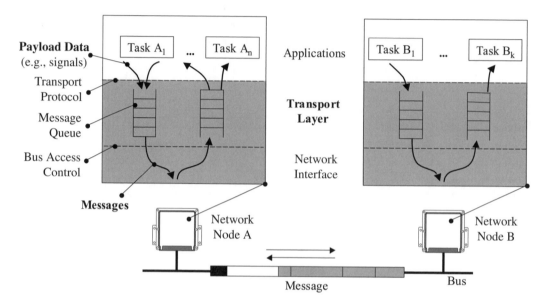

Fig. 2-49. *Communications model.*

This section discusses the structure of the transport layer (per OSEK) in greater detail. The latter follows the ISO reference model for data communications [46, 47], the so-called *open systems interconnection model*, also known as the *OSI model*.

OSEK-COM—the acronym "COM" standing for *communications*—defines software components for communications among network node software and standardizes the associated interfaces. OSEK-NM—the acronym "NM" denoting *network management*—provides corresponding definitions for network management. Figure 2-50 shows an overview of the software components.

Because almost all of the ECUs onboard a vehicle are networked, the vehicle-wide standardization of this communications layer architecture provides benefits in the areas of specification, integration, and quality assurance. In this context, the OSEK standards cover the realm of onboard communications. Standards for offboard communications (e.g., of the type requiring support for diagnostics or software updates in the service shop) were developed by ASAM and ISO [17, 25, 26].

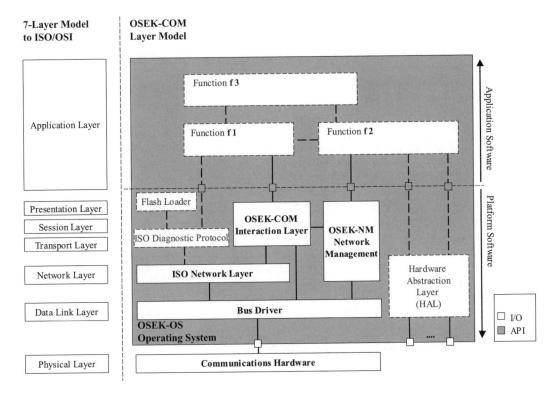

7-Layer Model to ISO/OSI

- Application Layer
- Presentation Layer
- Session Layer
- Transport Layer
- Network Layer
- Data Link Layer
- Physical Layer

OSEK-COM Layer Model

Function f 3
Function f 1
Function f 2
Flash Loader
OSEK-COM Interaction Layer
OSEK-NM Network Management
ISO Diagnostic Protocol
ISO Network Layer
Hardware Abstraction Layer (HAL)
Bus Driver
OSEK-OS Operating System
Communications Hardware

Application Software

Platform Software

□ I/O
■ API

Fig. 2-50. *Overview of software components (per OSEK-COM V3.0.1). (Ref. [16])*

2.5.5.1 Communications (per OSEK-COM)

OSEK-COM defines several variants of the message mechanism introduced in Section 2.4.6.3. Regarding communications among tasks, a differentiation is made between *queued messages* and *unqueued messages*.

- For unqueued messages, the size of the message receive buffer, the so-called *message queue*, is always limited to a single message. An unqueued message is overwritten with the *Send-Message()* service as soon as a new message arrives. The message contents can be read by the application with the use of the *ReceiveMessage()* service. Because the message is not deleted by the read access, it may be read as often as desired. This type of communication is especially suited to the communications among tasks subject to execution at different activation rates. For this reason, this is often the method of choice for communications among different tasks running on the same network node.

- However, in the case of queued messages, a message queue can accommodate several messages. The message queue is organized on the basis of the FIFO (First In, First Out) principle. Thus, the messages are read and processed in the order that they are received. The ReceiveMessage() service always reads the "oldest" message in the message queue. The message is deleted after reading, and the application always works with a copy of the message.

A further distinction is made between *event messages* and *state messages* on the basis of message type. Depending on whether the message refers to the occurrence of an event or the value of a state variable, the use of one or the other communications method makes good sense.

- In the event that each occurring event is of relevance, the loss of a single message may cause the loss of synchronization between sender and recipient. The messages ensuring this synchronization also are termed *event messages.*

  An application case in point is rotational speed measurement by means of incremental encoders. The loss of one event—here a transition of the speed signal—introduces a fault to the speed calculation.

- By contrast, if the current value of a state variable is of interest, the overwriting of an older value by the current value may be permitted. The messages used in this case also are termed *state messages*.

  One application case in point is temperature acquisition. Most of the time, the loss of one measured value from a temperature sensor may be permitted because this will not normally cause faulty temperature calculations.

2.5.5.2 Network Management (per OSEK-NM)

In addition to the communication-specific functions residing in the various layers of the OSI model, the operation of a communication system calls for a number of additional organizational functions. To facilitate the implementation of these functions, the communications model was extended by the so-called *network management* throughout all of its layers.

For example, the network management handles the setting of operating parameters and the control of the operating modes of the microcontroller onboard a network node. On one hand, this includes the switchover between the different operating states of the microcontroller, with a view to reducing current draw. On the other hand, it involves the operation of network segments by placing network nodes in *Wake Up* or *Shut Down* states. Further, the network management monitors the network nodes participating in communications. It also provides logging and reporting functions for errors detected in this process, to which application-dependent responses thus become possible.

Example: Node monitoring per OSEK-NM

OSEK-NM implements node monitoring by means of a logical ring (Fig. 2-51). This is accomplished by passing a special type of message—a so-called *token*—from one network node to the next (i.e., in each case, from the logical predecessor to the logical successor). When a token has been passed around the logical ring, a determination may be made whether all nodes are active and free or errors. If the token is no longer being received by a certain node for a defined period, this will be recognized as a fault or failure by the network management of that node. Appropriate responses are then possible in the application of the affected node.

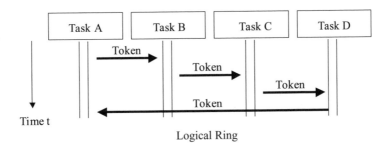

Fig. 2-51. *Logical ring for node monitoring (per OSEK-NM V2.5.2).*
(Ref. [16])

2.5.6 Strategies for Bus Arbitration

In the event that several nodes attempt to send a message on the bus, bus arbitration must be subject to unambiguous rules. Making the correct selection from a number of available approaches for resolving *bus access conflicts* is a major determinant in the deployment of this communication system in real-time systems. Thus, this section presents an overview of typical strategies. For a detailed discussion of the topic at hand, reference is made to the relevant specialized literature [48]. The commonly applied *bus access strategies* and their designations are described in Fig. 2-52.

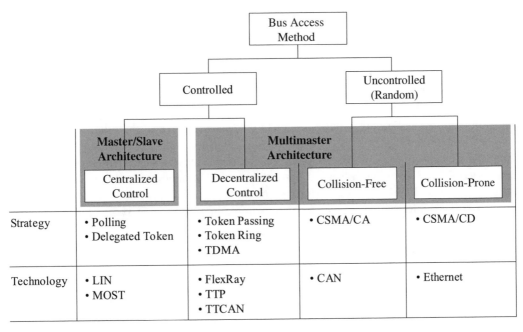

Fig. 2-52. *Organization chart of bus access strategies. (Ref. [48])*

2.5.6.1 Bus Access Strategies—Centralized or Decentralized Implementation

It is possible to make a general differentiation between two categories of bus access strategies. First, there are strategies that are implemented in a central network node, the so-called *master*. Second, there are the strategies with decentralized implementation. In the case of centralized implementation, the term *master/slave architecture* is also used, whereas the term *multimaster architecture* describes decentralized implementation. A master/slave architecture can easily be implemented, although it must be said that a failure of the master will bring down the entire communication system. As a rule, a decentralized multimaster architecture is more costly to implement, but, barring unforeseen outside influences, the communication system remains functional despite the failure or shutdown of a network node.

2.5.6.2 Bus Access Strategies—Controlled or Random

Although master/slave architectures always employ *controlled strategies* for bus access, the multimaster architectures allow for a differentiation between controlled and *uncontrolled* (i.e., random) bus access strategies.

With the multimaster strategies with random bus access, the various network nodes switch over to send access to the bus as soon as it becomes available. Due to the fact that several nodes may attempt bus access simultaneously, this strategy is also termed *carrier sense multiple access*, abbreviated as *CSMA strategy*.

Depending on whether or not such strategies may have the inherent potential of causing collisions on the bus, a differentiation is made between strategies with, and those without, collisions. Those strategies that, although not avoiding collisions, provide a means of detecting and handling collisions once they have occurred are termed *CSMA/collision detection strategies*, abbreviated as *CSMA/CD strategies*. The most famous example of an implemented CSMA/CD strategy is the Ethernet [48].

Strategies capable of avoiding collisions are known as *CSMA/collision avoidance strategies*, abbreviated as *CSMA/CA strategies*. This type of collision-free bus access may be implemented, for example, by enabling the network nodes to detect an impending simultaneous bus access. This occurs early during a so-called *arbitration phase* that precedes the actual transfer of payload data. On the basis of priorities that may be attached to the messages to be transmitted, only the one network node intending to send the message with the highest priority continues its send access to the bus. In this context, a prioritization on the basis of network nodes instead of messages is conceivable. The most well-known example of a CSMA/CA strategy using message prioritization is the CAN [2].

Among multimaster strategies with controlled bus access, a differentiation can be made between the so-called *token-controlled* and *time-controlled* methods.

A token is a message with special attributes that is passed from one network node to the next. As soon as a node has received a token, it will be permitted to access the bus for the purpose of sending messages for a defined time period. When this interval elapses, the node passes the token to its logical successor.

In the time-controlled method, fixed time windows for exclusive bus access are defined for each network node. Thus, this approach is termed *time division multiple-access strategy*, abbreviated as *TDMA strategy*. Examples of TDMA-based methods are FlexRay [49], Time Triggered Protocol (TTP) [50], and Time Triggered CAN (TTCAN) [51].

When associating the existing bus technologies with the strategies under discussion, observe that, similar to the processor scheduling in real-time systems, it also may be possible to implement a combination of strategies. A case in point is FlexRay, a TDMA method that uses a fixed time window for random bus access.

2.5.6.3 Bus Access Strategies—Event-Driven and Time-Controlled

Selecting the right communication system depends on many factors, that is, the required transmission performance, safety and reliability requirements, or the spatial expanse of the network. A determinant for real-time operating characteristics is the differentiation between *event-driven* and *time-controlled* access strategies. Introduced in Section 2.4.4.6, this differentiation criterion not only determines the predictability of the interval required for task execution on a network node. It also defines the time period—termed *communication latency*—required to transmit a message in a given communication system. For example, event-driven systems, such as the CAN, allow for estimates of the latency only in relation to the message with the highest priority. By contrast, the latency in wholly time-controlled systems can be estimated for all messages.

For time-controlled multimaster architectures accommodating multiple processors, a system-wide *global time*, or timebase, is required. Because the local real-time clocks may run out of sync due to minor deviations (Fig. 2-53), synchronization mechanisms for the real-time clocks on all network nodes are required. These mechanisms must be supported by the communication and real-time systems of all network nodes. OSEK-TIME [16] standardizes a variety of synchronization methods.

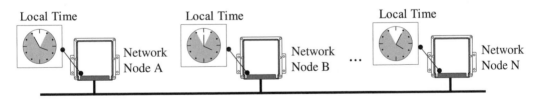

Fig. 2-53. Deviations among local system clocks in a network.

2.6 System Reliability, Safety, Monitoring, and Diagnostics

Despite the diversity of onboard control systems in a modern vehicle, the failure of even a single function, such as the braking or steering system, in a traffic situation may cause a catastrophic accident involving injuries and fatalities. For obvious reasons and independently of the technical implementation, great demands are made on the reliability and safety of the subject vehicle functions.

Therefore, the development of electronic systems contributing to increased road safety—such as the electronic stability program (ESP), a failure of which may nonetheless lead to dangerous situations—demands special consideration of applicable safety requirements.

This also applies to those vehicle functions that provide increasing degrees of driver assistance, assuming more and more "responsibility" in the process.

Example: Increasing safety relevance of electronic systems in the vehicle

The safety relevance of electronic system functions in automotive onboard systems is on the rise:

- From a situation analysis, such as the display of road speed, fuel level, engine, or outside temperature,

- To a situation assessment, such as a black-ice warning,

- To a recommendation for action, such as from the navigation system,

- To the execution of an action, such as acceleration and braking intervention by an adaptive cruise control (ACC) system, or even a corrective steering intervention in the case of an active front steering system (AFS) [22].

For all of these reasons, the reliability, safety, monitoring, and diagnostics of vehicle functions continue to gain in significance. When designing safety-relevant electronic systems, the characteristics of distributed and networked systems, such as the predictability of real-time behavior, must be investigated as judiciously as the failure and malfunction characteristics of subsystems and components. This requirement also stems from the need to develop the capability to support the rapid detection of faults, failures, and malfunctions occurring in systems, subsystems, and components in production and service with suitable diagnostic procedures. Thus, this section presents an introduction to the technical basics of reliability, safety, monitoring, and diagnostics. The discussion excludes other aspects that are beyond the scope of this book, such as legal conditions.

2.6.1 Basic Terms

In investigating the demands made on vehicle functions, it is critical to observe the differentiation among the terms *reliability*, *availability*, and *safety*. Reliability and availability are defined in the DIN 40041 and DIN 40042 standards, whereas safety is defined in DIN 31000, as follows [52]:

- *Reliability.* Denotes, with respect to an observation unit, the complement of properties concerning the suitability for the fulfillment of specified requirements for a defined time period.

- *Availability.* Denotes the degree of probability of encountering a system in a serviceable condition at a specified point in time.

- *Safety.* Describes a condition in which the risk is not greater than the limit risk. The limit risk is deemed equal to the greatest justifiable risk.

Furthermore, the terms *fault* or *defect*, *failure*, and *malfunction* must be distinguished:

- *Fault* or *defect.* Comprises the unallowable deviation of at least one property or feature of an observation unit. A fault is deemed a state. The unallowable deviation is equal to the difference between the actual value and the specified value of a feature or property.

  Differentiations are made among different fault categories, such as design flaws and construction, assembly, and manufacturing faults. Other types of faults include faulty maintenance, hardware and software faults, and operator error or faulty operation. A fault may, but must not necessarily, impair the function of the observation unit. The consequence of a fault may be failure or malfunction.

- *Failure.* Comprises, in an observation unit, the random discontinuation of the execution of a task subsequent to the commencement of its utilization due to a root cause inherent in the subject observation unit and within the specified limits of allowable utilization. As such, the failure comprises an infringement of the serviceability of an entity known to have been functional prior to fault manifestation or failure. A failure is deemed an event. A failure is a consequence of the occurrence of one or more faults.

  The various types of failures are differentiated in accordance with their manifestation:

  - Based on failure frequency, such as one-time, multiple, or consequential failures

  - Based on predictability, such as unpredictable failures occurring statistically independent of elapsed operating hours or other failures

  - Systematic failures, such as early and wear-out failures occurring in a frequency, depending on certain influencing variables

  - Deterministic failures, such as failures that may be predictable in certain conditions

  - Based on the size and extent of the resulting impediment

  - Based on chronological failure characteristics, such as catastrophic failures or degradation failures

- *Malfunction.* Comprises a temporary failure occurring after the commencement of utilization. A *functional* malfunction—*nomen est omen*—manifests itself as the temporary interruption of, or impediment to, a function. The commencement of utilization may coincide with the system commissioning or acceptance inspection.

Example: Fault versus failure

An incandescent lamp burns out. The filament breakage comprises a fault. A consequential failure of the lighting function occurs only at a later time when the lighting function is enabled.

2.6.2 System Reliability and Availability

Reliability is the capacity to perform the desired functions over a specific period of time. Reliability can be impaired by failures and malfunction, both a consequence of faults. Thus, measures aiming at increasing reliability constitute attempts to prevent the occurrence of failures and malfunctions.

In the systematic investigation of tasks related to reliability, observations based on statistical models have been quite successful [53–55].

In this context, the mean time to failure (MTTF), the reliability function R(t), and the failure rate $\lambda(t)$ represent essential statistical reliability characteristics.

2.6.2.1 Definition of Reliability Function R(t) and Failure Rate $\lambda(t)$

A large number $i = 1, 2, 3, ...$ N of observation units is investigated. The failure characteristics of an observation unit i may be described by the time T_i, during which the unit remains functional (Fig. 2-54). T_i is termed the *time to failure* (TTF) of observation unit i.

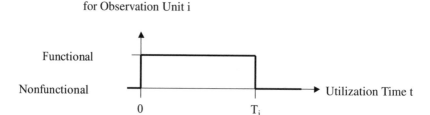

Fig. 2-54. *Definition of time to failure T_i.*

To obtain the *relative cumulative failure frequency* $\hat{F}(t)$ in the observation of a large number of similar units under identical conditions, the following formula will apply:

$$\hat{F}(t) = \frac{n(t)}{N_0} \tag{2.6}$$

where $n(t)$ is the number of failed observation units as per time t, and N_0 is the starting inventory of observation units at instant $t = 0$.

$\hat{F}(t)$ is also termed an *empirical failure function*.

This, the *empirical reliability function* $\hat{R}(t)$, is defined as

$$\hat{R}(t) = \frac{N_0 - n(t)}{N_0} = 1 - \hat{F}(t) \tag{2.7}$$

According to the law of large numbers, the *failure frequency* $\hat{F}(t)$ transitions for $N_0 \to \infty$ into the *failure probability* $F(t)$. Accordingly, the complement of failure probability is the *reliability function* $R(t)$

$$R(t) = 1 - F(t) \tag{2.8}$$

Thus, $R(t)$ expresses the probability with which an observation unit may be expected to be functional in the interval between 0 and t. Often, the failure rate $\lambda(t)$ is used instead of the reliability function $R(t)$. It has an important function in reliability and safety analyses.

The *empirical failure rate* $\hat{\lambda}(t)$ is defined by the ratio between the number of failures in interval $(t, t+\delta t)$ and the number of observation units that have not yet failed at instant t:

$$\hat{\lambda}(t) = \frac{n(t + \delta t) - n(t)}{N_0 - n(t)} \tag{2.9}$$

For $N_0 \to \infty$ and $\delta t \to 0$, the empirical failure rate $\hat{\lambda}(t)$ converges toward the *failure rate* $\lambda(t)$, the latter can be expressed, using the preceding definitions, by means of reliability function $R(t)$:

$$\lambda(t) = -\frac{1}{R(t)} \cdot \frac{dR(t)}{dt} \tag{2.10}$$

If the failure rate $\lambda(t) = \lambda = $ constant, the reliability function is derived as

$$R(t) = -\frac{1}{\lambda} \cdot \frac{dR(t)}{dt} \tag{2.11}$$

or

$$R(t) = e^{-\lambda t} \tag{2.12}$$

In this case, the failure probability follows a statistical exponential distribution.

In many cases, the failure rate $\lambda(t)$ changes over time. Figure 2-55 shows a typical progression that is also referred to as a *bathtub life curve*. Probability theory refers to this type of failure probability distribution as *Weibull distribution*.

Example: Empirical determination of failure rate

One thousand microcontrollers are tested simultaneously and under identical conditions for 1000 hours. The test yields 10 failures at a roughly constant failure rate. What is the failure rate?

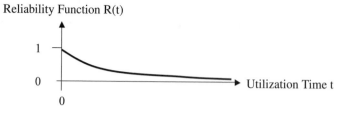

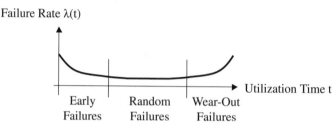

Fig. 2-55. *Definition of reliability variables.*

Using

$$N_0 = 1000$$

and

$$n(1000h) = 10$$

allows for calculation

$$\hat{R}(1000h) = \frac{N_0 - n(1000h)}{N_0} = \frac{990}{1000} = 0.99$$

Using

$$R(1000h) = e^{-\lambda \cdot 1000h}$$

yields for the failure rate

$$\lambda \approx 1 \cdot 10^{-5} \frac{failures}{h} = 10 \cdot 10^{-6} \frac{failures}{h} = 10 \, ppm \frac{failures}{h}$$

The abbreviation *ppm* denotes parts per million.

2.6.2.2 Definition of Mean Time to Failure (MTTF)

For the mean time to failure (MTTF) of a large number N of observation units, the following applies:

$$\text{MTTF} = \lim_{N \to \infty} \frac{1}{N} \sum_{i=1}^{N} T_i \tag{2.13}$$

With the failure rate being constant—and only then—the following applies:

$$\text{MTTF} = \frac{1}{\lambda} \tag{2.14}$$

Example: Empirical determination of MTTF

Thirty microcontrollers with a constant failure rate λ of 10^{-6} failures per hour are deployed in a vehicle. What is the value of the MTTF, assuming that the failure of one microcontroller can be tolerated?

Using

$$N_0 = 30$$

and

$$n(\text{MTTF}) = 1$$

allows for calculation

$$\hat{R}(\text{MTTF}) = \frac{N_0 - n(\text{MTTF})}{N_0} = \frac{29}{30}$$

Using

$$R(\text{MTTF}) = e^{-\lambda \cdot \text{MTTF}}$$

yields the value for

$$\text{MTTF} \approx 3.4 \cdot 10^4 \text{h} = 3.87 \text{ years}$$

2.6.2.3 Definition of Mean Time to Repair (MTTR)

In the case of repair-capable systems such as vehicles, the time to failure, that is, the failure-free operating time or uptime T_B as well as downtime T_A, must be considered (Fig. 2-56).

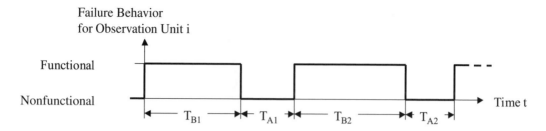

Fig. 2-56. *Uptimes and downtimes for repair-capable systems.*

Accordingly, the mean failure-free operating time is represented by the MTTF, and the mean failure time by the MTTR. The latter (i.e., the mean time to repair) is obtained as

$$MTTR = \lim_{N \to \infty} \frac{1}{N} \sum_{i=1}^{N} T_{Ai} \tag{2.15}$$

2.6.2.4 Definition of Mean Availability

The *mean availability* is then defined as

$$V = \frac{\text{mean operating time}}{\text{total time}} = \frac{MTTF}{MTTF + MTTR} = \frac{1}{1 + \dfrac{MTTR}{MTTF}} \tag{2.16}$$

Therefore, to attain a high availability value, the MTTF must be high compared with the MTTR. A high rating for the failure-free operating time MTTF may be attained through perfection—e.g., the deployment of highly reliable components—and a system architecture in which the failure of components may be tolerated. For example, the deployment of redundant system components may render failures tolerable.

A low rating for the failure or repair time MTTR may be attained by rapid and reliable fault diagnostics (e.g., by means of diagnostic support during service inspections) or by means of rapid and reliable troubleshooting (i.e., by the facilitation of simple repair procedures).

Example: Onboard diagnostics (OBD) requirements in engine management

Some reliability requirements to vehicle functions are imposed by legislation. A well-known example involves the so-called *onboard diagnostics* (OBD) requirements for all emission-related components around the engine. These requirements exert significant influence on the functions of engine ECUs. All emission-relevant components connected to the ECU are subject to continuous monitoring, and the same is true of the ECU. Failures and malfunctions must be recognized, stored, and displayed [56].

2.6.3 *System Safety*

In contrast to the considerations concerning reliability and availability for the definition of safety, the functionality of a unit under scrutiny is not addressed. In other words, from the safety standpoint, it is of no importance whether or not the observation unit is in serviceable condition—provided, of course, that this aspect does not represent an unjustifiably high risk.

With a view to a given automotive onboard system, this means that it may be deemed safe only if the consequence of both the fault-free and flawed states will be a risk that is at best negligible. This insignificantly negligible risk is accepted. The introduction of measures aimed at raising the level of safety is designed to prevent the hazardous effects of faults, failures, and malfunctions.

2.6.3.1 Definition of Terms in Safety Technology

The major terms used in conjunction with subjects germane to safety technology are defined in the DIN 31000 standard.

Safety engineering uses the less-than-expressive collective term *damage* to describe the negative consequences of faults, failures, and malfunctions. Defined differently, damage is deemed to represent a disadvantage suffered by virtue of the infringement of legally protected rights caused by a specific technical process or status. It is true that the referred legally protected rights encompass, in addition to human health, commodities such as property. Usually, however, and although ecological damages are often included, safety engineering appears to consider damages of a purely economic nature as taking a back seat to the priority concerns of damage to life and limb.

- *Risk.* The safety risk, briefly termed *risk* (i.e., the quantification of a hazard or peril), cannot be fully excluded. Safety engineering often defines *risk* as the product of the probability of the occurrence of a damage-causing event and the extent of damage that may be reasonably expected at the time of the event. Both of these characteristic quantities represent a means of measuring risk. An often-used alternative representation depicts risk as a multidimensional variable. An event that results in damage is termed an *accident*. Thus, the following applies:

$$\text{Risk} = \text{Probability of accident} \times \text{Accident damage} \qquad (2.17)$$

or, alternatively,

$$\text{Risk} = \left\{ \begin{array}{c} \text{Probability of accident} \\ \text{Accident damage} \end{array} \right\} \qquad (2.18)$$

- *Limit risk.* This represents the greatest justifiable risk. It may generally be said that the limit risk cannot be quantitatively defined. For this reason, it is indirectly described in terms of safety-specific requirements. These emanate from the entirety of all laws, directives, guidelines, standards, and rules applying in individual cases, and implicitly define the limit risk.

- *Hazard.* The term describes a situation in which there exists an actual or potential threat to humans and/or the environment. This hazard may lead to an accident with negative consequences for people, the environment, and the observation unit itself. Thus, a hazard constitutes a situation in which the risk actually exceeds the limit risk.

  A variety of hazards—such as electrical, thermal, chemical, or mechanical hazards—may originate from systems, that is, from a given system as a whole, and not from individual components. In most cases, therefore, it is virtually impossible to recognize and avoid—let alone prevent—all of the different types of hazards in advance. Thus, it may be argued that there is—in conjunction with any system of whatever nature—a residual hazard that must be accepted. The recognition of these hazards is the declared objective of the discipline of *hazard analysis*.

- *Safety.* The term describes a situation in which the limit risk exceeds the risk.

Figure 2-57 shows graphically a visualization of the correlation of the four basic terms: risk, limit risk, hazard, and safety.

Fig. 2-57. *Graph showing the correlation of the basic terms of safety engineering. (Ref. DIN 31000)*

The definition of the term *protection* closely follows that of risk. Protection constitutes the reduction of risk by means of such measures that limit the probability of occurrence (incidence rate), the extent of damage, or both.

2.6.3.2 Determining Risk

A risk analysis observing system-specific risks of malfunction and failure is carried out in accordance with DIN 19250 [18] and IEC 61508 [19]. The procedure uses the parameters designated Incidence Rate W, Extent of Damage S, Abode Time A, and Hazard Prevention G.

As shown in the example of the risk analysis plot in Fig. 2-58, these parameters can be used to determine the DIN requirement class, AK 0 through 8, or the IEC *Safety Integrity Level*, SIL 0 through 4. These two characteristic quantities represent a means of measuring risk.

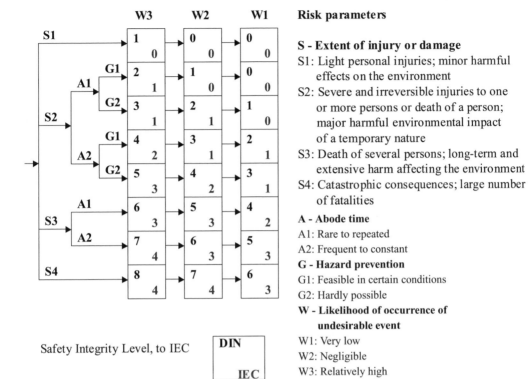

Risk parameters

S - Extent of injury or damage

S1: Light personal injuries; minor harmful effects on the environment

S2: Severe and irreversible injuries to one or more persons or death of a person; major harmful environmental impact of a temporary nature

S3: Death of several persons; long-term and extensive harm affecting the environment

S4: Catastrophic consequences; large number of fatalities

A - Abode time

A1: Rare to repeated

A2: Frequent to constant

G - Hazard prevention

G1: Feasible in certain conditions

G2: Hardly possible

W - Likelihood of occurrence of undesirable event

W1: Very low

W2: Negligible

W3: Relatively high

Safety Integrity Level, to IEC

Fig. 2-58. *Risk analysis plot and safety requirement classes (per DIN 19250, Ref. [18], and IEC 61508, Ref. [19]).*

The risk analysis must observe all system functions and evaluate their individual or collective hazard potential. This involves the evaluation of possible malfunctions through the application of appropriate risk parameters to each function provided by the system. The resulting findings then become the basis for the design of a suitable architecture for the system under scrutiny.

Example: Determining the requirement class for an electronic throttle control (ETC) system

The requirement class for an ETC system—also termed *electronic throttle control* or *electronic engine management system*—is to be determined. Figure 2-59 shows a simplified diagram of an ETC system for a gasoline engine.

In this example, a critical driving situation shall be assumed.

- *Driving situation:* Driving in a vehicle convoy at elevated road speeds

- *Possible hazard:* Inadvertent full acceleration and, as a result, rear-end collision or loss of vehicle control when negotiating curves

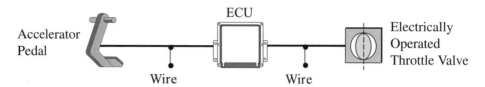

Fig. 2-59. *ETC system for a gasoline engine.*

- *Risk parameters:* S3—Injury or death of several persons
  A1—Abode time rare to repeated
  W1—Very low incidence rate

This evaluation yields requirement class AK 4 and SIL 2, respectively, for the *Accelera-tion* function. This classification becomes the basis for the safety requirements defined in standards such as IEC 61508, governing system structure (i.e., hardware, software, setpoint generators, sensors, and actuators).

2.6.4 System Monitoring and Diagnostics

In the event that a safety-related system is no longer capable of reliably performing the sum of its functions, and if this condition constitutes or tacitly implies the existence of a hazard both existent and conceivable, a response in accordance with a defined logical safety procedure will be required. As a prerequisite initiation of such safety response, malfunctions, failures, and faults must be reliably detected.

For this reason and because fault recognition is an essential function in the reliability and safety of electronic systems, it also comprises a central component of monitoring procedures [52]. In the discussion of monitoring, fault recognition, and troubleshooting, this book adheres to the terms and definitions originating from [52, 57].

2.6.4.1 Monitoring

Technical systems are subject to *monitoring* for the purpose of indicating current system status, recognizing undesirable or forbidden system conditions (e.g., faults), and initiating appropriate remedial actions wherever possible. Deviations from the "normal" system status occur as a con-sequence of a malfunction or failure, the root cause of which may be one or more of a variety of faults. It logically follows that the consequence of faults, absent appropriate countermeasures, will consist of malfunctions and failures over the short or long term. The objective of monitoring is to provide early fault recognition—that is, even before a malfunction or failure can occur—and to take the action necessary to prevent their manifestation to the extent possible.

Figure 2-60 shows a typical flow chart of monitoring functions.

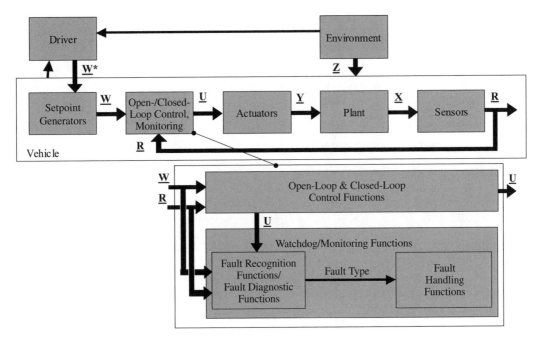

Fig. 2-60. *Diagram of monitoring functions.*

2.6.4.2 Fault Recognition and Fault Diagnostics

As a consequence of the monitoring objectives discussed in the preceding section, a *fault recognition method*—also termed *fault diagnostics,* or *diagnostics,* for short—is applied to verify whether or not the correlation existing between a minimum of two values can be confirmed. Deviations exceeding specifications are classified as fault symptoms.

Examples of *fault recognition* or *fault diagnostic measures* used in conjunction with electronic systems are as follows:

- **Reference value check**

   A question—having a known response—is posed (inquiry/response game). To determine the response, the system must perform the same functions or subfunctions used in normal operation. If the obtained response fails to match the known response, this is interpreted as a fault.

- **Redundant value check**

   Two or more comparable values are available, and their comparison facilitates the detection of errors. There are several ways in which this function can be software-implemented:

   1. Two or more algorithms with different principles are applied to the same input values. The property of being based on different principles is known as *diversity*. Because all

software faults are systematic faults, there is a mandatory requirement for diversity in this type of software-based fault recognition method.

2. If the algorithms are run on one and the same microprocessor, this is called *software diversity*; if they are executed on different microprocessors, this is called *software and hardware diversity*.

3. To facilitate the detection of spurious faults, the same algorithm can be run repeatedly on the same microprocessor while being applied to different input values.

• **Monitoring communication links**

Cases in point are parity and redundancy checks, such as the *parity check, cyclic redundancy CHECKSUM* (CRC CHECKSUM), or *Hamming codes* [58].

• **Handshake**

To inform the sender of a message of its receipt, of the message status, or his or her own status, the recipient of a message sends an acknowledgment to the sender. This communication is termed a *handshake*.

• **Monitoring physical properties**

A typical example would be a temperature sensor whose high temperature readings are indicative of faulty sensor signals. Another application would be a combination of checking a signal value with regard to the compliance to certain limit values and observing changes of the signal value over time, also known as *derivation*.

• **Monitoring program execution**

This is accomplished, for example, by a watchdog circuit that responds to excessively long program execution times by triggering a fault response, such as a microprocessor reset.

2.6.4.3 Error Detection and Correction

In digital communications, an error—occurring at the level of individual bits—is defined as a situation in which the received information fails to match the information dispatched by the sender. In this context, it is instructive to note the distinction that must be made between a *fault*, which manifests itself in the system, and its possible root cause, which may be an invalid transmission element or a fault in the software, termed *error*. Accordingly, the procedures used to locate the software-based origin of issues are known as *error detection* methods.

Error detection and *correction measures* include the following:

• **Redundant-value check**

In error correction, *redundancy*—or *parity*—checking is a method no less powerful than it is in error detection. To ensure error correction, a criterion must be defined and available that makes it possible to determine and apply the correct value. There are several ways in which this may be accomplished:

1. Error detection already provides the information identifying the incorrect results.

2. In some cases, it may be possible to respond to a fault situation by applying a fault-tolerant algorithm (i.e., acting "on the safe side"). An example would be the use of the first or higher value, value averaging, or similar algorithms.

*   **Disabling of subsystems or switching-off of the primary system**

*   **Remaining in the fault state or initiating a change of strategy**

*   **Fault storage**, such as in the fault memory of the ECU unit (see Section 2.6.6)

*   **Fault remedy,** such as through a microprocessor reset by means of a watchdog module

It also is possible to apply combinations of these measures.

2.6.4.4 Safety Logic

The safety logic defines the error correction measures applied to safety-relevant systems. Several system classes are distinguished.

As a first step, the so-called *safe state* is defined.

On systems capable of assuming this type of safe state, such as the defined emergency *shutdown*, which is also frequently called an *emergency stop*, a safety response may consist of the initiation of this state. It must be ensured that a safe state of this kind may be exited only in a controlled manner, that is, not as a consequence of additional faults, malfunctions, or failures. A system featuring this type of safety response is also known as a *fail-safe system* (FS system).

In some cases, the adoption of a safe state is naturally followed by the transition into a *degraded operating mode*. Whenever this results in continued—albeit restricted—system serviceability, such as the *limp-home* operating mode, this is termed *fail-reduced system* (FR system). Of course, there may be situations in which the degraded operating mode is deliberately introduced because of a scarcity of resources or with a view to risk minimization.

There are times when technical obstacles stand in the way of introducing a safe state. This applies, for example, to many vehicle functions that are mandatory while driving. If a system happens to fail, the adverse effect of the system failure on the behavior of the vehicle must be neutralized, and a fall-back switchover to a suitable backup system will be required. In principle, the implementation of the referred backup system may be similar to, or different from, the type of system suffering the failure. A system featuring this type of safety response is known as a *fail-operational system* (FO system).

For example, system requirements in terms of safety logic are frequently specified in the form of FO/FO/FS or FO/FO/FR. This means that a system meeting these specifications must remain fully operational, regardless of two successive internal failures. It is the occurrence of a third failure that would permit the system to transition into a safe state and/or enter the "limp home" operating mode.

When a manufacturer applies for general type approval as a prerequisite to vehicle registration, an "easy" safety verification is an absolute prerequisite. This requires that complex concepts are generally seen to originate from basically simple and easy-to-grasp mechanisms. Thus, simplicity is one of the fundamental design principles for safety-relevant systems [57].

Another design objective should be to limit the imposition of stringent safety requirements to as few components as possible. For this reason, encapsulation and modular construction are among other essential design principles for safety-relevant systems.

It would exceed the scope of this book to discuss additional principles and methods applied to the development systems with built-in malfunction and failure tolerance. Among these, only a few shall be mentioned here, that is, the *fault tree analysis*, the *cause-and-effect analysis*, or the *failure mode and effects analysis* (FMEA). For more details on these, reference is made to the specialist literature [59–61].

2.6.4.5 Functional Software Safety

Regarding functional safety, it is particularly interesting to observe the great differences exhibited by the development and design branches of classic disciplines such as mechanical, hydraulic, and electrical engineering, and of that of software engineering as a relative newcomer [59]:

- In open-loop and closed-loop control systems, the software frequently assumes the functions of a previous analog open-loop or closed-loop controller of varying configurations. This is an area where the conversion of the controller functions from analog to digital form produces inaccuracies or difficulties. Often, when translating continuous functions into discrete functions, this requires considerable effort. The reason is that the specifications for discrete functions are much more complex than their analog counterparts. It will suffice to name value discretization, time discretization, and the handling of quasi-concurrent functions.

- Compared with software testing, the physical continuity in analog systems facilitates general testing procedures. More often than not, physical systems work within delineated areas and tend to undergo physical distortion before they ultimately fail. In most cases, a small circumstantial change will result in a small change in behavior. These are the cases in which a few tests or experiments may be carried out at specific locations within the work area, and continuity testing may be pressed into service to close existing gaps, such as by applying the methods of interpolation and extrapolation [30]. This approach would be truly alien with software, which may fail as a result of some minor hiccup somewhere in the realm of input variable statuses. Furthermore, malfunctioning software may exhibit behavior that is totally and unpredictably different from its standard performance.

- Substantial modifications to physical systems are not normally possible without great effort and expenditure. This too does not apply to software because it is not subject to these "natural" restrictions.

- Software does not fail due to superannuation. Its quality is not affected by production and service aspects. Without exception, software faults exist already in the development phase. For this reason alone, the application of diligence and care is of paramount importance in software design and quality assurance.

In the development of reliable software, several major aspects must be taken into account:

- Development should proceed with great accuracy to ensure that the system will perform as specified in a variety of operating circumstances.

- There must be timely detection and remedy of runtime errors, such as deviations caused by malfunctions or failures; the same applies to previously unmanifested development flaws.

- Appropriate security measures must be put in place to prevent or detect system manipulations, such as unauthorized interference with the program or data version of an ECU.

2.6.5 Organization of a Monitoring System for Electronic Control Units

Monitoring systems for ECUs often are implemented through a combination of hardware components and software measures. Examples of hardware components would be the deployment of *intelligent* output modules or a watchdog circuit. The software implementation of monitoring functions allows for the realization of extremely flexible concepts for responses to faults, malfunctions, and failures.

As a definite benefit compared with components of a purely mechanical or hydraulic implementation, the combination with electronic components provides for the detection and troubleshooting of faults, malfunctions, and failures—not only in the mechanical and hydraulic components but in the electronic components.

For the reasons given, many contemporary applications place the task of designing suitable monitoring functions at the same high level of importance as the job of designing control functions. It is safe to say that the steady increase in software-implemented monitoring functions is exerting significant influence on the entire design of system and software architecture in electronics. Thus, it is necessary to consider the development of monitoring functions at an early stage and across all development phases. With monitoring rated so highly, any mention of *functions* in the text to follow should be understood to refer to the combination of open-loop/closed-loop control functions and monitoring functions.

This section discusses the software monitoring system that is frequently deployed in ECUs. Depicted in Fig. 2-61, the system distinguishes between two layers. The lower layer handles the task of microprocessor monitoring. The upper layer is the location where monitoring functions for setpoint generators, sensors, actuators, and control functions are implemented.

In most cases, microprocessor monitoring necessitates the use of a second computer, the so-called *monitoring computer*. This being the case, the implementation of software functions dedicated to microcontroller monitoring is distributed over both the function computer and the monitoring computer. This has the effect that both computers are watching each other closely.

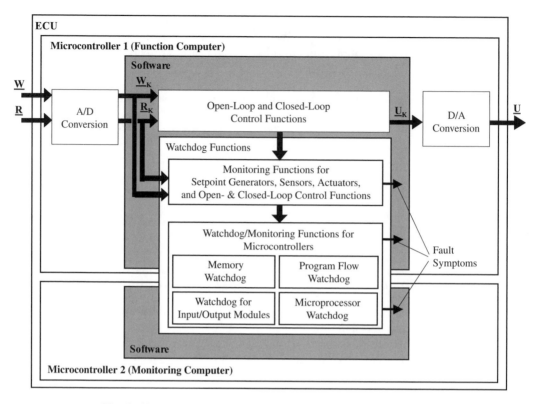

Fig. 2-61. *Overview of the software monitoring system in ECUs.*

If faults are detected, the appropriate corrective actions are triggered in both software layers on both the function computer and the monitoring computer. Again, these corrective actions may be implemented in the form of hardware or software functions. To this end, the fault symptoms are available as starting values for the monitoring functions.

2.6.5.1 Microcontroller Monitoring Functions

The dedicated microcontroller monitoring functions check the individual components, such as the memory areas onboard the microcontroller (e.g., Flash, EEPROM, or RAM), the input/output units, or the microprocessor. Many checks are run as part of the startup routine immediately after the ECU has been powered up. To ensure the detection of a component failure even during ongoing operations, some checks are repeatedly run while the ECU is performing its normal functions. Some checks requiring a relatively large contingent of computing time—such as EEPROM checks—are performed in the post-shutoff period, that is, when the vehicle has been parked. This prevents interference with other functions and dispenses with an otherwise required time delay when the vehicle is started.

In addition, program flow is monitored. For example, the function verifies whether or not a task is activated and executed as scheduled, or whether required messages (i.e., transmitted over the CAN bus) arrive at the anticipated regular intervals. A more detailed discussion of the implementation of error detection and error correction in real-time systems appears in Section 5.2.2 of Chapter 5.

2.6.5.2 Monitoring Setpoint Generators, Sensors, Actuators, and Control Functions

The setpoint generator and sensor monitoring functions verify, for example, continuity and plausibility. This may be accomplished on the basis of known physical correlations between the various setpoint generator and sensor signals. Implausible signal values will result in error routines, such as the imposition of values initiating the "limp-home" operating mode.

Actuators also must be monitored for correct functioning and functional wiring. On one hand, this requires sending test signals and checking the resulting responses. It stands to reason that the procedure must establish specific conditions to prevent the occurrence of hazardous situations. On the other hand, the current values produced by the actuators being logged during power-up can be compared with stored current limit values, with deviations serving as indicators of corresponding fault conditions.

Another area subject to monitoring is the calculation of control functions. For example, to check the plausibility of the calculated output values of a given control function, these are often referenced to the output values of a simplified monitoring function.

Example: Schematic of an engine ECU

The stringent safety and reliability requirements imposed on many engine management functions require the deployment of a monitoring computer in the engine ECU (Fig. 2-62).

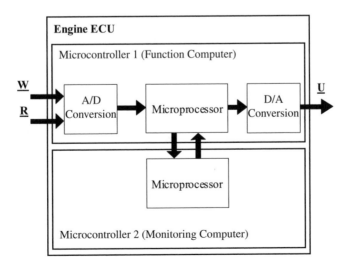

Fig. 2-62. *Simplified block diagram of an engine ECU. (Ref. [6])*

A detailed discussion of the methods used to analyze and specify the monitoring concept for safety-relevant functions of the engine ECU appears in Section 5.2.4 of Chapter 5.

2.6.6 Organization of a Diagnostic System for Electronic Control Units

The diagnostic system—as a subsystem of the monitoring system—comprises a part of the basic configuration of a production ECU. A distinction is made between onboard and offboard diagnostics (Fig. 2-63).

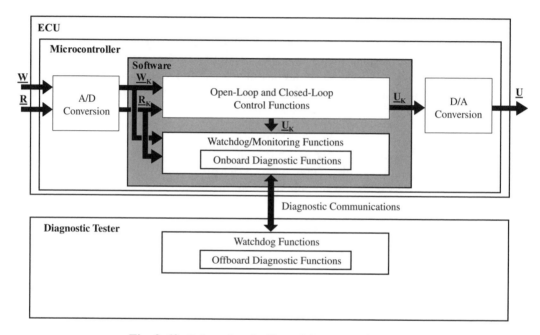

Fig. 2-63. Onboard and offboard diagnostic functions.

2.6.6.1 Offboard Diagnostic Functions

Whenever fault diagnostics are performed by interconnecting (either during vehicle manufacture or servicing) the ECU with a diagnostic tester, the procedure is termed *offboard diagnostics*. As a rule, the diagnostic tester, stationed in the service shop, is connected to a central diagnostic plug connector onboard the vehicle. This connector is the tap-in point for the entire ECU network in the vehicle. In this way, all diagnostics-capable ECUs can be diagnosed.

2.6.6.2 Onboard Diagnostic Functions

In the event that the fault diagnostics are conducted inside the ECU, the procedure is termed *onboard diagnostics*. If a fault, malfunction, or failure is detected, the onboard diagnostics initiates appropriate troubleshooting procedures. In most cases, the onboard diagnostics function also writes fault information into the fault memory for subsequent access and evaluation by means of a diagnostic tester in the service shop. Depending on the respective application, fault recognition functions are run at the time of system startup. However, they also may be cyclically conducted during standard system operation.

Figure 2-64 shows a typical organization of the onboard diagnostic system of an ECU. Aside from software functions for diagnostics on setpoint generators, sensors, and actuators, onboard diagnostics also include routines for verifying open-loop and closed-loop control functions. The diagnostic system also includes the fault memory manager handling read/write access to the fault memory, as well as the platform software components dedicated to offboard diagnostic communications with the diagnostic tester.

During standard operation, the onboard diagnostics check the I/O signals of the ECU. In addition, the entire system is constantly monitored for abnormal behavior, malfunctions, and failures.

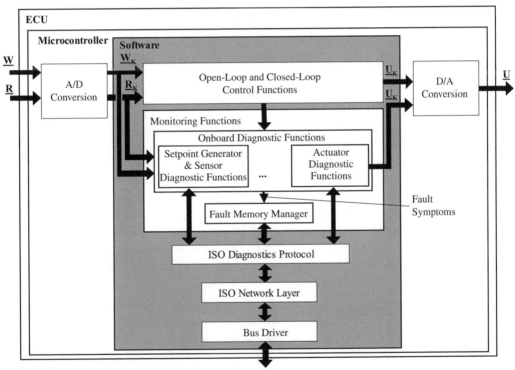

Fig. 2-64. Overview of an onboard diagnostic system for ECUs.

The automotive diagnostic system originally was intended as a support for quick and direct troubleshooting routines in the service shop. Over time and through the added impetus provided by legislation aimed at safety and reliability, it has matured into a comprehensive subsystem of the ECU.

2.6.6.3 Diagnostics for Setpoint Generators and Sensors

The setpoint generators, sensors, and wiring interconnection with the ECU can be monitored through the evaluation of input signals. In addition to the aforementioned functions, tests of this nature also can serve to detect short-circuits in battery voltage or vehicle ground connections, as well as wiring discontinuity. This may be accomplished in several ways:

- Supply voltage monitoring of the setpoint generator or sensor
- Verification of the permissible range of the acquired values
- Plausibility check, provided ancillary information is available

Setpoint generator and sensor diagnostics are accomplished by measuring the input signals of the ECU, as well as its internal variables. Offboard diagnostic communications then transfer the associated signals to the diagnostic tester. This device provides an online display of the transferred data. For the purpose of plausibility checks, the diagnostic tester also can be used for measuring live bus signals (bus monitoring). If it is desirable to run plausibility checks on additional signals, added diagnostic data acquisition modules may be installed in the vehicle.

2.6.6.4 Diagnostics for Actuators

Actuator diagnostics provide the vehicle service facility with pinpoint activation of individual actuators of the ECU to verify their proper functioning. This testing mode is initiated by the diagnostic tester. In normal circumstances, this device functions in only a standing vehicle and given that certain precautions are met. In the example of the engine ECU, the diagnostic tester will function only below a certain permitted engine speed or at engine standstill (key-on/engine-off condition), in which case—and by necessity—the testing of open-loop or closed-loop control functions ceases. However, absent the live actuator signals normally output by the ECU, these are simulated by the diagnostic tester. The actuator functions are audibly confirmed—for example, by solenoid valve clicks or movement of an actuator flap—or by means of other simple methods.

2.6.6.5 Fault Memory Manager

The fault symptoms recognized by the onboard diagnostic functions normally are entered in the fault memory of the ECU. In most cases, the fault memory is located in the EEPROM because this facilitates the permanent storage of entries. Figure 2-65 shows a diagram of a typical fault memory structure for engine ECUs. Statutory requirements (e.g., [56]) specify that each fault entry must be accompanied by supplementary information in addition to the diagnostic trouble code, or DTC. This information—the *vehicle test record*—includes indications of the operating and environmental conditions prevailing at the time of fault symptom logging. Examples of captured information would be engine speed and engine temperature, or the odometer reading

Pos. No.	Fault Symptom	Diagnostic Trouble Code (DTC)	Malfunction Indicator Light (MIL)	Stored	Active	Environmental Conditions		
1	Air Intake Temperature Sensor	P0110	Off	Yes	No			
2	Acceleration Information	P1605	Off	No	Yes			
3								
4								
⋮								

Fig. 2-65. Structure of ECU fault memory.

at the time of fault detection. Additional data committed to storage often consists of information regarding the fault type. Also of interest are the fault status (i.e., static or sporadic fault) or additional fault symptom characteristics. This includes indications of whether and how often the fault symptom has been captured on previous occasions, and/or whether it is currently manifested. The fault memory manager handles the entry and retrieval of fault symptoms in the fault memory. The function is normally implemented as a standalone software component.

Engine management is one area subject to exhaust emission standards that are often country specific. Emission standards contain the specifications for many faults influencing exhaust emissions, with the diagnostic trouble codes (DTC), and the blink codes of the so-called *malfunction indicator light* (MIL), provided as a means of driver information. Given certain specified conditions, such as when DTCs fail to recur during a specific number of driving cycles, the fault memory manager again may delete some of the fault symptoms—or malfunction indications—from storage.

Upon inspection of the vehicle in the service shop, this stored information can be retrieved by the diagnostic tester via the offboard diagnostic interface of the vehicle. This facilitates the actual troubleshooting and repair procedures. To effect the data transfer from ECU to diagnostic tester, the memory contents shaded grey in Fig. 2-65 must be transported by means of messages handled by offboard diagnostic communications. The fault memory manager handles all tasks required in conjunction with the use of the diagnostic tester. The memory contents visualizes the retrieved memory contents (e.g., directly in the form of the DTCs). However, a more widely understood display mode is the plain-text display as shown in Fig. 2-65, and a display of the environmental conditions in the form of physical variables. To this end, the diagnostic tester requires a description of the fault memory of the respective ECU.

With the troubleshooting procedures successfully concluded, a specific command, sent by the diagnostic tester to the fault memory manager, can clear the entire fault memory area.

2.6.6.6 Offboard Diagnostic Communications

The communications between the diagnostic tester and ECU are defined in standards [25, 26]. In compliance with the standards, automobile manufacturers generally define uniform offboard diagnostic communications for all ECUs onboard a given vehicle. This forms the basis for a similar vehicle-wide standardization of software components for the purpose of offboard communications between ECUs and diagnostic tester (see Fig. 1-22 in Chapter 1).

2.6.6.7 Model-Based Fault Recognition

This discussion would not be complete without a brief foray into *model-based fault* or *error recognition*—also termed *model-based diagnostics*. This method is increasingly deployed in ECUs. Figure 2-66 shows a block diagram of the required functions.

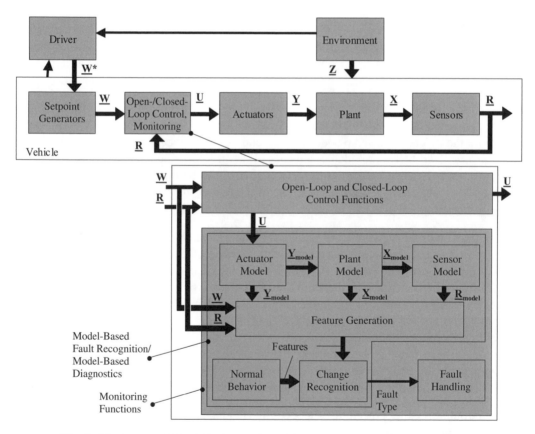

Fig. 2-66. *Principal block diagram of model-based fault recognition.* *(Ref. [52])*

Fault and/or error recognition exploits the known interdependencies of various measurable signals in both static and dynamic system behavior. These become the basis for the deployment of actuator, plant, and sensor models, with the application of methods from control engineering, such as model equations, state variable estimation, or state observers [34, 35]. Controller-based faults, or those in sensors, plants, and actuators, can be recognized on the basis of input variables. In most cases, these consist of controller output variables $\underline{U}$ and feedback variables $\underline{R}$, and in some cases, of reference variables $\underline{W}$ and manipulated variables $\underline{Y}$.

Model-based fault recognition compares the behavior of real-world components with that of modeled components and uses suitable methods to generate characteristics, so-called features. If these features deviate from the reference values or normal behavior, the result is the identification of fault types forming the basis for fault handling and troubleshooting.

2.7 Summary

As foreshadowed throughout the preceding sections, the task of designing automotive electronics and software systems represents a high level of difficulty, mainly because the requirements dictated by the various applications are both comprehensive and diverse. For this reason, the realization of the fulfillment of the diversity of communications requirements in distributed and networked systems by a single, cost-efficient, standardized, and multipurpose network technology has so far eluded the grasp of software engineers.

It is far from easy to define an optimization criterion for system design. For example, if real-time behavior were to be selected as an optimization criterion, this indeed would result in a design providing a minimal burden on processors and buses. However, this solution would fail to ensure sufficient consideration of reliability and safety aspects. In other words, requirements such as redundancy and aspects related to cost and quality assurance, such as component reuse, would be shortchanged.

A design issue of the demonstrated complexity calls for a structured approach. This should be a development process that spans the range of development phases, from the analysis of requirements and constraints to final system acceptance testing.

One approach, that is, the grouping of subfunctions sharing identical requirement specifications, has produced benefits in practical application. The electronic systems serving the respective subsystems are interconnected by means of a suitable communications technology. The implementation of specialized functions reaching beyond the referred subsystems is accomplished by interconnecting the subsystems by means of control units equipped with gateways.

Example: ECU network of BMW 7 Series [62]

Figure 2-67 shows a diagram of the ECU network featured in a recent model of the BMW 7 Series. It comprises roughly sixty ECUs organized in five subsystems.

Diagnostic information is queried via a point-to-point connection from the diagnostic tester to the central offboard diagnostic interface to a central gateway control unit. From that point

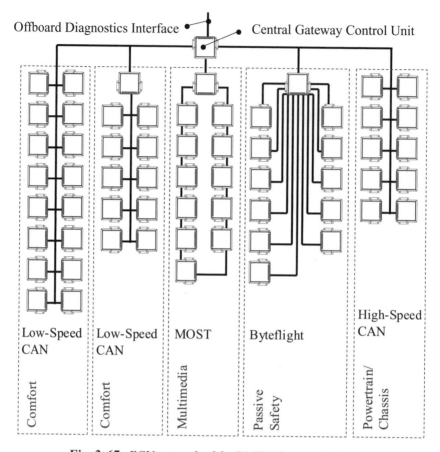

Offboard Diagnostics Interface • Central Gateway Control Unit

Low-Speed CAN — Comfort

Low-Speed CAN — Comfort

MOST — Multimedia

Byteflight — Passive Safety

High-Speed CAN — Powertrain/Chassis

Fig. 2-67. ECU network of the BMW 7 Series. (Ref. [62])

onward, communications continue via internal buses and gateway-equipped control units, with the respective control unit in the subsystem under diagnostics.

The subsystems utilize a variety of communications technologies and network topologies:

• The high-speed variant of the CAN bus [2] is deployed in the powertrain and chassis areas of the vehicle.

• The low-speed variant of the CAN bus [63] is the bus technology deployed in the area of comfort and convenience systems; it is organized in two segments.

• The star topology of the Byteflight bus [64] interconnects the control units of the passive safety systems.

• The multimedia systems require high data rates and accurate, time-synchronous data transmission. These systems are interconnected by means of a ring topology via MOST [65].

At the time of this writing (2005), the introduction of additional communications technologies has already occurred [66] or is foreseeable:

- In the field of multimedia applications, the discrepancy in innovation cycles—ranging from a few months for multimedia devices to several years for the classic vehicle systems—has resulted in a preference for the use of wireless communications technologies such as Bluetooth [67], restricting hardware changes onboard the vehicle to the lowest possible level.

- For application in the area of cost-sensitive body applications, the introduction of LIN [68] as a cost-efficient subnetwork technology is anticipated.

- For deployment in the area of safety-relevant systems, such as *brake-by-wire* or *steer-by-wire* systems, deterministic communication systems with failure-tolerant designs are required. Suitable networking technologies are FlexRay [49], TTP [50], and TTCAN [51].

CHAPTER THREE

SUPPORT PROCESSES FOR ELECTRONIC SYSTEMS AND SOFTWARE ENGINEERING

This section focuses on the processes supporting the development of electronic systems and software (Fig. 3-1). Before continuing, it is time to provide suitably accurate definitions of several colloquial terms related to system technology. The subjects to follow provide an overview of the processes used in configuration, project, subcontractor, and requirements management, including quality assurance. The discussion of these subjects remains largely independent of the topic of software development. Thus, it becomes much easier to apply the processes and methods under discussion to all system levels in the vehicle, and to the development of setpoint generators, sensors, actuators, hardware, and, last but not least, to software development.

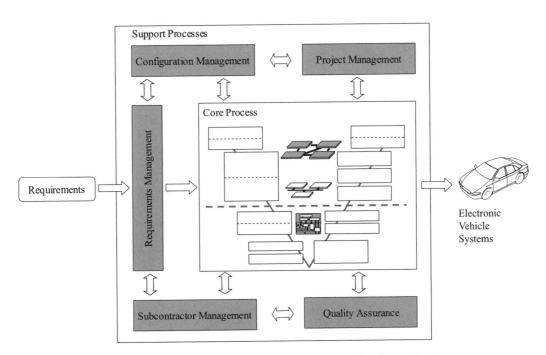

Fig. 3-1. *Support processes for electronic systems and software development.*

3.1 Basic Definitions of System Theory

System theory [59] furnishes processes designed to handle complexity. Without making histori-cal claims, the widely accepted approach to dealing with complexity may be likened to the old motto *Divide et impera* (divide and conquer). It is based on three important assumptions:

1. Dividing the system into components will not distort the issue being observed.

2. Regarded individually, the components are essentially identical to the components of the system.

3. The principles governing the assembly of components into a system are simple, stable, and well known.

These assumptions are deemed permissible for formulating a variety of practical questions.

The properties of a system exist as a consequence of the interrelations among the components forming the system (i.e., of the manner of component interaction and interplay). As the complex-ity of a system increases, the analysis of its components and their interdependencies becomes complex and expensive. That is exactly the type of system on which system theory brings its investigative efforts to bear. In this context, note that the components of one system may dif-fer entirely from the others. In fact, technical assemblies are as likely to be considered system components as are people or even the environment.

The following sections have technical systems as their point of focus. This book takes its ori-entation from the following system definitions [59, 60]:

- *System.* Comprises a group of interacting components that is separated from its surround-ings (Fig. 3-2).

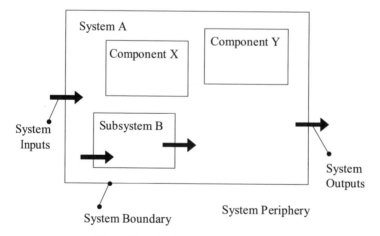

Fig. 3-2. *Block diagram of a system.*

- *System status.* At a given point in time, the system status is determined by a collection of properties used to describe the system at that respective point in time.

- *System periphery.* Also *periphery* for short. Describes a grouping of components and their properties that are not part of the system but whose behavior may influence the system status.

- *System boundary.* A delineation between system and system periphery.

- *System interface.* Any signal crossing the system boundary implicitly becomes a system interface by virtue of this action.

- *System input* and *system output.* Designation given to system interfaces, reflecting a differentiation on the basis of the inbound or outbound direction of data transfer they are handling.

- *Subsystem.* Because a system is almost always a part of its environment, it may be said to be a component of a larger system. Therefore, it would be safe to assume that any group of components that is considered a system also normally is a part of a hierarchy of systems. In this way, a system likewise may contain subsystems (i.e., represent an assembly of subsystems).

- *System level.* As a rule, system theory uses several so-called *observation* or *abstraction levels*, which are also called *system levels*.

- *Fractal proliferation.* This term is used if the different system levels exhibit similarities (i.e., show common characteristics). For example, Fig. 3-2 depicts a similarity between system A and subsystem B.

- *Interior view* and *exterior view.* These terms describe the differentiation between a system observation from within or without the system. In other words, being "on the outside looking in," it is not always possible to tell whether the item being examined represents a component or a subsystem. The outside view is an abstract *system view* of the system boundary and the system interfaces.

Thus, it follows that any system view comprises an abstraction that is analytically developed by the respective observer.

This makes it possible for different observers to develop differing system views of the same system. For example, the modeling perspectives introduced in Chapter 2—such as the open-loop/closed-loop control modeling approach on the basis of block diagrams, the microcontroller, and safety technology views—all present a diversity of approaches for looking at electronic vehicle systems.

Commonly accepted system modeling methods use the tools of abstraction through the formation of hierarchies—or *hierarchy-building*—and *modularization*. These basic principles are applied—often by intuition—to the bulk of tasks dedicated to the development of system views.

An essential aid to orientation in modeling is the so-called *7±2 rule*. In many cases, systems containing more than $7 + 2 = 9$ components appear complex to the human observer, whereas, by contrast, systems containing fewer than $7 - 2 = 5$ components often are perceived as trivial. Systems containing 5 to 9 components appear manageable (Fig. 3-3).

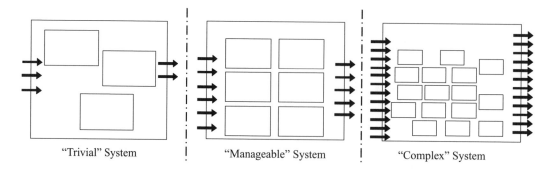

    "Trivial" System   "Manageable" System   "Complex" System

Fig. 3-3. Organizational clarity, the basic rule in system modeling.

The relations determining inclusiveness that exists between a system and its components are termed *aggregation relations* or *aggregations*. The division or parceling of a system into components is termed *partitioning* or *decomposition*. Conversely, the system-forming assembly of components is known as *integration* or *composition*.

Example: System levels in automotive electronics

Electronic systems onboard the vehicle can be observed at several system levels. The diagram in Fig. 3-4 labels the various levels in accordance with the sections that follow.

3.2 Process Models and Standards

System development avails itself of several specially developed process models and standards, such as the Capability Maturity Model Integration® (CMMI) [13], the Software Process Improvement and Capability Determination (SPICE) [14], or the V-Model [15].

Given the diversity of application options for each of these models, there must be an efficient means to determine which is most suited to an anticipated undertaking. Therefore, a process model must be assessed and evaluated—and possibly adapted—as a prerequisite for application to a specific project. There are numerous reasons for this. In many cases, the definitive focus of individual process steps varies, depending on their application. For example, the calibration of functions plays an important role in ECUs. In other fields of application (e.g., body electronics), the same process step is of comparatively low significance.

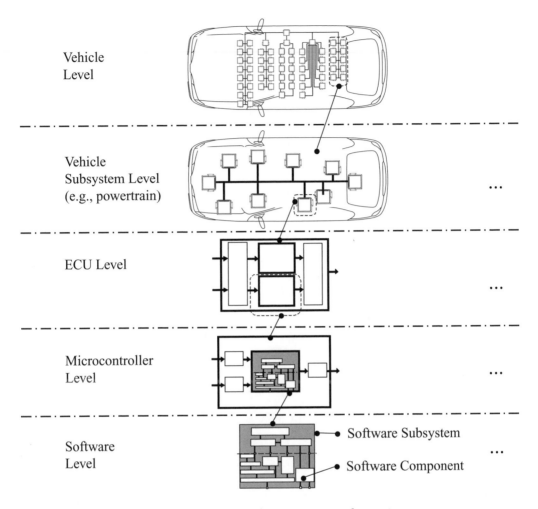

Vehicle
Level

Vehicle
Subsystem Level
(e.g., powertrain)

ECU Level

Microcontroller
Level

Software
Level

Software Subsystem

Software Component

Fig. 3-4. *System levels in automotive electronics.*

Note that as a rule, even the individual disciplines discussed in Chapter 2 of this book participate in development to varying degrees. An ECU requires the implementation of a multitude of different functions. However, in body electronics, distributed and networked systems are a single contributor of great importance.

The V-Model distinguishes between the areas of system design, project management, configuration management, and quality assurance. The so-called *key process areas* formulated in Level 2 of the CMMI differentiate between requirements management, configuration management, quality assurance, project planning, project tracking, and subcontractor management.

The following sections discuss the different aspects of configuration, project, subcontractor, and requirements management, including quality assurance, as depicted by Fig. 3-1.

This chapter does not attempt a comprehensive treatment of the subjects listed in the preceding paragraph. Instead, it intends to use real-life cases in point to demonstrate the benefits of the referred processes. Emphasis is given to those process steps that are of major consequence in vehicle development or those that incorporate specific individual features.

Example: Continual development and change management

Because of the long product life cycles of automobiles, the aspects of continual development and change management of onboard automotive systems are of great importance. It must be possible to manage the effects of change on a system and to track such changes. One example of how the changes made to one component can affect various other components in a system is shown in Fig. 3-5.

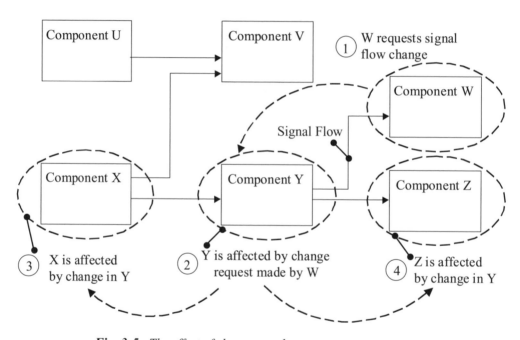

Fig. 3-5. *The effect of changes made to one system component.*

Initially, a required change made to Component W directly affects Component Y. The change that has occurred in Component Y then causes changes in Components X and Z. Changes also may have repercussions extending beyond subsystem boundaries or across system levels.

It stands to reason that, to safeguard continual system development and change management, the supporting processes discussed in the following sections must be interlinked with the core process. This is the only way in which lateral interdependencies among components within a system can be managed and tracked.

3.3 Configuration Management

3.3.1 Product and Life Cycle

The *life cycle of a product* allows for the differentiation of three phases: development, production, and operation and service (see Fig. 1-14 in Chapter 1).

The various components making up a system may have product life cycles of different durations. For example, the persistent technological advancements in electronics have resulted in product life cycles for vehicles that considerably exceed the life or change cycles of ECU hardware and software. Also, the system requirements in the individual development, production, and operational phases may vary.

Example: Differing requirements for ECU interfaces in development, production, and service

Quite often, the varying requirements for the interfaces of the ECU during development, production, and service can be met only by introducing different hardware features and software functionalities to accommodate the individual phases of the product life cycle. Figure 3-6 depicts some of the functional differences existing among development, production, operation, and service. Further demands arise, for example, in terms of different data transfer rates of the system interfaces.

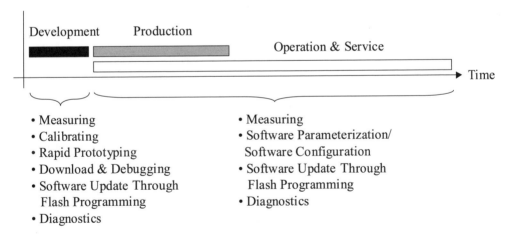

Fig. 3-6. *A diversity of requirements for ECU interfaces.*

3.3.2 Variants and Scalability

The combination of an increasing contingent of vehicle variants and rising customer expectations (i.e., regarding the availability of options for individualization and expandability) results in demands for a greater number of variants and a higher degree of scalability in onboard vehicle systems. The approach to meeting these system requirements may consist of introducing either additional *component variants* or *scalable system architectures*. In Fig. 3-7, the range of variants is extended by Component X, whereas the same result is achieved by the added Component Z in Fig. 3-8.

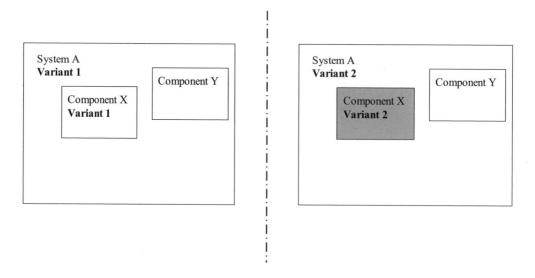

Fig. 3-7. *Creating system variants by assembling component variants.*

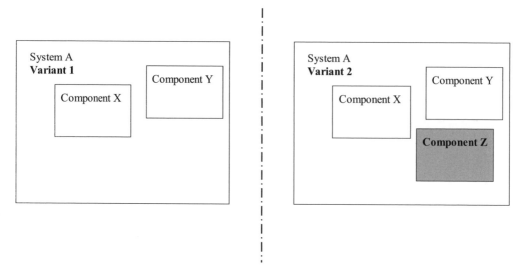

Fig. 3-8. *Creating system variants by exploiting scalability.*

3.3.3 Versions and Configurations

Because system variants may exist at all system levels, the *hierarchical relations* among system, subsystems, and/or components should be subject to closer scrutiny. Relations may take the shape of tree structures (Fig. 3-9) or network structures (Fig. 3-10).

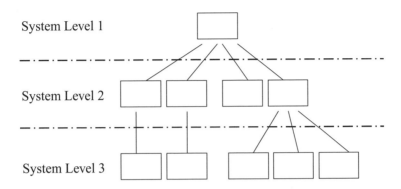

Fig. 3-9. *Tree structure.*

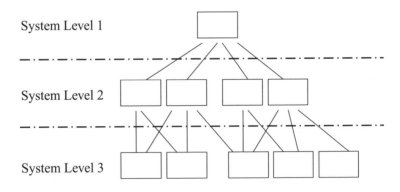

Fig. 3-10. *Network structure.*

In a tree structure, each component is assigned to only one system. In network structures, one component may belong to several systems. For this reason, tree structures comprise a special type of network structure, and the version management and configuration management handling system variants are based on network structures.

Over time, the continual development of systems and the introduction of new systems during the vehicle production phase results in the development of new generations of system components. As perceived from a vantage point at the component level, so-called component versions are introduced at certain points along the timeline (Fig. 3-11).

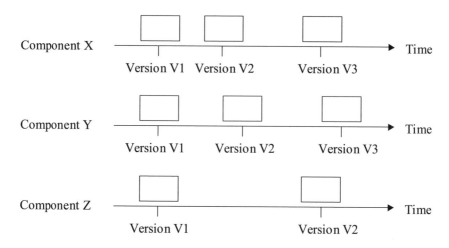

Fig. 3-11. *Various versions at the component level.*

The system level is also the area in which the relations—the *references*—with the contained components are managed.

In this context, the term *configuration* assumes special significance. Here, a configuration is defined as a *version-capable* or *versionable* component, which in turn references a group of other versionable components. In contrast to versions of components, configurations administer only the *references* to the component versions contained in the configuration and not the component versions themselves. A component cannot be changed after it has been versioned. Thus, it follows that a versioned configuration can reference only versioned components.

Based on these definitions, the term *configuration* may even apply to the collection of aggregate relations existing within a system. In other words, configurations matching this example contain only the hierarchical relations. However, note that hierarchical relations likewise can be subject to further development or change (Fig. 3-12).

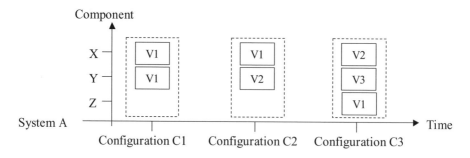

Fig. 3-12. *Various configurations at the system level.*

As a consequence of the conditions discussed in the preceding section, different versions of a given configuration evolve over time. These offspring can be observed at the primary system level in the same manner as a component or a subsystem.

The version and configuration management—*configuration management*, for short—facilitates the administration of the demonstrated relations between systems and components. This makes it an essential constituent of the development, production, and service processes. Configuration management not only provides for the parallel development of variants, it also handles the development of successive versions and ensures—at all system levels—the fulfillment of a variety of system requirements in individual phases of the product life cycle.

The configuration management covers all of the process steps necessary for filing, administration, restoration, and exchange of results produced as in the course of development procedures. This also includes the exchange of such information in all process phases, not only between the various organizational units of a company but between the different development partners. The configuration management also governs, in addition to the work-related findings and results, all of the materials and tools, such as the deployed development tools. This is the only way in which the reproducibility or repeatability of process steps can be ensured.

Several of the items managed by the configuration management are as follows:

- Requirements
- Specifications
- Implementations, such as program versions and data versions
- Description files, such as for diagnostics, software updates, and software parameterization
- Documentation, and so forth

Especially during software development, the configuration management is required to consider a variety of aspects. These include, for example, the simultaneous or concurrent work progression, the cooperation between vehicle manufacturers and suppliers, the separate handling of program and data versions, the tracking of historical version and configuration data related to software components (Fig. 3-13), and the administration of requirements and description files. For all of the reasons stated, the methodical integration of configuration management in the development process is an important prerequisite.

3.4 Project Management

The term *project* describes a collection of tasks that exhibits the following characteristics [69]:

- The envisioned undertaking contains an inherent risk and is characterized by uniqueness (i.e., it is not a routine situation).

- The task is defined in unambiguous terms.

- The accountabilities and objectives for a declared overall goal are clearly defined.

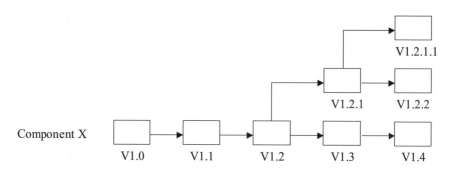

Fig. 3-13. *Version history of component X.*

- There is a clear limitation in time, providing a defined start date and end date.

- There is a limited deployment of resources.

- The organizational structure has been fine-tuned to suit the formulated objectives.

- In many cases, there exist discernible and differential contributory tasks—or *project segments*—and organizational units that are both interconnected and interdependent.

The objectives of a given project are expressed in the form of targets (Fig. 3-14):

- Quality targets: What are the requirements to be fulfilled by the overall project result?

- Cost targets: What is the budget approved for the attainment of the overall result?

- Target deadlines or milestones: When is the overall result expected for presentation?

Because any development endeavor is characterized by several of these characteristics, it may also be treated and handled as a dedicated project.

Fig. 3-14. *Project targets.*

On one hand, project management encompasses all aspects of project planning, which is the planning that concerns itself with the implementation of formulated project targets. It follows that there will have to be separate quality, cost, and deadline planning—also termed *project scheduling*—with concurrent organization planning, staff deployment scheduling, and risk analysis.

On the other hand, project management also includes the aspects of project control and project tracking, that is, the tracking and monitoring of quality, costs, and deadlines during the entire course of project implementation through the end of the project. This also entails being on the lookout for risks that may have been hitherto concealed or unrecognized. If such detriments are spotted, risk management will be trusted to apply the necessary course corrections.

3.4.1 Project Planning

To begin, the individual tasks making up a project must be defined. The sometimes arduous road that leads to the conclusion of a project is lined with *milestones*, that is, markers or events signifying the conclusion of individual project segments. Such a milestone typically may be a scheduled delivery date for partial shipments, testing procedures, or a customer's progress payment. The time period required to complete an individual project segment is termed the *project phase*.

Usually, it is possible to differentiate among at least four project phases (Fig. 3-15):

- Definition phase
- Planning phase
- Implementation phase
- Completion phase

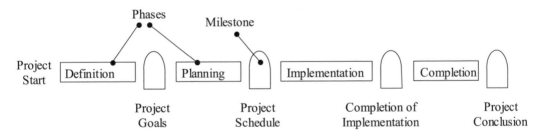

Fig. 3-15. *Project phases and milestones.*

Each of these four phases has its own concluding milestone:

- Definition of project objectives is concluded.
- Project planning has been completed.
- Project implementation has been successful.
- Project reaches its scheduled end date.

In some cases, the four major project phases are subdivided to create additional phases. This becomes necessary especially in situations where several organizational units and different corporate enterprises contribute to the project. More often than not, this is the case in automotive development.

3.4.1.1 Quality Planning

For the entire course of the project, quality planning defines all those measures intended to ensure that the overall project result will meet the formulated project requirements. Here, a differentiation is made between the quality assurance guidelines and the quality testing measures or methods. The actions required to serve quality assurance throughout all project phases are defined in a so-called *quality schedule*.

3.4.1.2 Cost Planning

Cost planning encompasses the planning for all resources and financial expenditures required to complete the project. The instruments most often used in this context consist of personnel deployment and fund disbursal schedules. Cost planning also must consider possible cost-saving measures, such as the reuse of findings from previous projects.

3.4.1.3 Project Scheduling

Project scheduling determines the length of time allowed for the completion of each project phase. It is a process that assigns specific start and end dates to each phase and milestone. For this planning step, it is crucial to consider, in addition to the possible ramifications of personnel deployment to different projects, the consequences of handling concurrent projects. As if this weren't enough, the additional need to account for interdependencies among the project phases turns project scheduling into a high-stakes juggling act.

Example: Project schedule—Development of a motor vehicle

Figure 3-16 shows an excerpt from the project scheduling of a motor vehicle development project. The deadline scheduling for the entire vehicle must be coordinated and synchronized with the scheduling assigned to all project segments. In this example, the development schedules of vehicle, electronics, and software must be fine-tuned to produce the required *meshing* of schedules.

As Fig. 3-16 indicates, several tasks are scheduled sequentially, whereas others are to be carried out simultaneously. In many cases, development time can be reduced only by planning for the concurrent handling of project tasks. For this reason, the scheduling and synchronization of parallel development steps—termed *simultaneous engineering*—constitutes a major challenge. This essential function is handled by a number of employees usually belonging to different teams, and it is often shared across the corporate boundaries of automobile manufacturers, suppliers, and other development partners.

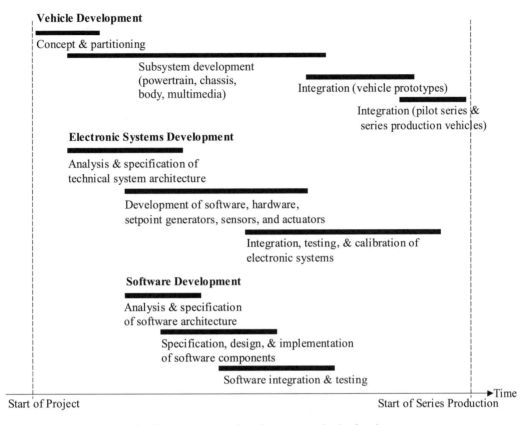

Fig. 3-16. *Project schedule for motor vehicle development.*

The job of accurately and completely defining the individual tasks, with the channels of information flow and the placement of interconnecting synchronization points, may be handled by a process model. Thus, it becomes an essential prerequisite for successful project management. The intricate meshing of software development with electronics and vehicle development represents a marked contrast to the approaches prevalent in other areas of industrial application—with telecommunications serving as an example. Therefore, it is safe to say that, by its very nature, automotive systems engineering exerts a significant influence on software engineering in the automobile industry.

Regarding the time-based synchronization of two project phases characterized by interdependencies, a differentiation may be made among the following three cases in point. However, it is not unusual for hybrid forms of these to occur in practical application.

Case 1: Phase B commences after the conclusion of Phase A (Fig. 3-17)

This scheduling approach is prescribed in situations where the completion of Phase A serves as the precondition for the start of Phase B, or in cases where the processing of Phase B is in large part dependent on the results produced by Phase A.

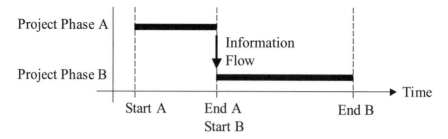

Fig. 3-17. *Project phases—sequential scheduling.*

Benefits: Provides sequential information flow without inherent risk

Drawbacks: Requires long processing times

Example:

The commencement of integration testing of the control unit software (Phase B) must wait until the integration of that software (Phase A) has run its course.

Case 2: Phase B commences with segment information from Phase A, without early decisions being taken in Phase A (Fig. 3-18).

This scheduling approach is applicable in situations where the working packet in Phase B is relatively robust and thus unaffected by subsequent modifications made to original decisions taken in Phase A.

Benefits: Shorter processing time

Drawbacks: Risk of delays caused by iterations in Phase B

Example:

Using a rapid prototyping system, the development of functions of the application software (Phase B) can be started prior to the completion of the platform software (Phase A).

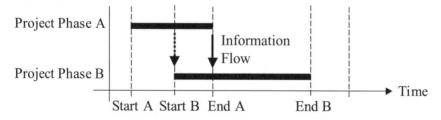

Fig. 3-18. *Project phases—parallel scheduling, absence of early decisions in Phase A.*

Case 3: Phase B commences with segment information from Phase A, prior decisions in Phase A having been frozen (Fig. 3-19).

This scheduling approach is advantageous in situations where decisions made in Phase A are rapidly approaching their final form, that is, decisions placed close to the start of the timeline are already close to reaching their final status, and the risk of subsequent changes is relatively low.

Benefits: Shorter processing times

Drawbacks: Risk of quality losses due to early constraints imposed in Phase A

Example:

> Even before all functions of the application software have been specified and implemented (Phase A), those functions that have already been implemented are ready for calibration (Phase B), albeit with the provision that there must be a very low likelihood of modifications occurring toward the end of the Phase A timeline.

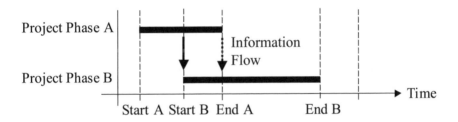

Fig. 3-19. *Project phases—parallel scheduling, presence of frozen prior decisions from Phase A.*

In all three of these cases, the information to be exchanged must be mapped onto the development process. The task of defining processes is the subject of a more detailed discussion in Chapter 4 of this book.

3.4.1.4 Development Roles and Responsibilities

As noted in Chapter 2, the development of vehicle functions requires in almost every instance the participation of several professional disciplines. Therefore, it is not unusual to note the interdisciplinary staffing of development teams. The individual team members contribute their various qualifications—they may be said to assume a variety of *roles*.

With regard to the performance of tasks and outline of responsibilities, all contributory roles require clearly defined demarcations. Table 3-1 presents an overview of various roles of the kind frequently differentiated on development projects.

TABLE 3-1
ROLES AND TASK RESPONSIBILITIES
IN THE DEVELOPMENT PROCESS

Role	Responsibilities
Function development	Analysis of user requirements, and specification of logical system architecture.
System development	Analysis of logical system architecture, and specification of technical system architecture.
Software development	Analysis of software requirements, plus software specification, design, implementation, and testing.
Hardware development	Analysis of hardware requirements, plus hardware specification, design, physical implementation, integration, and testing.
Setpoint generator, sensor, and actuator development	Analysis of requirements specific to setpoint generators, sensors, and actuators, with their specification, design, physical implementation, integration, and testing.
Integration, testing, and calibration	Integration, testing, and calibration of onboard vehicle systems and their functions.

The development of software functions for electronic systems is accomplished with the participation of all of the roles outlined in Table 3-1. Regarding the resulting role distribution, it must overcome the hurdle of interdisciplinary, and frequently cross-corporate, cooperation. For the reasons given, the interdisciplinary teamwork dedicated to the development of software functions is best conducted on the basis of graphical function models. These are replacing the previously used prose narrative specifications to an increasing degree.

In planning any project, the referred role distribution and the varying qualifications of the team members must be taken into account.

Another special feature indigenous to the automobile industry is the variety of development environments. For example, as shown in Fig. 1-18 in Chapter 1, virtual steps must be synchronized by means of simulation, with the use of laboratory-based development procedures, on the test bench or dynamometer, and in the vehicle.

3.4.2 Project Tracking and Risk Management

A *risk* comprises an event that may jeopardize the success of a project or even threaten the consequence of economic loss. Thus, a project risk may well constitute a quality, cost, or deadline risk.

Risk management encompasses all measures required to handle project-related risks. Because it is closely interlaced with project control, risk management coordinates appropriate countermeasures in the event that an actual versus target comparison in the course of a project reveals certain deviations. Function development may, as a measure of risk prevention, avail itself of the benefit of reused, previously validated functions. Another approach would be the early validation of new functions by means of prototype development. All of the preceding notwithstanding, there is no sure way to achieve a wholesale exclusion of project risks. Usually, the manifestation of risk necessitates project planning amendments. For a detailed discussion of the topic at hand, reference is made to the relevant specialized literature [69].

3.5 Subcontractor Management

The development of electronic systems in the automobile industry is frequently characterized by a pronounced division of labor between vehicle manufacturers and suppliers or subcontractors. Where the governing user requirements for a function to be developed are normally defined by the vehicle manufacturer, the implementation of the desired functions by means of electronic systems is frequently the exclusive domain of suppliers. However, the vehicle manufacturer usually is responsible for fine-tuning and acceptance testing of the functions implemented onboard the vehicle.

3.5.1 System and Component Responsibilities

Given the perils of this division of labor, a precise definition of the interfaces between the vehicle manufacturer and subcontractors is an indispensable prerequisite. This can be properly visualized by means of the V-Model diagram shown in Fig. 3-20. Whereas the vehicle manufacturer bears the responsibility for the vehicle (i.e., on both the left-hand and right-hand branch of the V-Model), the suppliers frequently are in charge of the component level.

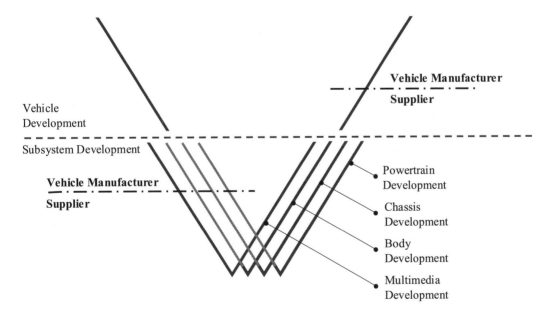

Fig. 3-20. *Distribution of responsibilities between the vehicle manufacturer and suppliers.*

The cooperation across corporate borders requires, in addition to the clarification of technical aspects, the settling of all issues addressing the organizational and legal levels of a project. For this reason, contractor management is an area of great importance in vehicle management. It encompasses all tasks to be considered in the context of interfaces between the vehicle manufacturer and suppliers and that of system development.

Although the referred interfaces may be defined differently on a case-by-case basis, they nevertheless require accurate and complete definitions in each case.

3.5.2 Interfaces for Specification and Integration

The cooperation between the vehicle manufacturer and suppliers distinguishes between two types of interfaces. In the example depicted in Fig. 3-20, these are as follows:

- The *specification interface* in the left-hand branch of the V-Model

- The *integration interface* in the right-hand branch of the V-Model

These interfaces may become extremely complex. This can be demonstrated simply by virtue of the great number of existing interrelations.

For example, if a system consists of n number of components made by n number of different suppliers, it will be necessary to control, within the auspices of system development, a 1:n relation on the side of the vehicle manufacturer—on both the specification side and integration side. Now, we shall assume that a subcontractor supplies a given component to m number of different vehicle manufacturers. This means that it will be necessary to control, within the auspices of component development, an m:1 relation on the side of the component manufacturer—again, on both the specification side and the integration side.

3.5.3 Defining the Cross-Corporation Development Process

The complexity of interfaces notwithstanding, this situation provides many benefits to both suppliers and vehicle manufacturers.

In most cases, electronic systems consist of embedded systems, that is, systems that are integrated in a given context and that do not overtly manifest their existence to the respective user. The value of the ECUs is rooted in the functions that they perform. In many cases, these functions represent differentiating competitive factors.

For good reason, vehicle manufacturers therefore are acutely interested in those ECU functions that have inherent properties providing a competitive edge. To software developers, this means that the focus of their customer is pinpointed on those functions of the ECU application software that hold the promise of competitive relevance.

To suppliers, this opens the door to a chance for the cross-customer development, testing, and standardization of ECU hardware, platform software, and segments of the application software. Customer-specific functions then can be added to and integrated into the application software.

The discussion in the preceding sections has addressed a number of factors affecting the cooperation between the customer—the vehicle manufacturer—and his or her suppliers. Despite their obvious complexities, the resulting interrelations between the vehicle manufacturer and suppliers can be depicted by means of a diagram. One such option is available in the so-called *line of visibility diagrams* (*LOV diagrams,* for short) [23], which use the graphical symbols shown in Fig. 3-21.

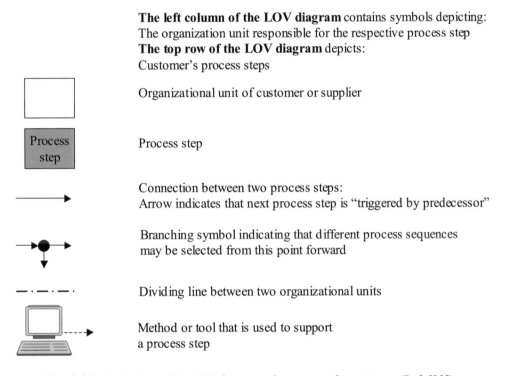

The left column of the LOV diagram contains symbols depicting:
The organization unit responsible for the respective process step
The top row of the LOV diagram depicts:
Customer's process steps

Organizational unit of customer or supplier

Process step

Connection between two process steps:
Arrow indicates that next process step is "triggered by predecessor"

Branching symbol indicating that different process sequences may be selected from this point forward

Dividing line between two organizational units

Method or tool that is used to support a process step

Fig. 3-21. *Symbols used in LOV diagrams for process description. (Ref. [23])*

Figure 3-22 shows an example of a LOV diagram. The top row depicts the *process steps* for which the vehicle manufacturer, in its function as the customer, assumes the responsibility. The rows that follow indicate the suppliers' and subcontractors' organization units, with the process steps assigned to them. The connecting lines and arrows indicate the sequence of the process steps. Each arrow represents the flow of an intermediate result, a so-called *artifact*. A separate row is dedicated to the definition of methods and tools deployed for the various process steps.

3.6 Requirements Management

By its nature, requirements management is not necessarily designed exclusively for automotive applications. This is a trait that it has in common with configuration management. A telltale sign

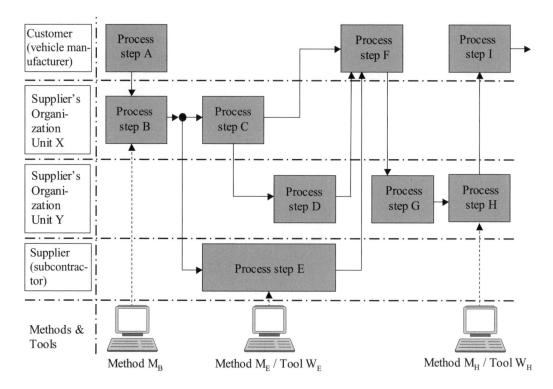

Fig. 3-22. *Process description using a LOV diagram. (Ref. [23])*

of this fact is the deployment of standard tools handling requirements management for vehicle-related projects. However, note that the necessity to consider the special demands of this type of projects is in no way diminished. Reference is being made here, for example, to the support of cross-corporate cooperation—in the field of requirements management—that even transcends location borders. Also worthy of note is the concerted action of requirements and configuration management for the purpose of versioning, not to mention the long product life cycles. All of these underscore the demand for the methodical integration of requirements management into the development process as a whole.

As its name implies, requirements management concerns itself with any and all tasks related to the following:

- Requirements logging and recording
- Requirements tracking

However, note that the analysis of requirements, as well as the task of defining the specifications for the logical and technical system architecture, belong to the core process of system and software development.

3.6.1 Mining, Recording, and Interpreting User Requirements

Any product that is sent to market with hopes of garnering acceptance and success must satisfy the requirements of its target user group. For this reason, it is essential to start defining, as accurately as possible, the intended users of a given system and their expectations. Therefore, the needs and wants of the future user are termed *user requirements*. Because it would be presumptuous to assume a certain level of technical background knowledge on the part of the user, user requirements must be expressed in the language familiar to users.

User wishes—and expectations—thus become the drivers for all development steps to follow. It also would appear logical that the process step concerned with the identification, recording, and interpretation of user requirements is decidedly different from all subsequent development steps. Therefore, always with an ear to the ground and an eye on the market, developers should conduct this step in a manner that combines intensive research and a high degree of interactivity. Even given the fact that not all requirements expressed by the target group may appear practical or feasible, they should still be recorded and evaluated, if only to get a better handle on the users' expectations as a whole. For this reason, user requirements in most cases are available only in the form of a motley assortment of list entries, resulting in a more or less structured, rudimentary tabulation.

Based on the point in time of their acquisition, three types of user requirements may be distinguished:

- Requirements expressed at the start of a project

- Requirements voiced during the course of a project, normally referred to as requests for change or supplemental requirements

- Requirements returned by way of feedback after the delivery of the finished product, normally called new requirements, fault reports, or suggestions for improvement

In the following discussion, all of the listed types of requirements are given equal treatment.

The term *user* applies to any and all persons who are in contact with the completed system in one capacity or another, with the provision that his or her wishes and/or instructions exert influence on the system. Often, it is possible to identify different *user groups*.

Example: User groups identified in conjunction with a vehicle

For a given vehicle, there are other user groups in addition to the group of drivers. For example, these include additional occupants and other road users such as pedestrians, cyclists, other vehicles, and service personnel, as well as legislators (Fig. 3-23). All of these groups impose their demands or requirements on the vehicle. Some requirement categories, such as statutory laws, also are termed *prerequisites*.

During this phase, which is also termed *opinion mining*, a differentiation between requirements and solutions provides a number of benefits. Users normally have a tendency to express their requirements by stating or suggesting solutions. If a user offers suggestions for solutions, these

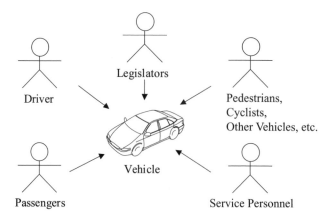

Fig. 3-23. *Identifying user groups for a given vehicle.*

should be scrutinized in such a way that the suggested solution may be used to formulate the underlying user requirement. Failing accurate mining, the technical implementation may be specified at an unsuitably early time, which would confine the space available for solutions.

Example: User formulation of a requirement concerning the fuel gauge

A user expresses the following suggested solution:

> *The fuel level should be indicated in liters instead of on a scale indicating readings of "¼ – ½ – ¾ – 1."*

The underlying user requirement might be as follows:

> *The indication of the road range of the vehicle should be more accurate, that is, stating miles or kilometers.*

User requirements may be mined in a variety of ways. First to come to mind are the tried-and-true interviews and workshops, followed by deductive derivation from existing systems and requests for change. There also is the potential inherent in user feedback from the field. Bear in mind that user requirements may arise from a variety of backgrounds, be they of a technical, organizational, or economic nature.

User requirements often are categorized on the basis of varying criteria, such as source, priority, urgency, stability, testability, acceptance, and so forth.

A closer look at developments during the past decade reveals that the number of user requirements increased with each successive vehicle generation. It is safe to say that this trend was not nourished by the increasing number of vehicle functions alone. Sizeable contributions also came from the increase in the number of vehicle variants and rising customer expectations, with vehicle customizing and scalability having been major factors (Fig. 3-24) [9].

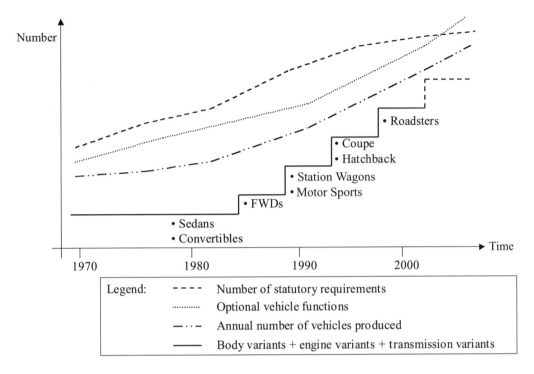

Fig. 3-24. *Increase in the number of vehicle-specific user requirements. (Ref. [9])*

Aside from the expectations of the customer group of a given vehicle, the design and development of electronic systems must consider a great number of additional prerequisites, such as technical specifications and statutory constraints.

As a case in point, Fig. 3-25 outlines the *requirement classes* that must be observed in most cases and that must be considered when designing electronic systems.

The various requirements imposed on electronic systems exhibit numerous interdependencies and reciprocal effects. It also may be possible for requirements to be mutually contradictory. If that is the case, the resulting goal-specific conflicts must be resolved before a technical implementation becomes possible.

The *accepted user requirements* become the basis for all subsequent development steps.

In the development of any system, the system requirements are formulated in the language of the participating engineering disciplines. For this reason, differentiation is required between the user requirements and those requirements that are imposed on a system from the development standpoint. Chapter 4 of this book introduces another differentiation between the logical and technical system architectures. The same chapter also provides a discussion of the analysis and specification procedures required for the mapping of user requirements onto a technical system

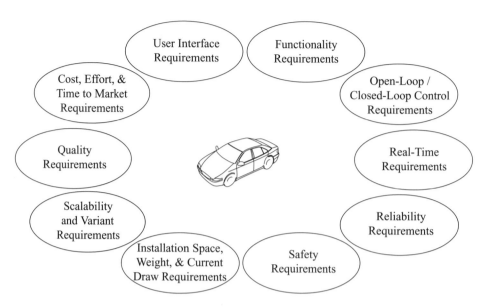

Fig. 3-25. *Various requirement classes for electronic systems.*

architecture. Accordingly, to facilitate the planning and tracking of requirements implementation, requirements management must support, in addition to a view of the user requirements, a view of the logical and technical system architecture (Fig. 3-26).

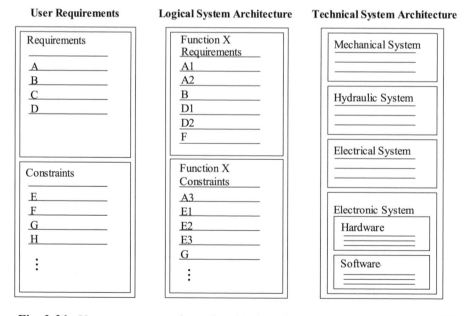

Fig. 3-26. *User requirements, logical and technical system architecture. (Ref. [12])*

3.6.2 Tracking User Requirements

The challenges of handling the system variants, scalability, and differing life cycles of the deployed components, as well as the reuse of components in a variety of vehicles, all result in prerequisites that must already be taken into account at the system design stage. At the same time, this often results in lateral interrelations among different vehicle projects. These relations must be considered in project planning to the same extent as the numerous interrelations between automobile manufacturers and suppliers, not to mention the simultaneous processing of design-related tasks, or *simultaneous engineering*.

Therefore, note that the single most important function of requirements management, in addition to the mining, recording, and interpretation of user requirements, consists of the tracking of requirements implementation.

For all entities contributing to development, this is the only common basis for making a determination about which requirements are being implemented with which program and/or data version, and which are not. This is a particularly important requirement in the integration and quality assurance of intermediate versions. As a prerequisite for the tracking of requirements, the interrelations between user requirements and the logical and technical system architecture must be managed. To this end, all system components must be connected to the respective requirements, as depicted in Fig. 3-27.

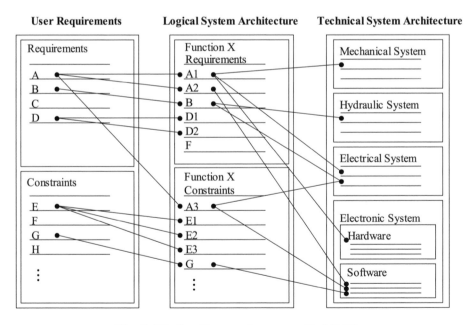

Fig. 3-27. *Tracking requirements. (Ref. [12])*

3.7 Quality Assurance

Quality assurance encompasses all measures ensuring that the product meets the specified requirements. It is quite true that quality can be "built into" a product, provided that quality assurance guidelines and appropriate quality testing procedures have been established.

Quality assurance guidelines also may be termed *preventive measures*. With regard to software products, this includes some or all of the following measures:

- Deployment of appropriately trained, capable personnel who possess the necessary experience and skills

- Provision of a suitable development process with defined testing procedures

- Availability of guidelines, measures, and standards to support the process

- Provision of a suitable tool environment to support the process

- Automation of both manual and fault-prone working steps

Quality testing procedures serve the purpose of fault detection. Therefore, quality testing should be conducted after as many steps in the development process as possible. Because a variety of quality testing methods are integrated in the V-Model, these will be discussed in more detail in conjunction with the core process in Chapter 4 of this book.

In the case of software products, a general differentiation is made between two types of faults:

- Specification faults
- Implementation faults

Research has shown that specification faults are predominant in most projects. For this reason, the V-Model differentiates between *verification* and *validation*.

3.7.1 Integration and Testing Procedures

After the user requirements for a given project have been explicitly defined, it is possible to test the product *vis-à-vis* its user requirements. The V-Model distinguishes four different test steps (see Fig. 1-15 in Chapter 1):

- The *component test* carries out testing against the component specification.

- The *integration test* carries out system testing against the specification of the technical system architecture.

- The *system test* carries out system testing against the specification of the logical system architecture.

- The *acceptance test* carries out system testing against the user requirements.

The component test, integration test, and system test comprise verification measures. The acceptance test is one of several validation measures.

Testing—without putting too fine a point on it—is a method of verifying the presence of faults. Because they focus on fault identification, tests contribute to the sustained attainment of product quality. For this reason alone, tests should be conducted at all system levels at the earliest possible juncture. In this context, however, note that the failure of a test to identify any faults whatsoever does not necessarily indicate an unequivocal absence of faults. Thus, tests must be planned in conjunction with additional quality assurance measures, such as reviews, with a view to forming an investigative entity.

The tests to be conducted may be described by means of application or testing cases in point that may be defined as early as in the design phase. This also means that the user requirements implicitly define the acceptance tests. The application cases for the system test are defined as part of the specification for the logical system architecture, the sample cases for the integration test become part and parcel of the specification for the technical system architecture, and so forth.

3.7.2 Software Quality Assurance Methods

The methods used in software quality assurance are closely related to the integration procedures. Especially in view of the increasing safety relevance of many software-based vehicle functions, the importance of software quality assurance is steadily increasing. There is a simple way to formulate the demand for safety: All components required for a given vehicle function, with all associated systems, must meet the technical safety requirements.

In electronics development, a high degree of system safety therefore cannot be attained simply by looking at the hardware involved. The parallel deployment of software quality testing methods is an absolute must.

For reasons emanating from the discussion throughout the preceding sections, the verification of software reliability and safety is steadily gaining in importance. It has become virtually impossible to guarantee a fault-free implementation, spanning the range from the analysis of user requirements to the completed program. Therefore, the only safe road to the creation of reliable software consists of the diligent application of software quality assurance methods and of uncompromising organizational measures, such as requirements management and configuration management. The combination of these and the deployment of software engineering methods will make the development process manageable.

An overview of possible software quality assurance methods as they relate to verification and validation is shown in Fig. 3-28 [70]. Some of these methods are discussed in more detail in Chapter 5 of this book.

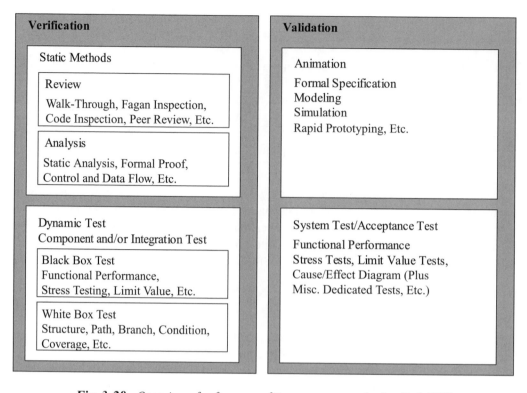

Fig. 3-28. Overview of software quality assurance methods. (Ref. [70])

CHAPTER FOUR

CORE PROCESS FOR ELECTRONIC SYSTEMS AND SOFTWARE ENGINEERING

In contrast to the practice of component development, which is the analysis and design of individual components, systems engineering concerns itself with the analysis and design of the system as a whole. The discussion in this chapter takes its orientation from the following definition of *systems engineering*, which closely follows the definitions in [12] and [71].

The definitions state that systems engineering is the dedicated application of scientific and technical resources for the purposes of:

- Transforming an operational requirement into the description of a system configuration, while considering, to the extent possible, all operational requirements in accordance with the benchmarks of the necessary effectiveness.

- Integrating all technical parameters, and ensuring the compatibility of all physical, functional, and technical interfaces in a manner optimizing, to the highest degree possible, the entire system definition and the system design.

- Achieving the integration of contributions from all participating engineering disciplines in a comprehensive development approach.

Thus, systems engineering is an interdisciplinary approach. It encompasses measures and methods employed by systems engineering practitioners and researchers for the sole purpose of facilitating the successful implementation of dedicated systems. In systems engineering, the development process aims at accomplishing an early definition of requirements and necessary functionalities, plus the documentation of requirements. Also included are the design and subsequent verification and validation of the system. Covering a cradle-to-grave life cycle of the system, the process encompasses every relevant aspect, such as development, performance features, costs, project schedule, testing, manufacture, operation, and servicing, as well as training and, finally, system disposal.

Systems engineering provides a structured development—or *engineering*—process, considering all phases of the product life cycle, spanning the arc from initial concept to production, down to operation and servicing. In its observations, systems engineering must consider both technical and organizational aspects. For example, the development of electronic systems for onboard automotive application requires the integration of engineering disciplines introduced in Chapter 2 of this book.

By contrast, software development comprises—as does the development of hardware, setpoint generators, sensors, and actuators—a separate engineering discipline integrated in systems engineering.

The unambiguous definition of the interfaces—of both the specification and integration type—between systems engineering and software engineering represents an indispensable prerequisite for a consistent development process. This so-called *core process* steps into the limelight in the present chapter. The following sections take their orientation from the overview and terminology shown in Fig. 4-1.

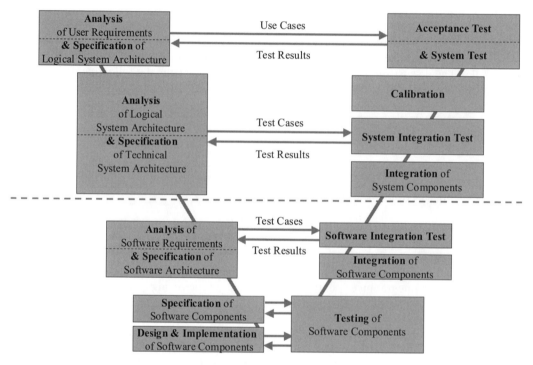

Fig. 4-1. *Overview of the systems and software engineering process.*

4.1 Requirements and Prerequisites

4.1.1 Shared System and Component Responsibilities

In vehicle development, the responsibility for given components often is shared by several partners (e.g., component suppliers). Needless to say, if suppliers happen to be engaged in a mutually competitive situation, this will affect the ways and means of cooperation. Therefore, the vehicle manufacturer normally takes charge of the overall systems responsibility, whereas the responsibility for subsystems often rests with the system suppliers (Fig. 4-2).

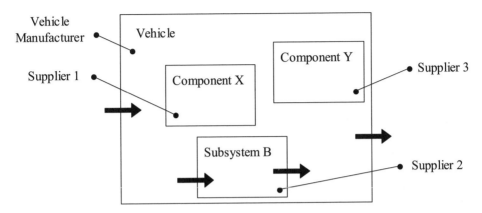

Fig. 4-2. *Distribution of responsibilities for components, subsystems, and systems.*

Thus, it is safe to say that, as a rule, the functions relating to vehicle systems specification, integration, and quality assurance are shared by several partners, each assuming one of the three roles of vehicle manufacturer, system supplier, or component supplier.

4.1.2 Coordination of Systems Engineering and Software Engineering

As depicted in Fig. 4-1, the objective of the early and late process steps is the observation of the system aspects related to vehicle functions. Here, the focus is on the interaction of the various components forming a system that facilitates the implementation of vehicle functions. Regarded individually, the system components may be implemented in a technically diverse manner, that is, based on mechanical, hydraulic, electrical, or even electronic principles. However, only the concerted interaction of the components of a system fulfills the user's expectations of a given vehicle function.

The ECUs onboard the vehicle interact with a variety of different components. Therefore, the basic design issue for vehicle functions is the replication of a logical system architecture in the form of a technical system consisting of ECUs, setpoint generators, sensors, and actuators. To this end, the interfaces connecting the systems and their components must be defined and subfunctions assigned.

This book limits the discussion of component development or subsystem development to those components and subsystems that are based on software implementation. This process necessitates the consideration of an abundance of reciprocal effects that cross the boundaries between the development of systems and software. Thus, the mastery of software development can be achieved solely with the aid of a systematic development methodology, which often is called *software engineering*. Actually, software engineering is not a new invention. For a long time, experienced software developers in all application areas have been using certain principles—mostly more or less intuitively and without subjecting these axioms to any kind of formal definition.

The decisive prerequisite for a consistent process is the detailed definition of the interfaces between systems engineering and its software counterpart. For this reason, the following sections pay particular attention to the specification and integration interfaces between systems and software engineering.

In Sections 4.5 through 4.10, the software, in its role as a component or subsystem, takes center stage. The discussion examines in greater detail those subfunctions that are carried out by microcontrollers onboard ECUs and whose description is software based. Because software opens the door to the random linking—both logical and arithmetical—of input signals for the purpose of calculating the output variables of a given function, the contribution by software functions to the entire functionality of a vehicle is steadily increasing. But there is a downside, which manifests itself in the rising complexity of the attendant software. The safe and predictable mastery of this complexity represents a challenge that necessitates the use of appropriate software engineering methods, such as the practice of extending the declaration and standardization of interfaces also to the software.

As the discussion has shown, software engineering shines its spotlight on mapping the logical system architecture onto a concretely defined software system, that is, onto the entire complement of programs and data being processed in a distributed, processor-controlled system onboard the vehicle. To this end, software engineering also can draw significant benefits from employing the general methods inherent in the support processes described in Chapter 3.

The following sections discuss the special prerequisites for the specification, design, implementation, testing, and integration of software for ECUs in series-produced vehicles. Particular attention is given to a clear delineation between the specification of software functions at the physical level, on one hand, and the design and implementation of programs and data for a specific microcontroller.

Stated differently, a separation of program version and data version can cause an enormous simplification of variant management in development, production, and service (e.g., through the implementation of physical variants in the form of data variants). This point is receiving appropriate consideration, too.

The V-Model was developed for embedded systems. Thus, it regards the software as a component of a system of information technology, gives equal weight to both software and hardware development, and integrates quality assurance testing in the system implementation.

For this reason, the V-Model is the preferred choice for systems that are characterized by high demands in terms of reliability and safety in conjunction with the prescription of appropriate testing steps, and for systems whose components are subject to distributed development.

In the presence of so much light, there is bound to be some shadow. A disadvantage is seen in the absence of feedback mechanisms with the early development phases, causing faults and/or changes occurring early on the timeline to be recognized or considered in a less than timely fashion. In this way, new requirements and change requests may be met and/or implemented only at the cost of great expenditures. In fact, they have a tendency to introduce unsavory consequences, ranging from high project risks to threatening the entire project. As a practical consequence, the V-Model is cycled through repeatedly in a given course of vehicle development. Various variants of possible endless loops are depicted by the flow of test results shown in Fig. 4-1.

In many cases, a first step is to develop a prototype that, despite its limited functionality, can be used for proving in a real-world environment at the beginning of the timeline. This aids the identification of deficits at an early stage. The limited prototype then is used to develop an improved prototype for validation in another iteration loop. This evolutionary prototyping cycle is repeated until all requirements or quality targets have been met. Alternatively, at least a software version with limited functionality can be shipped, even in the presence of looming time and cost constraints. This incremental and iterative approach allows for the timely reduction of development risks in software engineering. Other terms used to describe this iterative method are *prototype model* or *spiral model*.

The same model also is used in automotive systems engineering, and it is used in the initial development of components that are then tested in experimental vehicles. As a next step, vehicle prototypes are constructed and field tested, to be succeeded by pilot series and series production vehicles. As the number of iterations increases, the development risk and per-iteration expense diminishes. The prototypes developed for the respective integration versions also are termed *samples*. Depending of the progress of a project, a differentiation is frequently made between *A-*, *B-*, and *C-samples*. The series-produced version also is known as the *D-sample*.

In the development of software functions, a similar approach is supported by simulation and rapid prototyping tools; these are discussed in more detail in Section 5.3 of Chapter 5.

4.1.3 Model-Based Software Development

Software models facilitate the formulation of algorithms devoid of interpretation leeway. This is accomplished with the deployment of terminology and graphical notations that provide more clarity and distinction than plain-text descriptions or program code.

Because of these obvious advantages, model-based software development on the basis of graphical notations has gained widespread acceptance in the automobile industry in recent years. Software models describe a variety of views of a software system. The description of the software architecture of microcontrollers derives the greatest benefits from the context or interface view, the layer view, and the view of attainable operating states. The following sections present the essential terminology and notations used in these model views.

4.2 Basic Definitions and Notations

Before starting, there is the need to discuss one small matter of terminology. Now is the time to clarify the basic terms and notations used by the V-Model [15] for the purpose of process visualization.

4.2.1 Processes, Process Steps, and Artifacts

A *process*, as contemplated by a process model, represents a systematic and repetitive series of steps that follow each other in a logical sequence. A process may be said to:

- Serve the fulfillment of a requirement of an internal (in-house) or external customer

- Be initiated by a customer

- Deliver, to this customer, a performance in the form of a product or service, which is then paid for by that same customer (customer/vendor relationship)

A *process step* comprises a separate and complete individual sequence of activities whose result is an *artifact*. Subdividing a process step would not produce a useful artifact. An artifact represents an intermediate result that is passed on for use by other process steps. Examples of artifacts of electronic vehicle systems may be the specification or implementation of a software component. Other artifacts may be hardware components, setpoint generators, sensors, or actuators.

The different process steps are linked by interfaces that serve the purpose of exchanging artifacts. In the visualization used by the V-Model [15], process steps and artifacts are depicted as shown in Fig. 4-3.

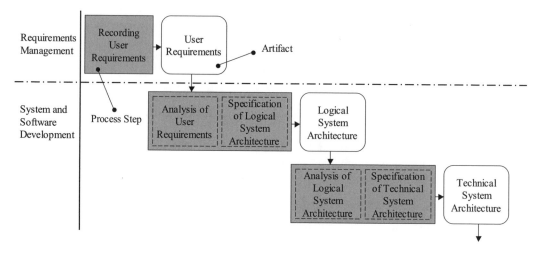

Fig. 4-3. *Visualization of V-Model (Ref. [15]) based processes using LOV diagrams. (Ref. [23])*

In the definition of process steps and artifacts, various prerequisites must be considered:

- Participants or responsibilities,   or   who produces/performs what?
- Competence and qualification,   or   who can contribute what?
- Precondition and result,   or   what is needed, and what is delivered?

4.2.2 *Methods and Tools*

For each individual process step or for a series thereof, a procedural approach—a so-called *method*—must be declared. Following the definition in [72], a method is a formalized, justified, and regularly scheduled procedural approach applied toward the attainment of defined targets, normally within the strictures of formulated principles.

Example: Simulation and rapid prototyping for a new vehicle function

The term *rapid prototyping* describes process steps pursuing the objective of achieving the rapid validation of a given specification through the application of predefined methods early on the timeline. In the case of software functions, these methods may be supported by rapid prototyping tools (see Fig. 1-20 in Chapter 1). In this context, typical process steps are those effecting the specification (i.e., through modeling) and simulation, as well as in-vehicle prototype integration and testing (Fig. 4-4).

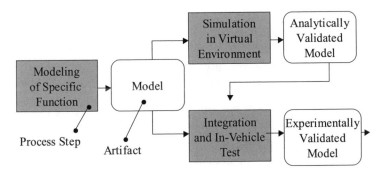

Fig. 4-4. *Simulation and rapid prototyping steps in the development process.*

The artifact resulting from this methodical approach is a specification that takes the form of a model and satisfies the demands imposed on a given function, in a manner that is both highly complete and devoid of contradiction. For example, the specification may take the form of an executable model offering analytical and/or experimental validation. For this reason, this approach is ideal for feasibility analyses of new functions. In addition to reducing the development risk for series developments, the use of this method provides the additional benefit of facilitating concurrent development and proving of software and hardware.

Regarding in-vehicle prototype integration and testing, several steps can be distinguished, such as the startup of the experimental system or test vehicle, and the actual performance of experiments (Fig. 4-5). Any steps that fail to produce artifacts suitable for evaluation by subsequent process steps are called *methodical steps*.

So-called *tools* contribute to the automated support of methods [72]. Tools can support the methodical processing of process steps, thus contributing to an increase in productivity. This

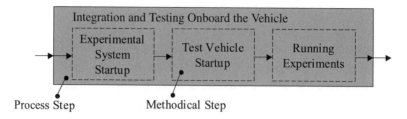

Fig. 4-5. *Methodical steps for integration and testing onboard the vehicle.*

is particularly useful in the automation of those methodical steps that require great accuracy or frequent repetition, or those necessitating verification.

4.3 Analysis of User Requirements and Specification of Logical System Architecture

As foreshadowed in Section 3.6 in Chapter 3, the replication of user requirements in the form of a concrete technical system architecture avails itself of the intermediate step of logical system architecture [12]. This differentiation has proven particularly useful in conjunction with complex systems and development projects of extended duration.

The term *user requirements analysis* describes the structuring process for both requirements and constraints during the early phase of system development, as perceived by a system user. The objective is to formulate the specification for a logical system architecture. This process defines the logical components and subsystems of a system, with their functions, requirements, and interfaces. Concurrent with this process, use cases forming the basis for the subsequent system and acceptance test are defined.

If required, this step may be cycled through repeatedly until a logical system architecture satisfying all user requirements has been assembled, and until the system and acceptance tests produce positive results (Fig. 4-6).

The logical system architecture describes an abstract solution, but it avoids specifying a concrete technical system architecture. In other words, the kind of performance the system will deliver is decided, but the specific manner of its implementation is not. The resulting creation may be described as an abstract logical model of the system and its functions. This model comprises the link between the user requirements and the design of the technical system architecture [12] that is the object of the succeeding step. The definition of the logical system architecture comprises a creative arranging and drafting process that is based on the accepted user requirements. In contrast to the user requirements, the requirements in the logical system architecture are expressed in the indigenous language of the various engineering disciplines contributing to the development process. Graphical notations, such as block diagrams and state machines, are suited to a model-based visualization.

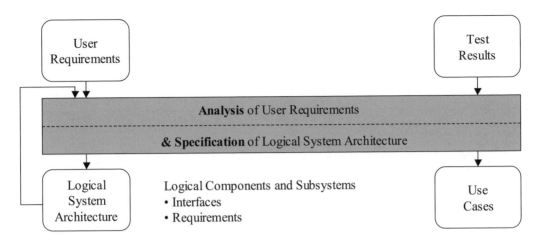

Fig. 4-6. *Analysis of user requirements and specification of logical system architecture.*

Logical system requirements may be formulated based on two different perspectives:

- Requirements that describe the properties the system is to possess
- Requirements that describe the properties the system may not possess

Another criterion is the differentiation between *functional* and *nonfunctional system requirements*.

The functional system requirements describe the *standard* and *nonstandard system functions*. The *standard system functions* manifest themselves in the course of normal system operations, whereas the *nonstandard system functions* define the system behavior that occurs as a consequence of faults, malfunctions, and failures.

The term *nonfunctional requirements* describes all additional demands imposed on the system; these also are called *constraints*. They form a category that includes, for example, variant and scalability requirements, as well as legal constraints imposed by legislation, such as reliability and safety requirements. The same category also embraces a multitude of requirements formulated by production and service. There are other nonfunctional requirements as diverse as those specifying operation in rough conditions, the voltage available in the onboard electrical network, limitation of installation space, and cost barriers. In electronic systems, these may have a direct influence on only the hardware, but their indirect influence on the software should not be overlooked. One example of a hardware requirement that also affects the software is the maximum allowable resources requirement, that is, memory and runtime requirements. In the development of automobiles, this category of logical system and software requirements particularly exhibits pronounced differences from its counterparts in other industries.

A widely used approach for this process step is the stepwise decomposition of system functions, with a view to determining not only the system components but also their interfaces and functions. The outcome of this process step is a logically structured, formal architectural model containing all of the functions to cover the various user requirements. The logical system architecture is also referred to as *function network*. If the logical system architecture refers to only a specific system version or variant, it is safe to assume that it covers only certain segments of the user requirements.

Example: Accepted user requirements and logical system architecture for the instrument cluster

Figure 4-7 shows some of the user requirements to be fulfilled by an instrument cluster in a vehicle. This fictitious instrument cluster is used as a basis for the discussion of the individual steps of the core process throughout this chapter.

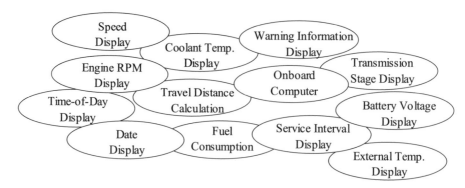

Fig. 4-7. Examples of user requirements for the instrument cluster.

Figure 4-8 shows the replication of user requirements in the form of a logical system architecture. The hierarchical structure of a block diagram was based on the consideration of design standards. One prerequisite, for example, is the stipulation that the type of visualization used shall provide the option of digital displays or pointer instruments. For this reason, provisions are already made in the logical system architecture for the processing of information to be displayed by a display or pointer instrument (e.g., through a filter or attenuation function).

If no provision is made for a delineation between user requirements and logical system architecture, it becomes more difficult to determine the user's erstwhile expectations as the project advances. What is more, it becomes downright impossible to divine which user requirements were accepted and which were not.

As a consequence, a differentiation between the user requirements and the logical system architecture—the latter being a product of technical prerequisites and constraints imposed by implementation—is no longer feasible at a later point in time.

The objective of this development step is to arrive at the definition for a logical system architecture that is at once unambiguous, noncontradictory, and as complete as possible. The effect

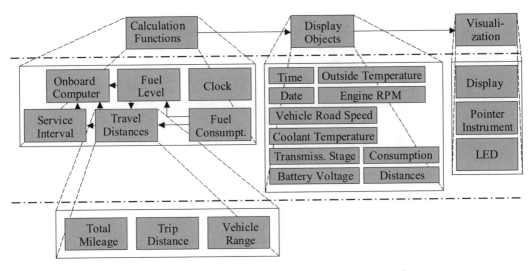

Fig. 4-8. *Logical system architecture of an instrument cluster.*

of this process step is the informal transition—although in many cases based on industry jargon and colloquialisms, incomplete, and unstructured—from the described user requirements to the first functional and structured models.

In this first crucial step, several structuring axioms, such as manageability, separability, and comprehensibility, provide essential guidance. The logical models created in this manner define both functions and function interfaces.

4.4 Analysis of Logical System Architecture and Specification of Technical System Architecture

On the basis of the logical system architecture, the specification of the technical system architecture establishes concrete implementation decisions.

After the logical system requirements have been assigned to technical components and subsystems, some basic analyses then can be performed. These may center around open-loop and closed-loop control tasks, or take the form of distributed and networked systems analyses, or reliability and safety analyses (Fig. 4-9). The main objective is the evaluation of various technical implementation alternatives, all of which are based on a standardized logical system architecture. Needless to say, any changes made to the implementation decisions would make it necessary to repeat this step.

The technical components and subsystems are defined for all system levels in a step-by-step progression. For example, with the implementation decisions completed at the upper system levels, an assignment to the hardware and software requirements can be defined for the electronics (Fig. 4-10).

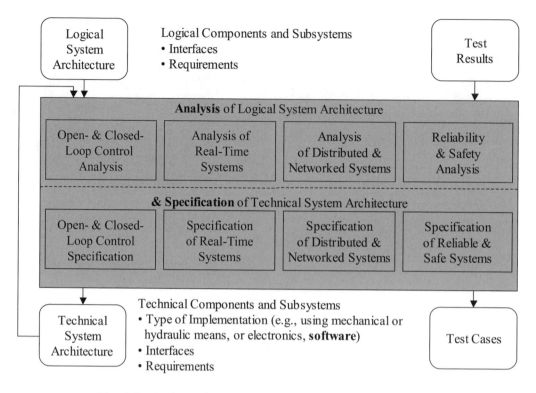

Fig. 4-9. *Analysis of logical system architecture and specification of technical system architecture.*

The technical system architecture must consider all constraints of a technical and economic nature, as well as those concerned with organizational structure and manufacturing technology.

The following are some typical constraints:

- Standards and design patterns
- Interdependencies among various systems and components
- Results of feasibility studies
- Production and service requirements
- Modifiability and testability requirements
- Expenditure and risk estimates

For all of these reasons, the expertise of the participating engineering disciplines is a precondition for the specification of the technical system architecture. More often than not, this process also entails the resolution of goal-specific conflicts.

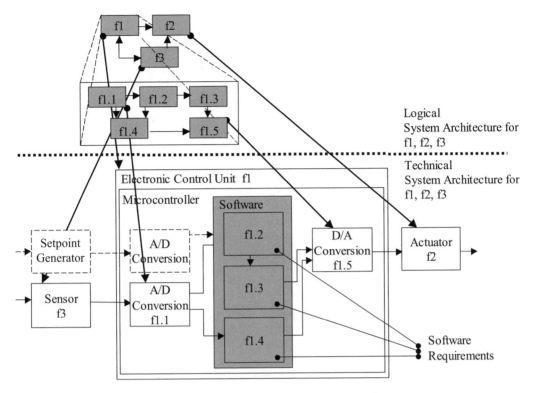

Fig. 4-10. Specification of technical system architecture.

Example: Constraints and conflicts of objectives in the specification of the technical system architecture

- **Reuse, or building-block use, of technical components in various vehicle series**

  The multiple use of engines and transmissions in different vehicle production series is dictated by cost considerations. Because this fact also influences the architecture of electronics, this often is the reason for the use of standardized engine and transmission ECUs that differ only in terms of program and/or data version.

- **Different vehicle variants within a vehicle series**

  The purchaser of an automobile can choose between an automatic or manual transmission. In many cases, this option alone causes a separation between engine and transmission ECU.

- **Optional extras versus standard equipment**

  Because the rain sensor, parking pilot, or electric seat adjustment are offered as optional extras, they require implementation by means of standalone ECUs. By contrast, several functions belonging to the standard equipment of the vehicle can be implemented in a single ECU.

- **Country-specific equipment variants**

  Differences in the standard equipment (e.g., between models for warm countries and those destined for cold countries, or between European and North American versions) influence the technical system architecture.

- **Component-oriented reuse**

  Often, the goal is to facilitate the use of components across the boundaries of brand and manufacturer. If this is the case, the component-oriented reuse takes precedence over any functional dissection. Figure 4-11 depicts the mandatory reuse of ECU 1. It covers the functions f1, f2, and f3. However, function f4 can be freely assigned to another ECU—in this example, ECU 3.

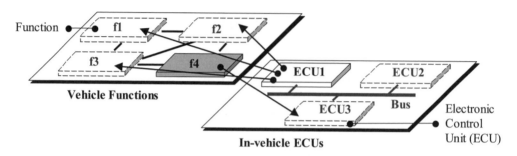

Fig. 4-11. *Component-oriented reuse versus functional decomposition.*

Example: Designing the technical system architecture for the instrument cluster

If the design procedure is started at the topmost hierarchical level, then the instrument cluster first must be defined as a component within the network of ECUs onboard the vehicle.

The engine RPM and coolant temperature are provided by the engine ECU via the CAN bus. The road speed of the vehicle is received from the ABS system, again via the CAN bus. Information addressing the driver shall be displayed partly in the instrument cluster and partly in a separate, centralized operating and display system, the so-called man/machine interface (MMI). In addition, there shall be an audible indication of warnings and fault messages to be signaled via the audio system of the vehicle. Video and audio signals are transferred via the MOST system. In consequence, the instrument cluster is designed to be a CAN bus station as well as a node on the MOST ring topology (Fig. 4-12).

Because of their sensory functions, the fuel level sensors are assigned to the instrument cluster. The same is true of the actuators (i.e., the pointer instruments and displays). All of the preceding results in the definition of the hardware architecture, as shown in Fig. 4-13.

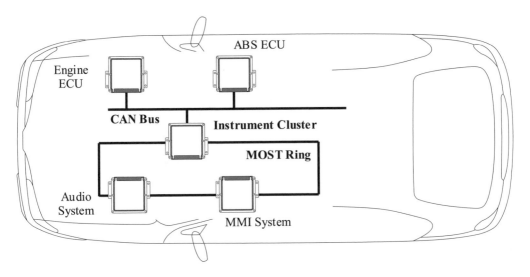

Fig. 4-12. *Technical system architecture for the ECU network of the vehicle.*

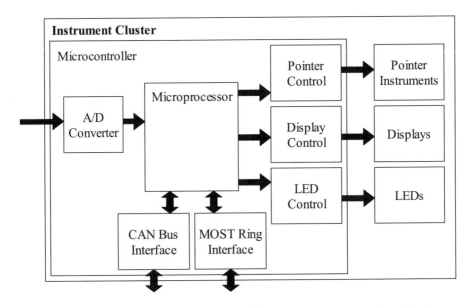

Fig. 4-13. *Technical system architecture defining the instrument cluster hardware.*

4.4.1 Analysis and Specification of Open-Loop/Closed-Loop Control Systems

The logical system architecture depicted in Fig. 4-14 forms the basis of any and all methods dedicated to the analysis of open-loop and closed-loop control systems.

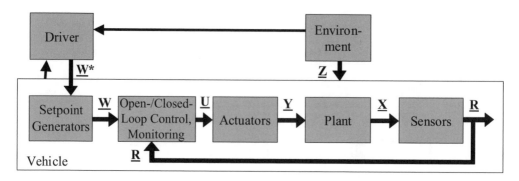

Fig. 4-14. Logical system architecture in open-loop/closed-loop control systems.

When specifying the technical system architecture for open-loop and closed-loop control systems, the specific implementation of setpoint generators, sensors, actuators, and the network of ECUs must be defined. This requires the replication of the logical system architecture in the form of a concrete technical system architecture, as shown in Fig. 4-15.

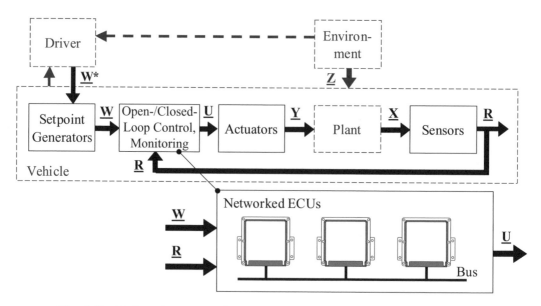

Fig. 4-15. Technical system architecture in open-loop/closed-loop control systems.

4.4.2 Analysis and Specification of Real-Time Systems

The process of analyzing and specifying control systems also includes the task of defining the sampling rates for the various control functions.

The sampling rate forms the basis for the definition of real-time requirements for the software functions to be executed by a microcontroller onboard the respective ECU. In cases where the implementation includes a distributed and networked system, the sampling rates also provide the real-time requirements for the data transmission among ECUs by means of the communication system.

Appropriate methods analyzing the schedulability in the presence of existing real-time requirements are shown in Section 5.2.2 of Chapter 5, using the real-time operating system in a microcontroller as a case in point. The results of this analysis become the basis for the assessment of technical implementation alternatives and for possible corrective modifications made to the configuration of the real-time operating system. In principle, the approach thus demonstrated also may be expanded to include the analysis and specification of the real-time characteristics of the communication system.

4.4.3 Analysis and Specification of Distributed and Networked Systems

The assignment of logical software functions to a network of microcontrollers comprises a development step requiring the consideration of multiple requirements, such as real-time, safety, and reliability requirements (Fig. 4-16). Additional factors to be taken into account when distributing software functions to the various microcontrollers exist in the form of certain prerequisites, such as limitations of installation space or the required computing power or communications capacity. Therefore, the assessment of various implementation alternatives plays an important role during the analytical phase.

After the software functions have been assigned to the microcontrollers, the next step consists of assigning the signals to messages. As mentioned, at the logical level of the system architecture, the developer's interest focuses on the signals to be exchanged among the software functions. Now, at the level of technical system architecture, the messages to be exchanged among the microcontrollers must be formed (Fig. 4-17).

4.4.4 Analysis and Specification of Reliable and Safe Systems

For many vehicle functions, the verification of the required reliability and safety is a mandatory requirement. For this reason, the reliability and safety analysis must be conducted at an early stage of the development process. Figure 4-18 shows a diagram of a typical approach to the reliability and safety analysis [70].

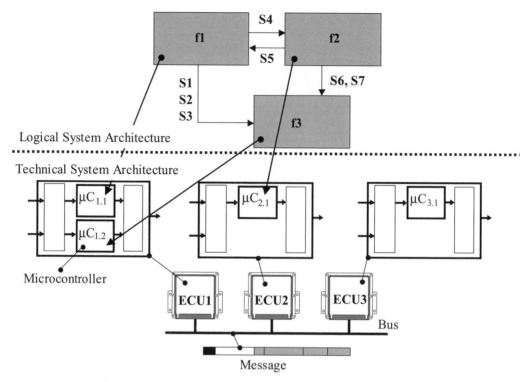

Fig. 4-16. *Assignment of software functions to microcontrollers.*

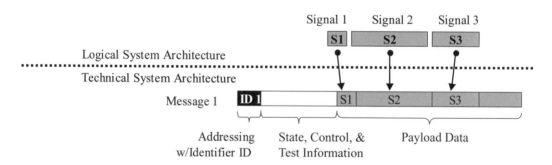

Fig. 4-17. *Assignment of signals to messages.*

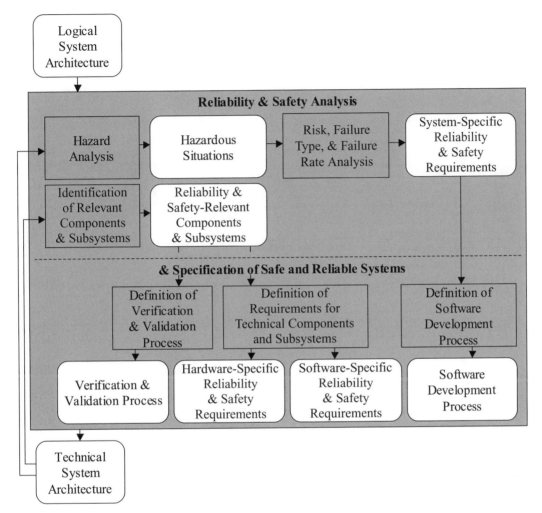

Fig. 4-18. *Reliability and safety analysis. (Ref. [70])*

4.5 Analysis of Software Requirements and Specification of Software Architecture

With the technical system architecture fully defined, the next step tackles the implementation of components and subsystems. On the basis of the software requirements (Fig. 4-10), the software design carries out an analysis of the same and establishes the specification for the software architecture (Fig. 4-19). For example, this step encompasses the specification of the software system boundaries, the software components and their interfaces, and the definition of software layers and operating states. Again, this procedure is carried out across all software system levels in a step-by-step progression.

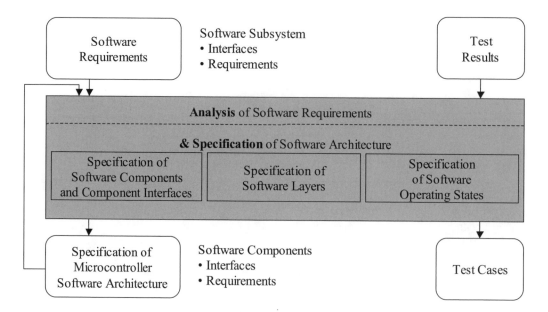

Fig. 4-19. *Analysis of software requirements and specification of software architecture.*

4.5.1 *Specification of Software Components and Associated Interfaces*

As foreshadowed in Section 2.3.3 in Chapter 2, programming must differentiate between two types of information, both of which require transmission by means of interfaces, and both of which influence program execution. These information fragments are termed as follows:

* *Data information*
* *Control information*

Accordingly, the software interfaces are differentiated as follows:

* *Data interfaces*
* *Control interfaces*

The flow of related pieces of data and control information occurring as a consequence of processing activities within a software system is termed *data flow* and *control flow*, respectively.

An example of control information would be an interrupt to a microprocessor that is triggered by a CAN bus module upon receipt of a CAN message. However, the contents of the CAN message, such as the value of a transmitted signal, may be qualified as data information.

This differentiation applies to both the input and output interfaces of a microcontroller and to the interfaces of the internal components of a software system.

An additional differentiation between *onboard* and *offboard* interfaces may be made in the context of designing the software architecture for microcontrollers used in ECUs (see Fig. 1-3 in Chapter 1).

4.5.1.1 Specification of Onboard Interfaces

As a first step, the boundaries of the software system must be accurately defined. This task requires the participation of all project participants. The objective is to decide which items are part of the software system, which items belong to the periphery or environment, and which items belong to the context of the software system. Only then will it be possible to define the input and output interfaces. The same approach may be used to define the onboard interfaces of the ECU, that is, the interfaces to the setpoint generators, sensors, and actuators, as well as the interfaces for onboard communications with other electronic systems onboard the vehicle.

Example: Context and interface model for instrument cluster software

Figure 4-20 presents the context and interface model for the onboard interfaces of the software driving the instrument cluster.

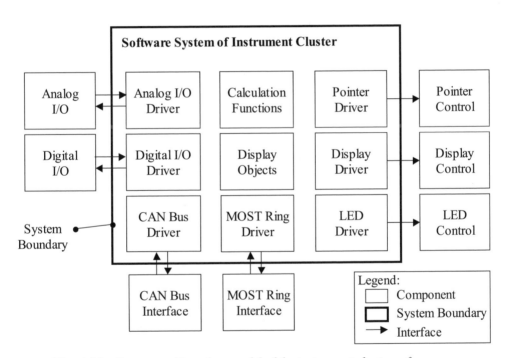

Fig. 4-20. *Context and interface model of the instrument cluster software.*

4.5.1.2 Specification of Offboard Interfaces

Another group of interfaces that may be subject to accurate definition is the group used for offboard communications. Accordingly, the software architecture for an ECU destined for installation in series-produced vehicles—the so-called *production ECU*—must support, in addition to the full complement of functions for onboard operation, all ECU interfaces required for the purpose of offboard communications in the development and production phases, or in service applications in repair facilities.

It stands to reason that not all development interfaces also are required for production and/or service. As a consequence, development avails itself of the use of several ECUs that are often referred to as *development ECUs*, or *prototype, sample,* or *calibration ECUs*. In practical terms, the named ECUs differ from the production ECU mainly with regard to the offboard interface that was modified to accommodate the respective development application, and whose deployment may introduce the need for adaptive hardware and software modifications.

The communications between a tool and a microcontroller onboard an ECU are then handled by a number of different interfaces. Functions such as measuring, calibration, diagnostics, and Flash programming are covered by standard ASAM-MCD procedures [17]. For a detailed discussion of these functions, reference is made to the relevant specialized literature (i.e., ASAM specifications). When designing the software architecture, the software components required for offboard communications also must be considered. Figure 4-21 provides an overview of frequently used tools that provide interfaces to the ECU.

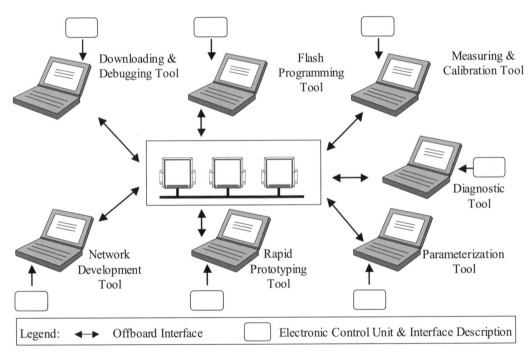

Fig. 4-21. *Overview of typical offboard interfaces of an ECU.*

Each of the listed tools requires a description of the offboard interface. This information is supplied primarily in the form of a so-called *description file*. On one hand, this file must describe the hardware and software aspects of the offboard interface; on the other hand, it must furnish information enabling tool access to the ECU data, such as the memory addresses of signals and parameter values.

4.5.2 Specification of Software Layers

A frequently used structural organization for the interrelations among software components consists of the assignment of software components to different layers. The result is a layer model. Software layers facilitate easy mutual access of the software components within a given layer. However, the rules governing access across different layers are somewhat more strict.

The layers are arranged in accordance with their abstraction level. There is no hindrance to access from layers with a higher abstraction level to those with a lower level. By contrast, access from lower layers to those with higher abstraction levels normally is severely restricted, if not entirely prohibited. Software structures permit access from a higher layer to all layers with lower abstraction levels; this is called a *strict-order layer model*. However, if the access is restricted to the next lower layer in each case, this is termed a *linear-order layer model* [72].

One example of a linear-order layer model is the seven-layer OSI Reference Model according to OSI/ISO (see Fig. 2-50 in Chapter 2), which also serves as the guiding structure for the OSEK-COM communications model. A layered architecture of this kind also is introduced frequently for other I/O interfaces in the platform software and within the application software. The introduction of abstraction levels can contribute greatly to the ease with which software components may be created, maintained, and reused.

Example: Software architecture of the instrument cluster

Taking into account applicable standards and design patterns, the design for the software architecture serving the instrument cluster is shown in Fig. 4-22.

Throughout the following sections, this hybrid layer and context model becomes the example on which the discussion of the software architecture is based.

4.5.3 Specification of Operating States

In both production and service, the parameterization of software variants as well as software updates are carried out mostly in a special operating state of the software. Due to safety considerations, the control and monitoring functions may be severely restricted or entirely prohibited for the duration of this state.

Thus, the software architecture for the microcontrollers onboard the ECU must be designed to support a variety of operating states. In addition to the standard operation, during which the control and monitoring functions—the so-called *driving program*—are executed, there often is a necessity for several other operating states in which the execution of the driving program is strictly prohibited. This is required, for example, for actuator diagnostics (see Fig. 2-64 in Chapter 2); it also is a requirement for software parameterization and updates, as mentioned.

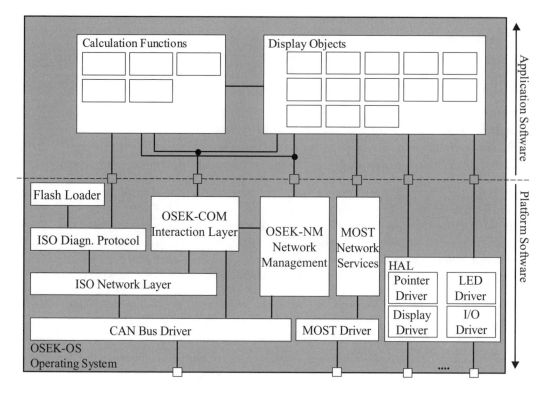

Fig. 4-22. *Software architecture of the instrument cluster.*

Even the "limp-home" operating state (see Section 2.6.4.4 in Chapter 2), which would facilitate a system operation with limited capabilities following the failure of safety-relevant components, may be perceived as a separate operating state.

In addition to defining the operating states, definitions also must be found for the permissible transitions between theses states, with the preconditions for such transitions. Therefore, so-called state machines are ideally equipped to support the specification of operating states and transitions.

Example: Operating states of the software driving the instrument cluster

For the instrument cluster, the following software operating states shown in Fig. 4-23 are required:

- The full display functionality is provided in the operating state labeled *Terminal 15* or *Ignition ON*.

- In the operating state labeled *Software Update*, only Flash programming for production and service purposes via the offboard diagnostic interface is supported.

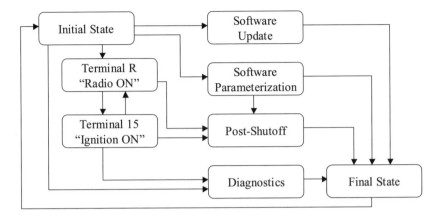

Fig. 4-23. *Operating states and transitions for the instrument cluster.*

- The operating state labeled *Software Parameterization* is designated for the setting of software parameters for production and service purposes via the offboard diagnostic interface. Examples would be switching the distance and speed displays from kilometers to miles, or the switchover between different language variants.

- The actual diagnostic function, such as the functions for sensor and actor diagnostics (see Fig. 2-64 in Chapter 2), with the downloading or flushing of fault memory contents, is available only in the *Diagnostics* operating state.

- In the operating state labeled *Terminal R*, turning the ignition key to the *Radio ON* setting on the ignition lock causes a number of monitoring functions to be performed. The transition to the *Terminal 15* operating state occurs only after all of these functions have run their course.

- Subsequent to shutting off the engine, the system assumes the *Post-Shutoff* operating state. This is the point, for example, at which the total mileage of the vehicle is stored in a manner that is both permanent and tamper-proof. In addition, time-intensive monitoring functions of the instrument cluster are carried at this juncture.

4.6 Specification of Software Components

In the specification of the software architecture, all of the software components, with their requirements and interfaces, were defined. The discussion now turns its spotlight on the specification of software components. Here, a differentiation may be made among a specification of the data model, the behavioral model, and the real-time model of a software component (Fig. 4-24).

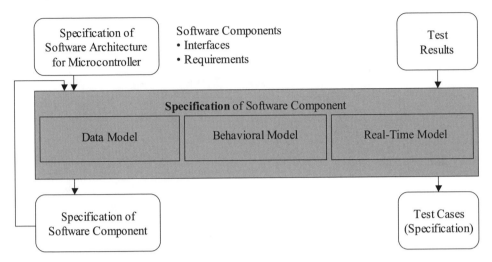

Fig. 4-24. *Specification of a software component.*

4.6.1 Specification of Data Model

Part of the specification of a software component is concerned with the definition of the data to be processed by that software component, that is, the data model specification. This is accomplished by first defining an abstract form of data—in effect, an abstraction of the real-world implementation of that data—so that the intended mode of processing the data can be abstracted in the form of a physical context.

Many applications in the vehicle require a variety of data structures. The following structures are used frequently:

- Scalar quantities
- Vectors, or one-dimensional arrays
- Matrices, or two-dimensional arrays (Fig. 4-25)

Interrelations also may exist among data fragments. The results are assembled data structures. For example, data structures for *characteristic curves* and *characteristic maps* are widely used (Fig. 4-26). In the case of the abstract specification of a characteristic curve or map, only

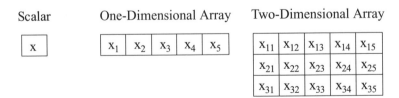

Fig. 4-25. *Simple data structures.*

Graphical Visualization:

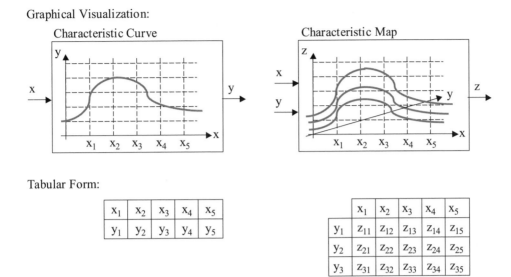

Fig. 4-26. Data structures of increased complexity.

the correlation between input and output variables is of interest; design and implementation require, for example, the specific tabular storage schematic and the method of interpolation. Various storage schematics and interpolation methods are discussed in detail in Section 5.4.1.5 of Chapter 5.

4.6.2 Specification of Behavioral Model

The discussion so far has introduced various methods for the specification of the static structure of software components. This section addresses the dynamic structure of software components, that is, the specification of their behavior or processing steps.

In this context, a differentiation is made between the specification of data flow and that of control flow.

4.6.2.1 Specification of Data Flow

Data flow diagrams provide two essential types of information. On one hand, they describe the paths of data information between software components. On the other hand, they show the processing flow of the data within software components.

There are several means of visualization and different symbols for data flow diagrams. For many vehicle functions, the control-specific modeling method on the basis of block diagrams and state machines is the most suitable. Therefore, this method also is used for the following examples.

Inputs, outputs, and data, as well as arithmetic and Boolean operations of a software component, are represented by blocks. Instances of data flow are shown as arrows.

Example: Data flow for a Boolean and an arithmetic instruction

Figure 4-27 shows the Boolean instruction

$$Y = X1 \, \& \, (X2 \parallel X3)$$

where

"&" represents a conjunction or logical AND operation, and

"∥" represents a disjunction or logical OR operation,

and the arithmetic instruction

$$c = a + b$$

as the data flow in a block diagram of the ASCET tool [73].

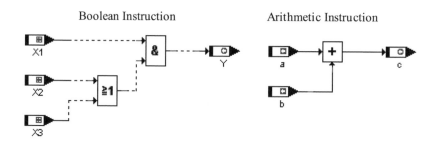

Fig. 4-27. *Data flow representing Boolean and arithmetic instructions in ASCET. (Ref. [73])*

Arithmetic data flows are drawn as arrows with solid lines; Boolean data flows are drawn as arrows with broken lines.

Although data flow diagrams are easily drawn and readily understood, they fail to provide a complete definition of the behavior of a software component.

For example, Fig. 4-27 does not indicate whether the Boolean or the arithmetic instruction is the first to be executed. It should be stated that, in this simple example, the result produced by the software component does not change by virtue of a change in the order of execution. However, if the results Y and c were to depend on one another in such a way that the value of c would enter into the calculation of Y, then a change on the order of execution also would change the behavior of the software component. The order of execution is determined by the control flow of a software component.

4.6.2.2 Specification of Control Flow

The purpose of control flow is to control the execution of instructions. The processing of instructions in a software component can be manipulated through the application of the control structures shown in the following list:

*   *Sequence*. Defines the order of processing.
*   *Branching*. Defines branches in the program sequence.
*   *Repetition* or *iteration*. Specifies processing loops.
*   *Call*. Summons the support of services residing in other software components.

Control flow structures of this kind are found in any of the high-level programming languages and lend themselves to graphical visualization. Well-known notations for the representation of control flow are *structograms* according to Nassi-Shneiderman—also termed *Nassi-Shneiderman diagrams* (Fig. 4-28) [72].

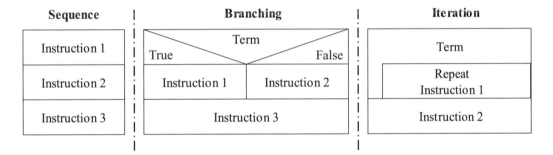

Fig. 4-28. *A Nassi-Shneiderman diagram: graphical representation of control flow constructs. (Ref. [72])*

However, note that for many software functions, the isolated depiction of the control flow is as insufficient as a dedicated diagram of the data flow. A visualization combining the benefits of both methods is needed.

Example: Control flow for a Boolean and an arithmetic instruction

Figure 4-29 shows that the sequencing information missing in the previous example has been entered in the block diagram. This control flow construct determines that the arithmetic instruction

$$c = a + b$$

is assigned the sequencing information /1/ of Process 1, and that it is executed prior to the Boolean instruction

$$Y = X1 \& (X2 \| X3)$$

based on the sequencing information /2/ of Process 1.

4.6.3 Specification of Real-Time Model

To complete the specification of a software component, its real-time model must be defined in addition to the data and behavioral models discussed in the preceding sections. This means that the instructions driving a software component must be assigned to specific processes. The processes, in turn, must be assigned to tasks. The tasks are subject to defined real-time requirements.

Example: Defining real-time requirements

In the introductory example in Fig. 4-29, both instructions are already assigned to Process 1. To complete the specification of real-time behavior, Process 1 still must be assigned to a task. This assignment is shown in Fig. 4-30. Process 1 is assigned to Task A, as are Processes 2 and 3.

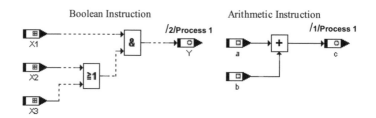

Fig. 4-29. *Control flow determining the order of execution in ASCET. (Ref. [73])*

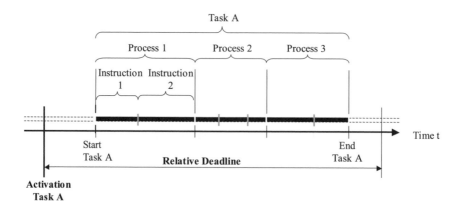

Fig. 4-30. *Assignment of instructions to processes and tasks.*

Reactive control and monitoring functions can be designed based on different execution models. The most common execution models are the state-dependent and state-independent reactive execution models.

4.6.3.1 State-Dependent Reactive Execution Model

Reactive software functions can be based on a general execution model, such as that presented in Fig. 4-31.

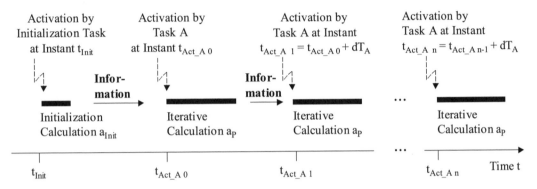

Fig. 4-31. *State-dependent reactive execution model for software functions.*

The software function differentiates between an initialization calculation that is carried out once after the system startup, and a so-called reactive calculation that is repeated, or iterated. The initialization portion, here Process a_{Init}, is activated by the initialization task at instant t_{Init}. The repeated portion, here Process a_P, is activated by a cyclical Task A in time interval dT_A. This interval may be fixed or variable. The first execution of Process a_P uses state information supplied by initialization Process a_{Init}. All subsequent executions utilize the state information of the respective previous execution of Process a_P. This information may consist of the results of the preceding calculation, or it may supply the length of time interval dT_A relative to the previous execution. Software functions exhibiting these characteristics also are termed *state-dependent reactive systems* [74].

As the discussion has shown, the software function must be divided into, at minimum, the two processes labeled Process a_{Init} and Process a_P. It also is quite common for software processes to be divided into more than two processes, which then are activated by different tasks. For example, the repeated iterative calculations of a given function may be divided for distribution to several processes and then activated by tasks with different real-time requirements in a quasi-parallel fashion.

4.6.3.2 State-Independent Reactive Execution Model

In some situations, it is both permissible and beneficial to assume that, after initialization has occurred, a process shall be executed only if a certain event occurs, without any relevance of prior history. If this is the case, a different execution model, such as the one depicted in Fig. 4-32, can be used. In this example, the division of the software function into two processes labeled Process b_{Init} and Process b_E again is required. However, Process b_E is activated only by the occurrence of Event E of Task B. This Event E may consist of the actuation of a switch—controlling the software function—by the vehicle operator.

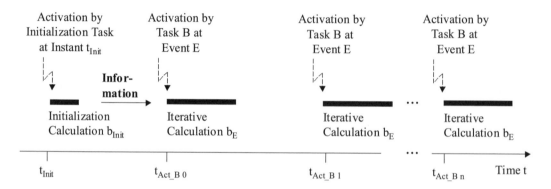

Fig. 4-32. *State-independent reactive execution model for software functions.*

Also, the Process b_E can be executed repeatedly. However, in contrast to the preceding example, the execution of this Process b_E does not use any kind of state information of the previous execution of Process b_E. Software functions exhibiting these characteristics also are termed *state-independent reactive systems* [74].

Hybrid forms of these two execution models commonly are used.

When modeling the interaction between the processes assigned to different tasks, real-time systems require the consideration of the mechanisms of the real-time operating system discussed in Section 2.4.6 of Chapter 2. Therefore, it would not be unusual for the real-time model to exert influence on the data model.

4.7 Design and Implementation of Software Components

During the design phase, all details of the specific implementation for the data, behavior, and real-time model of a software component must be defined (Fig. 4-33). With respect to the data, an additional differentiation now must be made between variables and fixed parameter values.

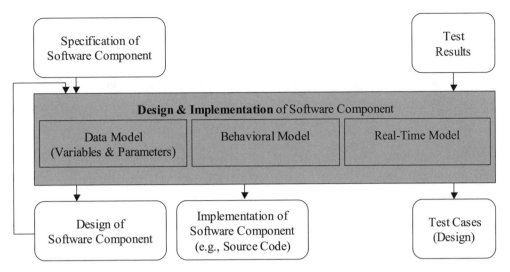

Fig. 4-33. *Design and implementation of software components.*

4.7.1 Consideration of Requested Nonfunctional Product Properties

When designing and implementing software components for production ECUs, consideration must be given, in addition to the specified software functions, to a number of further prerequisites that arise from the requested nonfunctional product properties. These include, for example, the separation of program version and data version. Another example would be cost barriers that frequently result in a limitation of available hardware resources.

4.7.1.1 Differentiation Between Program Version and Data Version

The separation of program version and data version is frequently used to facilitate the handling of software variants not only during development, but also in production and service.

Whereas other industries and application areas tend to develop program and data versions concurrently, the differentiation between program and data versions of ECUs in the automobile industry has produced benefits due to a number of reasons. Here, the data version encompasses all data that are not changed by the program, such as the parameter values of open-loop and closed-loop control functions.

In this way, a standardized program version can be adapted to a variety of applications (i.e., different vehicle variants) by applying different data versions. This produces cost and time benefits in development, such as in quality assurance, which is required only once for each program version.

Other considerations make this approach advisable:

- The actual instances—or points in time—at which the program version and data version are released may vary to a greater or lesser degree. For example, it often becomes necessary to modify the data version—in the course of running calibrations of software functions on a specific vehicle—occasionally very late on the timeline and independently of the program version.

- The creation of the program version and data version frequently occurs in vastly different development environments and is handled by different team members—at times even across corporate borders.

- The separation of the program version and data version makes good sense not only in development. It also provides tangible benefits with regard to the variant management in production and service.

4.7.1.2 Limitation of Hardware Resources

Design and implementation of software components frequently requires the consideration of optimization measures imposed by the limited availability of hardware resources. One of the root causes may be seen in the cost barriers that result in limited hardware resources in conjunction with high-volume production.

Example: Cost barriers for ECUs

By way of simplification, it could be stated that the cost of an ECU is the sum of development and manufacturing costs, divided by the total number n of units produced:

$$\text{Total cost per ECU} \approx \frac{(\text{development costs} + \text{manufacturing costs})}{n}$$

This has the effect that the final cost of an ECU is significantly influenced by the piece count-proportionate manufacturing costs (Fig. 4-34).

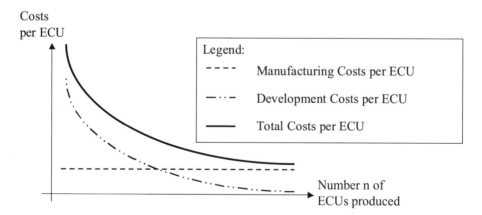

Fig. 4-34. *Cost per ECU relative to the number of units produced.*

In this context, the cost structures for hardware and software are quite different. If it is assumed that the cost for duplication of the software is close to negligible, the production costs are influenced mainly by the hardware costs, which are proportional to the number of units produced.

In many cases, high piece counts constitute the reason for the occasional insistent pressure to reduce the corresponding hardware manufacturing costs. Therefore, budget-priced microcontrollers supporting only integer arithmetic and featuring very limited computing power and memory capacity often are used. The inevitable consequence is a limitation of hardware resources.

In such cases, to handle the highest possible number of functions on a single microcontroller, software developers are called upon to spare no optimization effort with a view to putting the available hardware resources to most effective use. Depending on the prerequisites for the respective application, one of the objectives of software development is to reduce the RAM requirement, ROM requirement, or program runtime. A rule of thumb applicable to many of the microcontrollers in current use states that the RAM requirement demands much greater consideration than the ROM requirement because the area on the chip occupied by RAM is ten times that of ROM. The cost of RAM, so the rule, therefore is also ten times higher than that of ROM.

In all the relevant calculations, the corresponding rise in the development and quality assurance expenditures, as well as the increase of quality risks as a consequence of limited resources in the development phase, must not be overlooked.

Therefore, in practical application, the approach of combining the optimization of the piece count-proportionate manufacturing costs with a platform strategy for hardware and software components has proven beneficial. For example, standardized software components can be adapted to meet the requirements of a given application by means of various configuration parameters.

This discussion has touched on the many interdependencies and conflicts of objectives that exist among the various project targets, because there are quality, cost, and scheduling or deadline conflicts. Care also should be taken that an optimization measure is not overcompensated—or even negated—by the additional efforts and expenditures it creates.

Several of the numerous optimization measures deployed in practical application are discussed in the context of examples in Section 5.4.1 of Chapter 5. Also note that many optimization measures cause repercussions on the specification of the software architecture, as well as software components.

4.7.2 Design and Implementation of Data Model

When designing and implementing the data model of a software component, a differentiation must be made between variables and those parameter values that cannot be changed by the program. For each software component, design decisions must be made for all data concerning their internal representation on the processor, and regarding data storage in the memory segment of the microcontroller. Thus, variables must be deposited in a read/write memory such as RAM, whereas parameters and their settings can be stored in read-only memory, such as ROM.

Example: Function replicating the physical specification in the implementation

Figure 4-35 shows the representation of the engine temperature signal at both the level of physical specification and the level of concrete implementation.

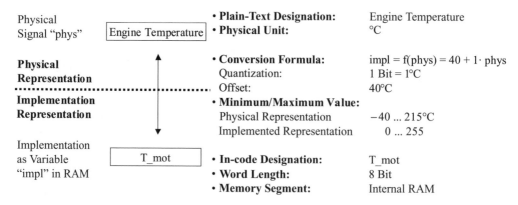

Physical Signal "phys"	Engine Temperature	• **Plain-Text Designation:**	Engine Temperature

• **Physical Unit:** °C

Physical Representation

• **Conversion Formula:** $impl = f(phys) = 40 + 1 \cdot phys$
  Quantization: 1 Bit = 1°C

Implementation Representation

  Offset: 40°C

• **Minimum/Maximum Value:**
  Physical Representation   −40 ... 215°C
  Implemented Representation   0 ... 255

Implementation as Variable "impl" in RAM   T_mot

• **In-code Designation:**   T_mot
• **Word Length:**   8 Bit
• **Memory Segment:**   Internal RAM

Fig. 4-35. *Physical specification of engine temperature transformed to implementation.*

In the case of measuring and calibration tools, for example, this transformation must be made in the direction from implementation to physical representation. The reason is that the implementation variables in measuring and calibration tools should be displayed as ECU external measurement signals in the specified physical units. To satisfy this display requirement, the measuring and calibration tools require all relevant data information. This information is stored in the description file. As the abbreviation *MCD* indicates, the ASAM-MCD 2 standard [17] defines description formats for the functional components of measuring, calibration, and diagnostics.

4.7.3 Design and Implementation of Behavioral Model

The design of the behavioral model must consider, in addition to the specification, the influence of the processor internal representation and calculation. An important consideration is the accuracy of arithmetic statements in the context of number processing. The accuracy of a result calculated by digital processors is limited by different types of errors. Differentiations are made among the following [75]:

• Errors in the input data of the calculation
• Rounding errors
• Approximation errors

Errors in the input data of a calculation are difficult to prevent if the input data consist of measuring variables with limited accuracy or resolution. This is almost always the case with sensors and microcontrollers of the type used in vehicles. Errors of this type also are termed *quantizing errors* (see Section 2.2.2 in Chapter 2).

Rounding errors occur in situations where calculations use a finite number of digit positions, which indeed is the case with the deployed microcontrollers. For example, rounding errors in fixed-point arithmetic are unavoidable (e.g., in divisions or with the necessary scaling of results due to the limited number of digit positions).

Approximation errors depend on the methods of calculation. Even with the use of methods that are free of rounding errors, many methods of calculation do not yield the problem solution actually sought. That is, instead of the solution of a problem P, they deliver only the solution to a simpler problem P*, which approximates the actual problem P. It often is possible to produce the approximating problem P* through the discretization of the original problem P. For example, differentials are approximated through difference quotients, or integrals through finite sums. Approximation errors are unavoidable in the context of fixed-point and floating-point arithmetic.

Example: Integration method according to Euler

One example is the integration method according to Euler shown in Fig. 4-36. It often is used in ECUs (e.g., for the purpose of implementing the integral-action component of the PI controller depicted in Fig. 2-2 of Chapter 2). Here, the integral of the function $f(t)$ is calculated approximately through the area $F^*(t)$ of the gray rectangles.

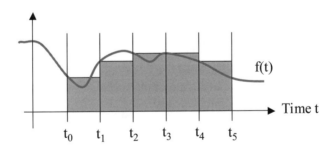

Fig. 4-36. *Integration method according to Euler.*

The calculation of the determined integrals of function $f(t)$

$$F(t_n) = \int_{t_0}^{t_n} f(t)\,dt$$

is approximated through the sum

$$F^*(t_n) = \sum_{i=0}^{n-1}(t_{i+1} - t_i) \cdot f(t_i)$$

The distance $(t_{i+1} - t_i)$ is called *step size* dT_i. Depending on whether a task has been activated with an equidistant or variable activation rate, the first approximation of step size dT_i is constant or variable. $F^*(t_{i+1})$ can be incrementally calculated through the use of the equation

$$F^*(t_{i+1}) = F^*(t_i) + dT_i \cdot f(t_i)$$

In the design and implementation of software components, the rounding errors deserve particular attention, in addition to the approximation errors and errors in the input data. Section 5.4.2 in Chapter 5 provides a detailed discussion of the in-processor numeric representation and the rounding errors that may occur in the processing of numerical values.

4.7.4 Design and Implementation of Real-Time Model

The task of designing and implementing the real-time model presupposes in-depth understanding of the hardware and software interrupt system of the microcontroller. If a real-time operating system is used, its configuration must be defined. The major configuration settings for real-time operating systems according to OSEK are described in Section 2.4 of Chapter 2.

4.8 Software Component Testing

Figure 3-28 in Chapter 3 provides an overview of several methods of software quality assurance. On the basis of the test cases defined during the specification and design phase, software components may be subjected to several static tests (Fig. 4-37).

4.9 Integration of Software Components

The assembly of software components, which may have been developed by a variety of partners, into a whole program and data version for a microcontroller is termed *integration*. This process requires that a program version and data version in a format suitable for acceptance by the microprocessor must be generated and documented. For the associated tools, which are connected later in production and service to the microcontroller of an ECU through offboard interfaces, appropriate description files must be generated, too (Fig. 4-38).

Thus, a software version for a production ECU normally encompasses the following:

• Program versions and data versions for all microcontrollers of the ECU

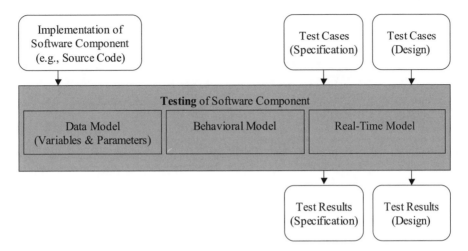

Fig. 4-37. *Software component testing.*

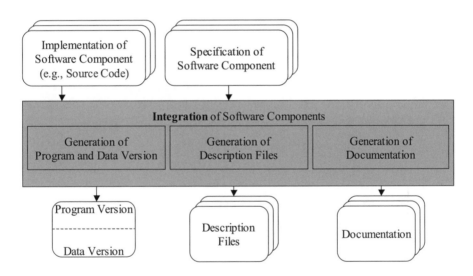

Fig. 4-38. *Integration of software components.*

- Documentation

- Description files for production and service tools (e.g., diagnostic, software parameterization, and Flash programming tools)

Development ECUs may require additional description files for the development tools, such as the following:

- Description files for measurement and calibration tools

- Description files of onboard communications for network development tools

- Description files of the so-called bypass interface, in the event that rapid prototyping tools are used. Rapid prototyping tools are discussed in detail in Section 5.3.8 of Chapter 5.

4.9.1 Generating Program Version and Data Version

Figure 4-39 shows the process steps required to generate a program version and data version.

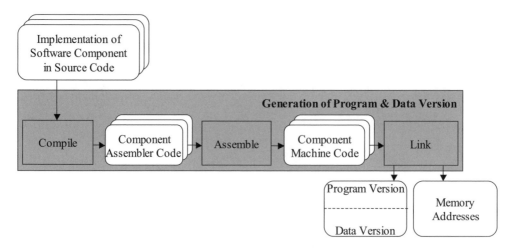

Fig. 4-39. *Generating a program version and data version.*

Any command that is executable by a microprocessor—a so-called *machine instruction*—is issued in the form of a numeric code in binary notation. This numeric code—also termed machine code—is analyzed by the control logic of the microprocessor (see Fig. 2-14 in Chapter 2), and causes, for example, the activation of the arithmetic logic unit. Thus, the executable program must be available in binary form (e.g., as a binary file in which the program is stored in machine code). However, because instructions in binary code tend to be cumbersome, confusing, and therefore error prone to a programmer, there are easily remembered abbreviations—so-called *mnemonics*—that can be used for each machine instruction. To generate the program for the microprocessor, the mnemonics are converted into machine code by a translation utility—the so-called *assembler*. Therefore, the source program is first written in an editor (e.g., on a PC) and then is translated into machine code. Even today, simpler applications that are either very hardware specific or require critical timing are still programmed, in whole or in part, in processor-specific assembler code.

Programs of higher complexity require the use of one of a dozen high-level languages, such as the C programming language [76]. Otherwise, extensive programs would no longer lend themselves to structured management, error-free writing, and acceptable maintenance effort.

Because the high-level languages are largely processor independent, they require the use of a translation utility—the so-called *compiler*—that translates the so-called *source code*, written in high-level language, into the processor-specific assembler code. This involves the replication of each high-level instruction in the form of a sequence of machine instructions. To this end, the following classes of machine instructions are needed:

- Data processing instructions: Arithmetic, logical, and conversion instructions

- Control commands: Branch and relational instructions

- Input/output commands: Instructions causing data to be read/copied and output, respectively

- Memory instructions: Memory read/write instructions

The high-level language source code can be implemented in the form of modules or components, in a manner that is largely independent of the microprocessor. A processor-specific compiler translates the source code components into assembler code components suited to the respective microprocessor.

To ensure the interaction of different program components existing in machine code, these components must be integrated—or "tied together"—to form a program version and data version. This is a job for the *linker*. It determines the symbolic memory addresses of all components and replaces them with real access addresses in machine code components. The linker also writes the address information into a separate file.

In many cases, the compiler, assembler, and linker are bundled, together with other tools, into a compiler tool set. For a detailed discussion of related topics, reference is made to the relevant specialized literature [77, 78].

4.9.2 Generating Description Files

The maintenance of data consistency between the program version and data version, and the description files for the offboard tools, comprises a requirement that is as basic as it is crucial. For this reason, the assembly of the software-specific part of the description files comprises a part of the software integration phase.

Figure 4-40 depicts a typical approach to generating a description file for measuring, calibration, and diagnostic tools according to the ASAM-MCD 2 standard.

Because the specification of a software component is used not only as the basis for design and implementation but also for the creation of a description file, the consistency among the program version, data version, and description file is virtually guaranteed.

As an alternative, the specification data required for the description file could be stored during implementation, that is, in the form of comments in the source code. This second path also is included in Fig. 4-40.

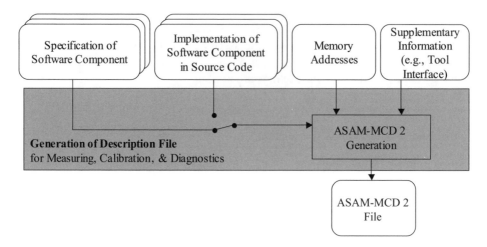

Fig. 4-40. *Generating description files for measuring, calibration, and diagnostic tools.*

The description file generation to the ASAM-MCD 2 standard utilizes the specification and design information for all data; thus, it requires no additional input. Both methods extract the necessary address information from the file that was generated by the linker.

4.9.3 Generating Documentation

The documentation of the software-implemented vehicle functions is required for a number of reasons:

- The documentation represents an artifact that is needed for all support processes during the actual software development. Other factors, such as the distinctive and often cross-corporate work sharing, the extensive product life cycles, and concurrent software maintenance phase, emphasize the need for detailed documentation.

- All of the subsequent development steps—such as system integration, testing, and calibration—are in need of documentation.

- One type of documentation is required for vehicle production and for distribution across a global network of service facilities.

- Another complement documentation is required for presentation to legislative authorities, that is, as a component of the application for the type approval certificate of a vehicle as a prerequisite for road registration.

To no one's surprise, the different user groups' expectations (Fig. 4-41) of the documentation are widely divergent. Simply for reasons of bulk and range of coverage alone, and because of the required differentiations to accommodate different levels of understanding of technical basics

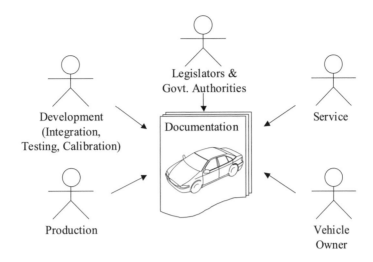

Fig. 4-41. *User groups of documentation describing software functions.*

and details, let alone different language versions and change cycles, calling for a standardized documentation that would be of equal usefulness to all of these user groups would be decidedly unrealistic.

However, one aspect is standardized. It is the function-oriented view of the vehicle, and it allows for a documentation structure that orients itself in terms of functionalities. Thus, the model-based specification can be used as a basis for the documentation of software functions.

The software documentation represents merely one part of the documentation of functions, which, given a suitable intermediate format, can be incorporated in the assembly of the specially tailored documentation for the different user groups.

As a result of efforts to standardize a suitable intermediate format within the framework of the MSR-MEDOC project [79], the MSR-Report format was introduced. It can be used to structure a documentation process, such as that outlined in Fig. 4-42, with the integration of supporting input from the development tools.

4.10 Software Integration Testing

The process of linking software components to form a software version usually is accompanied by a series of tests and verifications (Fig. 4-43). These may be conducted manually prior to the translation step or may also consist of automated routines run by suitable tools, such as the compiler tool set. Also included are checks confirming compliance with interface specifications or naming conventions for variables, as well as the use of standardized memory mapping. Because

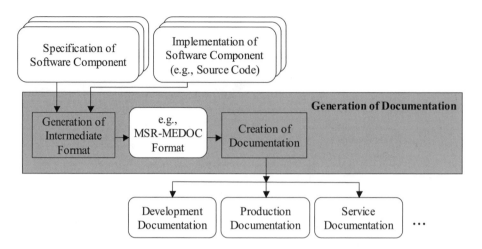

Fig. 4-42. *Generating documentation using an intermediate format.*

Fig. 4-43. *Software integration testing.*

the program is not actually executed during testing, all of the test procedures comprise static comparisons with implementation guidelines.

4.11 Integration of System Components

Subsequent to the interworked and parallel development of the system components, they undergo several component tests. The components are then integrated into the intended system, which, in turn, is subjected to integration tests, system tests, and acceptance tests. These steps are performed in stages across all system levels of the vehicle, that is, from individual components to subsystems, and from there to the overall vehicle system (see Fig. 3-4 in Chapter 3). Thus, the notions of integrating and testing are virtually inseparable.

With regard to software, this means that it first must be integrated with the hardware (e.g., the microcontroller, ECU, or experimental system).

The next step, ensuring that the interaction of the overall system with the plant can be tested, will be the integration of the various ECUs or experimental systems, as well as setpoint generators, sensors, and actuators. All other integration levels belong to the group of so-called *primary integration levels*, such as the vehicle subsystem level or the actual vehicle level (Fig. 4-44).

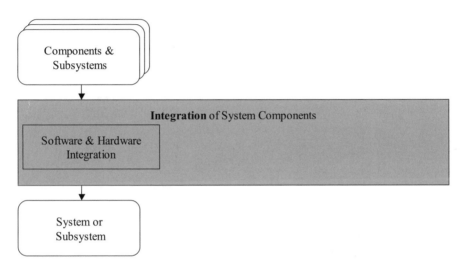

Fig. 4-44. *Integration of system components.*

4.11.1 Integration of Software and Hardware

The execution of the program, and thus the application of dynamic testing methods, becomes possible only after the integration of software and hardware has been completed. To facilitate the performance of these dynamic tests at an early stage, a variety of methods are used. One example would be rapid prototyping in conjunction with experimental systems. Figure 4-45 provides an overview of the methods applied to software and hardware integration.

4.11.1.1 Download

The process of downloading the program code to the microcontroller and its subsequent startup is supported by downloading and debugging tools. As a part of this procedure, a small loading and monitoring program in the firmware—the *boot loader*—program is executed on the micro-processor. It deposits the binary file, which is commonly transferred through a serial download

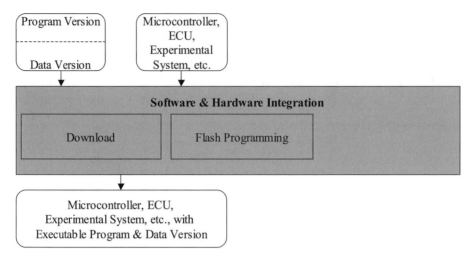

Fig. 4-45. *Software and hardware integration.*

interface, in the microcontroller RAM or Flash memory. In response to a request issued by the downloading tool, the boot loader also is capable of providing it with return data.

4.11.1.2 Flash Programming

The Flash memory is programmed by means of data from a connected Flash programming tool and internal programming routines in the microcontroller. This technology makes it possible, for example, to update the software in an ECU while installed in the vehicle. In this procedure, great care must be taken to prevent the inadvertent deletion of the memory area containing the actual Flash programming routines. A detailed discussion of Flash programming of ECUs appears in Section 5.6 of Chapter 5 and Section 6.3 of Chapter 6.

4.11.2 *Integration of ECUs, Setpoint Generators, Sensors, and Actuators*

One of the consequences of the interworked and cross-corporate development of components—such as ECUs, setpoint generators, sensors, and actuators—consists of a number of special requirements calling for suitable integration and testing tools for the electronic systems onboard the vehicle:

- In many cases, one of the test routines depicted in Fig. 4-1 also represents the vehicle manufacturer's approval test for the component or subsystem provided by the supplier.

- In the course of development, those prototype vehicles that do exist are available only in very limited numbers. In many cases, the companies supplying the components do not have the benefit of access to a complete or current environment for the component to be supplied. To add even more of a challenge, this environment changes with each component (Fig. 4-46).

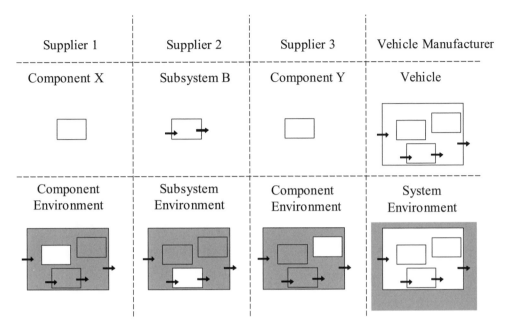

Fig. 4-46. *Differences in component, subsystem, and system environments.*

The cited limitations with respect to the testing environment may tend to reduce the number of feasible testing procedures on the part of the supplier.

• The component integration serves as a synchronization point for all contributory component developments. The integration, system, and acceptance test cannot be performed until and unless all components are available. Because of the resulting ripple effect, the late completion and shipment of a single component will delay the integration of the entire system and thereby the performance of all subsequent testing procedures (Fig. 4-47).

4.12 System Integration Test

In accommodating the special prerequisites discussed in the preceding section, integration and testing tools for vehicle systems reduce both the existing interdependencies and the development risk. Tests can be conducted with the automated support of appropriate tools. Figure 4-48 shows the artifacts forming the basis of integration testing.

Available components, subsystems, and components of the system environment are integrated as physical components existing in the real world. Those components, subsystems, and components of the system environment that are nonexistent are replicated by means of modeling and simulation (i.e., as *virtual components*).

The testing environment for a physical component is connected to a virtual integration platform, which simulates the components appearing with grey shading in Fig. 4-49. In this context, any

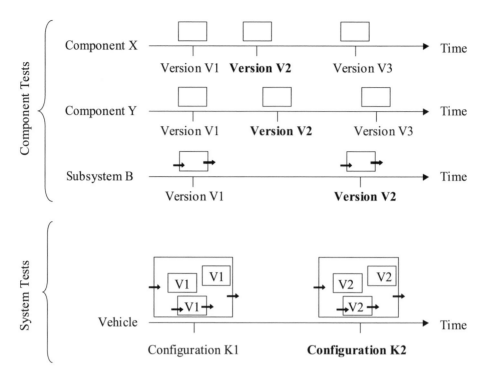

Fig. 4-47. *Interdependencies of the component test and the system test.*

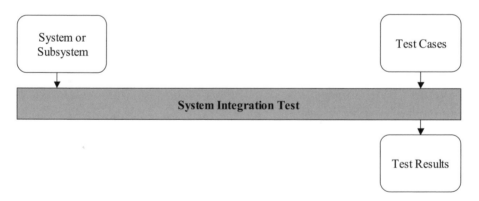

Fig. 4-48. *System integration testing.*

combination is conceivable. For example, system components or those belonging to the system periphery may be of the virtual type. With their use as stand-ins, the existing requirements for testing the system as a complete entity can be met:

- The virtual testing environment is available to all development partners. One of the testing steps shown in Fig. 4-1 may be freely selected to serve as the approval test. The approval test may be performed on the supplier's or vehicle manufacturer's premises through the use of the same virtual testing environment.

- Each of the partners has access to the same full complement of virtual components. He or she may then configure testing environments to accommodate the unique requirements of his or her situation (Figs. 4-49(a) and (b)).

- Because the system test also allows for the initial replacement of nonexistent physical components with virtual stand-ins, the risk of a delay in integration as a consequence of the late completion of individual components can be lessened (Figs. 4-49(c) and (d)). A system combined of both real and virtual components also is conceivable.

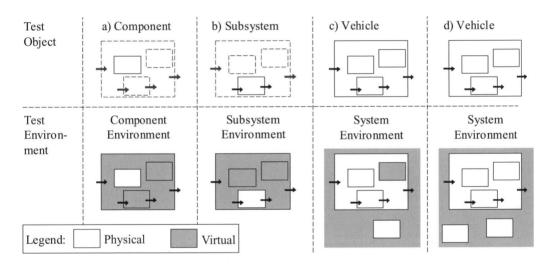

Fig. 4-49. *Test object and testing environment.*

- The initially completely virtual environment is replaced by real components in a step-by-step fashion. This gradual replacement occurs at all system levels.

Example: Virtual network environment for the instrument cluster

Figure 4-50 depicts the components of a virtual network environment for the instrument cluster. A testing environment of this type also is known as a *residual bus simulation*. The function models—introduced in former sections—can be used as a basis for the replication of nonexistent system components.

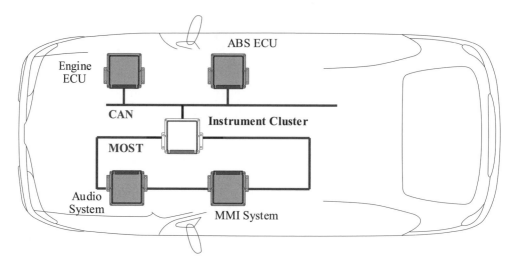

Fig. 4-50. *Virtual network environment for the instrument cluster.*

Integration and testing procedures of this kind provide additional benefits:

- Many testing procedures, which, in the absence of a testing environment, would need to be performed in the vehicle, can now be moved to the laboratory or test bench.

- Compared with driving tests, this practice—in addition to making test cases and application cases possible in the first place—definitely improves their reproducibility. Also, the added benefit of test automation should be noted.

- Extreme situations may be tested without the risk of danger to test drivers and/or prototype vehicles.

In this way, a consistent testing process that commences with virtual steps, and progresses from simulation through intermediate stages in the laboratory and on the test stand to the actual vehicle, has become a reality (Fig. 4-51).

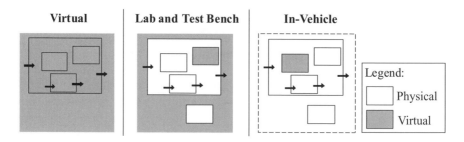

Fig. 4-51. *Consistent integration and testing process.*

All of the scenarios depicted in Fig. 4-51 replace real components with virtual ones. At the system level of the ECUs, the components ECU (software and hardware), setpoint generators, sensors, and actuators, as well as the system environment, can be discerned.

In conjunction with hardware, the term *virtual hardware* is used as follows: If the target system is replaced by a development platform, such as a PC or an experimental system, this execution platform is termed *virtual hardware platform*. In similar circumstances, this definition also applies to sensors and actuators.

In the presence of real-world software and hardware, it will be possible to execute the program. However, many test procedures will be possible only after integration with sensors, actuators, and the system environment. Integration and testing tools are discussed in Section 5.5 of Chapter 5.

After the successful conclusion of these test procedures, the program version and data version can be released for subsequent steps. However, the data version may still be modified in the course of calibration procedures during the late phases of development, whereas the program version remains unchanged and is released for the following process steps.

4.13 Calibration

In many cases, the fine-tuning of software functions implemented by means of a single ECU or an entire ECU network thereof—that is, the custom tweaking of the parameter settings that influence the software functions on a specific vehicle—can be performed only at a late juncture. This step often is possible only immediately in-vehicle, and with all electronic systems running.

For this reason, it must be possible to modify the data version of many ECUs, even into the very late phases of development. This step is termed *calibration* (Fig. 4-52).

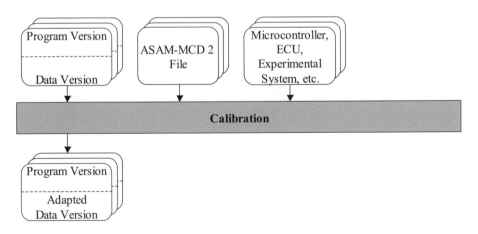

Fig. 4-52. *Calibration.*

Calibration is accomplished in the late phases of development through the use of calibration systems. Calibration systems must be capable of modifying the data versions that were unalterably deposited at their final destinations in read-only memory, such as ROM, EEPROM, or Flash memory. For this reason, a calibration system consists of an ECU equipped with a suitable offboard interface to a measuring and calibration tool. A detailed discussion of the various calibration methods appears in Section 5.6 of Chapter 5. The calibration phase concludes with the release of the data versions for the subsequent steps, as shown in Fig. 4-1.

4.14 System and Acceptance Test

A model is always short of detail and thus is always incomplete. It reduces the modeled components to specific aspects at the expense of neglecting others. For this reason, the model-based simulation of nonexistent components is fraught with uncertainties. Specific situations and scenarios are taken up, while others are overlooked. Thus, a simulation answers only the questions that were actually asked. As a consequence, results are always burdened with the residual risk arising from the imprecision of simulation models and from situations escaping consideration.

By contrast, test procedures conducted in the real-world operating environment of the system—this being the vehicle for vehicle systems—provide answers to questions that were not asked in advance. The in-vehicle system test eliminates the risks of ignoring specific perceptions due to the shortcomings of modeling. This makes in-vehicle testing indispensable. In the final analysis, the validation of the electronic systems onboard the vehicle can be achieved only by means of an acceptance test that is conducted from the user's perspective in his or her native operating environment (i.e., the vehicle) (Fig. 4-53).

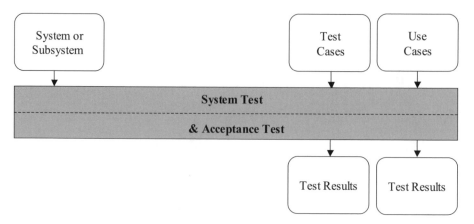

Fig. 4-53. *System and acceptance testing.*

This approach imposes special requirements on both development methodology and tools, such as the support of vehicle-compatible access to the ECUs and ECU networks onboard the vehicle, mobile measurement technology suited to deployment in rough environmental conditions, and vehicle-compatible operating and visualization elements.

As a final step, the release and approval of the entire system must take place in the vehicle. This also includes a system and acceptance test of the electronic systems, with all offboard interfaces and tools needed in production and service. Figure 4-54 provides an overview of those components and interfaces that must be tested as part of the system and acceptance test for the instrument cluster.

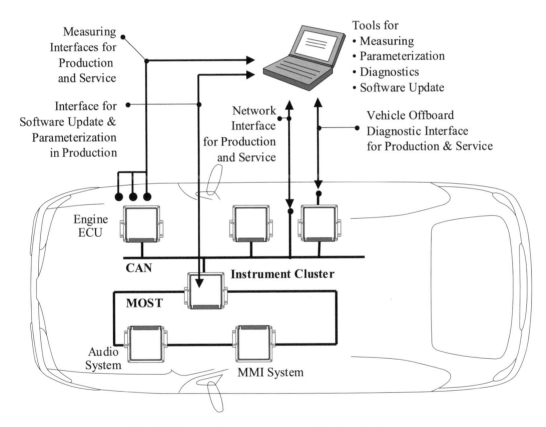

Fig. 4-54. *Interfaces requiring verification during system and acceptance test of the instrument cluster.*

CHAPTER FIVE

METHODS AND TOOLS
FOR DEVELOPMENT

Taking its orientation from selected process steps first introduced in Chapter 4, the present chapter introduces the methods and tools used in the start-to-finish engineering of software-implemented vehicle functions. Two types of process steps are examined. On one hand, these are the steps known to be essential in the development of application software functions for ECUs and, on the other hand, the process steps supporting the requirements and prerequisites characteristic of vehicle development.

Section 5.1 provides an initial overview of the various requirements and available options for the implementation of the *offboard interfaces between development tools and ECUs*. Various methods and tools are discussed throughout the following sections, with some methods supporting several process steps.

The development of systems and software for applications that impose high demands in terms of safety and reliability—that is, of the type often found in vehicles—requires that quality control measures for systems and software be deployed in every development phase. This chapter gives special consideration to this requirement.

Section 5.2 examines the methods available for logical system architecture analysis and technical system architecture specification:

- Analysis and specification of open-loop and closed-loop control systems
- Analysis of schedulability and specification of real-time systems
- Analysis and specification of communications in distributed and networked systems
- Reliability and safety analyses, and specification of reliability and safety concepts

To effect the *specification of software functions* and the *validation of the resulting specification*, model-based methods can be employed. In addition to providing an unambiguous and precise formulation of requirements, these facilitate the early validation of a given software function. To this end, Section 5.3 discusses suitable methods, such as the following:

- Formal specification and modeling
- Simulation and rapid prototyping

Section 5.4 focuses on methods and tools that support the *design and implementation of software functions*. Because this involves mapping a specification to specific algorithms, attention also must be given to the required nonfunctional product properties. These include, for example, the following:

- Optimization measures during software development with respect to required hardware resources.

- Utilization of limited subsets of programming languages to accommodate stringent reliability and safety requirements. A case in point is the MISRA-C Guidelines [80].

- Reduction of quality risks through the standardization and reuse of software components.

Section 5.5 discusses selected methods of *software function integration and testing*. These include the following:

- Testing in parallel with development, such as a component test, integration test, or system test conducted at various system levels

- Integration, system, and acceptance testing in the laboratory, on test benches, and in the vehicle

Section 5.6 examines suitable methods and tools for the task of *calibrating software functions*, which requires the following:

- Interface between the microcontroller and tools for so-called *online calibration*

- Vehicle-compatible measuring and calibration procedures for software functions

The practical significance of the methods and procedures presented is illustrated by examples taken from the powertrain, chassis, and body application areas.

5.1 Offboard Interface Between Electronic Control Units and Tools

The deployment of numerous tools throughout the various phases of development requires the availability of an offboard interface to the microcontroller of the respective ECU. This interface serves several purposes:

- Program download and debugging tools
- Software update tools for Flash programming
- Development and testing tools for ECU network interfaces
- Rapid prototyping tools
- Measuring and calibration tools for development ECUs
- Parameterization tools for production ECUs
- Offboard diagnostic tools

The interfaces between a given tool and the respective ECUs must be supported by hardware and software components on both ends. Some examples of the varying requirements imposed on these offboard interfaces in the various phases of development are listed as follows:

- Deployment in the laboratory, and in-vehicle in harsh environments

- Tool access to the microcontroller, with or without interruption of program execution by the microcontroller

- Varying demands on interface transmission speed

- Application only during development, or also in production and service

- Tool access to the ECU, with or without physical removal from the vehicle

The development phase for any electronic vehicle system concludes with the production approval and subsequent service release. For the development of ECUs, this means that the acceptance test performed at the end of development must use the same offboard interfaces and tools that will be used in the course of production and as a part of service procedures.

There is a basic difference between many of the items making up the requirements for the offboard interface formulated for in-vehicle operation and those formulated for laboratory conditions. For example, in-vehicle applications are subject to higher demands in terms of temperature range, shock and vibration, power source stability, and electromagnetic compatibility (EMC). Also, the location of the installed ECU onboard the vehicle results in restrictions regarding the installation space for the offboard interface, with the additional consequence of a larger spatial distance between the ECU and the respective tool.

For this reason, a variety of interface technologies is used in the course of development. Figure 5-1 shows an overview of those microcontroller components that bear on the design of an offboard interface. These are the microprocessor, the internal and external ROM and/or Flash memory and RAM, the internal and—as the case may be—external bus of the microcontroller, and the various serial interfaces of the microcontroller.

Section 5.6 discusses the special requirements and the design of offboard interfaces used to calibrate software functions. Further, detailed information about the offboard interfaces for deployment in production and service appears in Chapter 6.

5.2 Analysis of Logical System Architecture and Specification of Technical System Architecture

The initial development step is that of defining the logical system architecture, that is, the function network, the function interfaces in the form of signals, and the communications among the functions for the entire vehicle or for a vehicle subsystem.

The next step consists of replicating—or mapping—these abstract logical functions in the form of a specific technical system architecture. Support in this step comes from the analysis and specification methods of the various engineering disciplines participating in the development process. On one hand, this aids the early assessment of technical feasibility, while on the other hand providing for contrasting, comparing, and evaluating different implementation alternatives. The next few sections introduce several analysis and specification methods that influence the implementation of software functions.

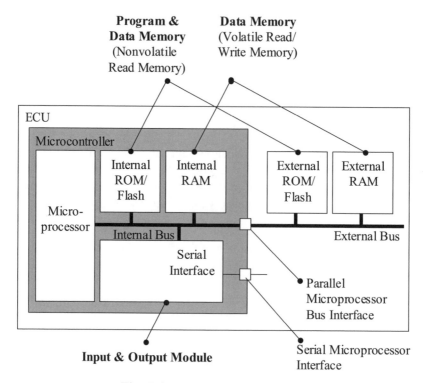

Fig. 5-1. *Microcontroller interfaces.*

5.2.1 Analysis and Specification of Open-Loop and Closed-Loop Control Systems

A closer look at the nature of many vehicle functions reveals that they represent open-loop or closed-loop control functions. Because the implementation of all types of control functions is increasingly handled by software, the analysis and design methods indigenous to control technology, which may be supported by tools using numerical simulation methods, exert a significant influence on the development of many software functions.

This section does not intend to cover the details of the numerous analysis and design methods. For a detailed discussion of these, reference is made to the relevant specialized literature [34, 35]. Instead, the focus of this section highlights those criteria that must be considered early in the analysis and design of control functions onboard vehicles, provided the said functions are intended for implementation on the basis of software and electronic systems.

The quest for solving control tasks is independent of the construction-related aspects of the respective plant. Instead, the static and dynamic behavior of the plant is of primary importance. For this reason, the first step of control technology-specific analysis methods consists of examining the plant. When the system boundaries for the plant have been established, the input and output parameters (I/O parameters), as well as the components of the plant, are defined. Identification methods are then used to establish physical model equations depicting the static and dynamic interrelations among the components. The resulting model view of the plant becomes the foundation for any and all subsequent design procedures.

In the course of this procedure, all components of an electronic system that contribute to the solution of a given control function—such as setpoint generators, sensors, actuators, and ECUs—initially are assigned to the control system to be designed. During the early phase, this practice simplifies the system view of the components, interfaces, and interrelations shown in Fig. 5-2. The specific technical structure of the control system being designed is defined only in the course of designing the technical system architecture.

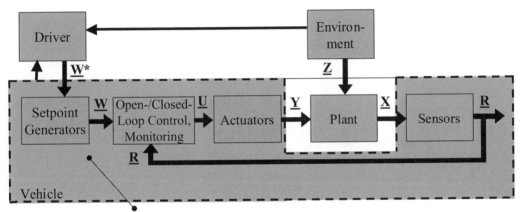

Model of controller in open-/closed-loop control analysis phase

Fig. 5-2. *View of logical system architecture in the open-loop*
and closed-loop control analysis phase.

For example, when using this approach of contemplating a gasoline engine as being synonymous with a plant, the manipulated variables Y—such as fuel injection volume, ignition point, and throttle valve position—are readily identified. Frequently, as a consequence of the numerous reciprocal effects existing among the various components, the internal structure of the plant can be rather complex. Figure 5-3 shows a comparatively simple example of a plant. It consists of seven components that are labeled Plant 1 through Plant 7. This is the basis for the design of the logical control system architecture. Figure 5-3 provides for seven controllers (labeled Controller 1 through Controller 7).

The initial steps are followed by the stepwise design of the control system strategy for the individual control components. The final step consists of the design of the technical system architecture. This involves the required setpoint generators, sensors, and actuators, and the design of the ECUs and their software functions. Figure 5-4 illustrates this step on the example of Controller 3.

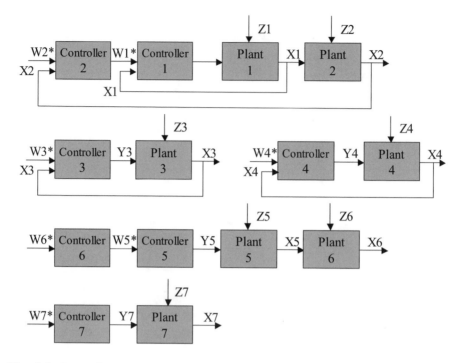

Fig. 5-3. *Logical system architecture of an open-loop and closed-loop control system.*

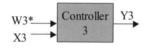

Logical System Architecture

Technical System Architecture

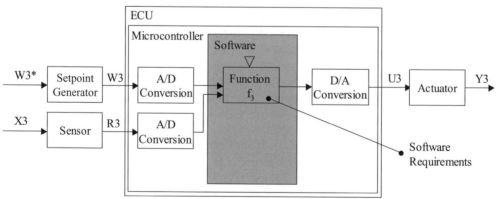

Fig. 5-4. *Design of the technical system architecture for Controller 3.*

The methods applied to the specification of software functions are discussed in Section 5.3.

In the context of this design step, note that the transfer function of the components making up an electronic system may not simply be deemed "ideal" in many in-vehicle applications. Due to cost considerations, setpoint generators, sensors, actuators, and hardware modules often provide limited resolution and dynamics. In addition, the time and value-discrete function of the microcontrollers must be taken into account. All of these make it imperative to consider the following properties of the deployed setpoint generators, sensors, and actuators—plus microcontroller A/D and D/A converters—early in the design phase of a control system:

- Effects caused by the value-discrete operation (e.g., due to limited resolution)
- Nonlinearities (e.g., caused by limitations)
- Delay or dead times caused by limited dynamics

In many cases, the implementation of software functions is adversely influenced by the limited hardware resources of the deployed microcontrollers. Accordingly, the following items should be kept in mind:

- Errors caused by rounding or the handling of underflows or overflows (e.g., when using integer arithmetic)

- Approximation errors (e.g., caused by the limited accuracy of algorithms)

- Effects caused by the time-discrete operation of microcontrollers

The time constants of the plant determine the necessary sampling rate dT of the control system, and thus the sampling rate dT_n for a given software function f_n.

Figure 5-5 shows the external view of a software function in this development phase.

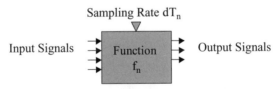

Fig. 5-5. *External view of software function f_n.*

The control components shown in Fig. 5-3 also may be jointly implemented in a single ECU, as shown in Fig. 5-6. The seven control components (Controller 1 through Controller 7) are to be implemented with the use of setpoint generators, sensors, actuators, A/D and D/A converters, and the software functions f_1 through f_7.

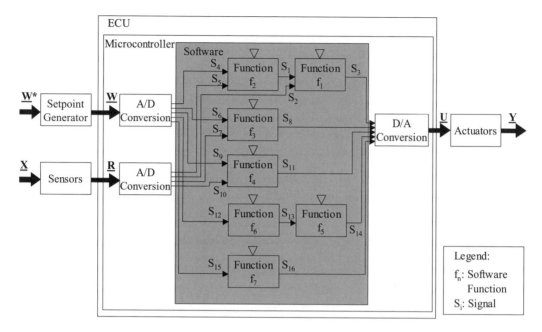

Fig. 5-6. *Design of the technical system architecture of an open-loop and closed-loop control system.*

As shown in Fig. 2-60 of Chapter 2, this approach also can be used in the specification of monitoring and diagnostic functions.

The result provides, for all software functions f_n, *a specification of the control and monitoring strategy, I/O signals, and the necessary sampling rate dT_n.* The procedures described in the following sections are based on the information thus obtained.

5.2.2 *Analysis and Specification of Real-Time Systems*

In the event that several software functions using different sampling rates must be implemented either by a single ECU or an entire ECU network, the software functions are activated by a variety of tasks that are subject to different real-time requirements.

For many in-vehicle applications, compliance with the real-time requirement of a given task is extremely important. Therefore, it stands to reason that analysis and specification of real-time systems must be carried out with the conscientious observance of the repercussions resulting from the arbitration and scheduling strategy of both the operating system and the communication system.

Specific methods facilitating a schedulability analysis make it possible to assess and evaluate compliance with the real-time requirements defined in Fig. 2-18 of Chapter 2 in a timely manner, that is, long before the real-time system enters actual operation.

In this context, a differentiation may be made between the analysis of processor scheduling for a variety of tasks and the analysis of bus arbitration between the nodes of a communication system. The methods applied to both task settings are quite similar. The present section discusses a possible approach that avails itself of processor scheduling. In practical application, however, these analytical procedures are complemented by suitable design, verification, and monitoring principles.

The result is a *specification of the real-time system*, for which all software functions may have been divided into processes, and these processes assigned to tasks.

Without limitation of universal applicability, it is first assumed that the standardized definition of real-time requirements for each task of the real-time system is based on the following:

- The constant or variable interval between two activations of a given task, labeled *activation rate* in Fig. 5-7, and

- A time barrier established relative to the activation point, up to which the execution of a task shall be completed. This time barrier is termed the *relative deadline*.

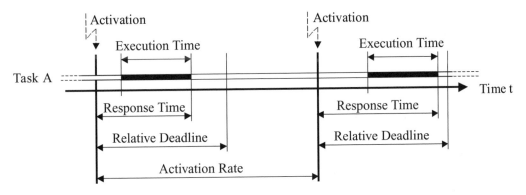

Fig. 5-7. *Definition of real-time requirements for schedulability analysis—Example: Task A.*

A violation of the real-time requirement for a given task is deemed to exist in the event that the execution of that task is not concluded within the specified time limit, that is, if

$$\text{Response time} > \text{Relative deadline} \qquad (5.1)$$

Rather than being a constant variable, the response time is influenced by various factors. Figure 5-8 shows a typical distribution of the response time for a given task. The critical determinant for the violation of the real-time requirement is the largest response time value, known as the *worst-case response time* (or WCRT, for short).

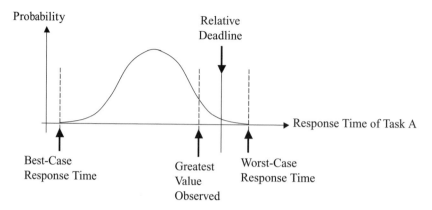

Fig. 5-8. *Probability distribution of response time for Task A.*

In some cases, proof of compliance with the real-time requirements at a degree approximating certainty cannot be obtained by means of testing in limiting conditions and with simultaneous response time measuring. As the number of tasks increases, and with the rising complexity of real-time requirements and scheduling strategies, obtaining such proof through testing often is virtually impossible. Even after "successful" testing, it may be possible in critical situations that the execution of a task is concluded only after the deadline has passed. Because, in such critical cases, the greatest response time value obtained and measured in prior testing is not identical to the largest value, the result is a violation of the real-time requirement.

Therefore, a combination of three corrective measures is employed in practical application:

• Schedulability analysis for the assessment of implementation alternatives

• Measurements after implementation to verify the results of the schedulability analysis

• Online deadline monitoring by the real-time operating system, and application-specific response to deadline violations

5.2.2.1 Schedulability Analysis

The purpose of the schedulability analysis is to use all known parameters to provide a before-the-fact estimate of the compliance with real-time requirements.

Thus, the requirement for a real-time system is

$$\text{Worst-case response time (WCRT)} \leq \text{Relative deadline} \qquad (5.2)$$

This requires that the WCRT be determined or estimated.

In the simple case depicted in Fig. 5-7, the response time is determined by the interval between the activation point and the start of task execution on one hand, and by the task execution time on the other hand.

The commonly encountered case is more complex because the task execution may be interrupted by the execution of one or more tasks of higher priority, with the added obstacle that those tasks may be time or event-activated. The WCRT is further influenced by the resulting dead times and the execution time required by the operating system for the task transition.

It normally takes two steps to determine or estimate the WCRT of a given task:

1. The first step involves a determination or estimation of the maximum execution time required for each task (termed *worst-case execution time*, or WCET). In addition, the execution times required by the operating system must be determined or estimated.

2. Taking into account the real-time requirements and scheduling strategy, the second step facilitates an estimation of whether or not the condition (Eq. 5.2) for all activations of the respective tasks can be fulfilled.

Example: Schedulability analysis

A manager's daily schedule shall be examined for schedulability. The manager sleeps 8 hours in a 24-hour period. He eats for 30 minutes in 8-hour intervals. Each time 1.5 hours have elapsed, he drinks for 15 minutes, and he talks on the telephone for 30 minutes during each 2-hour interval.

As a condition, it is permissible to delay the meal by a maximum of 30 minutes and drinking by 30 minutes, but telephoning by only 15 minutes. The required sleep interval shall be concluded with a 24-hour period. This results in the following deadlines: Sleep = 24 hours, Eat = 1 hour, Drink = 45 minutes, and Phone = 45 minutes.

Assuming the application of a preemptive scheduling strategy in accordance with the basic task state model as per OSEK-OS (see Fig. 2-20 in Chapter 2), the intent is to examine whether the manager is able to handle appointments in addition to the ones that are known. As matters stand, the manager must perform a total of four tasks:

- Task A: Sleep
- Task B: Eat
- Task C: Drink
- Task D: Phone

The assigned priorities are Phone, followed by Eat, Drink, and Sleep. Table 5-1 summarizes the entire daily schedule, with priorities and activation, deadline, and execution times.

The schedulability may be examined with the aid of the following execution scenario (Fig. 5-9):

- Task D—Phone, having the highest priority, is executed in 2-hour intervals, without violating the real-time requirement.

TABLE 5-1
MANAGER'S TASK LIST

	Activation Time	Deadline	Execution Time	Priority
Task A	Every 24 h	24 h	8 h	1
Task B	Every 8 h	60 min	30 min	3
Task C	Every 1.5 h	45 min	15 min	2
Task D	Every 2 h	45 min	30 min	4

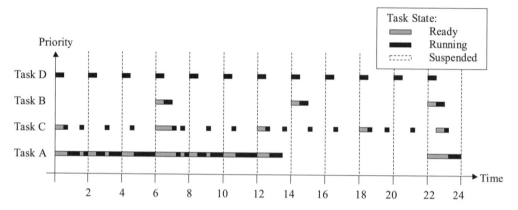

Fig. 5-9. *Schedulability diagram prior to optimization.*

- Task B—Eat is activated simultaneously with Task D at 0600, 1400, and 2200 hours. However, because of its low priority ranking, it is executed with a 30-minute delay. Execution is finished just before the deadline.

- Task C—Drink is activated in 90-minute intervals. However, because of its low priority ranking, the execution may be interrupted or delayed by Task B or Task D. In four of the cases, violation of the 45-minute deadline is barely avoided. The worst-case scenario manifests itself at 0600 hours. Here, the response time is 75 minutes, which results in a deadline violation. Task C is again activated as early as 15 minutes after the completion of task execution.

- Task A—Sleep has the lowest priority and is started only after a delay of 75 minutes. As expected, the task is frequently interrupted. More than 15 hours elapse between the task activation point and the end of execution.

The critical situation with Task C at 0600 hours, and the borderline situations of the real-time requirements of Task B, may be diffused through the introduction of a variety of measures. Figure 5-10 depicts a scenario in which Task B is not activated at the same time as Task D,

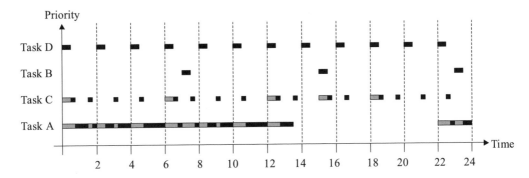

Fig. 5-10. *Schedulability diagram subsequent to optimization.*

but instead with a one-hour offset—that is, at 0700, 1500, and 2300 hours. This ensures the safe fulfillment of the real-time requirements for Task B at all times. The critical situation of Task C at 0600 hours is alleviated in the same way. However, it is true that there continue to be five cases where a deadline violation is barely avoided. Additional measures to remedy critical situations would be extending the Task C deadline to, say, 60 minutes. Another possible action would be raising the priority, if that is possible. And, as may be expected, the newly introduced measures do not affect Task A with its lowest priority ranking.

It also is now possible to answer the original question, namely, that of scheduling additional appointments in the form of Task E. As Fig. 5-10 shows, the schedule density now permits additional daily tasks to be scheduled between 1400 and 2200 hours. To achieve a more balanced schedule for our busy manager, the Sleep task might be split into two tasks named NightSleep and AfternoonNap. It also is possible to estimate the effect of unforeseen interruptions of higher priority, such as a customer's phone call to the manager.

Although the situation surrounding the fictitious manager in our example was deliberately abstracted, it does serve the purpose of elucidating the errors of interpretation that may occur in conjunction with real-time systems specification, as well as the effect of optimization measures.

In addition to providing schedulability details for each of the tasks at hand, this analysis also facilitates closer scrutiny of schedule density information, that is, overload and underload situations. These, in turn, may be used to improve the specification of real-time requirements. As a result, the total system load is more evenly distributed. In certain circumstances, a smoother load situation may even reduce the complement of required hardware resources, such as processor clock rate.

It would be misleading to entertain the assumption that tasks of lower priority may be interrupted at any point by tasks having higher priority. In fact, practical applications frequently exhibit limitations. With respect to our example, this means that the Sleep task can be interrupted only every two hours.

Also, it would not be realistic to assume that the switch from one task to another occurs entirely without delay. Here, too, limitations crop up in real-world applications which—in our example—would require the insertion of a delay or wake-up phase into the task transition between Sleep and Phone.

When transposing this procedural approach to a practical in-vehicle application, additional consideration must be given to the execution times required by the real-time system. These may be substantial, depending on numerous parameters, and especially on the selected scheduling strategy.

Another issue is the estimation of the worst-case execution time (WCET) required for a given task. More often than not, it also depends on a variety of parameters.

All of the methods undertaking the calculation or estimation of the execution times (e.g., based on the compiler-generated instructions) tend to be time-intensive and costly. These are feasible only when tailored to specific situations. This subject matter is the object of multifaceted research activities.

In this context, it should be basic practice to strictly limit the employment of any program constructs, such as repeat loops or wait states, whose processing may take an arbitrary length of time. For this reason, iterative algorithms should be implemented in a manner ensuring the calculation of only one or a finite number of iteration steps per task activation [57]. If this is not possible, a worst-case estimation of the execution time of iterative algorithms cannot be performed.

5.2.2.2 Verifying Schedulability by Means of Measurements

The verification of real-time behavior can be accomplished on the basis of measurements of activation times and execution times in the real-world system, and by plotting an arbitration diagram. In this way, flagrant design flaws can be identified and iterative steps taken toward improving the parameter settings of the real-time system.

The foregoing notwithstanding, remember that, as shown in Fig. 5-8, the measured or observed execution times provide only a ballpark figure of the maximum execution time and response time.

Furthermore, in most cases, it is not even possible to ensure that a given system was actually in the critical load phase while being measured. This situation is typical of event-controlled systems that are subject to variable task activation times and events, such as interrupts.

5.2.2.3 Monitoring and Handling Deadline Violations in the Operating System

For a given task, the risk of deadline violations can be reduced by changing various attributes, such as the priority or the deadline, or by setting an activation delay. Exception handling can be used to define behavior in overload situations. These include so-called *debouncing measures*, such as defining a maximum number of repeat activations for a task or specifying a minimum time period between two activations of a given task.

To identify exception situations of this kind at the earliest possible point during the development phase, the exception conditions often are made decidedly tighter during development than later in series production.

However, even in series production, and even in the presence of a software version that has been approved for production, it may not be possible in all cases to dispense with online deadline monitoring by the real-time operating system, especially for tasks that are subject to hard real-time requirements. The same is true of the application-specific handling of deadline violations.

Appropriate implementations may utilize function-specific error hooks, which are called by the real-time operating system in response to an identification of deadline violations. In such cases, these software monitoring functions augment the hardware-implemented monitoring measures (e.g., program execution monitoring by means of a watchdog module).

5.2.3 Analysis and Specification of Distributed and Networked Systems

The acquisition of input parameters for ECU software functions may be accomplished by sensors that are directly assigned to the ECU. An alternative would be the utilization of signals produced by sensors assigned to other ECUs. These signals would be transmitted via the onboard communications network of the vehicle, and their use might be described as indirect. Similar options exist with respect to actuators. In addition, all of the signals and states internally calculated by the ECUs may be transmitted through the communications network.

Although this results in appreciable degrees of freedom with respect to the design of functions, it also tends to create new design problems, that is, those of the most efficient distribution of software functions over a network of ECUs and/or microcontrollers, and of the abstraction of sensors and actuators. For this reason, this section focuses on the analysis of various distribution and networking alternatives. Figure 5-11 shows some of the degrees of freedom provided by virtue of the flexible direct or indirect implementation of logical communications links between electronic system components. The graphical visualization differentiates between sensors and intelligent sensors, and between actuators and intelligent actuators.

Another factor of far-reaching consequence is the influence of the communications system, such as the value discretization of signals during message transmission or the transmission times (response characteristics) of the communications system. These should be considered as early as possible in the design of a distributed and networked system.

Methods facilitating the analysis of distributed and networked systems provide a means of evaluating the referenced influencing factors. They also require the observation of numerous requirements and constraints, such as installation space, real-time, safety, and reliability requirements.

As an introductory example, it shall be assumed that the software functions of the control system depicted in Fig. 5-6 need to be distributed to different microcontrollers. As a first step, those requirements that already exist for the software shall be identified. These consist of the input and output signals, and of the sampling rate dT. These requirements are summarized in table form in Fig. 5-12.

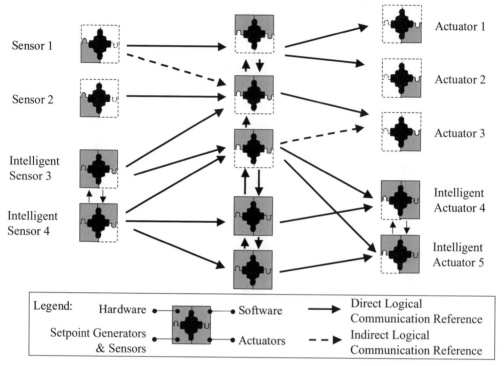

Fig. 5-11. *Analysis of logical system architecture of distributed and networked systems.*

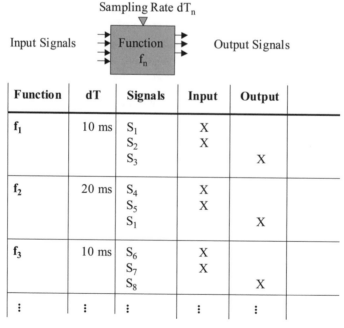

Function	dT	Signals	Input	Output
f_1	10 ms	S_1	X	
		S_2	X	
		S_3		X
f_2	20 ms	S_4	X	
		S_5	X	
		S_1		X
f_3	10 ms	S_6	X	
		S_7	X	
		S_8		X
⋮	⋮	⋮	⋮	⋮

Fig. 5-12. *Table of software functions with sampling rate and signals.*

To assign these software functions to various microcontrollers, a new column is added to this table, as shown in Fig. 5-13. The information in this column indicates the specific locations in which the functions shall be implemented. Function f_1 is calculated on microcontroller $\mu C_{1.1}$, function f_2 on microcontroller $\mu C_{2.1}$, and function f_3 on microcontroller $\mu C_{1.2}$. In this distribution, the prerequisites of the existing hardware architecture must be considered. This may cause the distribution of functions to be restricted by the pre-existing assignment of sensors and actuators to specific microcontrollers. For example, this may result in the direct assignment of a sensor signal preprocessing function to the microcontroller that also handles the respective sensor.

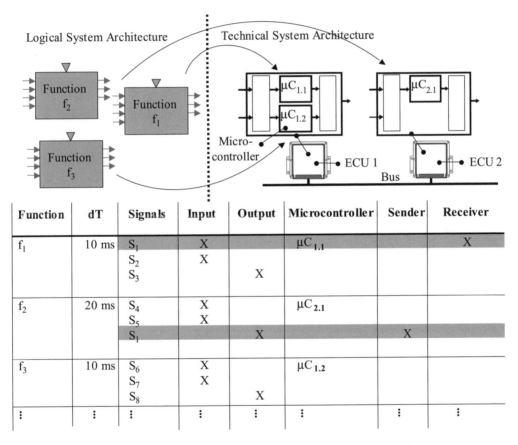

Function	dT	Signals	Input	Output	Microcontroller	Sender	Receiver
f_1	10 ms	S_1	X		$\mu C_{1.1}$		X
		S_2	X				
		S_3		X			
f_2	20 ms	S_4	X		$\mu C_{2.1}$		
		S_5	X				
		S_1		X		X	
f_3	10 ms	S_6	X		$\mu C_{1.2}$		
		S_7	X				
		S_8		X			
⋮	⋮	⋮	⋮	⋮	⋮	⋮	⋮

Fig. 5-13. *Assignment of software functions to microcontrollers.*

As the discussion continues, two cases in point must be differentiated:

1. In the event that signals occur not only repeatedly but also on different microprocessors in the table shown in Fig. 5-13, these must be communicated over the network. In this way, the set of all signals to be transmitted by the communications system is obtained. In the simplified example in Fig. 5-13, this applies only to signal S_1, which must be transmitted from microcontroller $\mu C_{2.1}$ to microcontroller $\mu C_{1.1}$.

2. However, if signals occur repeatedly on a given microcontroller in the table shown in Fig. 5-13, addressing different functions for which different sampling rates have been specified, these must be communicated across task boundaries. In this way, the set of all signals that must be transmitted by via inter-task communications is obtained.

The former case raises the immediate question of the timing requirements (e.g., the transmit rate, at which the signal transmission through the network is to be accomplished). In our example, in which function f_2 calculates the signal S_1 at a sampling rate of 20 ms, it would make little sense to transmit the signal S_1 at a faster rate. This would hold true even if—as depicted in Fig. 5-13—the receiving function f_1 were to be calculated at the faster sampling rate of 10 ms. In this case, the resulting specification will call for the transmission of signal S_1 at the sampling rate of 20 ms.

By contrast, if the receiving function f_1 were to be calculated at a slower sampling rate, the burden on the communications system would be lightened by transmitting the signal at the sampling rate of the receiving function. Thus, it has been demonstrated that a differentiation must be made in each case between the sampling rate of the signal transmission, the required transmission time, and the sampling rate dT for the calculation of transmitting and receiving functions.

A second definition concerns the signal resolution and value range during transmission. Here, too, the resolution expected by the receiver of a message must be considered.

These definitions at the signal level suffice as a basis for estimating the communications load and evaluating distribution alternatives.

The next step consists of defining the communications system. This also requires that the messages to be transmitted by the communications system be formed. In other words, it must be defined which message will be used to transmit a given signal.

For reasons of efficiency, it will be natural to attempt the bundling of various signals that a microcontroller must send with identical time requirements and to the same group of receivers, for transmission with one message or the least possible number of messages.

To this end, it is useful to rearrange the rows and columns of the table in Fig. 5-13 and to expand it into a communications matrix. This will place the microcontroller sending the signals in the left-hand column. The signals are arranged in ascending order of sampling rates for signal transmission (transmit rate) and by signal receivers.

The formation of messages produces the communications matrix shown in Fig. 5-14. Signal S_1 is transmitted via message N_3. Figure 5-14 shows several additional signals and messages that may be derived from additional functions that have not been discussed at this point.

A sizeable contingent of additional aspects must be considered when analyzing the network onboard a real-life vehicle. First, the true number of signals, messages, senders, and receivers is considerably larger than that discussed in this section. The situation is further complicated by the fact that the signals transmitted by a given sender are normally processed by several receivers at various sampling rates. Also, note that the leeway with respect to the distribution of functions is normally restricted by numerous additional prerequisites.

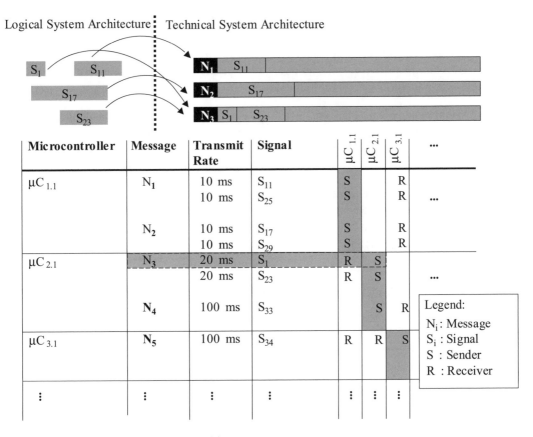

Microcontroller	Message	Transmit Rate	Signal	$\mu C_{1.1}$	$\mu C_{2.1}$	$\mu C_{3.1}$	...
$\mu C_{1.1}$	N_1	10 ms	S_{11}	S		R	
		10 ms	S_{25}	S		R	...
	N_2	10 ms	S_{17}	S		R	
		10 ms	S_{29}	S		R	
$\mu C_{2.1}$	N_3	20 ms	S_1	R	S		
		20 ms	S_{23}	R	S		...
	N_4	100 ms	S_{33}		S	R	
$\mu C_{3.1}$	N_5	100 ms	S_{34}	R	R	S	
⋮	⋮	⋮	⋮	⋮	⋮	⋮	

Legend:
N_i : Message
S_i : Signal
S : Sender
R : Receiver

Fig. 5-14. *Communications matrix.*

The massive obstacles embodied in the concerted effect of the aforementioned drawbacks lend even greater significance to the early analysis of the requirements, the evaluation of the implementation alternatives, and the iterative improvement of the network design.

After the communications system, messages, and network topology have been defined, the information contained in the communications matrix can be enhanced to a point where the deployment of simulation will facilitate initial statements regarding the bus load or expected communications latencies.

The result obtained in this manner comprises a *specification of the distributed and networked system,* in which all of the software functions are assigned to a microcontroller, and where the communications matrix is fully defined.

5.2.4 Analysis and Specification of Reliable and Safe Systems

Reliability and safety requirements for vehicle functions arise as a consequence of the interplay between customer desires and the consideration of technical, legal, and financial prerequisites.

For example, reliability requirements are imposed in the form of short repair times or long service intervals. By contrast, safety requirements define the safe operating characteristics of the vehicle in the event of component malfunction or failure. From the beginning, the reliability and safety requirements for vehicle functions also define requirements concerning technical implementation and verification requirements.

For this reason, systematic methods facilitating a reliability and safety analysis have a growing influence on software development (e.g., on the implementation of monitoring, diagnostic, and safety concepts). In the case of complex electronic systems, the activities safeguarding reliability and safety must be planned early, with subsequent integration into the entire project plan.

Reliability and safety analyses encompass failure rate and failure mode analyses, plus the examination and evaluation of specific means of improving reliability and safety. The group of failure mode analyses also includes the so-called *failure mode and effects analysis* (FMEA) [61] and the *fault tree analysis* (FTA) [53, 54].

5.2.4.1 Failure Rate Analysis and Calculation of Reliability Function

The systematic scrutiny of the failure rate of an observation unit facilitates a prediction of its reliability on the basis of calculation. This forecast is an essential prerequisite in the early identification of weak points and the evaluation of alternative solutions. It also aids in the quantitative acquisition of the interdependencies of reliability, safety, and availability. In addition, investigations of this type are necessary when assistance in the formulation of reliability requirements for components is warranted.

Remember that, because of deliberate neglect and simplifications, as well as the poor reliability of input data, the calculated and predicted reliability may be used as a mere estimation of the true reliability, which can be determined only with the aid of reliability testing and field trials. However, for the purpose of comparative investigations during the analysis phase, absolute accuracy is not a major concern. As a result, the calculation of the predicted reliability is especially useful in the context of evaluating implementation alternatives.

For the purpose of this section, the observation unit always comprises a technical system or system component. Normally, however, a more general view may set wider margins and even include the vehicle operator.

The failure rate analysis encompasses the following steps:

- Defining the boundaries and components of the technical system, required functions, and the requirement profile

- Establishing the reliability block diagram

- Determining the load conditions for each component

- Determining the reliability function or failure rate for each component

- Calculating the reliability function for the entire system

- Remedial actions to eliminate weak points

The failure rate analysis comprises a multistage procedure. It is performed in a top-down progression from the system level through the various subsystem levels to the component level of the technical system architecture. In the event that changes are made to the technical system architecture, the failure rate analysis must be repeated.

Defining system boundaries, required functions, and requirement profile

Indispensable prerequisites for the theoretical considerations needed for the reliability forecast are detailed knowledge and in-depth skills with respect to the system, its functions, and the specific options providing for improvements in reliability and safety.

The required system skills also include familiarity with the system architecture and its operational principles, the working and load conditions of all system components, and the reciprocal effects among components, possibly in the form of signal flows and the inputs and outputs of all components.

The improvement options include the limitation or reduction of static or dynamic component operating loads, interface loads, the deployment of components of higher suitability, the simplification of system or component design, the pretreatment of critical components, and the introduction of redundancy.

A required function specifies the system task. Because the definitions of system boundaries and required functions also are used to define failure, they form the starting point for any reliability and safety analysis.

In addition, because the environmental conditions for all of the system components define component reliability, these likewise must be defined. For example, the temperature range exerts a significant influence on the failure rate of hardware components. In the vehicle, the required temperature range, operation in humidity, dust, and corrosive atmosphere, or shock and vibration loads or fluctuations of operating voltage all belong under the same umbrella term. In cases where the required functions and environmental conditions also are time dependent, a requirement profile must be established. One example of requirement profiles prescribed by statutory law is the driving cycles used in the verification of compliance with exhaust emission directives. In such cases, the term *representative requirement profiles* is used.

Establishing the reliability block diagram

The reliability block diagram answers the questions of which components of a given system must always function in order to fulfill the required function, and which components would not severely impede the function in the event of their failure because they are available in redundancy. The reliability block diagram is established by observing the components of the technical system architecture. These components are then arranged in a block diagram and are interconnected in such a fashion that the components required for the fulfillment of functions are switched in series, and redundant components are connected in parallel.

Example: Establishing the reliability block diagram for an electromechanical braking system

As a first step in establishing the fictitious brake-by-wire system shown in Fig. 5-15, the system boundary is defined. The system consists of the components brake pedal unit (C_1), ECU (C_2), the wheel brake units (C_5, C_7, C_9, and C_{11}), and the electrical connections (C_3, C_4, C_6, C_8, and C_{10}).

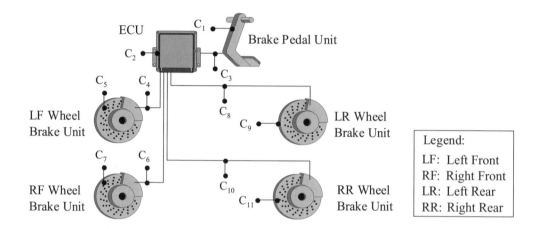

Fig. 5-15. *System view of a brake-by-wire system.*

Instead of providing the customary hydraulic line connections among the brake master cylinder, the brake pedal, and the wheel brakes, electromechanical braking systems employ electrical connections. Brake actuation causes the operator command issued by brake pedal unit C_1, and processed onboard ECU C_2, to be conveyed "by wire" to wheel brake units C_5, C_7, C_9, and C_{11}, with the electrical energy required for braking. This process has one major objective: In conventional braking systems, the "information and energy conveyance" function between the brake pedal unit and wheel brakes is performed by mechanical and hydraulic means. The brake-by-wire implementation by means of electrical and electronic components C_2, C_3, C_4, C_6, C_8, and C_{10} must under no circumstances introduce an additional safety hazard but provide a certain safety gain. Therefore, the absolute safety of transmitted braking instructions constitutes a mandatory requirement. Similarly, the required operational safety also must be guaranteed in the case of component failures.

The "braking" function shall be investigated. To this end, the overall reliability of the system must be determined. It shall be assumed that the failure rates λ_1 through λ_{11} of components C_1 through C_{11} are known.

For its remainder, this example will be greatly simplified. Its intended function is to illustrate the basic approach to the reliability analysis. For this reason, this examination focuses on the transmission of information, whereas the aspects of energy supply and transmission, as well as prerequisites related to driving dynamics (e.g., the distribution of braking forces to the front and rear axles, which must naturally be considered in the context of the reliability analysis) shall be disregarded.

In this simplified view, the fulfillment of the "braking" function makes the functioning of the components brake pedal unit C_1 and ECU C_2, plus the connections C_3 between the brake pedal unit C_1 and ECU C_2, a mandatory requirement.

The function of the wheel brake units, and the connections between the ECU and wheel brake units, are protected by redundancy. As a consequence of the strongly simplified assumption that the secondary braking effect for the vehicle can be accomplished with only one wheel brake unit, the components C_4 and C_5 are required, whereas components C_6 and C_7, C_8, and C_9, and/or C_{10} and C_{11} are available as redundant units. This type of arrangement is known as *one-of-four redundance*.

Based on the foregoing, the reliability diagram for the "braking" function will appear as shown in Fig. 5-16.

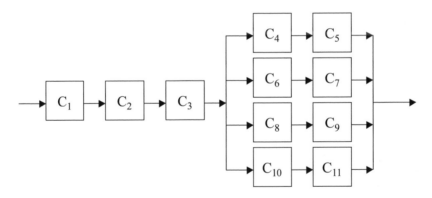

Fig. 5-16. *Reliability block diagram for the "braking" function of a brake-by-wire system.*

Calculating the reliability function for the system

Subsequent to specifying the load conditions and defining the reliability functions $R_i(t)$ for all of the components C_i, the system reliability function $R_S(t)$ can be calculated in consideration of the basis rules for reliability block diagrams [54] shown in Fig. 5-17.

For the example in Fig. 5-16, the system reliability function R_S can be calculated. Based on the assumptions $R_4 = R_6 = R_8 = R_{10}$ and $R_5 = R_7 = R_9 = R_{11}$, R_S is derived as follows:

Reliability Block Diagram	Reliability Function $R_S = R_S(t)$, $R_i = R_i(t)$	Failure Rate λ_S if λ_i = constant: $R_i(t) = e^{-\lambda_i t}$	Example
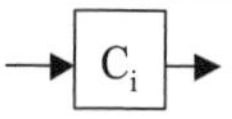 $\rightarrow \boxed{C_i} \rightarrow$	$R_S = R_i$	$\lambda_S = \lambda_i$	
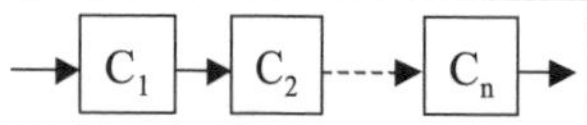 $\rightarrow \boxed{C_1} \rightarrow \boxed{C_2} \dashrightarrow \boxed{C_n} \rightarrow$	$R_S = \prod_{i=1}^{n} R_i$	$\lambda_S = \sum_{i=1}^{n} \lambda_i$	$R_1 = R_2 = 0.9$ $R_S = 0.9 \cdot 0.9 = 0.81$
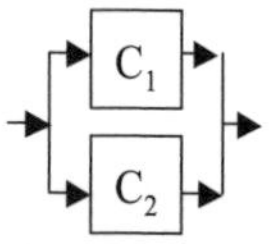 $\boxed{C_1}$ $\boxed{C_2}$ one-of-two redundancy	$R_S = 1-(1-R_1)(1-R_2)$ $= R_1 + R_2 - R_1 * R_2$		$R_1 = R_2 = 0.9$ $R_S = 1- (1-0.9)(1-0.9) = 0.99$
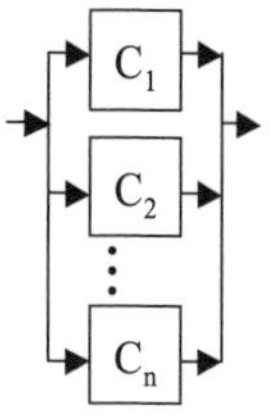 $\boxed{C_1}$ $\boxed{C_2}$ $\vdots$ $\boxed{C_n}$ k-of-n redundancy	$R_1 = R_2 = ... = R_n = R$ $R_S = \sum_{i=k}^{n} \binom{n}{i} R^i (1-R)^{n-i}$ For $k = 1$: $R_S = 1- (1-R)^n$		$R_1 = R_2 = R_3 = R_4 = 0.9$ at one-of-four redundancy $R_S = 1- (1-0.9)^4 = 0.9999$

Fig. 5-17. *Basic rules for calculating the system reliability function. (Ref. [54]).*

$$R_S = R_1 R_2 R_3 \left[1 - \left(1 - R_4 R_5\right)^4 \right] \qquad (5.3)$$

As this simplified example demonstrates, the system reliability for a given function is increased by the presence of redundant components in the reliability block diagram, as compared with component reliability. By contrast, the system reliability of the components connected in series is reduced *vis-à-vis* component reliability. Therefore, it stands to reason that it will be necessary to demand a high degree of reliability of the serial components already in the reliability block diagram or to introduce a technical system architecture that provides for redundant structures also in this situation.

5.2.4.2 System Safety and Reliability Analysis

With regard to the safety analysis, it is of little importance whether or not an observation unit actually does fulfill the functions being demanded of it, as long as this does not introduce an unacceptable high-risk factor. Any actions taken with a view to increasing safety are termed *protective measures* and are aimed at reducing the risk level.

The reliability and safety analyses comprise iterative and contiguous processes of several steps, as depicted in Fig. 4-18 of Chapter 4 [70]. They influence hardware and software requirements, as well as the software development process for electronic systems. Furthermore, the safety analysis of a system often is carried out by applying methods for failure mode analysis. The failure mode analysis produces a risk assessment for all functions within a system.

The permissible limit risk is normally implicitly prescribed by safety technology stipulations, such as laws, standards, or directives. The risk level obtained for the functions of the system and the permissible limit risk then become the basis for deriving safety requirements for the system (e.g., in accordance with standards such as IEC 61508 [19]). In many cases, such standards exert significant influence on system and software design in electronics development.

For the so-called *safety-relevant* functions of the system, which are defined and isolated by the failure mode analysis, special protective measures must be introduced. These may be implemented in both hardware and software. The verification of safety is a prerequisite for the approval for road registration of vehicles. Therefore, appropriate verification and validation procedures must be planned as early as in the analysis phase.

Example: Monitoring concept for an electronic throttle control system (ETC)

In Chapter 2, the requirement class for an ETC system was determined (see Fig. 2-59). A possible hazard was assumed to be inadvertent acceleration, with a resulting accident. To the engine ECU, this means that all control functions f_n leading to an inadvertent increase in engine torque are to be considered safety relevant. Therefore, a concept for monitoring these functions is needed.

For the purpose of this example, the monitoring concept that has been in use in engine ECUs for several years [81] has been slightly modified. It will be investigated with respect to safety and reliability. Under the auspices of the "E-Gas" Working Committee of the German Association of the Automotive Industry (VDA), this basic concept developed by Robert Bosch GmbH is currently subject to advanced development as a standardized monitoring concept for gasoline and diesel engine ECUs (see Fig. 2-62 in Chapter 2).

Figure 5-18 shows the monitoring concept for safety-relevant control functions f_n.

The safety-relevant control functions f_n are subject to constant monitoring by the monitoring functions $f_{\ddot{U}n}$. Although the monitoring functions $f_{\ddot{U}n}$ utilize the same input variables as the control functions f_n, they work with different data and algorithms.

In addition to checking RAM, ROM, and microprocessor functions, the microcontroller monitoring functions also verify whether or not the control functions f_n and monitoring functions $f_{\ddot{U}n}$ are actually running. This necessitates the deployment of a second microprocessor, a so-called *monitoring computer*, in the engine ECU. The dedicated microcontroller monitoring functions are distributed to the function computer and monitoring computer. Both computers conduct a question-and-answer routine in a mutual monitoring process.

A defined safe state is the power shutoff to the electromechanical throttle valve. The throttle valve is constructed in such a way that it automatically assumes the idle position in the event of being de-energized. Therefore, the transition to the safe state can be initiated in the ECU

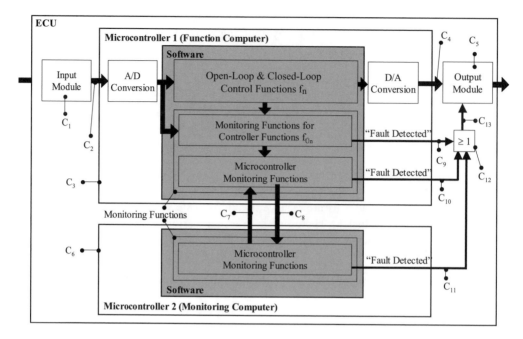

Fig. 5-18. *Monitoring concept for safety-relevant functions of an engine ECU. (Ref. [81])*

by powering down the output modules driving the throttle valve. In this way, the engine can continue to be operated in the limp-home operating mode.

Thus, it has been demonstrated that not only the monitoring functions $f_{\ddot{U}n}$ but also the dedicated microcontroller monitoring functions on the function and monitoring computer can disable the throttle valve output modules of the ECU.

In the event that a fault is detected, an entry is written into the fault memory in addition to the safety response previously discussed. In most cases, an appropriate message is output to the vehicle operator (e.g., by means of an indicator in the instrument cluster).

To assess the reliability of this monitoring concept, three types of functions must first be differentiated:

- The control functions f_n
- The monitoring functions $f_{\ddot{U}n}$
- The microcontroller monitoring functions

When this is done, the reliability block diagrams for these different functions can easily be determined (Fig. 5-19).

To determine system reliability, all three of these functions will be challenged at the same time. Accordingly, the system reliability results from an in-series connection of these block

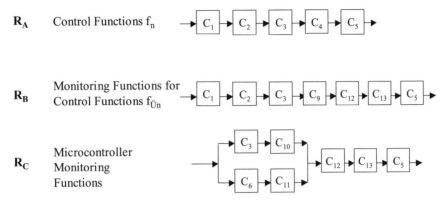

R_A Control Functions f_n

R_B Monitoring Functions for Control Functions $f_{Ün}$

R_C Microcontroller Monitoring Functions

Fig. 5-19. *Reliability block diagrams for engine management functions.*

diagrams. What is more, the components C_7 and C_8, which do not appear in the block diagrams of the individual functions, also must be connected in series.

The system reliability $R_{S\ Reliability}$ is a product of the multiplication of the reliability of the three functions $R_{x;\ x\ =\ A,B,C}$ shown in Fig. 5-19 by the reliability of components C_7 and C_8. Because $R_x < 1$, it is in any case lesser than the respective reliability of the functions R_x. When calculating system reliability, the rules for calculating with repeated elements in reliability block diagrams must be observed [54].

By contrast, assessing safety merely requires the reliable detection of a failure and the reliable transition to a safe state. The reliability $R_{S\ Safety}$ of this safety response is specified by the reliability of the monitoring functions $f_{Ün}$ or by the microcontroller monitoring functions. For this reason, it is higher than the reliability of the functions R_x. In addition, the reliability of components C_7 and C_8 does not enter into the calculation of $R_{S\ Safety}$.

As this example demonstrates, measures aimed at increasing safety can reduce system reliability. It also is evident that measures aimed at increasing reliability can cause the safety of a system to be reduced.

Although the reliability and safety analyses focus only on hardware components, they exert great influence on software development. In a distributed and networked system, for example, they influence *the assignment of software functions to microcontrollers*; in *software development*, they dictate the necessary *quality assurance measures*. For a detailed discussion of related subjects, reference is made to suggested reading and advanced literature [57, 59, 82, 83].

5.3 Specification of Software Functions and Validation of Specification

After the interfaces and sampling rates for the software functions, with their assignment to a microcontroller, have been accomplished, the next question addresses the manner in which the data and the behavior of software functions, such as the linking of input signals with algorithms for the calculation of output signals, may be specified. Topics centered on this subject are the main focus of the following sections.

Several methods may be employed in the specification of software functions. Figure 5-20 shows one classification. A differentiation must first be made between formal and informal specification methods. The former consist of strict mathematical methods used in the formulation of algorithms (i.e., methods permitting the unambiguous formulation of algorithms without leeway for interpretation). By contrast, informal methods are not subject to such strictures. For example, a formal method would be the expression of algorithms in a high-level language, whereas expressing an algorithm in colloquial language is deemed an informal method.

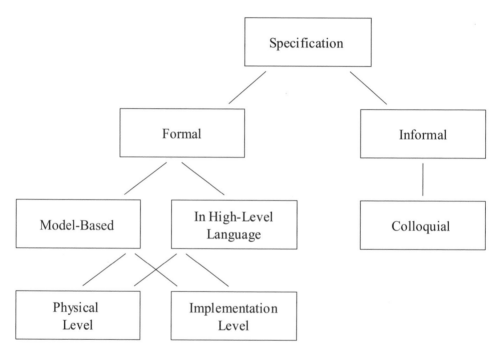

Fig. 5-20. *Outline of specification methods for software functions.*

As discussed in Section 4.6.2 of Chapter 4, simple examples may be used to demonstrate that interpretative leeway inherent in the informal description of algorithms may result in differing implementations. These, in turn, produce different results or output signals despite identical input signals. For this reason, the following discussion is restricted to the investigation of formal specification methods, in which a differentiation is made between high-level language and model-based specification methods. Examples of specification methods that are frequently used to describe software functions in vehicle development are block diagrams, decision tables, or state machines.

A third differentiation criterion is the abstraction level of the specification. Because in most cases vehicle functions are implemented by means of a technical system comprising a number of components of varying technical implementation, the specification requires a standardized abstraction level. Taking a cue from the modeling and design methods for control systems, the first step consists of the useful specification of software functions at the physical level. A detailed discussion of several methods facilitating the model-based specification of software functions appears in the following sections. This discussion initially ignores many implementation details that are defined in a subsequent design and implementation phase. These are discussed in greater detail in Section 5.4.

The consistent development of software functions—spanning the range between specification, design, and implementation—can be ensured only if software-specific requirements and prerequisites are already considered early in the process of specifying the software functions. This is reflected in the following sections, for example, which already take into account the software architecture, the definition of real-time characteristics, or the specific differentiation between data flow and control flow.

The formal specification of software functions offers additional development benefits. For example, the completed specification can be executed early on the timeline in a simulated environment, and it becomes a tangible experience in the vehicle with the aid of rapid prototyping systems, thus facilitating timely validation of the specification. In this context, a graphical model offers easier comprehension than a high-level language description. A model also may serve as a basis for common understanding among the various engineering disciplines participating in the development of software functions.

The differentiation between the physical level and the implementation level also aims at the abstraction of numerous implementation details, some of which are hardware dependent. This provides the option of using the specified software functions in a variety of vehicle projects, for example, by porting the software functions to microcontrollers using a different word length.

5.3.1 Specification of Software Architecture and Software Components

Starting with the established logical software function model with its defined real-time requirements and I/O signals, the manner in which the architecture of a given software function is visualized must be determined. The starting point is the software architecture for the microcontrollers onboard ECUs, as shown in Fig. 1-22 of Chapter 1. To handle comprehensive software functions, a suitable modularization and hierarchy concept is an indispensable necessity. Therefore, the consistent use of the component view and interface view also is needed at the software level. The definition of the interfaces for all software components used in the specification of a given software function likewise is a pivotal prerequisite for the distributed development of a software system of this type. An example of the fulfillment of this requirement, with the added benefit of reusability of the specified software components, is object-based modeling.

5.3.1.1 Object-Based Software Architecture Modeling

In view of the foregoing, the major terms related to object-based software models shall be introduced. A software system is divided into so-called *objects*, that is, software components that are at once clearly structured, independent of each other, and self-contained within themselves. The objects interact with the purpose of performing a specific task. Objects encompass the software structure and its behavior [72].

The term *structure* indicates that objects may contain *attributes* in which the object data is stored. In other words, attributes are the internal storage areas within objects. The term structure also denotes that objects may contain other objects. This type of entity relation between objects is termed *aggregation*. Therefore, the structure describes the static properties of an object.

By contrast, the term *behavior* describes the dynamic properties of an object. Interfaces are required for objects to access other objects. The interfaces of an object are defined by its so-called *public methods*. Methods are capable of adopting input data from outside an object. They also can modify object attributes or provide object output data. To modify any of the attributes of a given object, a method of that object must be called. This ensures object modularity, flexibility, and reusability. For this reason, objects are suitable for deployment in a variety of environments without side effects.

A *class* is the abstraction of a collection of similar objects. It identifies the common attributes and methods provided by each object. Objects represent copies, or *instances*, of a class. It may be said that a class is the specification for an object instantiation guideline.

Example: Calculating wheel revolutions per minute (rpm) and vehicle speed for an antilock braking system (ABS)

> The graphical visualization of object-based software models makes widespread use of the notations of the Unified Modeling Language™ (UML) [84]. Figure 5-21 shows the "Wheel" class with the "Speed n" attribute, with the methods for initialization "init_n()," computation "compute_n()," and output "out_n()" of the wheel rotational speed, in the notation of a UML class diagram. A software component of this type might be deployed in an antilock braking system (ABS).

> For the purpose of calculating the vehicle speed, a "Vehicle" class is defined. The "Vehicle" class must represent the four wheels of the vehicle. The result is a 1:4 aggregation between the "Vehicle" and "Wheel" classes.

> The "Vehicle" class also must represent the engine of the vehicle. To this end, the "Engine" class is specified. For the "Engine" class, the "Speed n" attribute for engine speed, with the methods for initialization as "init_n()," computation as "compute_n()," and output as "out_n()" of the engine speed are defined.

> Figure 5-22 shows the class model for the "Vehicle" class in UML notation. For the "Vehicle" class, the attributes "Velocity v" and "Gear g," with the methods for computation of vehicle velocity and selected gear—"compute_v()" and "compute_g()"—are defined. These calculations utilize the methods of the "Wheel" and "Engine" classes.

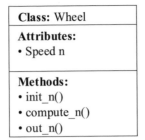

Fig. 5-21. *"Wheel" class and methods for calculating wheel rotational speed (revolutions per minute). (Ref. [84]).*

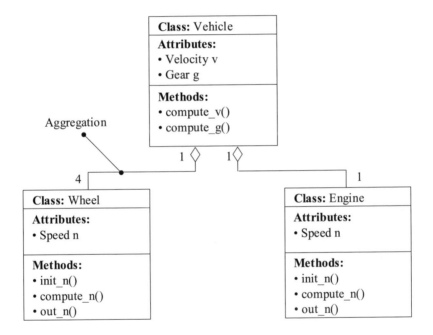

Fig. 5-22. *Class diagram for the "Vehicle" class. (Ref. [84]).*

Software models of this type are used as a basis for the visualization of contexts within software functions. In this way, for example, a software function f1 can be hierarchically assembled from software components. This is accomplished by instantiating the classes. Thus, the instantiation of the "Vehicle" class creates the object named "Vehicle_1." This object contains four instances of the "Wheel" class and one instance of the "Engine" class. The objects thus created are "RF_Wheel," "LF_Wheel," "RR_Wheel," and "LR_Wheel" for the right front, left front, right rear, and left rear wheels, respectively, plus the object "Engine_1" for the engine.

In the following sections, the representation of the software architecture including objects uses a graphical visualization similar to that shown in Fig. 5-23. The class designation of a given object is stated after the object name and is separated by a colon.

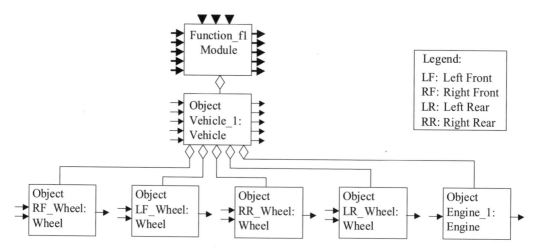

Fig. 5-23. *Graphical visualization of software architecture with object diagrams.*

5.3.1.2 Module-Based Specification of Interfaces to Real-Time Operating System

The software components at the primary hierarchy level of a software function require the definition of interfaces to the real-time operating system in the form of processes and to the communications system in the form of messages (see Fig. 2-36 in Chapter 2). Assigning these processes to tasks facilitates the specification of real-time requirements. By replicating the input and output signals of the software function in the form of messages, the communications across the boundaries of tasks or even microcontrollers can be supported.

Interfaces of this type are not required for levels other than the primary level of a software function. Therefore, the software components at the top level of a software function are termed *modules*. In the discussions to follow, modules are depicted graphically as in Figs. 5-23 and 5-24. The processes P_1 through P_m are shown as triangles. The messages M_1 through M_n are shown as arrows, with the direction of the arrowhead providing the identification of Receive and Send messages.

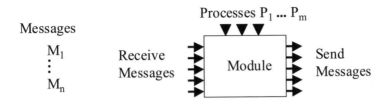

Fig. 5-24. *Graphical depiction of modules contained in the specification.*

5.3.1.3 Class-Based Specification of Reusable Software Components

At the lower levels, objects are defined that can be accessed by means of methods. A given method can be assigned interfaces in the form of several arguments and a return value. The differentiation between modules and objects in conjunction with software components facilitates the reuse of objects in a variety of contexts through the instantiation of classes. In the discussions to follow, classes and objects are graphically depicted as shown in Fig. 5-25 [73]. Arguments are shown as arrows that point at the class or object. Return values are shown as arrows that point away from the class or object.

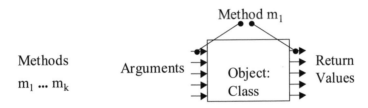

Fig. 5-25. *Graphical depiction of classes and objects contained in the specification.*

As an alternative to the visualization of the function architecture shown in Fig. 5-23, the following discussion also may use the block diagram as shown in Fig. 5-26. In addition to showing the aggregation and hierarchy relationships, this diagram also provides for the inclusion of the data flows and control flows between methods and arguments and/or return values of object methods. These paths are shown in the form of lines in Fig. 5-26.

Depending on the type of context that must be described, several different modeling techniques are suited to the specification of the behavior of modules and classes. Block diagrams, decision tables, and state machines are among the most important techniques.

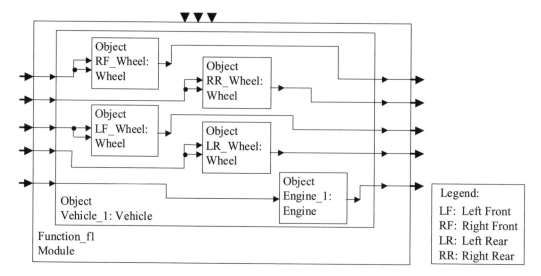

Fig. 5-26. *Graphical depiction of software architecture with block diagrams. (Ref. [73]).*

5.3.2 Specification of Data Model

The task of specifying the data model for a software component also begins at the physical level. In object-based modeling, the data are presented by the attributes of objects and/or modules.

5.3.3 Specification of Behavioral Model Using Block Diagrams

If the data flow is featured in the formulation of the behavior of a software component, block diagrams are suited to graphical visualization. This occurs frequently at the abstract level. For this reason, numerous interrelations between software components discussed in the preceding chapters of this book were depicted in the form of block diagrams.

Block diagrams also can be used to provide a clearly structured visualization of complex algorithms within a software component, allowing for differentiation between arithmetic and Boolean functions.

5.3.3.1 Specification of Arithmetical Functions

As an example of the specification of arithmetic algorithms, the integration method according to Euler (see Fig. 4-36 in Chapter 4) shall be continued with the use of block diagrams.

Example: Specification of "Integrator" class

The integration method according to Euler is frequently employed as an approximation procedure for the calculation of integrals.

The calculation of the definite integral of function $f(t)$

$$F(t_n) = \int_{t_0}^{t_n} f(t)\,dt \tag{5.4}$$

is approximated by the sum of

$$F^*(t_n) = \sum_{i=0}^{n-1} (t_{i+1} - t_i) \cdot f(t_i) \tag{5.5}$$

The distance $(t_{i+1} - t_i)$ is termed *step size* dT_i.

$F^*(t_{i+1})$ may be calculated incrementally using the equation

$$F^*(t_{i+1}) = F^*(t_i) + dT_i \cdot f(t_i) \tag{5.6}$$

Because this integration method is deployed repeatedly and with varying context, it shall be specified as a class in the form of a block diagram. This causes a number of additional requirements to be imposed on this software component:

- It shall be possible to weight the integration of an input variable "in" with a constant K, and the current integration value shall be stored in the variable labeled *memory*.

- The integration value *memory* shall have an upper boundary of MX and a lower boundary of MN.

- The integration value in, integration constant K, and the boundaries MN and MX are specified as default arguments for the "compute()" method. In this way, the "compute()" method calculates the current integration value, using the equation

$$\text{memory}(t_{i+1}) = \text{memory}(t_i) + K \cdot dT \cdot \text{in}(t_i) \tag{5.7}$$

and subsequently limits the same by means of boundaries MN and MX.

- The step size dT comprises the interval that has elapsed since the preceding execution of the "compute()" method; the same value was termed execution rate in Fig. 2-18 of Chapter 2. The real-time operating system shall calculate and provide the step-size dT for each task.

- Using a second method labeled "out()," it shall be possible to output the current integration value labeled *memory* independently of the integration calculation.

- An "init()" method is required for the initialization of *memory* with the initialization value IV, which is transferred in the form of an argument.

- The methods "init()" and/or "compute()" shall be executed, depending on a Boolean argument I or E, which is in each case transferred to these methods in the form of an additional argument.

A visualization of this integrator in the form of a block diagram in the ASCET tool [73] appears in Fig. 5-27. Arithmetical and Boolean data flows are depicted by solid and dashed arrows, respectively, whereas control flows are represented by dash-and-dot arrows.

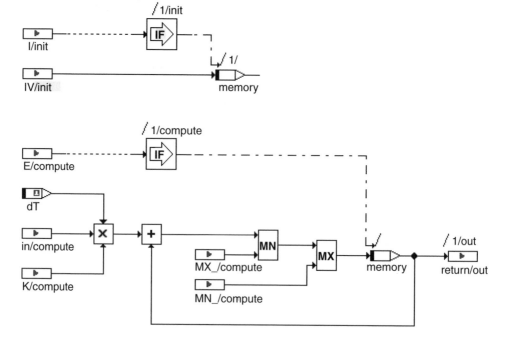

Fig. 5-27. *Specification of the "Integrator" class as a block diagram in the ASCET tool. (Ref. [73]).*

Figure 5-28 shows the external view of this software component. The assignment of arguments to the methods "init()," "compute()," and "out()" is depicted in Fig. 5-27.

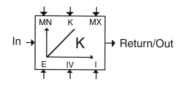

Fig. 5-28. *External view of the "Integrator" class in the ASCET tool. (Ref. [73]).*

Note that the arithmetic algorithms were defined at the physical level. Thus, the preceding example does not reflect any definitions about the subsequent implementation, such as a definition of the word length or a decision regarding fixed or floating-point arithmetic. For this reason, a software component specified in this manner may be ported to a variety of microcontrollers. Another procedure that occurs at the physical level is the limitation of the integration value. It is performed also in the context of implementation with floating-point arithmetic and may not be confused with possible limitations in the context of the implementation of overflow or underflow treatment in integer arithmetic. However, the sequential order of the individual arithmetic operations, or control flow, has already been defined.

5.3.3.2 Specification of Boolean Functions

Aside from the specification of arithmetic operations, block diagrams also can be used in the definition of logical operations, or so-called *Boolean operations*. In many cases (i.e., when actions depend on Boolean arguments taking the form of "IF … THEN" relations), a combination of Boolean operations and arithmetical operations is needed to describe a function.

A Boolean variable can assume only the values of the two elements of set B = {TRUE, FALSE}. Boolean variables can be linked to Boolean operators to form Boolean arguments. For the Boolean operators *conjunction* (logical AND operation), *disjunction* (logical OR operation), and *negation* (logical NOT operation), the following sections make use of the graphical symbols—also termed *switching functions*—shown in Fig. 5-29.

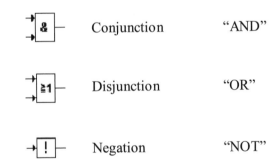

Fig. 5-29. *Graphical symbols for the switching functions in the ASCET tool. (Ref. [73]).*

Example: Specification of Boolean arguments using block diagrams

The specification of Boolean arguments with the use of symbols representing switching functions is also termed *switching network*. Figure 5-30 shows a switching network visualizing two Boolean arguments in the form of a block diagram in the ASCET tool [73].

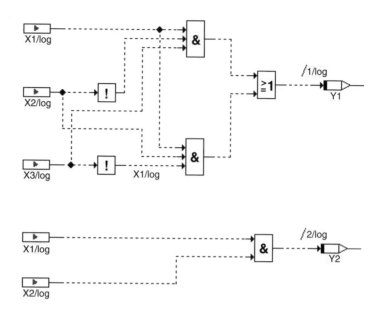

Fig. 5-30. *Specification of Boolean instructions as a block diagram in the ASCET tool. (Ref. [73])*

5.3.4 Specification of Behavioral Model Using Decision Tables

As an alternative, any actions whose execution depends on the compliance or noncompliance with several conditions lend themselves to a compact and clearly structured definition by means of so-called *decision tables* [72, 73]. The input and/or output variables of a decision table comprise Boolean variables X1 through Xn and/or Y1 through Ym, respectively.

Each of the input variables X1 through Xn, also termed *conditions*, are shown as columns in the decision table. Thus, each row of input variables in the decision table represents a conjunction—or logical AND function—of the input variables in the columns. Therefore, a row comprises a Boolean argument, the so-called *rule* R, whose truth value determines the output variables Y1 through Ym, which also are termed *actions*. These output variables are shown as additional columns in the decision table.

A maximum of 2^n combinations can be formed between n input variables. Therefore, the complete decision table encompasses 2^n rows or rules. The output values are assigned to one or more rules. In the event that one output variable is assigned to several rules, this represents a disjunction—or logical OR operation—of the respective rules. Figure 5-31 shows the Boolean arguments taken from Fig. 5-30 in the form of a decision table. Thus, the specifications in Figs. 5-30 and 5-31 are equivalent.

Decision tables can be optimized by the same procedure used for Boolean arguments. Thus, in Fig. 5-31, only the last three rules R6 through R8 are of relevance, because only these rules determine whether or not one of the actions Y1 or Y2 will be executed (Fig. 5-32).

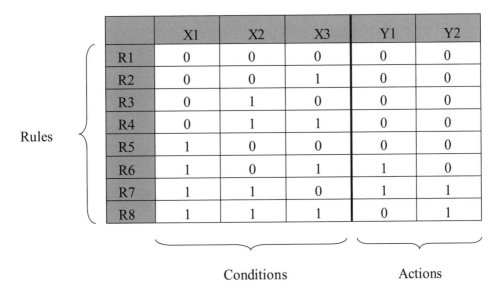

	X1	X2	X3	Y1	Y2
R1	0	0	0	0	0
R2	0	0	1	0	0
R3	0	1	0	0	0
R4	0	1	1	0	0
R5	1	0	0	0	0
R6	1	0	1	1	0
R7	1	1	0	1	1
R8	1	1	1	0	1

Rules

Conditions — Actions

Fig. 5-31. *Specification of Boolean instructions as a decision table.*

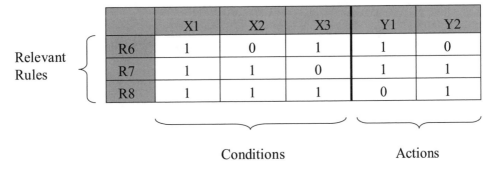

	X1	X2	X3	Y1	Y2
R6	1	0	1	1	0
R7	1	1	0	1	1
R8	1	1	1	0	1

Relevant Rules

Conditions — Actions

Fig. 5-32. *Optimizing the decision table.*

If a given action occurs repeatedly in different rules, the decision table can be further optimized. Initially, the rules for this action are examined in pairs. Both rules can be combined in an OR circuit. Therefore, if both rules differ only in a single condition, they can be simplified because this means that the differing condition is irrelevant. In Fig. 5-32, each of the actions Y1 and Y2 occurs twice. In the case of action Y2, the two rules differ only in condition X3, rendering the condition irrelevant. It follows that further simplification is possible at this point. Irrelevant conditions are marked with an asterisk character (" * ") in the decision table (Fig. 5-33). However, action Y1 does not provide for further optimization.

A number of decision tables also may be linked sequentially, as shown in Fig. 5-34.

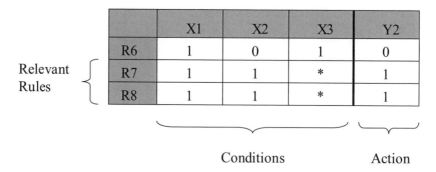

	X1	X2	X3	Y2
R6	1	0	1	0
R7	1	1	*	1
R8	1	1	*	1

Relevant Rules

Conditions   Action

Fig. 5-33. *Optimizing the decision table for action Y2.*

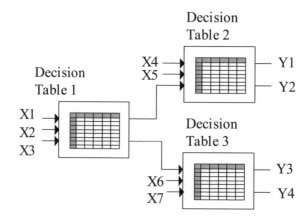

Fig. 5-34. *Sequential linking of decision tables.*

Decision tables are ideally suited to the specification of functions in which a number of combined conditions cause the execution of a number of different actions.

Interrelations of this type are a frequent occurrence in monitoring functions. For a detailed discussion of decision tables, reference is made to suggested reading and advanced literature ([72, 73]).

5.3.5 *Specification of Behavioral Model Using State Machines*

In many software functions, the result depends not only on the inputs but also on an event and the history up to that point. Interactions of this type are suitable for description by means of state machines. The state machines discussed in this section take their orientation from the finite state machines according to Moore, Mealy, and Harel [72, 73, 85].

State machines may be drawn as state diagrams, where the *states* are shown as labeled rectangles with rounded corners. Available *transitions* are represented by arrows with text labels. The occurrence of a transition depends on a *condition* that is assigned to that transition. Depending on the current state or the performed transition, an *action*—assigned to a state or a transition—may be performed.

The conditions and actions may be specified in several ways, that is, either in the form of a block diagram or decision table, or even as an underlying state machine. As an alternative, the specification of conditions and actions also may be written in a high-level language.

5.3.5.1 Specifying Flat State Machines

As an example of the specification of software functions by means of state machines, the control of the low-fuel indicator lamp (see Fig. 2-9 in Chapter 2) shall be continued here.

Example: Specification for controlling low-fuel indicator lamp by means of state machine

For the specification of the low-fuel indicator lamp control to this end, only the conditions "Signal value > 8.5V" and/or "Signal value < 8.0 V" and the previous state "Lamp Off" or "Lamp On" are deemed relevant (Fig. 5-35).

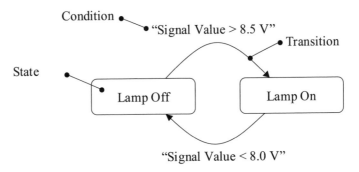

Fig. 5-35. Specification of states, transitions, and conditions.

- So far, no point in time for the execution of the so-called *actions* "Switch Lamp On" and "Switch Lamp Off" has been defined. As is the case with conditions, these actions can be assigned to the transitions, and the applicable term is *transition actions*. State machines of this type are known as *Mealy state machines*. As an alternative, the actions may be assigned to the states, the applicable term being *state actions*. State machines of this type are known as *Moore state machines*. Mealy and Moore state machines also can be combined, that is, actions may be assigned to states and transitions. To suit the purpose of this example, the actions "Switch Lamp On" and "Switch Lamp Off" shall be assigned to the transitions.

- In addition, the state that the state machine occupies at the start requires definition. This state is termed *start state*. To monitor the functioning of the low-fuel indicator lamp, the definition will specify that the lamp must be energized for a specific time period each time the engine of the vehicle is started. In this way, the proper functioning of the lamp is confirmed independently of the actual fuel level. The first possible state transition shall occur only after a two-second delay, that is, the lamp shall remain illuminated for a minimum of two seconds after starting the engine. For this reason, a new state labeled "Function Check," with a transition to the start state "Lamp On," is introduced. As a result, the action "Switch Lamp On" is executed in the "Function Check" state. The start state in a state machine is marked with an "(S)."

Figure 5-36 shows the state machine enhanced by means of the preceding procedure.

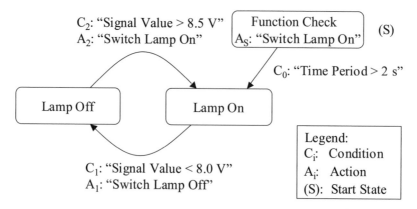

Fig. 5-36. *Assignment of actions and definition of start state.*

The following differentiations can be made when assigning actions to a state:

- Actions executed only upon entry into a state (entry actions)
- Actions executed upon exiting a state (exit actions)
- Actions executed while dwelling in a state (static action)

Figure 5-37 demonstrates that an entry action is the equivalent of a transition action that is assigned to all transitions leading to a given state. Similarly, the exit action of a state is the equivalent of a transition action that is assigned to all transitions leading away from a given state.

If there is only one state transition between each state for each set of input variables, the behavior of state machines is said to be deterministic.

Nondeterministic situations may arise, for example, if several conditions of different transitions leading away from a state are true at the same time. Situations of this type may be excluded

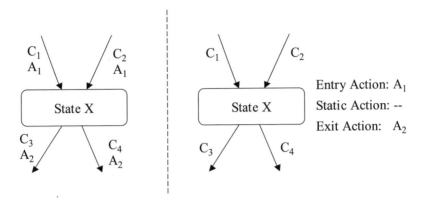

Fig. 5-37. *Equivalent actions in state machines.*

through the assignment of priorities, that is, by assigning a different priority to a transition leading away from a state. The priority levels are normally specified with the use of numerals. In our example, a higher number indicates a higher priority.

In Fig. 5-38, three transitions lead away from state X. If condition C_2 were true, the behavior of the state machine pictured in the left half of the diagram would not be deterministic because two transitions would be possible. The introduction of a priority, as shown in the right half of the diagram, defines the execution of the transition with priority (3), with the execution of action A_2.

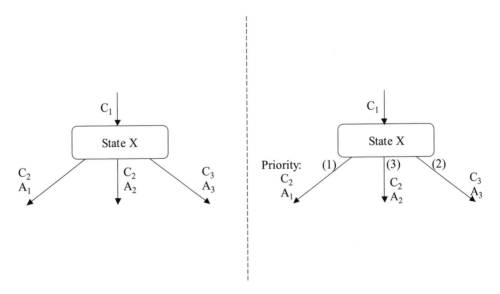

Fig. 5-38. *Deterministic state machines through priority assignment.*

A state machine also requires the definition of a so-called *event* at which the conditions of the transitions leading away from the current state are verified and, if applicable, at which the respective actions and transitions are executed. In Fig. 5-39, for example, this *event*, which triggers the calculations in the state machine, is specified by the "trigger()" method that is assigned to each transition.

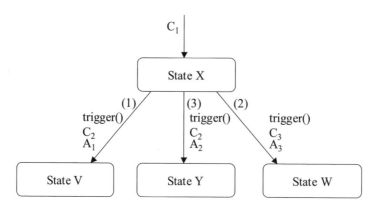

Fig. 5-39. *The "trigger()" method for state machine calculation.*

Each time the "trigger()" method is called, the following calculations are performed:

- Verification, by descending priority, of conditions for the transitions leading away from the current state

- If a condition is TRUE

    - Execution of exit action of current state
    - Execution of transition action of transition
    - Execution of entry action of new state
    - Transition to new state

- If none of the conditions is TRUE

    - Execution of static action of current state

This demonstrates that a maximum of one state transition is executed each time the "trigger()" method is called.

5.3.5.2 Specifying Transitions with Branching Instructions

If conditions such as those taking the form C_1 and C_2, and/or C_1 and C_3 occur at transitions leading away from the same state, this may be more clearly structured with the use of branched transitions and junction points. Both diagrams in Fig. 5-40 are equivalent.

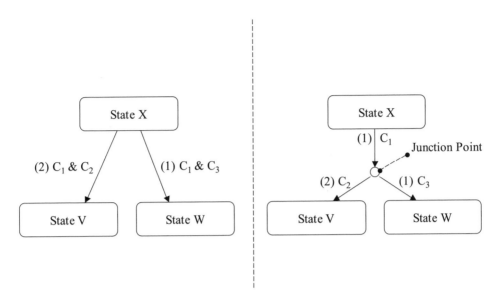

Fig. 5-40. *Equivalent state transition modeling.*

5.3.5.3 Specifying Hierarchy State Machines

With a rising number of states and transitions, state diagrams quickly become complex and confusing. However, clarity can be maintained through the use of hierarchically nested states, which results in hierarchical state diagrams that differentiate between base states and hierarchy states:

- For each hierarchy state, a base state is defined as a start state. Those transitions that lead to a hierarchy state cause a transition to this start state.

- As an alternative, a hierarchy state with a memory may be defined. Each transition leading to a hierarchy state marked "H" for "History" causes the last active base state to again be assumed in this hierarchy state. Thus, the start state defines the base state for the first entry into the hierarchy state.

Transitions also may be defined across hierarchical boundaries. Therefore, the priority of transitions leading away from a base state must be unambiguously differentiated from those leading away from a hierarchy state. The same is true of the sequence in which the actions defined for hierarchy state and base state are executed.

Figure 5-41 shows an example of a hierarchy state machine. States X, Y, and Z are defined at the highest hierarchical level. State X is also the start state. States V and W comprise base states of hierarchy state Z. Therefore, the transition from state Y to hierarchy state Z leads to a transition into this start state V, which also is true of the direct transition from state X to state V, across the hierarchical boundary of state Z.

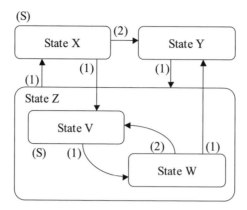

Fig. 5-41. *Hierarchy state machine.*

For a detailed discussion, reference is made to suggested reading and advanced literature [73].

5.3.6 Specification of Behavioral Model Using High-Level Languages

In many cases, the use of a high-level language is the preferred manner of defining the behavior of a software component. This applies especially to situations where the formulation of a behavior lends itself only to a cumbersome or unintelligible data flow-oriented or state-based description. With their numerous loops and branches, search or sorting algorithms serve as a case in point.

Example: Specification of "Integrator" software component in the C programming language

>   Figure 5-42 shows the methods used by the "Integrator" software component from Fig. 5-27 in C language notation [76].

5.3.7 Specification of Real-Time Model

In addition to the specification of the data model and behavioral model for a software compo-nent, specification of the real-time model is required (see Figs. 4-31 and 4-32 in Chapter 4). If a real-time operating system is used, its configuration must be defined. Aside from the various operating modes, transitions, and transitional conditions, the specification of the arbitration strategy, as well as the task process list for each operating mode, must be defined.

The specification of real-time requirements can be separated from the behavioral specification of models and classes by means of the process and message interfaces, as well as the calculation of the step size dT.

```
/* Variables */

extern real64 memory;

extern real64 dT;


/* Method compute() */

void compute (real64 in, real64 K, real64 MN, real64 MX, sint8 E)

{

  real64  temp_1;

  if E {

    temp_1 = memory + in * (K * dT);

    if (temp_1 > MX){

      temp_1  = MX;

    }

    if (temp_1 < MN){

      temp_1  = MN;

    }

    memory = temp_1;

  }

}


/* Method out() */

real64 out (void)

{

  return (memory);

}


/* Method init() */

void init (real64 IV, sint8 I)

{

  if I{

    memory = IV;

  }

}
```

Fig. 5-42. *Method specification of "Integrator" class in C language [76].*

The initialization process and cyclical processes for the various operating modes also must be defined.

5.3.8 Validating the Specification Through Simulation and Rapid Prototyping

The analysis of software requirements and their formal specification (e.g., by means of software models) frequently are not detailed enough to provide a sufficiently clear idea of the software system to be developed or to facilitate an advance estimate of the required development expenditures. For this reason, efforts often are aimed at deploying methods and tools permitting an animation or simulation of the formally specified software functions. The same efforts extend to making the referenced functions tangible in the vehicle, thus providing a means of early validation of a software function.

The computer-based replication and execution of a function is termed *simulation*. By contrast, the execution of a software function on a so-called *experimental system* (i.e., a computer that is interconnected with the vehicle through interfaces) is termed *rapid prototyping*.

In the event that the software model is to be used as a basis for simulation and rapid prototyping processes, model compilers are required. These facilitate the direct or indirect translation of the specification model into machine code suitable for execution on a simulation or experimental system. In this process, the design decisions required for the model compiler either are implicitly defined in the model or are initially formulated by the model compiler in a manner ensuring the most accurate replication of the specified model.

Figure 5-43 shows the organization of a rapid prototyping tool [73]. Initially specified with the use of a modeling tool, the software function model is in the first step translated in source code by a model compiler. In a second step, a compiler tool set translates this source code into a program version and data version for the experimental system. Program and data versions are then downloaded to the experimental system by means of a download tool or Flash programming tool, rendering them "ready to run." The subsequent program execution can be controlled, parameterized, animated, and observed by means of a so-called *experimentation tool*.

In this case, the software models, in addition to representing the basis for the subsequent design and implementation, also provide the foundation for simulation and rapid prototyping methods. The use of an experimental system allows for the validation of software functions that is both timely and independent of the ECU. As an added benefit, the experimental system can subsequently serve as a reference for ECU verification.

5.3.8.1 Simulation

In many cases, the purpose of the simulation is not merely the replication of the software function per se; beyond this, the focus is also on the interaction among the software functions with the hardware, with setpoint generators, sensors, and actuators, and with the plant.

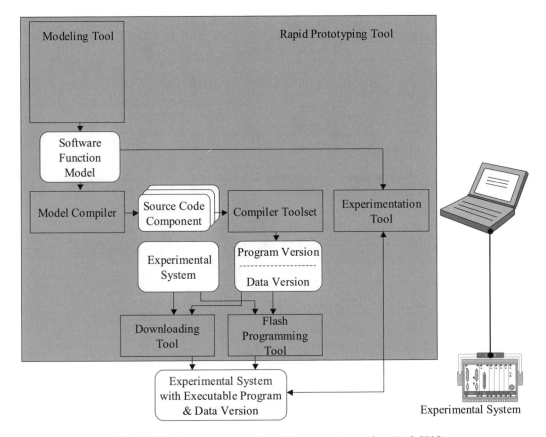

Fig. 5-43. *Organization of rapid prototyping tools. (Ref. [73])*

This means that modeling also must be carried out for these elements which, from the viewpoint of software development, are termed *environmental components*. The result is a virtual vehicle, driver, and environmental model that is linked to both virtual ECU model and software model. This model can then be run on a simulation system such as a PC (Fig. 5-44). This approach, also termed *model-in-the-loop simulation*, likewise is suited to the development of vehicle functions that are not software implemented.

The details of modeling practices and the simulation of environmental components would exceed the scope of this book. For a detailed discussion of these subjects, reference is made to suggested reading and advanced literature [35].

5.3.8.2 Rapid Prototyping

Because the automobile industry uses the term *prototype* in a variety of contexts, its use in conjunction with software development requires a more accurate definition and demarcation.

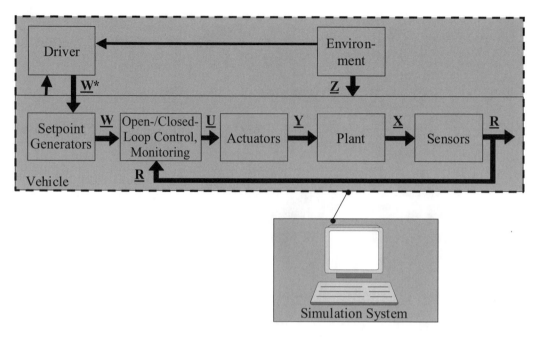

Fig. 5-44. *Modeling and simulation of software functions and environmental components.*

In vehicle manufacture, it is generally held that a prototype represents the first sample of a large series of products (i.e., of a mass-produced commodity). A software prototype is characterized by the differentiation that the duplication of a software product does not present any technical issues.

Generally speaking, a prototype is a technical model of a new product. In this context, a differentiation can be made between nonfunctional prototypes (e.g., aerodynamic models for wind tunnel use), functional prototypes (e.g., prototype vehicles or studies), and pre-series prototypes (e.g., pilot series vehicles).

In the context of the discussion throughout this book, a *software prototype* is always deemed a functional prototype that demonstrates software functions—although with varying purpose and application—in situations of practical deployment. In the same context, the designation *rapid prototyping* describes a collection of methods dedicated to the specification and execution of software functions in the physical vehicle, as shown in Fig. 5-45. A variety of methods are discussed in the following sections. On one hand, these are methods that use development ECUs (shaded gray). On the other hand, these are methods designated for use on experimental systems.

Because of the interfaces to the physical vehicle, the execution of the software functions on the experimental system must comply with real-time requirements. The experimental systems used for this purpose are mostly real-time computer systems whose computing power far exceeds that of the ECUs. This dispenses—at least initially—with the need for software optimization due to

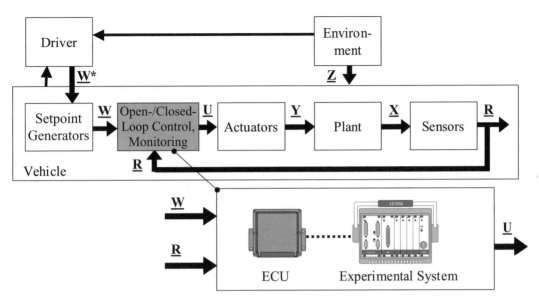

Fig. 5-45. *Rapid prototyping of software functions in the physical vehicle.*

hardware resource limitations. Given this circumstance, the model compiler is able to translate the model with the assumption of standardized design and implementation decisions. It must be ensured, however, that the specified behavior is replicated as accurately as possible.

Modular experimental systems can be configured to suit specific applications (e.g., to accommodate the required interfaces for input and output signals). The entire system is designed for in-vehicle use and is operated via a PC, for example. In this way, the specifications of software functions are available for immediate in-vehicle validation and modification as required. At the same time, modifications made to the program version and data version also may be carried out.

5.3.8.3 Horizontal and Vertical Prototypes

Prototype development differentiates between two procedural objectives:

1. *Horizontal prototypes* aim at the representation of a broad range of a given software system. However, they provide only an abstract view and neglect details.

2. *Vertical prototypes* provide a very detailed representation of a limited area of the software system.

Using a section of a software system, Fig. 5-46 depicts the procedural objectives of horizontal and vertical prototypes.

Software Architecture   Horizontal Prototype   Vertical Prototype

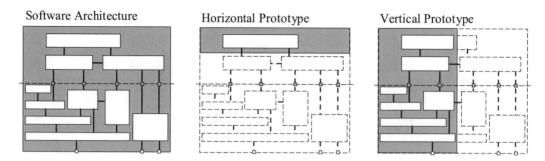

Fig. 5-46. *Horizontal and vertical prototypes of a software system.*

Example: Development of a horizontal prototype in the "Bypass" mode

Early on the timeline, a new software function must be in-vehicle tested and validated. Therefore, for the time being, issues concerning details of the subsequent implementation in the software system of the production ECU, such as its software architecture, are deemed irrelevant.

This problem can be solved by developing a horizontal prototype. The software function is specified by a physical model. Many aspects of prototype implementation are implicitly predefined either by the model itself or the model compiler.

Such an approach can be supported by employing the so-called *Bypass mode* in function development. As a prerequisite, an ECU must provide a fully validated basic functionality of the software system, operate all of the sensors and actuators, and support a so-called *bypass interface* to an experimental system. The functional concept is developed with the aid of a rapid prototyping tool and is executed on the experimental system in Bypass mode (Fig. 5-47).

This approach also is suited to the further development of existing ECU functions. In such a case, the existing functions are still calculated in the ECU but are modified in such a way that the input values are transmitted through the bypass interface, and the output values of the newly developed bypass function are used.

The required modifications on the ECU side are termed *bypass implementation* or *bypass hooks*.

In many cases, the calculation of the bypass function is triggered by the ECU through a control flow interface (labeled "Trigger" in Fig. 5-47). The ECU monitors the output values of the bypass function for plausibility. In this case, both the ECU and experimental system are running synchronized. As an alternative, unsynchronized communications—without the trigger—can be implemented.

When working with safety-relevant functions, the ECU is able to respond to incoming implausible output values with an automatic switchover to the existing internal function or to substitute values as a fallback level. For example, this is the case when the bypass

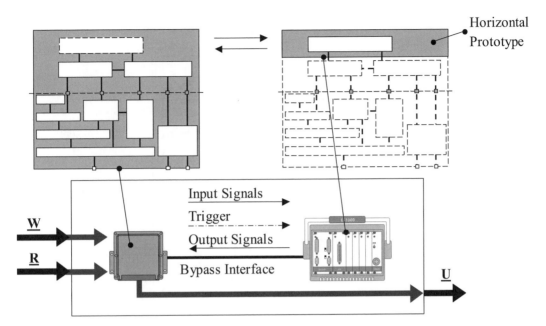

Horizontal Prototype

Input Signals

Trigger

Output Signals

Bypass Interface

W

R

U

Fig. 5-47. Prototype development using a bypass system.

function supplies illegal output values; it also may occur in the event of a communications failure between the experimental system and ECU, or if the calculation of the bypass function requires an excessive amount of time.

The use of such a monitoring concept can ensure that, during field trials and test drives, even a failure of the experimental system would result in only a limited personal injury hazard or risk of damage to any of the components of the vehicle. Thus, it is demonstrated that the function development in Bypass mode also can be deployed in the validation of safety-relevant functions.

In the context of *bypass communications*, remember that a software function onboard the ECU is often divided into several processes, which are calculated in separate tasks. In such cases, the bypass communications must support the respective sampling rates of the various tasks. Figure 5-48 shows a typical bypass communications sequence for a given sampling rate between development ECU and experimental system.

Example: Development of a vertical prototype in "Fullpass" mode

If a new function must be developed from scratch, or if an ECU equipped with a bypass interface is not available, then the experimental system can be used to develop a vertical prototype. In this case, the experimental system must support all of the sensor and actuator interfaces required by the respective function. Also required is the definition of the real-time behavior, adherence to which must be ensured by the experimental system (Fig. 5-49).

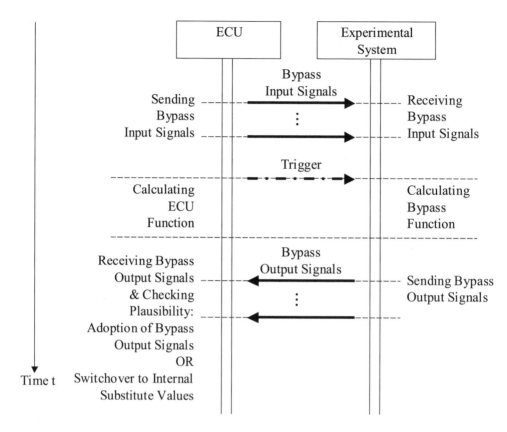

Fig. 5-48. *Communications between the ECU and experimental system.*

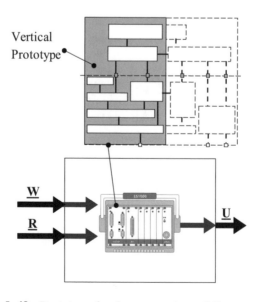

Fig. 5-49. *Prototype development using a fullpass system.*

Bypass applications are preferred in cases where only a few software functions must be developed, and where an ECU with validated software functions—such as one used in a previous project—is available. This ECU then must be modified to enable the support of a bypass interface. Bypass applications are suited to situations of high complexity, such as cases where extensive sensor and actuator systems integrated in an ECU can be provided by an experimental system only at high cost. For example, this would be true of an engine ECU.

If such an ECU is not available and additional sensors and actuators must to be validated given the presence of sensor and actuator systems of limited complexity, fullpass applications are often preferred. In such cases, the real-time behavior must be ensured by the fullpass computer of the experimental system and may require additional monitoring. For this reason, a real-time operating system is normally running on the fullpass computer.

Because hybrid forms of bypass and fullpass systems offer a high degree of attainable flexibility, these often are employed (Fig. 5-50). This facilitates the integration of additional sensors and actuators. On an experimental system so equipped, new software functions can be tested and then executed together with the existing software functions of the ECU.

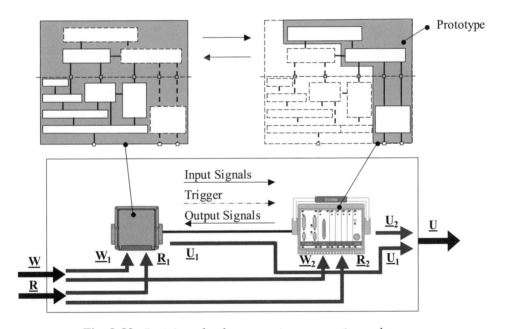

Fig. 5-50. *Prototype development using an experimental system.*

When compared with a development ECU, an experimental system provides significantly more computing power. Therefore, many requirements that would need to be considered in the context of implementing a software function on the ECU—such as fixed-point arithmetic or limited hardware resources—may be safely ignored. Thus, modifications to the software functions become simpler and quicker. Also, the integration of additional I/O interfaces in experimental systems facilitates the early evaluation of various implementation alternatives (i.e., in the case of sensors and actuators).

5.3.8.4 Target System Identical Prototypes

In most instances, the development for series production calls for the highest possible degree of congruence between the behavior of the experimental system and the ECU. Only in such cases will the experiences gathered with the prototype be similar to the behavior to be expected by the subsequent implementation in the production ECU. It need not be emphasized that any deviation between the experimental system and the ECU—as the target system—represents a development risk.

For example, a high degree of congruence with respect to the real-time behavior of the experimental system and ECU can be achieved by deploying a real-time system—e.g., according to OSEK—on both platforms. In such a case, the real-time behavior prototype is said to be *target system-identical*. Also, explicitly specified design decisions, as in the subsequent implementation on the ECU, and their consideration in prototype implementation, contribute to reducing the development risk. Rapid prototyping methods exhibiting this orientation also are known as target system-identical prototyping.

5.3.8.5 Throw-Away and Evolutionary Prototypes

Another decision criterion determines whether or not a prototype shall be used as a basis for product development. If the answer is positive, the prototype is said to be *evolutionary*. If the answer is negative, the designation *throw-away prototype* is used. For example, a prototype that is used exclusively in functional or engineering specifications is deemed a throw-away prototype because its results fail to become part and parcel of the completed product. The automotive industry makes widespread use of both approaches. The most well-known example of an evolutionary approach to development is the progression of A-, B-, C-, and D-samples for ECU hardware and software (Figs. 5-51 and 5-52).

With the deployment of experimental systems, the development progress is accompanied by the switchover to a development ECU. The validated specification provides the basis for design and implementation accounting for every last detail of the microcontroller.

This transition is becoming increasingly fluid because the use of code-generating technologies provides for the generation of source code for experimental systems and/or ECUs from a single software model. The process also allows for the consideration of many implementation details already on the experimental system.

5.3.8.6 Reference Prototype for ECU Verification

Target system identical prototyping provides for the use of a software function validated with the bypass method as a test reference for the verification of the corresponding ECU function that has been implemented by means of automated code generation. To accomplish this, a software

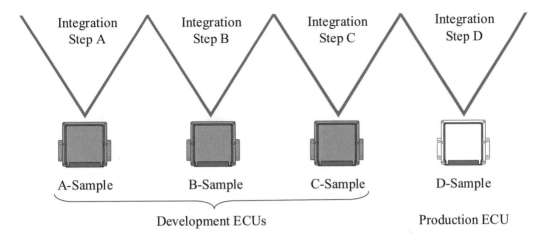

Fig. 5-51. *Evolutionary prototype development using development ECUs.*

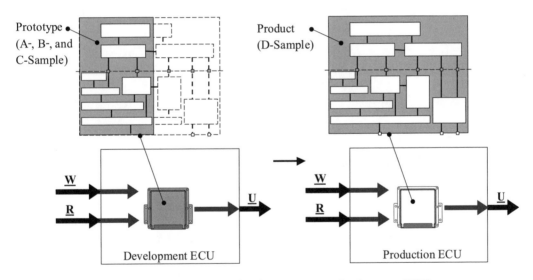

Fig. 5-52. *Evolutionary development using development ECUs.*

function is calculated in parallel and in synchronization on both the ECU and experimental system. The experimental system is used to compare the intermediate and output variables of a software function calculated in the ECU with the results obtained by the bypass function. To this end, the bypass communications must be extended, as depicted in Fig. 5-53.

In conjunction with this technique, a high degree of test coverage may be achieved through the additional deployment of code coverage analysis tools on the experimental system.

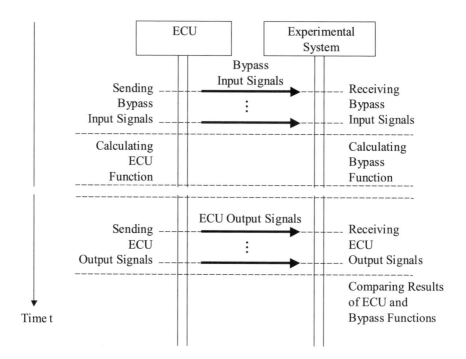

Fig. 5-53. *Verifying the ECU function by comparing the bypass function of an experimental system.*

5.4 Design and Implementation of Software Functions

Before the software functions specified at the physical level can be implemented on a microcontroller, design decisions are required. This also involves the consideration of the nonfunctional product properties for production ECUs, such as the separation of program and data versions, implementation of program and data variants, support for the required offboard interfaces, implementation of algorithms in floating-point integer arithmetic, or the optimization of required hardware resources. To a degree, these nonfunctional requirements also have repercussions on the specification, necessitating an iterative and cooperative approach between specification and design. One example of this would be the objective to prevent, as early as possible in the specification, the need for the resource-intensive characteristic curves and maps discussed in Section 5.4.1.5.

The following sections discuss methods and tools for the design and implementation of software architecture, and the data model and behavioral model of software functions.

5.4.1 Consideration of Requested Nonfunctional Product Properties

As a major example of nonfunctional product properties, the first item to be examined in detail is the influence exerted on software engineering by cost barriers for electronic in-vehicle systems. As a consequence, frequent limitations of hardware resource often have a restrictive effect on available options when mapping physically specified software functions to numerical algorithms. This section presents examples of a variety of optimization measures aimed at reducing required hardware resources. The implementation of data variants is discussed in the context of data model implementation.

5.4.1.1 Runtime Optimization Through Consideration of Varying Access Times to Different Memory Segments

Often, access times for the various memory segments of a microcontroller (i.e., RAM, ROM, or Flash memory) are different. The consequence may be an influence on the program runtime that is anything but negligible. When designing the software, a runtime optimized solution may be obtained by depositing frequently executed program sections, such as interpolation routines for characteristic curves and maps, in memory segments featuring short access times. In the case of software components that are deployed on a variety of platforms, this requirement may be met by means of appropriate configuration options.

Example: Architecture of ERCOS^EK real-time operating system [86]

Through its modular structure, the architecture of the ERCOS^EK real-time operating system [86] allows for a variety of access times to different memory segments. Figure 5-54 demonstrates the storage of individual components of the operating system in different memory segments of the microcontroller.

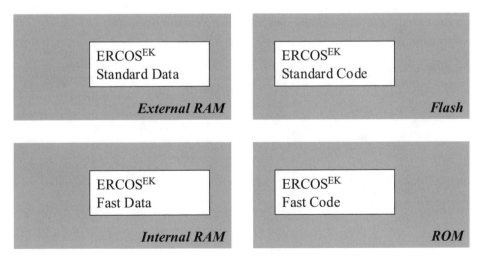

Fig. 5-54. *Example of memory configuration of ERCOS^EK real-time operating system. (Ref. [86])*

Because the execution of program code from the ROM of microcontrollers is characteristically faster than that from Flash memory, frequently called routines of the operating system are bundled in the ERCOS^{EK} Fast Code component and deposited in ROM. Routines subject to less frequent calls are bundled in the ERCOS^{EK} Standard Code component and may be deposited in Flash memory. Depending on access frequency, the data structures of the operating system also may be assigned to the various RAM segments (i.e., internal or external RAM) with different access times.

5.4.1.2 Runtime Optimization Through Distribution of Software Function to Several Tasks

Another runtime optimization measure consists of splitting a software function into several tasks to which different real-time requirements are assigned. The sampling rate needed for the execution of a subfunction depends on the physical characteristics of the plant. For example, temperature changes in the ambient atmosphere occur slowly, whereas internal pressure fluctuations manifest themselves almost instantly. In such cases, any subfunctions depending on changes in the ambient air temperature may be assigned to a "slow" task; subfunctions depending on internal pressure readings must be executed by a "faster" task.

Example: Distribution of a software function to several tasks

Figure 5-55 shows the division of a software function into three Subfunctions a, b, and c that are assigned to Tasks A, B, and C. The tasks have different activation rates. Task A is activated every 100 ms, Task B every 10 ms, and Task C every 20 ms. Subfunction a calculates an intermediate variable that is communicated via message X to Task B, where it is subject to further use by Subfunction b. Subfunction c calculates message Y, which is also used in Subfunction b. Compared with the calculation in the "faster" Task B, this provides for a reduction of the required runtime, provided the net time savings are not exceeded by the required "additional" runtime of inter-task communications.

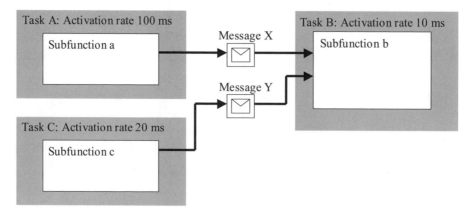

Fig. 5-55. *Distribution of software functions to several tasks, and specification of message-based inter-task communications. (Ref. [86])*

It is safe to say that many optimization measures are successful only if overall "resource costs" are reduced. For example, in many instances, the inevitable consequence of runtime reduction is an increase in needed memory capacity, and vice versa. This fact should be kept in mind with respect to all examples and deliberations to follow.

5.4.1.3 Resource Optimization Through Division into Online and Offline Calculations

To optimize runtime, many optimizations are also performed offline (i.e., prior to their actual execution). For this reason, a differentiation between online and offline calculations is useful. One example from the realm of real-time operating systems comprises dynamic online task scheduling *vis-à-vis* static offline task scheduling, as discussed in Section 2.4.4.6 of Chapter 2.

Example: Offline optimization of unnecessary message copies

Another example consists of the offline optimization of unnecessary message copies (see Fig. 2-36 in Chapter 2). The priorities of Tasks A, B, and C are entered in the diagram in Fig. 5-56. If a preemptive processor scheduling strategy is used, Task B—with its higher Priority 2—can interrupt Task A with its lower Priority 1 ranking. In turn, Task B may be interrupted by Task C because of its Priority 3 ranking. Because Task C is capable of changing the value of message Y, Task B is required to store a local copy of message Y at its starting point; Task B thus will be working with the unchanged value of message Y during the entire course of the execution. Because Task A—due to its lower priority—is unable to interrupt Task B, a change of the value of message X during task execution is not possible, which dispenses with the necessity for a local copy of message X in Task B. Therefore, when the scheduling strategy is known, it may be decided offline whether or not a message copy is necessary. In this way, unnecessary message copies can be avoided, with the consequence of savings in terms of runtime and required memory capacity.

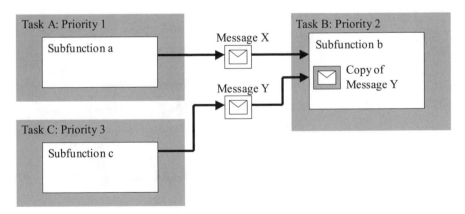

Fig. 5-56. *Offline optimization of unnecessary message copies. (Ref. [86])*

5.4.1.4 Resource Optimization Through Division into Onboard and Offboard Calculations

Additional optimization potential is provided by a division into onboard and offboard calculations. Those variables and calculations that are not required in the onboard ECU network—and are used only by offboard tools such as measuring, calibration, and diagnostic tools—can be swapped from the ECU to these tools. This results in a conservation of ECU resources. Examples of this consist of the specifications of dependent parameters or calculated signals, which are required only for offboard use.

Example: Dependent parameters [73, 87]

Figure 5-57 shows an example of interdependencies existing among parameters, where the physical equations are divided into onboard and offboard calculations. To accomplish this, the parameters d and U, which are dependent on parameter r and constant π and are calculated in the calibration tool, are introduced to the ECU. This results in a reduction of the calculations required onboard the ECU and thus a reduction in runtime.

As another benefit of this arrangement, only parameter r must be adapted in the calibration tool, while the tool ensures the consistent tracking of the values of dependent parameters d and U.

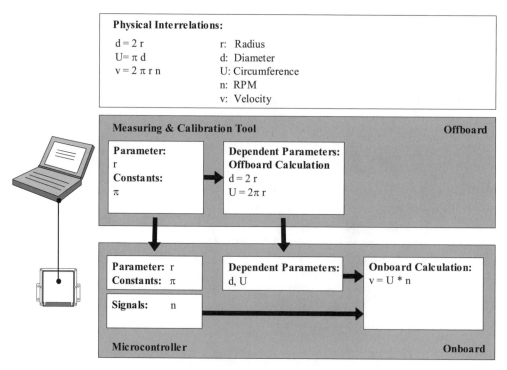

Fig. 5-57. *Dependent parameters. (Refs. [73, 87])*

Example: Calculated signals [87]

Similar optimization options can be exploited through the offboard calculation of signals based on measured variables, as shown in Fig. 5-58. The signals torque M and RPM n are present in the ECU, whereas performance P is calculated offboard in the measuring tool.

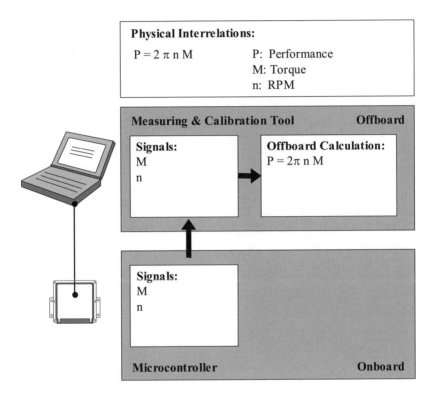

Fig. 5-58. *Calculated signals. (Ref. [87])*

5.4.1.5 Resource Optimization for Characteristic Curves and Maps

A large variety of optimization measures are used in the area of data structures. Characteristic curves and maps (see Fig. 4-26 in Chapter 4) are deployed in large numbers in conjunction with many functions. A similarly large optimization potential applies to the reduction of memory and runtime requirements in the context of characteristic curves and maps.

The following examples introduce several practical options in the context of characteristic curves. All of the measures described may be similarly applied to characteristic maps.

Data structure and interpolation and extrapolation of characteristic curves

In standard practice, characteristic curves are stored in a tabular data structure, as shown in Fig. 5-59. The first row of the data structure accommodates the entries of the values on the

Tabular Visualization	Axis Point x	x_1	x_2	x_3	x_4	x_5	x_6	x_7	x_8
	Characteristic Value y	y_1	y_2	y_3	y_4	y_5	y_6	y_7	y_8

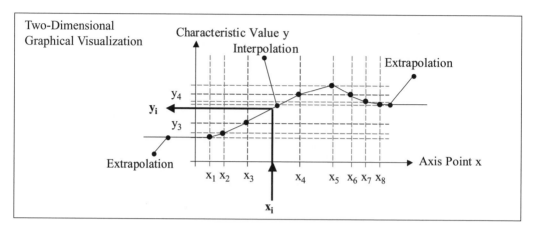

Fig. 5-59. *Data structure and interpolation and extrapolation of characteristic curves.*

independent axis, or *x-axis points*, for the input variable in the form of an ascending sequence of strict monotony. As is the case with the characteristic curves input values, the x-axis points are mostly labeled "x." The second row contains the value of the characteristic curve for each x-axis point. This value is labeled "y," as is the output value of the characteristic curve.

Additional elements of characteristic curve data structure are auxiliary variables for output value calculation, such as the number of x-axis points. Aside from tabular visualization, characteristic curves are frequently plotted on a graphical x–y diagram.

Those input variables that are located outside the x-axis point distribution—which, in Fig. 5-59, affects the values for $x < x_{min} = x_1$ or $x > x_{max} = x_8$—normally are extrapolated. Figure 5-59 depicts a constant extrapolation of the type used in many applications. Input values located between two x-axis points are interpolated. Figure 5-59 shows the linear interpolation, which is most frequently used.

The following discussion neglects extrapolation and instead looks at interpolation. The interpolation algorithm used to determine the output value y_i for an input value x_i identifies three steps.

Step 1: Searching for x-axis points

Relative to input variable x_i, an adjacent x-axis point (i.e., the next-lower or next-higher one) is determined. In the example in Fig. 5-60, the next-smaller x-axis point x_u to x_i is x-axis point x_3. Because of the strictly monotonic x-axis point storage, the next-higher x-axis point $x_o = x_4$ also is known.

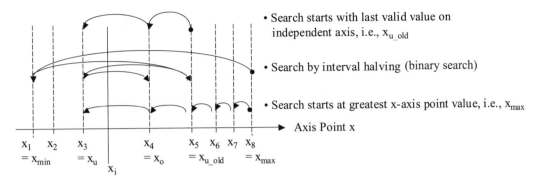

- Search starts with last valid value on independent axis, i.e., x_{u_old}

- Search by interval halving (binary search)

- Search starts at greatest x-axis point value, i.e., x_{max}

Axis Point x

$x_1 = x_{min}$ x_2 $x_3 = x_u$ x_i $x_4 = x_o$ x_5 x_6 x_7 $x_8 = x_{max}$ $= x_{u\_old}$

Fig. 5-60. *Various x-axis point search methods.*

To perform the x-axis point search, several search algorithms can be used. Some examples are as follows: "Search starting with the last valid value on the x-axis," "Search by interval halving (binary search)," and "Descending search, starting with the greatest value on the x-axis," or vice versa (Fig. 5-60).

Selecting a suitable search method depends on x-axis point distribution and application, among other factors. For example, the runtime in engine ECUs is very short in the presence of high engine speeds. For this reason, in the case of characteristic curves with RPM input, it would make good sense to search starting from higher to lower RPM. Thus, with lower RPM, the longer search time that "comes with the territory" is deemed less critical.

In some application cases, the presence of limited execution times causes the output variable of the characteristic curve to be stated as being $y_u = y(x_u)$ or $y_o = y(x_o)$. A more accurate value is obtained with the use of an interpolation algorithm. In general practice, the interpolation is linear between two x-axis points, with a clear differentiation between Steps 2 and 3.

Step 2: Calculating slope a

For the linear interpolation, the following differences must be calculated:

$$dx = x_i - x_u \qquad \text{(in Fig. 5-59:} \qquad dx = x_i - x_3) \qquad (5.8)$$

$$DX = x_o - x_u \qquad \text{(in Fig. 5-59:} \qquad DX = x_4 - x_3) \qquad (5.9)$$

$$DY = y_o - y_u \qquad \text{(in Fig. 5-59:} \qquad DY = y_4 - y_3) \qquad (5.10)$$

The slope a of the characteristic curve is calculated by division

$$a = \frac{DY}{DX} \qquad (5.11)$$

Step 3: Calculating characteristic curve value y_i through linear interpolation

$$y_i = y_u + a * dx \quad \text{(in Fig. 5-59:} \quad y_i = y_3 + a * dx \quad (5.12)$$

The variable dx can be calculated only online. If DX, DY, and a also are calculated online, this means that online calculation of three subtractions, one division, one addition, and one multiplication will be required for each interpolation.

An alternative is to calculate DX, DY, and a both offline and offboard. This option is exploited for the purpose of optimization. The following methods are widely used.

Storing slope a in an extended characteristic curve data structure

The practice of storing slope a in an extended characteristic curve data structure saves online computing time during interpolation. As a result, only one subtraction, one addition, and one multiplication must be calculated online. In time-sensitive applications, the resulting increase in required memory capacity is tacitly accepted (Fig. 5-61).

Axis Point x	x_1	x_2	x_3	x_4	x_5	x_6	x_7	x_8
Characteristic Value y	y_1	y_2	y_3	y_4	y_5	y_6	y_7	y_8
Slope a	a_1	a_2	a_3	a_4	a_5	a_6	a_7	

Fig. 5-61. *Extended data structure with stored slope a for characteristic curves.*

Fixed characteristic curves

The distance between the x-axis points $DX = x_o - x_u$ is supplied as a constant. Thus, x-axis point x_u can be calculated. A search procedure is not required. The reciprocal value of DX can be calculated both offline and offboard, and stored with the characteristic curve data. The interpolation no longer requires a division. Online calculation of two subtractions, one addition, and two multiplications is required.

The x-axis point distribution can be defined and stored on the basis of the value of the minimum x-axis point x_{min}, the number of x-axis points n, and the x-axis point distance DX. This data structure is the selection of choice, especially for characteristic curves exhibiting a large number of x-axis points (Fig. 5-62).

Group characteristic curves

A uniform x-axis point distribution is specified for various characteristic curves having identical input variables. The x-axis point search and the calculation of differences on the x-axis are required only once. Each time, the interpolation calculation is carried out for each output variable y_i (Fig. 5-63).

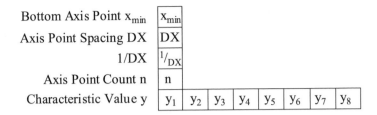

Bottom Axis Point x_{min}	x_{min}							
Axis Point Spacing DX	DX							
1/DX	$1/_{DX}$							
Axis Point Count n	n							
Characteristic Value y	y_1	y_2	y_3	y_4	y_5	y_6	y_7	y_8

Fig. 5-62. *Data structure for fixed characteristic curves.*

Axis Point x	x_1	x_2	x_3	x_4	x_5	x_6	x_7	x_8
Characteristic Value y_1	y_{11}	y_{12}	y_{13}	y_{14}	y_{15}	y_{16}	y_{17}	y_{18}
Characteristic Value y_2	y_{21}	y_{22}	y_{23}	y_{24}	y_{25}	y_{26}	y_{27}	y_{28}
$\vdots$	$\vdots$	$\vdots$	$\vdots$	$\vdots$	$\vdots$	$\vdots$	$\vdots$	$\vdots$
Characteristic Value y_n	y_{n1}	y_{n2}	y_{n3}	y_{n4}	y_{n5}	y_{n6}	y_{n7}	y_{n8}

Fig. 5-63. *Data structure for group characteristic curves.*

The use of combinations of fixed and group characteristic curves is also conceivable.

Additional optimization measures consist of adjustment and/or reduction of the x-axis point count subsequent to calibration. This saves calculating time during x-axis point search and reduces the required memory capacity. When the calibration is completed, it also is possible to reduce the physical value range, increase the quantization, or reduce the word length for x-axis points and values.

The numerous combinations of possible word lengths for the internal representation of x-axis points and values for characteristic curves in the processor lead to a large number of different interpolation routines in conjunction with a high demand for memory capacity. Therefore, it is standard practice to reduce in advance the number of possible combinations by limiting the permissible data structures for characteristic curves and maps.

5.4.2 Design and Implementation of Algorithms for Fixed-Point and Floating-Point Arithmetic

This section focuses on the design of algorithms in fixed-point and floating-point arithmetic. The discussion highlights basic methods used in today's practical online applications—that is, in the microcontroller onboard the ECU. Aside from basic arithmetical operations, online applications mainly include interpolation methods for characteristic curves and maps, numerical differentiation and integration methods, and numerical filtering procedures. For example, a library of graphical modeling blocks addressing this set of functional features was standardized under the auspices of the MSR-MEGMA project [79]. However, the scope of this section is limited to several basic issues that occur in the context of design and implementation of machine-based arithmetic.

5.4.2.1 Representation of Numbers in Digital Processors

All digital processors work with numbers in the binary system, in which the coefficients a_i of the binary decomposition are used to represent a number x:

$$x = \pm\left(a_n {}^* 2^n + a_{n-1} {}^* 2^{n-1} + \ldots + a_0 {}^* 2^0 + a_{-1} {}^* 2^{-1} + a_{-2} {}^* 2^{-2} + \ldots\right) \tag{5.13}$$

Example: Binary notation of the number x = 9

After decomposition, the number x = 9

$$9 = 1 * 2^3 + 0 * 2^2 + 0 * 2^1 + 1 * 2^0$$

has the binary notation **1001**.

To allow for the ready differentiation between decimal and binary notations, binary notations always appear in **boldface printing** in the following text.

For the internal representation of a number, digital processors provide only a fixed finite number n of binary positions. This number is referred to as *word length*. It is determined by processor construction and can be expanded to full multiples (e.g., 2n, 3n) of n. Accordingly, microprocessors with a word length of 8 positions are termed 8-bit microprocessors, those with a word length of 16 bits are called 16-bit microprocessors, and so forth.

There are several ways to use the word length of n positions to represent a number.

- In *fixed-point representation*, not only the number n but also the numbers n_1 and n_2 of the positions before and after the decimal point are fixed, where $n = n_1 + n_2$. In most cases, $n_1 = n$, or $n_1 = 0$.

  To this day, the functions of many microprocessors deployed in ECUs are limited to the fixed-point representation and processing of numbers.

  Without restrictions on general validity, the following discussion shall assume $n_1 = n$ to be true for fixed-point notation. Thus, the number n determines the set of numbers represented.

  For example, for n = 8, the numbers 0 through 255 can be represented by binary numbers **0000 0000** through **1111 1111**. Accordingly, this notation is referred to as *8-bit unsigned integer* notation, or *uint8,* for short.

  The representation of negative numbers makes use of a sign encoding bit. This bit is known as the *sign bit*. Thus, for n = 8, the numbers −128 through 0 through +127 can be represented. Accordingly, this notation is referred to as *8-bit signed integer* notation, or *sint8,* for short.

Similarly, 16- and 32-bit notations of numbers are termed *uint16, sint16, uint32,* and *sint32*. Table 5-2 lists the available value ranges.

TABLE 5-2
FIXED-POINT NOTATION OF INTEGERS AND AVAILABLE VALUE RANGES

No. of Binary Positions	Abbreviation	Available Value Range
8-bit unsigned integer	uint8	0 ... 255
8-bit signed integer	sint8	−128 ... 127
16-bit unsigned integer	uint16	0 ... 65 535
16-bit signed integer	sint16	− 32 768 ... 32 767
32-bit unsigned integer	uint32	0 ... 4 294 967 295
32-bit signed integer	sint32	− 2 147 483 648 ... 2 147 483 647

- In *floating-point representation,* the decimal point floats in accordance with the value that a given number assumes. Therefore, information indicating the placement of the decimal point (i.e., the number of positions after the first digit) must be provided for each number. This is accomplished with the use of the so-called *exponent.* This practice exploits the fact that a real number x can be expressed as the product of

$$x = a * 2^b \qquad (5.14)$$

with $|a| < 1$ and b as an integer.

The exponent b indicates the position of the decimal point in the mantissa a.

Example: Binary representation of the number x = 9.5

$$9.5 = \mathbf{1} * 2^3 + \mathbf{0} * 2^2 + \mathbf{0} * 2^1 + \mathbf{1} * 2^0 + \mathbf{1} * 2^{-1}$$

produces binary notation **1001.1** or **0.10011 * 2^{100}**.

As is the case with fixed-point representation, any digital processors provide, for the floating-point notation of numbers, only a fixed finite number m and/or e of binary positions for the representation of mantissa a and/or exponent b, where n = m + e.

Whether or not ECUs are equipped with microprocessors capable of supporting floating-point representation and processing of numbers depends on the requirements of the respective application.

Floating-point representations of a given number are not necessarily unique. In the last example, the notation **0.010011 * 2^{101}** might have been chosen. For this reason, the floating-point notation of any number for which the first digit of mantissa a is unlike 0 ("nonzero") is termed *normalized*. In the binary system, $|a| \geq 2^{-1}$ applies. Thus, all numbers of mantissa a, excluding the leading zeros, are termed *significant digits*.

Without restrictions on general validity, the following discussion shall always assume normalized floating-point representation and attendant floating-point calculation.

The numbers m and e, together with base $B = 2$ of the notation, determine the set A of numbers that can be accurately represented in the machine. This set A comprises a subset of the real numbers $\mathbb{R}(A \subseteq \mathbb{R})$. The elements of which set A is composed are termed *machine numbers*.

For $n = 32$ and $n = 64$, floating-point representations are defined in the IEEE standard. In a manner similar to fixed-point numbers, 32-bit and 64-bit floating-point numbers are termed *real32* and *real64*, respectively.

Because the set A of the numbers available for the representation of fixed-point and floating-point numbers is finite, the design and implementation of the behavior of a software component presents the immediate issue of how to approximate a number $(x \notin A)$, which is not a machine number itself, with a machine number. This issue manifests itself not only at the time of data entry in the computer, but also during internal data handling in the processor.

It can be demonstrated by means of simple examples that there are cases where even the result c of simple basic arithmetical operations with two numbers a and b (i.e., the addition a + b, subtraction a – b, multiplication a * b, and division $\frac{a}{b}$) do not belong to A, although both operands a and b are machine numbers $(a, b \in A)$.

Therefore, of an approximation for a number x that is not a machine number $(x \notin A)$ by a machine number $\text{rd}(x)$ with $\text{rd}(x) \in A$, it is demanded that

$$|x - \text{rd}(x)| \leq |x - g_k| \qquad (5.15)$$

for all $g_k \neq \text{rd}(x) \in A$ (Fig. 5-64).

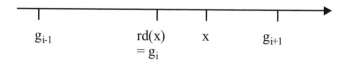

Fig. 5-64. *Approximation of x through rd(x).*

It is normal for $\text{rd}(x)$ to be determined by *rounding* or by limiting the result within limits of the so-called *overflow or underflow handling*. The following sections use simple examples to discuss rounding errors, as well as the treatment of overflows and underflows. The foreground objective is to obtain the most accurate result possible.

Rounding errors, overflows, and underflows occur with all numbers in fixed-point representation. To enhance the clarity of presentation, the following examples are based primarily on numbers in uint8 representation.

5.4.2.2 Rounding Errors in Integer Division

The integer division $c = \dfrac{a}{b}$ results in a rounding problem because it is possible that the exact result of the operation $\dfrac{a}{b}$ is not an integer.

Example: Integer division and rounding

Variables a, b, and c shall be represented in uint8 notation.

The division

$$c = \frac{a}{b}$$

where a, b, c $\in$ A = {0, 1, 2, ..., 255} yields the following results:

Test case 1:	a = 100,	b = 50	$\rightarrow c = 2$	$\in$ A
Test case 2:	a = 19,	b = 2	$\rightarrow c = 9.5$	$\notin$ A
Test case 3:	a = 240,	b = 161	$\rightarrow c = 1.49...$	$\notin$ A
Test case 4:	a = 100,	b = 201	$\rightarrow c = 0.49...$	$\notin$ A
Test case 5:	a = 100,	b = 1	$\rightarrow c = 100$	$\in$ A (trivial)
Test case 6:	a = 100,	b = 0	Division by 0 is not defined	

- In test case 1, the result is an integer. It can be represented as a uint8 number. A rounding error does not occur.

- In test case 2, the result is not an integer. Thus, rounding is required.

  This is accomplished by forming, for the representation of c = 9.5 in normal binary representation

  $$c = (a_n * 2^n + a_{n-1} * 2^{n-1} + ... + a_0 * 2^0 + a_{-1} * 2^{-1} + a_{-2} * 2^{-2} + ...)$$

  Thus, in the present test case,

  $$c = 9.5 = \mathbf{1} * 2^3 + \mathbf{0} * 2^2 + \mathbf{0} * 2^1 + \mathbf{1} * 2^0 + \mathbf{1} * 2^{-1} \quad \text{or } \mathbf{1001.1}$$

Therefore,

$$a_3 = \mathbf{1},\ a_2 = \mathbf{0},\ a_1 = \mathbf{0},\ a_0 = \mathbf{1},\ a_{-1} = \mathbf{1}$$

the rounded value $\mathrm{rd}(c)$ is formed by

$$\mathrm{rd}(c) = a_n\, a_{n-1} \dots a_0 \qquad\qquad \text{if } a_{-1} = 0 \qquad\qquad\qquad (5.16)$$

$$\mathrm{rd}(c) = a_n\, a_{n-1} \dots a_0 + 1 \qquad\qquad \text{if } a_{-1} = 1 \qquad\qquad\qquad (5.17)$$

Therefore, in the present test case, the calculation would be $\mathrm{rd}(c) = 10$, or **1010** rounded.

An integer division in many microprocessors produces, instead of a rounding, a simple truncation of the positions after the decimal point. Amounts are always rounded off.

$$\mathrm{rd}(c) = a_n\, a_{n-1} \dots a_0 \qquad\qquad \text{for all values of } a_{-1} \qquad\qquad\qquad (5.18)$$

Therefore, in the present test case, the calculation would be $\mathrm{rd}(c) = 9$, or **1001**.

- In test case 3, $\mathrm{rd}(c) = 1$ is calculated for rounding and truncation of the decimal places in integer division. In this case, however, the so-called *relative rounding error*
$$\varepsilon = \frac{(\mathrm{rd}(c) - c)}{c} = \frac{(1 - 1.49)}{1.49} \approx \frac{-1}{3} \text{ (which determines the accuracy of the result) has}$$
already become sizeable.

- In test case 4, $\mathrm{rd}(c) = 0$ is calculated. Here, the relative rounding error $\dfrac{(0 - 0.49)}{0.49} = -1$
is particularly large. It shall become clear that this test case is especially critical for error propagation (e.g., when further processing the intermediate result in a multiplication).

- In test case 5, the division by 1 is almost negligible.

- The division by 0, as in test case 6, is not defined and must be excluded through *exception handling* in the algorithm.

For $c > 1$, the relative rounding error ε calculates thus:

$$|\varepsilon| = \left| \frac{\mathrm{rd}(c) - c}{c} \right| \le \frac{1}{3} \qquad\qquad\qquad (5.19)$$

For $c > 1$, the following applies to relative error ε upon truncation:

$$|\varepsilon| = \left|\frac{rd(c) - c}{c}\right| \leq \frac{1}{2} \tag{5.20}$$

Thus, the result for $c > 1$ is $rd(c) = c(1 + \varepsilon)$ with $|\varepsilon| \leq \frac{1}{3}$ with rounding, or $|\varepsilon| \leq \frac{1}{2}$ with the truncation of decimal places. Accordingly, the relative rounding error is slightly smaller than with the truncation of decimal places. In both cases, the relative error becomes smaller as the result increases.

5.4.2.3 Overflow and Underflow in Addition, Subtraction, and Multiplication

If the operands $a, b \in A$ are available in the form of machine numbers in fixed-point integer representation, then the results obtained with the basic operations addition $a + b$, subtraction $a - b$, and multiplication $a * b$ are integer values. A rounding error does not occur. However, because of the finite number n of binary positions, there are always numbers $x \notin A$ that are not machine numbers.

Example: Addition, subtraction, and multiplication

The variables a, b, and c shall be represented in uint8 notation.

The addition $c = a + b$ with $a, b, c \in A = \{0, 1, 2, \ldots, 255\}$ yields the following results:

Test case 1: $a = 100, \ b = 100 \rightarrow c = 200 \in A$

Test case 2: $a = 100, \ b = 157 \rightarrow c = 257 \notin A$

The subtraction $c = a - b$ with $a, b, c \in A = \{0, 1, 2, \ldots, 255\}$ yields the following results:

Test case 3: $a = 100, \ b = 100 \rightarrow c = 0 \in A$

Test case 4: $a = 100, \ b = 102 \rightarrow c = -2 \notin A$

In test case 2, the result for c is too great for representation by a uint8 integer. This is termed *overflow*.

In test case 4, the result for c is too small for representation by a uint8 integer. This is termed *underflow*.

Similar situations may occur in conjunction with multiplications.

The implementation in floating-point arithmetic is another area in which errors in the input data as well as approximation errors have such an effect on the selected calculation modes. However, when compared with fixed-point arithmetic, the rounding errors occurring in floating-point integers and floating-point arithmetic are smaller by several orders of magnitude.

5.4.2.4 Shift Operations

Because of the binary representation in the processor, multiplications taking the form a * b and divisions of the form $\frac{a}{b}$ may be handled quite efficiently by means of *shift operations*—provided that the operand b assumes a value from the set $\left\{2^1, 2^2, ..., 2^n\right\}$.

Example: Shift operations

The number x = 9 is decomposed thus:

$$9 = 0 * 2^4 + 1 * 2^3 + 0 * 2^2 + 0 * 2^1 + 1 * 2^0$$

and has the binary notation **01001**.

The product of 9 * 2 can be represented through a left-shift operation **01001≪1**. The result obtained is **10010**, or **18.**

The division $\frac{9}{2}$ may be similarly calculated through a right-shift operation **01001≫1**. The result obtained is **00100**, or 4. Thus, right-shift operations also cause the decimal positions to be truncated.

In the context of signed integers, such as sint8, sint16, or sint32, remember that, in right-shift operations ≫ in certain circumstances, the sign bit itself may become a normal digit in the numerical representation. Therefore, it should be scrupulously examined whether a normal division might not be better in this case.

5.4.2.5 Handling Overflows and Underflows

The actions taken in the event of a value range violation due to overflow or underflow depend on the processor. The algorithm may provide different responses. Using the addition example, some of the frequently used options for overflow handling are discussed here.

Example: Overflow handling

Variables a, b, and c shall be represented in uint8 notation.

The addition c = a + b with $a, b, c \in A = \left\{0, 1, 2, ..., 255\right\}$ yields the following results:

Test case 1: $\qquad$ a = 100, b = 100 $\rightarrow$ c = 200 $\in$ A

Test case 2: $\qquad$ a = 100, b = 157 $\rightarrow$ c = 257 $\notin$ A

The following optional responses to the overflow in test case 2 are possible:

- Overflow with or without overflow detection

  Overflow is permitted. Most microprocessors output c = a + b − 256 = 1. A compare operation $(c < a)$ & &$(c < b)$ can be used to detect and handle an overflow of unsigned integers in the algorithm.

- Limiting the result

  The overflow is recognized in the algorithm, and the result c is limited to the maximum representable value c = 255.

- Extending the value range of the result

  The result c is represented in a variable with extended value range (e.g., in a uint16 or sint16 variable). Thus,

  $$c = a + b \qquad \text{at} \qquad a,b \in A_{uint8} = \{0,\ 1,\ 2,\ ...,\ 255\}$$

  and

  $$c \in A_{uint16} = \{0,\ 1,\ 2,\ ...,\ 65535\}$$

  or

  $$c \in A_{sint16} = \{-32768,\ ...,\ 0,\ 1,\ 2,\ ...,\ 32767\}$$

  An overflow can no longer occur. In the event that c is represented as a variable of the sint16 type, an underflow can no longer occur in a subtraction also.

- Rescaling the result

  The overflow is recognized, and the result c is rescaled to $rd(c)$. To do this, a quantification or resolution q for c at $|q| > 1$ is introduced. By rescaling the result c to the equation $c = q * rd(c)$, the value range of c can be extended, and overflow no longer occurs. Rescaling with factors q from the set $\{2^1,\ 2^2,\ ...,\ 2^n\}$ can be realized by means of shift operations. Thus,

  $$rd(c) = \frac{(a + b)}{q}$$

  with $a, b, rd(c) \in A_{uint8} = \{0,\ 1,\ 2,\ ...,\ 255\}$ and q = 2

  $$c \in A_c = \{0,\ 2,\ 4,\ ...,\ 510\}$$

An overflow can no longer occur. On the downside, the accuracy of the result $\mathrm{rd}(c) = 256$ is reduced. The relative error ε is as follows:

$$|\varepsilon| = \left|\frac{\mathrm{rd}(c) - c}{c}\right| \le \frac{q - 1}{c} \tag{5.21}$$

As in a previous example, the relative error decreases as the size of the result increases.

5.4.2.6 Error Propagation with Algorithms in Fixed-Point Arithmetic

The investigation now focuses its attention on the manner in which errors propagate within a given algorithm. However, a closer definition of the term *algorithm* shall first be given. The following discussion deems an algorithm to be a clearly defined sequence of a finite number of "simple" operations, which can be used to produce the solution to a problem through the calculation of specific input data.

Example: Definition of the term algorithm

The example to be used shall be the expression $d = a + b + c$.

Although the methods $d = (a + b) + c$ and $d = a + (b + c)$ are mathematically equivalent, they may produce divergent results due to numerical reasons in fixed-point calculation.

Algorithm 1 differentiates the following steps:

> Step 1.1: $\eta_1 = a + b$
>
> Step 1.2: $d = \eta_1 + c$

Algorithm 2 differentiates the following steps:

> Step 2.1: $\eta_2 = b + c$
>
> Step 2.2: $d = a + \eta_2$

Note that a, b, c, and d shall be represented in sint8 integer notation. Thus,

$$a, b, c, d \in A = \{-128 \ldots + 127\}$$

Overflows and underflows are detected and reduced to the values $-128 \ldots +127$.

In the test case of a = 101, b = –51, and c = –100, the results are as follows:

Algorithm 1: $\eta_1 = a + b$ $= 101 - 51$ $= 50$

                $d = n_1 + c$ $= 50 - 100$ $= -50$

Algorithm 2: $\eta_2 = b + c$ $= -51 - 100$ $= -128$ (underflow limitation)

                $d = a + \eta_2$ $= 101 - 128$ $= -27$

The examination of the reasons why different algorithms normally supply divergent results quickly reveals that the propagation of rounding and limitation errors is an essential factor. Therefore, some criteria for the evaluation of algorithm accuracy shall be formulated here.

In fixed-point calculation, an approximation value $rd(d)$ is obtained instead of d. For Algorithm 1, $rd_1(d)$ can be determined thus:

$$rd(\eta_1) = (a + b)(1 + \varepsilon_{1.1})\tag{5.22}$$

$$
\begin{aligned}
rd(d_1) &= \left(rd(\eta_1) + c\right)(1 + \varepsilon_{1.2}) \\
&= \left[(a + b)(1 + \varepsilon_{1.1}) + c\right](1 + \varepsilon_{1.2}) \\
&= (a + b + c)\left[1 + \frac{a + b}{a + b + c}(1 + \varepsilon_{1.2})\varepsilon_{1.1} + \varepsilon_{1.2}\right]
\end{aligned}
\tag{5.23}
$$

Therefore, the relative error ε_{d1} is

$$\varepsilon_{d1} = \frac{rd(d_1) - d}{d} = \frac{rd(d_1)}{d} - 1 = \frac{a + b}{a + b + c}(1 + \varepsilon_{1.2})\varepsilon_{1.1} + \varepsilon_{1.2}\tag{5.24}$$

As the first approximation, when disregarding higher order terms such as $\varepsilon_{1.1} * \varepsilon_{1.2}$, ε_d yields for Algorithm 1

$$\varepsilon_{d1} \approx \frac{a + b}{a + b + c}\varepsilon_{1.1} + 1 \cdot \varepsilon_{1.2}\tag{5.25}$$

Therefore, Algorithm 2 produces

$$\varepsilon_{d2} \approx \frac{b + c}{a + b + c}\varepsilon_{2.1} + 1 \cdot \varepsilon_{2.2}\tag{5.26}$$

The amplification factors $\dfrac{(a + b)}{(a + b + c)}$ and 1, and/or $\dfrac{(b + c)}{(a + b + c)}$ and 1, indicate how strongly the rounding errors of the intermediate results affect the relative error ε_d of the result. The critical factor is $\dfrac{(a + b)}{(a + b + c)}$, and/or $\dfrac{(b + c)}{(a + b + c)}$. Depending on whether $(a + b)$ or $(b + c)$ is smaller, it is more beneficial because it is "numerically more stable" to calculate the sum $a + b + c$ using the formula $(a + b) + c$, and/or $a + (b + c)$.

In the preceding test case, $a + b = 50$ and $b + c = -151$. Because of the limitation, $\varepsilon_{2.1}$ is particularly large, in the preceding test case, $\varepsilon_{2.1} = \dfrac{(-128 + 151)}{(-151)} \approx -0.15$. By contrast, $\varepsilon_{1.1}$, $\varepsilon_{1.2}$, and $\varepsilon_{2.2}$ are 0.

Thus, the result obtained for error $\varepsilon_{d2} = \left[\dfrac{(-151)}{(-50)}\right] * (-0.15) = -0.45$.

Thus, it is demonstrated that the relative error $\varepsilon_{2.1}$ of Step 1 of the calculation enters the result of Algorithm 2 with an amplification factor of ≈ 3, although Step 2 of the calculation is executed without a relative error. This explains why Algorithm 1, considering the input values of this test case, is more beneficial in numerical terms.

Although this method is suited to systematic extension, it will quickly become cumbersome. While it may be used to estimate the effect of a few rounding errors, with a typical algorithm, the number of arithmetic operations and thus the number of individual rounding errors are too large to determine the influence of all rounding errors in this manner. Such cases may be better served by other techniques, one of them being interval calculation [75], although a detailed discussion would go beyond the scope of this section. The following examples are limited to the examination of the relative error ε_i in the calculation step i of a given algorithm.

Example: Algorithm 3

However, rescaling and not limiting the intermediate result in Algorithm 2 of the preceding example by a factor of 2 produces the following Algorithm 3:

Step 3.1: $\quad b_1 = \dfrac{b}{2} = -\dfrac{51}{2} = -25 \qquad\qquad \varepsilon_{3.1} = \dfrac{[-50 - (-51)]}{(-51)} = -\dfrac{1}{51}$

Step 3.2: $\quad c_1 = \dfrac{c}{2} = -\dfrac{100}{2} = -50 \qquad\qquad \varepsilon_{3.2} = 0$

Step 3.3: $\quad n_2 = b_1 + c_1 = -75 \qquad\qquad\qquad \varepsilon_{3.3} = 0$

Step 3.4: $\quad a_1 = \dfrac{a}{2} = \dfrac{101}{2} = 50 \qquad\qquad\quad \varepsilon_{3.4} = \dfrac{[100 - 101]}{(101)} = -\dfrac{1}{101}$

Step 3.5: $d_1 = a_1 + \eta_2 = 50 - 75 = -25$ $\varepsilon_{3.5} = 0$

Step 3.6: $d = d_1 * 2 = -25 * 2 = -50$ $\varepsilon_{3.6} = 0$

With these input values, the selected rescaling produces a much more accurate result than Algorithm 2 with a limitation of the intermediate result. Limitations of this type must be watched closely because they may implicitly occur in algorithms (e.g., through the transfer of arguments in conjunction with subprogram calls).

5.4.2.7 Physical Interrelation and Fixed-Point Arithmetic

It is a frequent occurrence that two physical signals that occur in the microprocessor as variables with different scaling must be handled in an arithmetical operation. The following example discusses the addition of two signals. Operations using more than two operands can be dissected into several operations with two operands each.

Example: Addition of two signals of different scaling

A simple example is the addition of the two signals a and b. The intent is to implement the physical relation $c_{phys} = a_{phys} + b_{phys}$.

In the microprocessor, the signals a, b, and c are available in the form of fixed-point variables a_{impl}, b_{impl}, and c_{impl} in uint8 representation.

The interrelation between the physical continuous variables and the implementation variables in discrete fixed-point notation is specified by a linear formula and by the lower and upper limits. Figure 5-65 shows this interrelation for the variable a.

With respect to limits, the value range resulting from the representation at the implementation level must be observed. In Fig. 5-65, a_{impl} uses uint8 representation with the value range $\{0, 1, 2, ..., 255\}$, or general value range $\{a_{impl\ MIN}, ..., a_{impl\ MAX}\}$. Accordingly, this example yields the upper and lower limits for the physically representable value range:

$$a_{phys\ MIN} = \frac{\left(a_{impl\ MIN} - K_{0a}\right)}{K_{la}} = \frac{\left(-K_{0a}\right)}{K_{la}} \tag{5.27}$$

$$a_{phys\ MAX} = \frac{\left(a_{impl\ MAX} - K_{0a}\right)}{K_{la}} = \frac{\left(255 - K_{0a}\right)}{K_{la}} \tag{5.28}$$

This value range must not be confused with the range of physically occurring values with the limits $a_{phys\ min}$ and $a_{phys\ max}$, to which the value range $\{a_{phys\ min} ... a_{impl\ max}\}$ can be assigned at the implementation level.

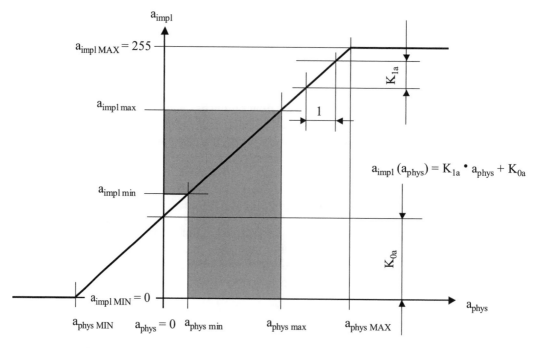

Fig. 5-65. *Interrelation between a physical variable and implementation.*

Similar interrelations apply to the variables b and c. For the linear range, the following applies:

$$a_{impl}\left(a_{phys}\right) = K_{1a} * a_{phys} + K_{0a} \qquad (5.29)$$

$$b_{impl}\left(b_{phys}\right) = K_{1b} * b_{phys} + K_{0b} \qquad (5.30)$$

$$c_{impl}\left(c_{phys}\right) = K_{1c} * c_{phys} + K_{0c} \qquad (5.31)$$

Because only fixed-point values can be represented at the implementation level, each case requires a rounding that was omitted in the diagram in Fig. 5-65. $\dfrac{1}{K_{1i}}$ is also termed a *quantization* or *resolution*, and K_{0i} is known as *offset*.

The addition of the physical variables at the implementation level can be accomplished with the following algorithm:

Step 1: Removing offset from a_{impl} and b_{impl}

$$a_{impl\_1} = a_{impl} - K_{0a} \tag{5.32}$$

$$b_{impl\_1} = b_{impl} - K_{0b} \tag{5.33}$$

Step 2: Approximating quantization of a_{impl_1} and b_{impl_1}

$$a_{impl\_2} = a_{impl\_1} * \frac{K_{1b}}{K_{1a}} \tag{5.34}$$

Step 3: Addition

$$c_{impl\_1} = a_{impl\_2} + b_{impl\_1} \tag{5.35}$$

Step 4: Approximating quantization of c_{impl}

$$c_{impl\_2} = c_{impl\_1} * \frac{K_{1c}}{K_{1b}} \tag{5.36}$$

Step 5: Allowing for offset of c_{impl}

$$c_{impl} = c_{impl\_2} + K_{0c} \tag{5.37}$$

As an alternative, calculations after Step 2 also may be based on the quantization of a_{impl}. In this case, b_{impl} must be approximated to the quantization of a_{impl}. Step 4 will change correspondingly. Because of the higher accuracy, it would be standard practice to approximate to the quantization having the higher resolution.

A third alternative would be to use the quantization of result c_{impl} after Step 2 for calculation.

The judicial selection of one of these alternatives assists in keeping the number of requantizations to a minimum.

If the quantizations by K_{1a}, K_{1b}, and K_{1c} are adroitly chosen, the necessary conversions can be effected with shift operations. Thus, it is recommended to choose the quantizations in such a way that the relations $\frac{K_{1b}}{K_{1a}}$, $\frac{K_{1c}}{K_{1b}}$, and so forth assume values from the set $\left\{ 2^1, 2^2, ..., 2^n \right\}$. Provided that identical quantizations are chosen, Step 2 and/or Step 4 can be omitted.

Interval arithmetic applied to barriers $a_{impl\,min}$ and $a_{impl\,max}$ can be used for prior verification of whether or not the intermediate results having the value range $a_{impl\,MIN}$ and $a_{impl\,MAX}$ of the selected operand representation can be represented with the use of the value range in the selected representation of operand a without requiring overflow handling. A correction of parameter values K_{1i} and K_{0i} allows for the specification of intervals, which are more suitable numerically, thus increasing the accuracy of the calculated results.

Limitations and overflow handling can be avoided, provided that the intermediate calculations are carried out using a representation with a wider value range.

Separating online and offline calculations may achieve further optimizations. For example, the divisions in Eqs. 5.34 and 5.36 can be calculated offline. To enhance the clarity of presentation, optimizations of this type were deliberately omitted from the last example.

5.4.2.8 Physical Model Level and Implementation Level

As the preceding example demonstrates, the differentiation between the physical level and implementation level for algorithms makes good sense. The reason is that in this way, physical interrelations and implementation details indigenous to microprocessors, such as the choice of quantization method, word length, and strategy for integer arithmetic, can be subjected to separate scrutiny.

At the physical level of a model, a differentiation may be made between continuous-value, discrete-value, and Boolean variables:

- In most cases, continuous-value variables represent physical signals of continuous value, such as temperatures, revolutions per minute, or pressures.

- Value-discrete variables represent natural variables, such as the number of cylinders in an engine or the number of stages (shift levels) in a transmission.

- Boolean variables describe state pairs, such as a switch position to which the state of the respective pair (On/Off, High/Low, TRUE/FALSE) may be assigned.

If a continuous-value variable is to be implemented in fixed-point representation, it first must be discretized. For this reason, this aspect of value discretization often gains central significance in data modeling.

This means that each physical value X_{phys} must be assigned exactly one discrete implementation value

$$X_{impl} \text{ of the set } \{X_1, X_2, X_3, \ldots, X_n\} \text{ with } X_{impl\,min} \leq X_{impl} \leq X_{impl\,max} \qquad (5.38)$$

that is unique and unambiguous.

This transformation is normally described by means of a conversion formula and by the specification of minimum and maximum values at the physical model level or implementation level.

Where the design of software components calls for the transformation from physical model level to implementation level, the measuring of internal ECU variables during subsequent development phases—including in production and service—necessitates the conversion from implementation variables to physical units.

5.4.2.9 Notes on Implementation in Fixed-Point Arithmetic

The relative error is the determining quality factor for the result produced by an algorithm. As shown in the preceding sections, integer divisions, as well as overflow and underflow handling, limit the numerical accuracy. From these truths, a number of pointers, rules, and guidelines for implementation may be derived:

Useful pointers on integer divisions

- Because the relative error in integer divisions is large, every effort should be made to avoid their utilization.

- Divisions by 0 (zero) are not defined and therefore must be handled as an exception. One option consists of exclusion by way of limitations or queries.

- With unsigned integers, divisions by values from the set $\left\{2^1,\ 2^2,\ ...,\ 2^n\right\}$ can be effectively performed by means of shift operations.

- If the use of divisions is unavoidable, the division operations should occur as late in the algorithm as possible. In this way, the relative error enters the result only at a very late stage.

- The larger the result of the integer division, the smaller the relative error. Therefore, if possible, the value of the numerator should be considerably larger than that of the denominator. This may be accomplished by defining an offset or through a requantization by means of a shift operation prior to the actual division. Needless to say, the original offset or quantization must again be established in the course of the algorithm.

Example: Calculating the division $c_{phys} = \dfrac{a_{phys}}{b_{phys}}$

The variables a_{impl} and temp are available in uint16, and the variables b_{impl} and c_{impl} are in uint8 representation.

The physical values are as follows:

$$a_{phys} = 79$$

$$b_{phys} = 5$$

The exact value of c_{phys} would be $\dfrac{79}{5} = 15.8$.

The conversion formulas are as follows:

$$a_{impl}\left(a_{phys}\right) = K_{1a} * a_{phys} + K_{0a} = 1 * a_{phys} + 0 \qquad (5.39)$$

$$b_{impl}\left(b_{phys}\right) = K_{1b} * b_{phys} + K_{0b} = 1 * b_{phys} + 0 \qquad (5.40)$$

$$c_{impl}\left(c_{phys}\right) = K_{1c} * c_{phys} + K_{0c} = 1 * c_{phys} + 0 \qquad (5.41)$$

The value range is as follows:

$$a_{impl\,min} = 0 \qquad \text{and} \qquad a_{impl\,max} = 255$$

$$b_{impl\,min} = 2 \qquad \text{and} \qquad b_{impl\,max} = 10$$

To calculate $c_{phys} = \dfrac{a_{phys}}{b_{phys}}$, the following algorithm is chosen:

- Step 1: Shift operation by 8 places for a_{impl} to take advantage of the full 16-bit value range

$$a_{impl} = a_{impl} \ll 8 = a_{impl} * 2^8$$

Thus, $a_{phys} = 79$ yields $a_{impl} = 79 * 2^8 = 20\ 224$.

- Step 2: Executing the actual integer division

$$\text{temp} = \frac{a_{impl}}{b_{impl}}$$

Thus, $b_{phys} = 5$ yields $\text{temp} = \dfrac{20\ 224}{5} = 4\ 044$.

This is the equivalent of $15.7968... * 2^8$.

Compared with the integer division $\dfrac{79}{5} = 15$, rescaling the variable temp aids in obtaining significantly higher accuracy.

- Step 3: Rescaling the result by 8 decimal places

  As the algorithm progresses, the variable temp must be rescaled to the scale of c_{impl}:

$$c_{impl} = temp \gg 8$$

  This causes a relative error and loss of accuracy. Therefore, this step should be inserted in the algorithm at the latest possible time. From this point onward, any calculating steps should use the more accurate intermediate temp variable.

Useful pointers on additions, subtractions, and multiplications

- Overflow and underflow handling limit the accuracy of additions, subtractions, and multiplications.

- Several strategies for overflow and underflow handling are available. Among them are rescaling, limitation, or extension of the value range by means of type conversion, or permitting overflow or underflow with or without detection and response in the algorithm.

- Rescaling the value range reduces the relative accuracy across the entire value range, even if overflow or underflow does not occur.

- Limiting the value range causes a drop in relative accuracy only if an overflow or underflow occurs.

- Using the conversion relation of physical signal in implementation variables, the offset can be set in such a way that the calculations at the implementation level occur "in the middle" of the chosen value range. This also aids the in-processor representation using a shorter word length. This benefit is particularly apparent in the case of large data structures, such as with characteristic curves with offsets and with characteristic maps, and it manifests itself in the form of lower memory requirements. However, offsets may cause additional conversion operations when linking different signals. Aside from characteristic curves and maps and another few exceptions, it is good practice to avoid offsets in conversion formulas to the extent possible.

- Multiplications and divisions using values from the set $\left\{2^1,\ 2^2,\ ...,\ 2^n\right\}$ can be effectively performed by means of shift operations. Right-shift operations with signed integers should be avoided whenever possible. In such cases, the use of the normal division is recommended.

Useful pointers on error propagation

- Even with accurately executed operations such as additions, subtractions, and multiplications, a relative error in the input variables may quickly become amplified.

- In this context, it also is advisable to pay particular attention to limitations of the kind that may become implicitly active by virtue of argument transfer in subprogram calls and to estimate their influence on intermediate results.

5.4.2.10 Notes on Implementation in Floating-Point Arithmetic

The implementation in floating-point arithmetic is another area where it must be remembered that the machine number set A is finite for floating-point numbers. The unavoidable consequences are rounding errors in the arithmetical operations. As is the case with fixed-point arithmetic, the associative and distributive laws do not apply here because the exact arithmetical operations are approximated by floating-point operations.

Even given the fact that not all numerical problems are solved by means of floating-point arithmetic, the larger numerical value range does present the advantage of reducing the influence of numerical rounding errors, as well as overflows and underflows, making them negligible in most cases. Also, the scaling of physical variables—a frequent source of error in the implementation in integer arithmetic—is not required.

On the downside, the higher numerical accuracy comes at the cost of greater word length, which in turn means increased requirements in terms of memory capacity and runtime. For example, in the presence of a preemptive arbitration strategy, backing up and restoring floating-point data may have a significant influence on runtime in real-time systems.

Thus, a solution that combines fixed-point and floating-point arithmetic is used for many applications. For this reason, an awareness and understanding of general numerical methods will always be an essential asset in solving problems such as the following [88]:

- Conversion of fixed-point integers to floating-point integers, and vice versa

- Handling "division by zero" conditions

- Propagation of approximation errors that may be generated by filter and integration algorithms

- Propagation of rounding errors

Useful pointers on compare and division operations

- Where compare operations of fixed-point numbers are noncritical, compare operations of two floating-point numbers a and b should be avoided in many cases. Instead, it is recommended to compare the difference $\delta = |a - b|$ *vis-à-vis* a barrier ε, which also requires consideration of the relative accuracy (e.g., in the form of $\delta = |a * \varepsilon|$ or $\delta = |b * \varepsilon|$).

- Divisions by 0 (zero) must be excluded by means of conditions and queries.

5.4.2.11 Modeling and Implementation Guidelines

The optimizations for production ECUs depend on the application on one hand, and on the hardware platform on the other. For this reason, close cooperation is necessary between the function developer responsible for the model-based physical specification and the software engineer in charge of the design and implementation.

Modeling and implementation guidelines are vital prerequisites for dedicated optimization measures. The function model must facilitate the explicit specification of all software relevant information without unnecessarily impeding physical understanding. Examples of modeling guidelines are the so-called *MSR standards* [79], whereas the *MISRA Guidelines* constitute an example of implementation guidelines [80].

The separation between specification and design facilitates the porting to new hardware platforms that may become necessary. In a best-case scenario, only the adaptation of the hardware-specific design decisions will be required to accomplish this.

The consistency of specification and design represents a basic problem in function development. A variety of data and behavioral modeling tools support these design steps. Tools also facilitate the definition of guidelines in the form of libraries of graphical modeling blocks, scaling recommendations, and naming conventions for variables, as well as formula libraries, data structures, and interpolation routines for characteristic curves and maps, memory segmentation, and so forth.

5.4.3 Design and Implementation of Software Architecture

The software architecture, too, must be specified in consideration of the features of the designated microprocessor and the properties of the ECU, with a view to taking into account all requirements imposed on the production ECU. Due to the frequent large variety of different requirements, only a few tentative beginnings of standardized software architecture are discernible at the time of this writing.

5.4.3.1 Platform and Application Software

The differentiation between two software layers, that is, platform and application software, is widely accepted. Earlier in this chapter, the specification in Section 5.3 defined an architecture for the software functions. In the design phase, the software components thus specified, which are needed for the implementation of a software function, can be integrated as application software components in the software architecture introduced in Chapters 1 and 2. Figure 5-66 shows an example of an architecture design in which the software functions are implemented as modules and communicate by means of messages. The models are depicted with the use of the graphical representation first introduced in Fig. 5-24.

The following sections discuss methods for the implementation and configuration of software components, especially those methods that may be suited to automated support from appropriate tools. In this manner, it becomes possible to ensure the consistency between specification and implementation, constituting a crucial contribution to the improvement of software quality.

5.4.3.2 Standardization of Platform Software Components

The standardization of the platform software components provides a host of benefits. Standardization becomes possible because the platform software components do not represent a

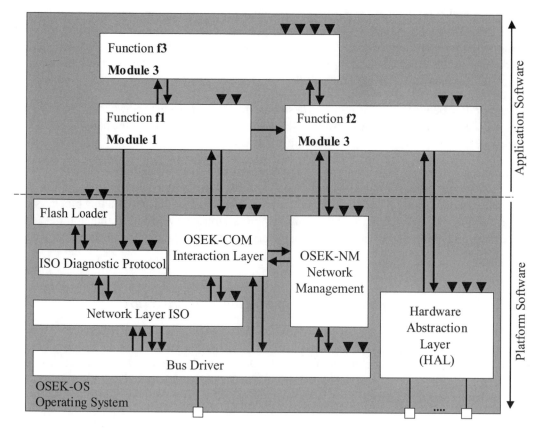

Fig. 5-66. *Software architecture composed of standardized software components.*

differentiating competitive factor to vehicle manufacturers. Standardization of platform software components facilitates the integration of ECUs developed by a variety of vendors in the vehicle. Also, quality assurance for platform software components can be handled at a central point. For example, the following platform software components have already been standardized:

- Operating systems, communications, and network management, per OSEK standards [16]

- Diagnostic protocols, per ISO standards [25, 26]

The software components are adapted to a variety of applications with the aid of configuration parameters.

Another area in which numerous benefits are waiting to be solidified is that of standardized Flash programming procedures, including the required platform software components and the necessary security mechanisms preventing unauthorized access.

This standardizes the software components that support, during the production and service phases, the offboard interface for a number of functions provided by a production ECU:

- Diagnostics
- Software parameterization
- Software update

In the course of development, support for additional interfaces, such as for measuring and calibrating, or for bypass applications, is frequently called for. Measuring and calibration protocols, such as the CAN Calibration Protocol (CCP, for short) or the Extended Calibration Protocol (XCP), are standardized under the auspices of ASAM [17]. The integration of the software components required for these functions in the software architecture is necessary only during the development phase. Their presence is no longer required in the production and service phases.

Standardization potential also is evident in the context of application software components. For example, suitable candidates would be interpolation routines and data structures for characteristic curves and maps, or the elements of a system library for control technology, of the type specified under the auspices of the MSR-MEGMA working group [79].

The software modules used for controlling the peripheral modules of the microcontroller are often collected in a hardware abstraction layer (HAL). Their implementation may be standardized for a given microcontroller or microcontroller family.

5.4.3.3 Configuration of Standardized Software Components

The use of configuration parameters facilitates the adaptation of standardized software components to a specific application. The configuration step may be automated through the use of configuration tools. Cases in point would be a real-time operating system configuration or that of platform software components for communications and diagnostics.

Figure 5-67 outlines the automatic generation of the configuration settings required for the software components handling communications within the ECU network. To this end, the ECU communications matrix is stored in a centralized database. Editing utilities facilitate the modification of communications parameters in accordance with varying views of the communications matrix. In this way, configurations with a specific orientation for signal view, message view, bus view, node view, or function view become possible. Export interfaces support a variety of data exchange formats—such as description files for development or measuring tools—used to distribute the communications matrix to the various development partners. Conversely, import interfaces can be used to merge functional subsets to verify their consistency. A documentation interface assists in the automated adoption of data to be included in specification and design documents.

Together, all of these options ensure the consistency among implementation, documentation, and description formats of the data describing communications within the ECU network. Transfer errors of the type that may occur in the manual configuration of software components thus can be avoided.

Similar requirements exist in the realm of diagnostic data (Fig. 5-68). The administration of diagnostic data in a centralized database provides a range of benefits. The first automated function comprises the configuration of software components for diagnostic purposes. For example, it

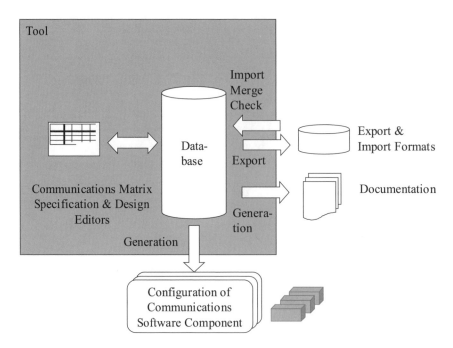

Fig. 5-67. *Automated configuration of communications layer.*

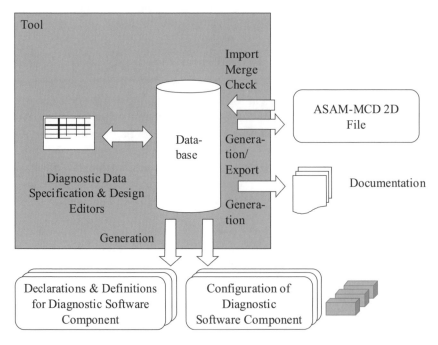

Fig. 5-68. *Automated configuration of diagnostic layer and generation of a diagnostic description.*

ensures data consistency between the fault memory description for the diagnostic tester (e.g., in the ASAM-MCD 2D format) and the implementation onboard the ECU. A second task that may be automated is the integration of diagnostic data from several ECUs into a single data version, complete with subsequent consistency checking.

5.4.4 Design and Implementation of Data Model

Country and customer-specific equipment options confront both production and service with a multitude of vehicle variants, over which complete command is required at all times. By-products of vehicle variants are the software versions for the ECUs.

To master the multiple vehicle variants, specific procedures reducing the number of ECU types required by a given vehicle manufacturer for production and service are required. This section introduces those methods that become available by virtue of forming a data variant for ECU software.

- For all procedures deployed in production, requirements with regard to the length of time needed to set up a program or data version for an ECU constitute important prerequisites. The maximum permitted time is dictated by the production time cycle. The setup procedure may be inserted before or after the physical installation of the ECU in the vehicle.

- In the case of procedures to be used by vehicle service facilities, the logic of worldwide logistics clamors for the smallest number of different ECU hardware types. As an inherent benefit of software, the global distribution of program and/or data versions is decidedly more cost efficient than that of hardware components. An added benefit is the fact that the cost-intensive demounting and replacement of ECUs from a vehicle is no longer necessary if it is considered in the overall concept. For this reason, a concept that facilitates the setup, modification, or download of program and data versions—dispensing with the need for ECU replacement or removal and repair—provides a number of advantages.

- In addition, the users of a vehicle (i.e., the operator and other occupants) increasingly wish to configure and store individual personal profiles for a number of software functions. This may include the settings of seat and steering column or mirror position coordinates, as well as settings of the heating system, air conditioning system, or favorite radio stations. Personal profiles such as these may be managed by means of driver ID information that is stored in the ignition key.

All of these considerations are required in the context of data design and implementation.

Sections 5.4.4.2 and 5.4.4.3 introduce two different methods for data version setup or configuration in greater detail:

1. Setting data variants through Flash programming

2. Setting data variants via configuration parameters

In addition, the combined use of both methods is conceivable.

5.4.4.1 Definition of Memory Segment

Aside from the type of representation used by the microprocessor, the specification for each piece of data must identify the memory segment of the microcontroller in which it shall be stored.

Accordingly, it must be decided whether a variable shall be stored in volatile read/write memory (e.g., in RAM), in nonvolatile read memory (e.g., in ROM, PROM, EPROM, or Flash memory), or in a nonvolatile read/write memory (e.g., in EEPROM or battery-backed RAM).

5.4.4.2 Setting Data Variants via Flash Programming

The first solution is based on a method that can be used on ECUs equipped with Flash memory. For this purpose, the entire Flash area containing the program version and the variant-specific data version may be programmed. As an alternative, only a subsection of the Flash memory (e.g., only the data version) may be programmed at the time the vehicle rolls off the assembly line. This gave rise to the term *end-of-line programming*.

The same method also is used increasingly for software updates in service shops, where programming utilizes the central diagnostic interface of the vehicle, dispensing with the need to remove the ECU for reprogramming. The Flash programming procedure used in service shops is discussed in detail in Section 6.3 of Chapter 6.

To reduce the time required for Flash programming, the program version and data version are frequently programmed in separate sessions. In a production situation, for example, the variant independent program version can be programmed already during ECU manufacture, whereas only the vehicle-specific and variant-dependent data version is subject to end-of-line programming.

Using a characteristic curve as a case in point, Fig. 5-69 shows an example of variant management through Flash programming.

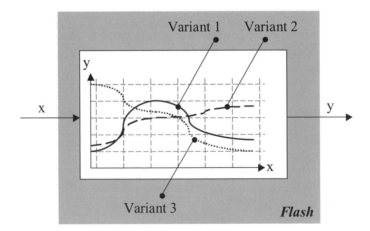

Fig. 5-69. *Data version programming using the example of a characteristic curve.*

5.4.4.3 Setting Data Variants via Configuration Parameters

The second solution consists of the concurrent deposit of different data variants in the non-volatile read-only memory onboard the ECU. Only one of these data variants is chosen for the subsequent end-of-line parameterization. The respective software parameter may be stored in EEPROM. Because this causes one of several possible configurations (as shown in Fig. 3-12 of Chapter 3) to be chosen only as the vehicle is about to leave the assembly line, this method is referred to as end-of-line configuration.

As an alternative, the respective configuration may be chosen upon starting the engine of the vehicle. In this case, the described procedure deposits the configuration data for all ECUs onboard the vehicle in a central ECU. From there (e.g., after switching on the ignition), the data will be distributed by means of a message to the receivers on the network, which, upon receipt of the information, select the required configuration.

This method also is employed for the purpose of software configuration on vehicles in the field. Here, too, the central diagnostic interface serves as the connecting point. In addition, this method enables the vehicle operator to set his or her individual function parameters.

Using a characteristic curve as a case in point, Fig. 5-70 shows an example of configuration management by means of software parameters.

5.4.4.4 Generation of Data Structures and Description Files

The centralized management and automated generation of data structures and description files for measuring and calibration data facilitate the automation of another development step (Fig. 5-71).

The measuring and calibration data of a microcontroller are stored in a central database. In this process, the physical specification, and the design and implementation decisions for all of the data, as well as the definition of the transformation rule (e.g., through the use of conversion formulas) are managed together. The database records then can be used to generate data structures for a development environment (e.g., in C language), on one hand (see Fig. 4-35 in Chapter 4). On the other hand, once the address information has been loaded, all of the information required for the generation of a description file in the ASAM-MCD 2MC format, which is used by measuring, calibration, and diagnostic tools, is available. In this way, consistency between the description files for measuring and calibration tools and the implementation of data in the microcontroller onboard the ECU can be ensured.

5.4.5 Design and Implementation of Behavioral Model

The data consistency among specification, documentation, and the complete implementation of software components can be ensured through the use of code generation tools (Fig. 5-72).

The same model-based specification that is used for simulation or rapid prototyping provides the basis for automated code generation. This means that the necessary design decisions must be made for the data specified at the physical level and for the algorithms. The data require the definitions shown in Fig. 5-71. The algorithms require the design decisions for arguments and

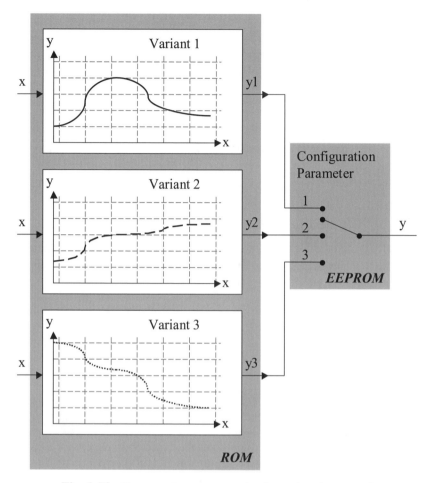

Fig. 5-70. *Data version parameterization using the example of a characteristic curve.*

return values, as well as the assignment to the memory segments of the microcontroller onboard the ECU. If the implementation uses integer arithmetic, additional definitions must be made (e.g., with respect to the strategy for handling rounding errors, underflows, and overflows, as discussed in Section 5.4.2). A design tool supports the subject definitions.

On the basis of this information, the automated generation (e.g., in source code) of complete software components is possible. These may then be subjected to further processing in a conventional software development environment and finally integrated to form a program version and data version for the respective microcontroller. Accordingly, this method is known as the *Additional Programmer Method* (Fig. 5-72).

Provided that the description of the software architecture also is possible and that the components of the platform software can be integrated and configured, the integration of a compiler toolset

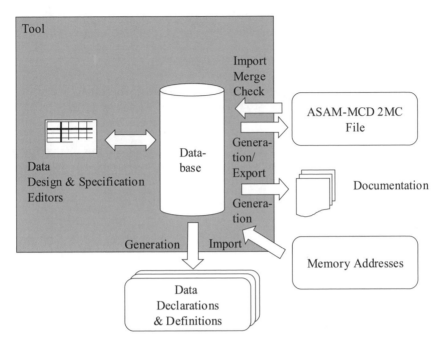

Fig. 5-71. *Automated generation of data structures and a description file. (Ref. [89])*

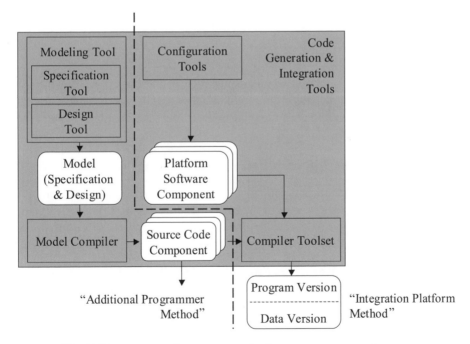

Fig. 5-72. *Automated generation of software components plus program and data version. (Ref. [73])*

for the respective microprocessor will facilitate the generation of a complete program and data version (Fig. 5-72). Accordingly, this method is known as the *Integration Platform Method*.

Example: Design and implementation of "Integrator" class

The objective is to implement the "Integrator" class already specified in Fig. 5-27. Thus, the design decisions shown in Fig. 5-73 are made with respect to the data.

Designation X	Notation	Formula $X_{impl}(X_{phys}) = K_1 \cdot X_{phys}$	Value Range at the Physical Level X_{phys}	Value Range at the implementation Level X_{impl}
E/compute()	uint8	$K_1 = 1$	true/false	1/0
in/compute()	uint16	$K_1 = 256$	0 ... 100	0 ... 25 600
K/compute()	uint16	$K_1 = 256$	0 ... 255.996	0 ... 65 535
MN/compute()	uint32	$K_1 = 256$	0 ... 16 777 215.99	0 ... 4 294 967 295
MX/compute()	uint32	$K_1 = 256$	0 ... 16 777 215.99	0 ... 4 294 967 295
return/out()	uint16	$K_1 = 256$	0 ... 255.996	0 ... 65 535
I/init()	uint8	$K_1 = 1$	true/false	1/0
IV/init()	uint16	$K_1 = 256$	0 ... 100	0 ... 25 600
memory	uint32	$K_1 = 256$	0 ... 16 777 215.99	0 ... 4 294 967 295
dT	uint16	$K_1 = 1024$	0 ... 63.999	0 ... 65 535

Fig. 5-73. Design decisions for data and interfaces of "Integrator" class.

Figure 5-74 shows a possible C language implementation using the "compute()" method in fixed-point arithmetic. Concerning the algorithms, additional design decisions, such as overflow or underflow handling, are taken into consideration.

5.5 Integration and Testing of Software Functions

This section discusses verification and validation methods applied to software functions during the integration and test phases. Because of the cross-corporate applicability of integration and test procedures, methods employing modeling and simulation techniques that turn nonexistent physical components into virtual entities provide a crucial function in vehicle development.

The structure of this section takes its orientation from the following integration and test environments:

- Simulation tools

- Laboratory vehicles and test benches

- Experimental, prototype, and production vehicles

```
/* Variables */

extern uint32 memory;

extern uint16 dT;


/* Method compute() */

void compute (uint16 in, uint16 K, uint32 MN, uint32 MX,

uint8 E)

{

  uint32 t1uint32, t2uint32, t3uint32;

  if E {

    /* Overflow handling 15 Bits */

    t1uint32 = MX >> 1;

    /* min=0, max=2147483647, impl=128phys */

    t2uint32 = (( (uint32) (in >> 5)

                 *( ( (uint32) K * dT) >> 10)

                 ) >> 4)

          + (memory >> 1);

    /* min=0, max=2357192447, impl=128phys+0 */

    t3uint32 =
(uint32)((t2uint32<t1uint32)?t2uint32:t1uint32)<<1;

    /* min=0, max=4294967294, impl=256phys+0 */

    memory = (t3uint32 > MN) ? t3uint32 : MN;

    /* min=0, max=4294967295, impl=256phys+0 */

  }

}
```

Fig. 5-74. *Implementation of the "compute()" method of "Integrator" class as a function in C language.*

The necessary synchronization—among all development partners and across all development environments—of the various verification and validation steps (e.g., the coordination of component models and test cases) must be considered as early as possible along the timeline in project planning.

Some validation methods, such as rapid prototyping for specified software functions that can be employed during the specification phase, were discussed in Section 5.3. Those methods already discussed can be combined with the ones described in this section. The methods highlighted here facilitate the timely verification and validation of implemented software functions in an environment that is part virtuality and part reality. The discussion features several typical intermediate steps, and the starting situation and final objectives are depicted in Fig. 5-75.

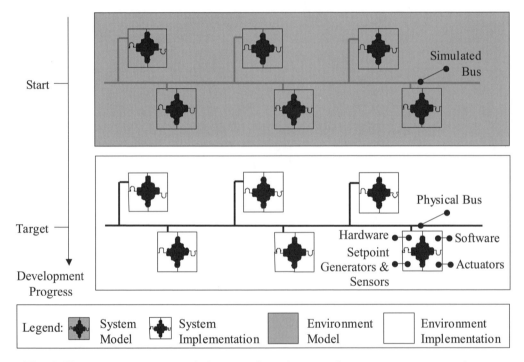

Fig. 5-75. *Starting situation and objectives for software and systems integration and testing.*

Figure 5-76 presents an overview of the various intermediate steps occurring in integration. The models representing the logical system architecture may provide the basis for the simulation of nonexistent system components. The following sections discuss widely accepted integration, verification, and validation methods, using the selected sample segments from Fig. 5-76.

The earliest possible validation step consists of a simulation of the model of a control function, with a model of the system to be controlled. The simulation model permits the replication of

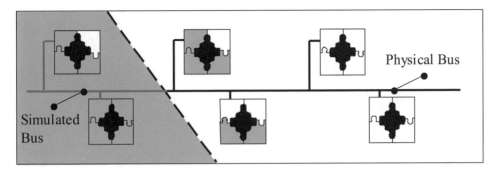

Fig. 5-76. *Intermediate steps in software and systems integration and testing.*

components such as setpoint generators, controllers or monitors, actuators, plant, and sensors. The simulation also attaches relevance to the influence that vehicle operator and environment exert on system behavior. To this end, the operator and environment may be considered additional components, as shown in Fig. 5-44.

Because virtual models represent all of the components, real-time requirements with respect to suitable modeling or simulation techniques are nonexistent. At this juncture, however, a detailed discussion of the modeling of vehicle components would exceed the scope of this book. For a detailed discussion of function modeling, reference is made to the relevant specialized literature [35].

5.5.1 Software-in-the-Loop Simulations

The execution of implemented software components in a simulated environment is known as *software-in-the-loop simulation* (*SiL simulation*, for short).

If one contemplates a closed-loop control function, then this designation makes sense. For example, a software component of the application software layer that represents a closed-loop control function implementation may be modeled and executed as a component in the "loop," as shown in Fig. 5-77.

However, this approach can be put to good use with a number of other application cases in point, too, even if no control loop exists as such. For example, in the event that software components used to implement open-loop control or monitoring functions, or software components of the platform software (e.g., the communications layer) are to be verified and validated in this manner, it becomes apparent that the designation *SiL simulation* fails to adequately describe that situation.

In this case, the structure of the simulation model does not greatly differ from that shown in Fig. 5-44. However, a significantly stricter specification of the model components is called for. For example, the modeling procedure for the ECU must be brought to a point of concretion where the analog/digital and digital/analog signal conversion, as well as the "real-time behavior" are accounted for as precisely as possible. Only then will it be possible to integrate implemented

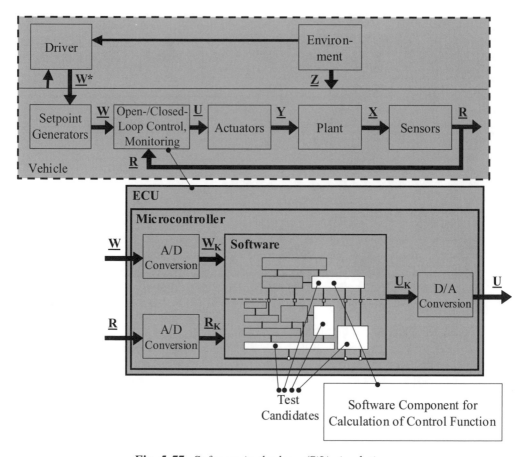

Fig. 5-77. *Software-in-the-loop (SiL) simulation.*

software components in this system environment and to execute these, as shown in Fig. 5-77. The implemented software component, having thus become a test candidate, is then executed in a development and simulation platform in a simulated environment (e.g., on a PC). There are no real-time requirements concerning the execution of the simulation.

The use of software-in-the-loop simulations facilitates the execution of a number of dynamic software tests, that is, early on the timeline and without a real-life ECU (e.g., component tests in conjunction with code coverage analyses).

5.5.2 Laboratory Vehicles and Test Benches

An entire class of methods and tools is used for verification and validation as soon as the hardware and software of a given ECU are available. These are grouped under the collective designation laboratory vehicles and test benches. As shown in Fig. 5-78, the attendant objective may be the

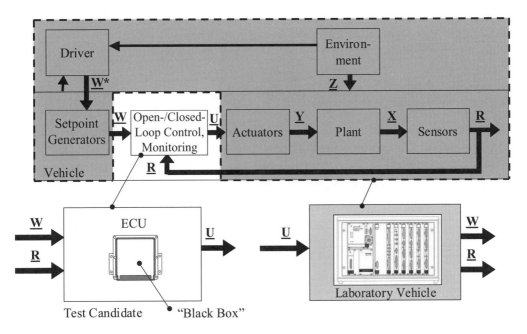

Fig. 5-78. *Operation of an ECU in a virtual environment. (Ref. [90])*

operation of a real-world ECU in a partly virtual and partly real environment. For this reason, in contrast to the aforementioned simulation methods, real-time requirements must be considered during modeling and execution of the simulation of environmental components.

If the focus is on the verification and validation of control functions, then the ECU must be viewed and treated as a component in the control loop, as shown in Fig. 5-78. For this reason, this approach is often referred to as *hardware-in-the-loop simulation* (*HiL simulation*, for short). However, it shares with the SiL simulation the fact that this method is not limited to control functions but can be deployed in a number of other applications, some examples of which are discussed here. This book groups these different methods under the designation *laboratory vehicles*.

Regarding ECU software, a variety of aspects are highlighted, such as the verification and validation of real-time behavior, onboard and offboard communications behavior on the network, or the verification of control and monitoring functions.

5.5.2.1 Test Environment for Standalone ECUs

The laboratory vehicle can be used as a software and hardware test bench for a standalone ECU (Fig. 5-78). It produces real-time simulations of static and dynamic processes of the ECU environment.

The input signals of the ECU are replicated by an environmental model, which is used to stimulate the ECU. The signal vectors $\underline{W}$ and $\underline{R}$ form the inputs of the ECU, as shown in Fig. 5-78. The output signal vector $\underline{U}$ is used as an input variable for the environment simulation in the laboratory vehicle.

Figure 5-79 shows the structural principle of the laboratory vehicle named LABCAR [90]. The environmental model is translated and executed on a real-time computer system. In addition to executing the models, that system outputs the signal vectors $\underline{W}$ and $\underline{R}$ of the ECU and acquires the signal vector $\underline{U}$. An operating host computer permits the interactive control of experiments by the user, as well as automated control of experiments. Modeling tools support modifications to the models of the environmental components.

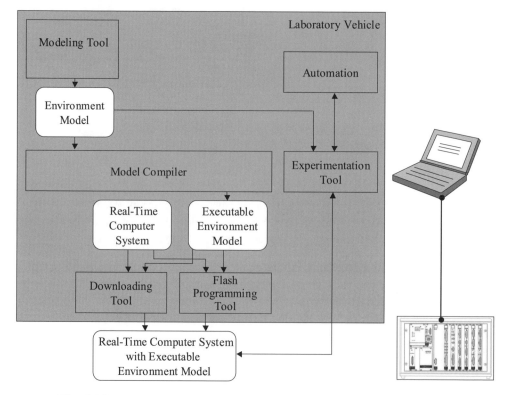

Fig. 5-79. *Structural diagram of the LABCAR laboratory vehicle. (Ref. [90])*

Example: Test environment for ECU control functions

A typical application for a laboratory vehicle consists of testing the dynamic characteristics of the control functions provided by an ECU. In addition to the software functions in the application software, this includes signal processing by both platform software and ECU hardware.

The available freedoms in terms of presetting options for ECU input signals afford the tester a liberal scope for freedom of experimentation:

- The preselection of environmental conditions for the ECU (e.g., temperature, atmospheric pressure, or humidity) and the random stimulation of input signals facilitate the testing of software functions in extreme conditions.

- In this way, borderline-driving situations can be simulated without hazard to test drivers or prototype vehicles.

- It also is possible to randomly specify aging or failure situations on setpoint generators, sensors, actuators, or wiring connections. The preselection of aging effects for adaptive control function components facilitates the evaluation by changes of the respective signals.

- Monitoring functions can be systematically checked by entering implausible signals.

- Component tolerances (e.g., of setpoint generators, sensors, and actuators) can be preset to any value. The effect of these components on the robustness of control functions thus can be verified.

- In contrast to physical test bench trials or in-vehicle testing, the working points can be randomly entered without limitation, such as for the full revolutions per minute and load range of a given engine.

All tests are fully reproducible and can be run in automated mode. No other hardware components or assemblies nor physical vehicles are required for LABCAR testing.

In the context of a laboratory car structure as shown in Fig. 5-78, the ECU is deemed to be a "black box." The only way to evaluate the functional behavior of an ECU is to analyze its input and output signals. Although this method will suffice for simple ECU functions, the scrutiny of more complex functions requires the integration of a measuring procedure for intermediate internal ECU variables.

5.5.2.2 Test Environment for ECUs, Setpoint Generators, Sensors, and Actuators

The method described in the preceding section also may be expanded to include the setpoint generators, sensors, and actuators of a given ECU. To accomplish this, the real-life counterparts of these components are "installed in the loop" and are regarded as test candidates (Fig. 5-80).

As a consequence, modeling procedures in the laboratory vehicle are limited to models representing the plant, vehicle operator, and environment. Models representing setpoint generators, sensors, and actuators are no longer required. In this particular case, the laboratory vehicle is called on to support the output variables $\underline{W}^*$ and $\underline{X}$ and the input variables $\underline{Y}$. This, in turn, requires a suitable adaptation of the hardware structure.

Rounding out the available options, the combined use of both simulated and real-world setpoint generator, sensor, and actuator components also is conceivable.

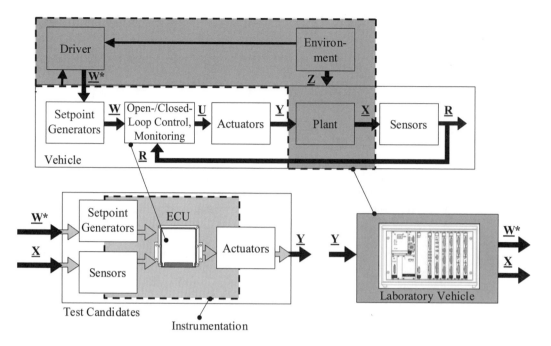

Fig. 5-80. *Operation of ECU, setpoint generators, sensors, and actuators*
in a virtual environment. (Ref. [90])

Example: Test environment for control and monitoring systems

Compared with the specialized purpose of the preceding example, this setup provides for the comprehensive testing of electronic control and monitoring systems. Testing the setpoint generators, sensors, and actuators requires the in-process measurement of a diversity of signals occurring in these components. In most cases, these signals are acquired by an additional set of sensors—the so-called *instrumentation*—such as on the sensors and actuators of a vehicle system. Likewise, the process of acquiring intermediate internal ECU variables is termed *ECU instrumentation*.

This can be accomplished by integrating an instrumentation of these components and of the ECU in the laboratory vehicle with a measuring, calibration, and diagnostic system. The ECU can be accessed by one of several offboard interfaces, such as the offboard diagnostic interface.

The test cases that can be shown in a diagram exceed to some degree the test situation of the preceding example. However, the point could be made that these shortcomings are again outweighed by limitations imposed in other areas (e.g., with respect to the presetting of aging effects in sensors, or the specification of extreme situations and fault occurrences).

5.5.2.3 Test Environment for ECU Network

If the functions to be tested are implemented in the form of a distributed and networked system, this means that the procedure must be expanded to handle the simultaneous testing of several ECUs. That is, the instrumentation must be extended to cover several ECUs (Fig. 5-81).

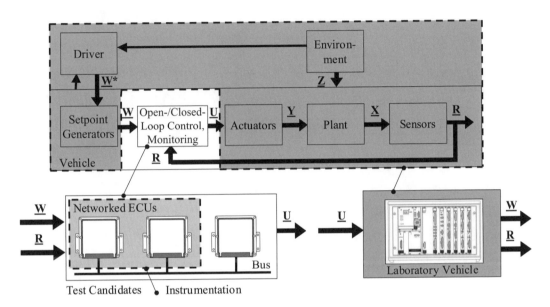

Fig. 5-81. *Operation of multiple ECUs in a virtual environment. (Ref. [90])*

Tests frequently are conducted in phases. For example, the first phase concentrates on testing the communications over the bus between ECUs and the relevant components of the platform software. The application software components are then tested in a second phase (Fig. 5-66).

In both cases, nonexistent ECUs may be replaced by their simulated counterparts. These become components of the environmental model that is executed on the real-time computer system. For this purpose, the real-time computer system must be provided with an interface to the bus, which comprises the communications system.

To describe the virtual replication of the communications characteristics of ECUs and the functional interconnections forming an implemented subsystem for the purpose of checking communications on the ECU network, the term *residual bus simulation* [91] is used. Figure 5-82 shows one application case in point.

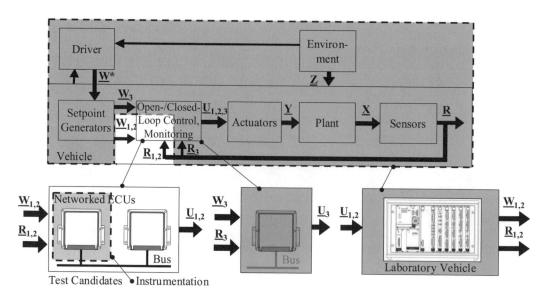

Fig. 5-82. *Operation of physical and virtual ECUs in a virtual environment. (Refs. [90, 91])*

5.5.2.4 Test Bench

The transition from laboratory vehicles to test benches may be described as fluid. In situations where electrical signals are insufficient to drive the actuators (e.g., in the case of electrohydraulic actuators), a suitable test environment would be termed *hydraulic test bench*.

Working with laboratory cars is one thing. Quite another situation is the integration of additional, real-world components in the test environment, such as the plant depicted in Fig. 5-83, which serves as test candidates. Furthermore, the predefinition of environmental status variables (e.g., the ambient temperature in the case of subzero or extreme heat test facilities) is possible. Similar options exist for the presetting of desired values by a flesh-and-blood driver (e.g., on chassis dynamometers).

Nonexistent real-world components are replicated in virtual form, such as by means of a driver or environmental model, both of which provide for the presetting of a dynamic load profile. The resulting virtual components can be used as standardized modules in laboratory vehicles and test benches alike. To accomplish the simulation, a real-time computer system (e.g., a laboratory vehicle) is integrated in the test bench (Fig. 5-83).

Example: Engine test bed

The engine test bed installation depicted in Fig. 5-83 regards ECU, setpoint generators, sensors, actuators, and the engine as test candidates. The remaining vehicle components, environmental conditions, and driving profiles are replicated, some as real and others as virtual. At this point, the instrumentation also includes the engine.

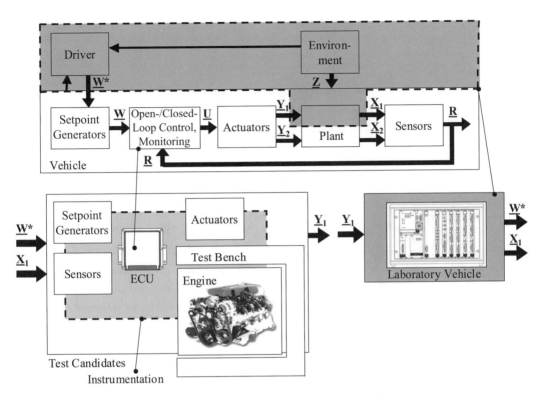

Fig. 5-83. *An ECU in an engine test bed installation.*

5.5.3 Experimental, Prototype, and Production Vehicles

The integration, verification, and validation of electronic systems in the real-world vehicle require an instrumentation of the participating vehicle system components. In this context, the instrumentation is frequently expanded to include the environment and the driver. This often requires, in addition to a measuring and diagnostic system, a calibration system for the fine-tuning of internal ECU parameters, as shown in Fig. 5-84.

It stands to reason that the measuring, calibration, and diagnostic systems must be suited to the integration of functions residing on a variety of networked ECUs. To be compatible, they must support the simultaneous instrumentation and calibration of multiple ECUs. A detailed discussion of measuring and calibration systems appears in Section 5.6.

Such a measuring, calibration, and diagnostic system also may be combined with a rapid proto-typing system, as shown in Fig. 5-47.

In many cases, the transition from prototype to production vehicle, and the associated switch from development ECU to production ECU, also results in a change in the offboard interface available for instrumentation. In contrast to the prototype vehicle, the production vehicle often restricts ECU access to the central offboard diagnostic interface and, in some cases, to the access to the communications systems.

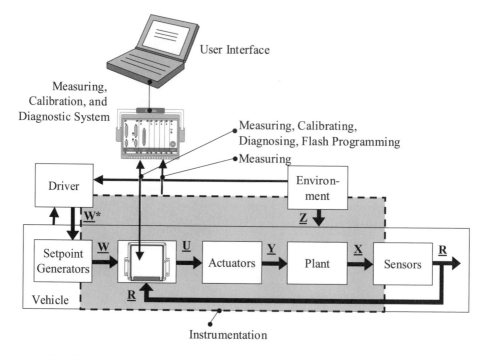

Fig. 5-84. *Onboard instrumentation in an experimental vehicle. (Ref. [87])*

Whereas the aforementioned transition results in reduced transmission speeds for the offboard interface, it limits the parameters selectable for the calibration functions and changes the operating principle of that function.

5.5.4 Design and Automation of Experiments

The definition of test cases should be considered as early as in the initial design phase. The structure of the experiments may orient itself on the basis of various criteria, such as vehicle functions, vehicle system components, or driving situations.

Examples of *function-oriented testing* of software functions serve as test cases for the following:

- Control functions
- Monitoring and diagnostic functions

Examples of *system and component-oriented testing* serve as test cases for software components, such as the following:

- Real-time operating system
- Communications layer and network management
- Diagnostic layer

Examples of *situation-oriented testing* of software components can be divided into the following:

- Normal cases
- Extreme cases
- Fault situations

The automation of test routines depends more on the test environment than on the test case. It requires that experiments must be formally described. Automation is more easily accomplished on the laboratory vehicle or test benches than it is on the vehicle.

Automated testing offers a significant potential for cost reduction. However, it would exceed the scope of this book to engage in a detailed discussion of the design and automation of experiments. For such a discussion of experiment design, reference is made to the relevant specialized literature [30, 31].

5.6 Calibration of Software Functions

The various deployment options for measuring and calibration systems in conjunction with laboratory vehicles, test benches, and the physical vehicle were outlined in Section 5.5. The present section discusses the functional principles of measuring and calibration systems.

A measuring and calibration system consists of a measuring and calibration tool and one or more ECUs, each featuring one or more microcontrollers equipped with suitable offboard interfaces. Added to this is auxiliary measuring technology that is bundled under the term *instrumentation*.

For all of the signals acquired by means of the instrumentation, a standardized mode of representation in the tool must be ensured. This applies not only to the value range but also to the timeline of signals comprising the acquired measurements, or *measurement signals*. With regard to the captured discrete measuring signals of the microcontroller program, this means that a conversion from the notation used for implementation to the physical representation used by the measuring tool is needed.

The tool is required to provide editor support at the implementation level and—for the representation of measurement signals—at the physical level, for any changes in parameter values (e.g., the values of characteristic values, curves, and maps). Figure 5-85 shows an example of both the physical view and the implementation view of a characteristic curve KL and a measured signal S.

In this context, it is quite useful to make a logical distinction between onboard operations carried out by the microcontroller in the ECU and those handled offboard by the measuring and calibration tool (Fig. 5-85).

This development phase has as its objective the generation or adaptation of the data version, which encompasses all of the parameter values that were stored in the microcontroller memory in the form of characteristic values, curves, and maps. The microcontroller program uses this data as the basis for its operations.

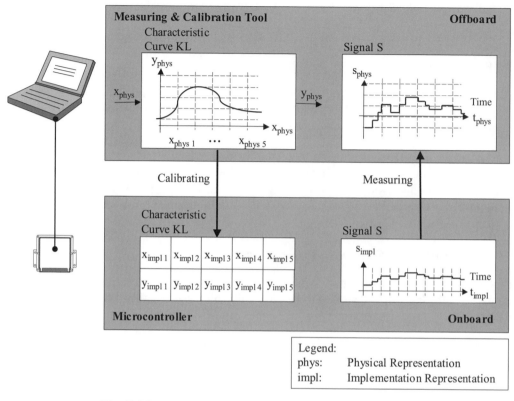

Fig. 5-85. *Onboard and offboard calculations for measuring and calibration systems. (Ref. [87])*

To accomplish the calibration of software functions that are implemented by means of distributed and networked systems, measuring and calibration systems must support an entire network of microcontrollers and ECUs. For the sake of clarity, the following sections use the simplified approach of regarding only one microcontroller and one ECU.

The starting point consists of the provision of an ECU, that is, of a hardware and software version. The software version encompasses a program version and an initial data version for each microcontroller onboard the ECU. The measuring and calibration system also requires a description of the software version, which may be available in the form of a separate file in ASAM-MCD 2 file format. The file not only contains information for the conversion between the physical level and implementation level for all measuring, calibration, and diagnostic data, it also provides information concerning the interface between the tool and the microcontroller.

The purpose of this at times demanding and costly development step is the adaptation of the data version. In this play of many actors, several aspects take center stage. Among them are the adaptation to various working points, the long-term operation of systems aimed at compensating aging effects by way of parameters and algorithms, fleet trials facilitating the evaluation of component manufacturing tolerances, or the adaptation of data versions to vehicle variants.

5.6.1 Offline and Online Calibration Procedures

When working with calibration systems, a general distinction between online and offline calibration can be made.

In offline calibration, the execution of the control and monitoring functions of the ECU—the so-called drive program—is interrupted while parameter values are modified or calibrated. Thus, offline calibration is fraught with a number of limitations. Especially when used on test benches or in-vehicle testing, setting or changing of parameters always requires that the test bench or drive trial operation be interrupted.

For this reason, a testing procedure that supports the more versatile approach of online calibration is much more useful. In online calibration, parameter values can be modified "on the fly," that is, while the microcontroller onboard the ECU is running the drive program. In other words, the setting or changing of parameters, and the simultaneous execution of control and monitoring functions, is possible even while normal test bench and drive trial operation is ongoing.

During the operation of the calibration tool, exception situations may develop where short-term failures in the ascending sequence of strict x-axis point monotony on characteristic curves and maps call for a certain robustness of the program running on the microcontroller. For this reason, online calibration makes greater demands on the stability of the control and monitoring functions.

Online calibration is ideally suited to protracted tuning tasks on parameters associated with functions of somewhat lower dynamics (e.g., for fine-tuning engine control functions on an engine test bed).

Although parameter settings are not changed during the active execution of control functions with high dynamics or safety relevance, here, too, the online calibration of parameters can dispense with the need to interrupt the drive program.

One pertinent example is the fine-tuning of ABS functions in braking applications. In this case, although adjustments do not occur during the actual ABS control action, online calibration can reduce the interval between two road tests.

Figure 5-86 depicts two contrasting examples of the procedures involved in online and offline calibration. The diagram outlines the different requirements existing for online and offline calibration systems. For example, offline calibration systems "make do" with the available functions, such as measuring, offboard calibration of parameters, and downloading the program and data versions—that is, by means of Flash programming—into the microcontroller. By contrast, online calibration calls for additional functions facilitating on-the-fly calibration without requiring the drive program to be interrupted. The following sections are oriented in line with the functions required for online and offline calibration procedures.

5.6.2 Software Update Through Flash Programming

To initialize the ECU, the program version and data version first must be downloaded to the respective memory areas of the microcontroller. In standard practice, development ECUs are

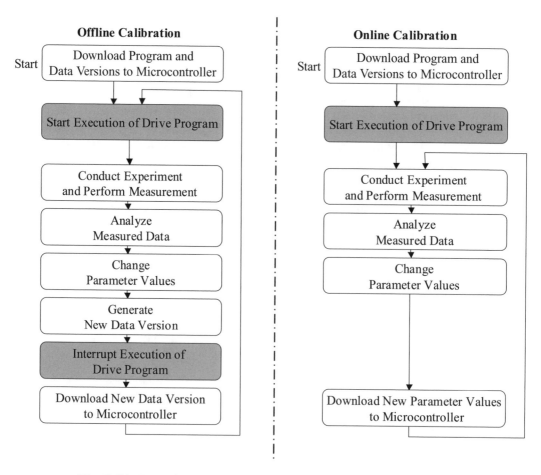

Offline Calibration

Online Calibration

Fig. 5-86. Procedural differences between offline and online calibration.

equipped with Flash memory. The software update for the program and data versions can be accomplished through Flash programming (Fig. 5-87).

Figure 4-23 in Chapter 4 showed that, for any software update using Flash programming, a dedicated software operating state is defined, in which the execution of the control and monitoring functions required for normal vehicle operation is interrupted. The transition to the Software Update operating state is initiated by the Flash programming tool and may occur only in certain conditions. For example, in engine ECUs, such a condition would consist of the detection of engine standstill, that is, engine RPM = 0.

When the Software Update operating state has been entered, the program version and the initial data version are downloaded into the Flash memory on the microcontroller. Afterward, triggered by the Flash programming tool, the microcontroller again exits the Software Update state and transitions to the Normal Operating state, in which the control and monitoring functions of the drive program are executed. Section 6.3 in Chapter 6 discusses the actual Flash programming procedure for the software update.

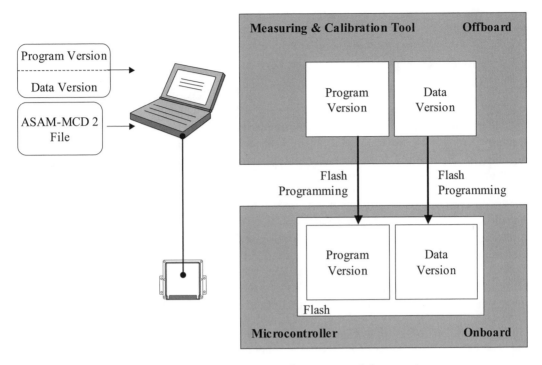

Fig. 5-87. *Flash programming of program and data versions.*

The capabilities of the Flash technologies in current use are limited to the erasing or reprogramming of entire memory areas, the so-called Flash segments. In situations where it is necessary to facilitate separate programming of program and data versions, this means that the data version must be stored in a Flash segment that is different from that of the program version. Thus, Flash programming requires the addressing of specific memory areas. At its current state of the art, Flash technology is incapable of programming changes made to the values of individual parameters.

5.6.3 Synchronous Measuring of Microcontroller and Instrumentation Signals

In standard practice, the effect of changes to parameter values is evaluated by means of measurements. The objective is to analyze the concerted interaction of all vehicle system components in the execution of a specific vehicle function on the basis of a diversity of measurement signals. A typical example of this kind of experimental observation is that of checking the engine ECU with regard to oxygen control in cold starting conditions. This experiment may be conducted either in a subzero testing facility, or it may be carried out through in-vehicle testing in the course of arctic field trials.

In most situations, however, evaluating a function in this manner is hardly possible without the instrumentation of all participating vehicle components by means of a suitable measuring technology. Also needed in this context is the synchronous logging of measurement data in the microcontroller, as well as in the instrumented components.

The measuring system must support the capture of fluctuating signals in the microcontroller (e.g., the measurements of variables stored in the RAM onboard the microcontroller) with a suitable measuring technology. To add to the challenge, these measurements also must be taken synchronously with additional signals originating in the instrumentation in the periphery of the ECU (Fig. 5-84). Finally, these measurements may include the acquisition of signals related to the driver or environment.

These additional signals are frequently picked up at the sensors and actuators associated with the vehicle function being tested. In many cases, the current environmental conditions, such as atmospheric pressure and air temperature, are deemed to be relevant, as are additional signals such as those representing torques, pressures, temperatures, or exhaust emissions, all of which are picked up at a diverse number of measuring points in the vehicle. Also, the data traffic linked to a function under test can be picked up on the onboard communications network of the vehicle; it is subject to synchronized recording, in many cases.

Thus, it stands to reason that a performance class exceeding that of the vehicle sensors is demanded for the instrumentation. From the standpoint of measuring technology, major challenges must be met in two areas. There is the task of synchronizing the various capture rates of microcontroller signals on one hand, and the acquisition of measured values of the spatially distributed and decentralized instrumentation on the other. This also involves the placement of time stamps and the synchronization of the system time (see Fig. 2-53 in Chapter 2).

5.6.4 Downloading and Evaluating Onboard Diagnostic Data

In addition to the setting of parameter values for control functions, calibration of the monitoring and onboard diagnostic functions (e.g., threshold values for plausibility checks) also is required.

In addition to the measuring technology discussed in the preceding section, the experimental verification of the serviceability of the onboard diagnostic system requires diagnostic data to be downloaded for analysis from the fault memory of the microcontroller. It also should be possible to clear the fault memory in preparation for an experiment. This means that the basic functionality of an offboard diagnostic system is already required during calibration (see Fig. 2-64 in Chapter 2).

The description file in ASAM-MCD 2 format contains the descriptive information required for the plain-text display of fault memory contents and for the conversion of signals to enable the physical representation by the measuring and calibration tool. Chapter 6 discusses the architecture of offboard diagnostic tools in greater detail.

5.6.5 Offline Calibration of Parameters

The information contained in the description file forms the basis for the description of values of the parameters of the data version—that is, the values of characteristic values, curves, and maps—at the physical level of the calibration tool. The tool also provides a comfortable means of visualizing changes in parameter values by means of graphical or table-based editing functions.

The following sections refer to the data version held in the Flash memory of the microcontroller as the *reference version* (also the *reference page*). Likewise, the data version in the calibration tool is termed the *tool reference page* (Fig. 5-88). To change parameter values, a copy of the reference page—termed the *working page*—is created in the calibration tool. The data version of the working page can be modified, whereas the reference page remains unchanged.

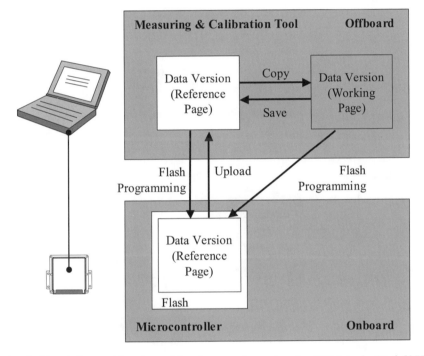

Fig. 5-88. *Offline calibration of the data version using the INCA tool. (Ref. [87])*

The changes made to the working page can be backed up to the tool reference page. In this way, the tool reference page represents a basis for comparison with the other changes made to the working page.

Conversely, when the current values have been uploaded from the microcontroller, the reference page comprises a true reflection of the current state of the ECU.

The reference page or working page of the tool is downloaded into the microcontroller with only a subsequent Flash programming session. This again will require changing the operating state of the microcontroller, with an interruption of the drive program.

5.6.6 Online Calibration of Parameters

If the online modification of parameter values also must be available, this will require an expansion of the working page/reference page concept on the microcontroller.

This is accomplished by copying the data for online calibration from the ROM or Flash memory area to a RAM segment that is not used by the program, that is, the segment where the working page resides (Fig. 5-89). In this RAM area, which is also termed *calibration RAM* (*CAL-RAM*, for short), both the microcontroller and calibration tool work in sync with the calibration data (Figs. 5-1 and 5-89).

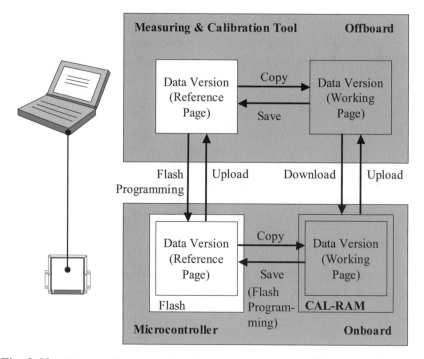

Fig. 5-89. *Online calibration of the data version using the INCA tool. (Ref. [87])*

As a result, although parameter value changes on the microcontroller reference page (stored in Flash memory) require exact memory addressing and an interruption of the drive program, on-the-fly calibration on the microcontroller working page (stored in CAL-RAM) is capable of addressing individual parameters without interfering with or interrupting the drive program.

To this end, the microcontroller software is required to access the working page during the execution of the drive program; this may be accomplished through modifications to the microcontroller software or hardware. Some of the available methods are introduced in the next section.

5.6.7 Classification of Offboard Interfaces for Online Calibration

The calibration tool can avail itself of several interfaces of the microcontroller to access the CAL-RAM area. A basis differentiation can be made whether or not a CAL-RAM segment is present onboard the microcontroller, and whether a tool uses the parallel bus or a serial interface of the microcontroller to access the CAL-RAM (Fig. 5-90).

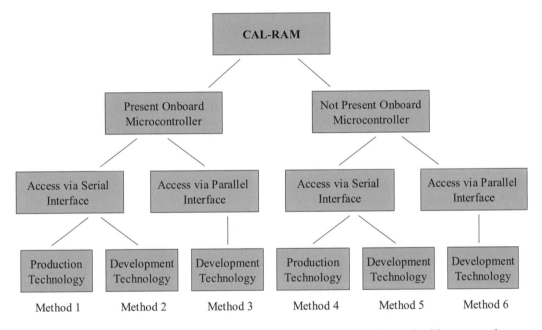

Fig. 5-90. *Classification of interfaces between the microcontroller and calibration tools.*

With respect to the serial interfaces, another distinctive feature should be considered. It is possible to choose a specific serial interface technology that also is deployed in the production ECU, where it is used for offboard diagnostic communications or for onboard communications. Widely used examples of such a serial technology are the K-Line [5] or CAN (Controller Area Network) [2]. It also is possible to use an interface that exists only during the development phase and that is used for software downloading and debugging. Examples of this are NEXUS [92] or JTAG [93]. By contrast, the parallel bus of the microcontroller is used for access only during the development phase.

In this way, the classification results in the overall view shown in Fig. 5-90. All of the interfaces occurring in practical real-world applications may be assigned to one of Methods 1 through 6. After a short introduction by way of simplified block diagrams, these are subject to a brief evaluation throughout the following sections.

As an example of the simplification of the block diagrams in question, only the CAL-RAM present or not present onboard the microcontroller is mentioned, whereas no further differentiation is made. This simplification ignores whether the CAL-RAM—to the extent that the existence of both variants is technically feasible in conjunction with the deployed microcontroller type—is implemented by means of internal or external RAM. The simplification further ignores the type of implementation (e.g., through an ECU extension or a microcontroller extension in the development phase) that is used.

5.6.7.1 Serial Preproduction Interface with Internal CAL-RAM (Method 1)

In conjunction with the internal CAL-RAM, Method 1—that is, the use of a serial interface that is also deployed in the production ECU—has the inherent advantage that hardly any modifications are necessary on the ECU as compared with the production ECU and that the technology is suited to in-vehicle deployment (Fig. 5-91). The CAL-RAM is no longer required in the production ECU. Due to cost considerations, development ECUs can be equipped with microcontroller development samples equipped with additional CAL-RAM. However, if this is not possible, this CAL-RAM in certain circumstances will result in higher hardware costs in the production ECU.

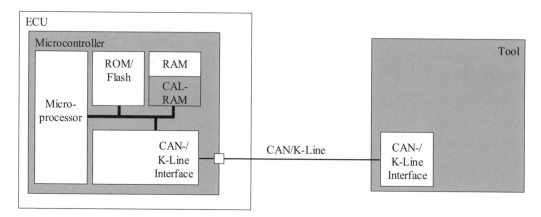

Fig. 5-91. *Serial preproduction interface with internal CAL-RAM (Method 1).*

Because cost considerations tend to limit the transmission rate of the interface, it does not always fulfill the high demands imposed on the measuring technology during the development phase. With increasing frequency, the K-Line [5], which also is used for offboard communications, or the CAN interface, which is used for onboard and increasingly for offboard diagnostic communications, are used for this purpose.

If the interface also is put to concurrent use for onboard communications, as is the case with the CAN interface, it may already be found to be severely burdened. For this reason, a second CAN interface often is used, which is exclusively dedicated to offboard communications with the development tool. In this way, no additional traffic burden is imposed on onboard communications.

On the downside, the microcontroller is burdened in both cases by the implementation of communications between the microcontroller and tool through software components that occupy additional resources, such as runtime and memory capacity.

In many cases, online calibration is subject to limitations caused by the limited size of the CAL-RAM area. This effectively restricts the number of characteristic values, curves, and maps that can be calibrated at any one time. Although the dynamic management and allotment of the CAL-RAM capacities may take the edge off this issue, it should not be overlooked that—in each case, and in a manner reminiscent of offboard communications—CAL-RAM management also allocates additional microcontroller resources.

CAL-RAM management methods are discussed in Section 5.6.8.

5.6.7.2 Serial Development Interface with Internal CAL-RAM (Method 2)

Method 2, that is, the use of a serial development interface in conjunction with internal CAL-RAM, also provides the advantage of necessitating only small hardware changes on the ECU side, as compared with the production ECU. However, parts of the development interfaces such as NEXUS [92] or JTAG [93] are specified for other areas of application, with debug operations being one example. Other microcontroller interfaces are specifically designed for the microcontroller. In most cases, these do not fulfill all of the requirements with respect to in-vehicle testing in rough conditions. Accordingly, the conversion to an interface that is specially configured for in-vehicle use must be effected in the ECU itself. One solution based on this principle, using a so-called *Serial ETK* [94], is shown in Fig. 5-92.

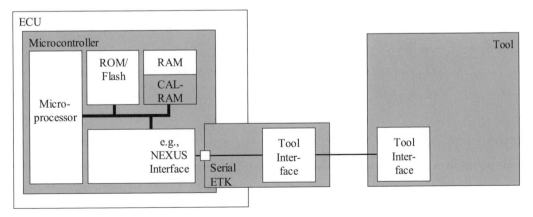

Fig. 5-92. *Serial development interface with internal CAL-RAM (Method 2).*

Almost without exception, the transmission rate of development interfaces is considerably higher than that of production interfaces, thus fulfilling the greater all-around demands made on measuring technology in the development phase.

In the event that this type of development interface is used, and if the communications between the microcontroller and tool utilize a hardware implementation, then no extensions of or modifications to the microcontroller software are required. It also goes without saying that the influence of this method on runtime is much smaller than with other methods.

However, as is the case with Method 1 discussed previously, online calibration continues to be restricted by the limited size of the CAL-RAM area, and the microcontroller continues to be burdened with the CAL-RAM management.

5.6.7.3 Parallel Development Interface with Internal CAL-RAM (Method 3)

As an alternative, and to the extent possible, a parallel development interface as per Method 3, depicted in Fig. 5-93, may be employed. Although the performance features are similar to those of Method 2, the required hardware modifications in the ECU are considerably more extensive than they would be with access through a serial interface. For this reason, the practical value of Method 3 might be deemed negligible.

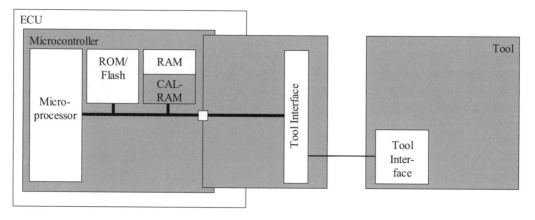

Fig. 5-93. *Parallel development interface with internal CAL-RAM (Method 3).*

5.6.7.4 Serial Preproduction Interface with Additional CAL-RAM (Method 4)

The restrictions imposed on online calibration by virtue of the limitation of internal CAL-RAM size may be remedied through the installation of additional CAL-RAM capacity in development ECUs and through the use of development samples of the microcontroller, which feature additional CAL-RAM, as shown in the diagram of Method 4 (Fig. 5-94).

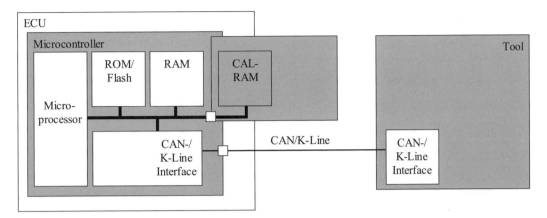

Fig. 5-94. *Serial preproduction interface with additional CAL-RAM (Method 4).*

The use of a preproduction interface, as shown in Fig. 5-94, does not provide a remedy to the aforementioned restrictions in terms of transmission performance and microcontroller burden. These issues persist unabated.

5.6.7.5 Serial Development Interface with Additional CAL-RAM (Method 5)

The restrictions with respect to transmission rate and microcontroller load again can be avoided through the use of a serial development interface of the kind described in Method 5. Such a solution, which uses a Serial ETK [94] and additional CAL-RAM, is shown in Fig. 5-95. However, because this method requires not only additional CAL-RAM but also an interface conversion, the associated modifications to the ECU hardware are quite extensive.

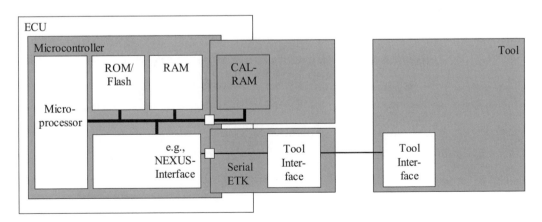

Fig. 5-95. *Serial development interface with additional CAL-RAM (Method 5).*

5.6.7.6 Parallel Development Interface with Additional CAL-RAM (Method 6)

Method 6, that is, the use of a parallel development interface in conjunction with additional CAL-RAM, provides the benefit that calibration data, as well as independent CAL-RAM access by the microcontroller and tool, may be combined while keeping the microcontroller burden low to moderate. Such a solution, which uses a so-called *Parallel ETK* [95], is shown in Fig. 5-96. Here, too, the required modifications to the ECU hardware are relatively extensive.

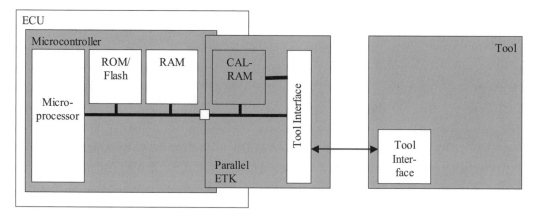

Fig. 5-96. *Parallel development interface with additional CAL-RAM (Method 6).*

5.6.7.7 Communications Protocols for Calibration Tools and Microcontrollers

The communications between calibration tools and microcontrollers are governed by several standardized protocols. Table 5-3 provides an overview.

TABLE 5-3
STANDARDIZATION OF COMMUNICATIONS BETWEEN
TOOL AND MICROCONTROLLER

Interface	Parallel Interface	Serial Interface	
Physical layer	Dependent on microcontroller	CAN [2]	K-Line [5]
Protocol		ASAM-MCD 1a: CCP/XCP [17]	
		ISO: Diagnostics on CAN [26]	ISO: KWP 2000 [25]

5.6.8 CAL-RAM Management

Regardless of the selected method, the microcontroller, once initialized, starts working on the basis of the reference page parameters. In this way, operation also is possible without a calibration tool being connected. Upon initialization, the working page is overwritten with the data from the reference page. Afterward, the procedures to be carried out may use the parameters from either the reference page or the working page. This requires a switchover of the drive program from working page to reference page, and vice versa. It can be implemented through software or hardware modifications of the microcontrollers. Some microcontrollers provide full hardware support for this function. The switchover is controlled by the calibration tool.

A monitoring concept on the microcontroller side may be structured in such a way that any implausible behavior of drive program functions in response to changes in parameter values on the working page (e.g., in the event that control function instabilities are detected) will cause an automatic switchover to the reference page as "limp-home" operating state.

If implausible behavior occurs after parameter value changes, the user of the calibration tool can quickly restore the system to a serviceable state by switching to the reference page of the system.

5.6.8.1 CAL-RAM Management with Sufficient Memory Resources

Provided that the available CAL-RAM area is sufficiently dimensioned—that is, having at least the size of memory capacity required by the data version in the Flash memory of the microcontroller—then the effort expended on the microcontroller side for CAL-RAM management is essentially limited to three tasks: (1) copying the entire reference page to the working page, (2) backing up the working page to the reference page via Flash programming, and (3) toggling between these two pages (Fig. 5-97).

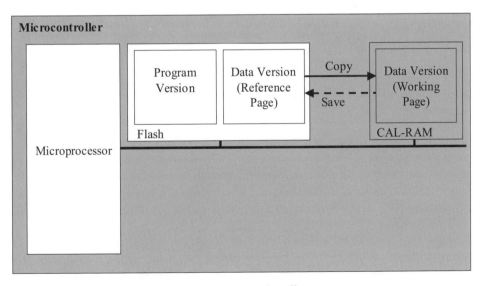

Fig. 5-97. *CAL-RAM management with sufficient memory resources.*

5.6.8.2 CAL-RAM Management with Limited Memory Resources

However, if the size of the CAL-RAM area is limited, meaning that it will not be possible to copy the entire data version into CAL-RAM, then the CAL-RAM management must be extended—in both microcontroller and calibration tool—through the addition of functions that facilitate the management of a segment of the data version, that is, a parameter subset (Fig. 5-98).

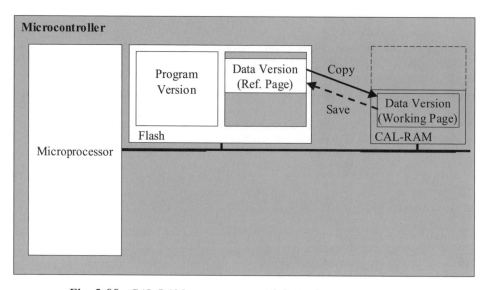

Fig. 5-98. *CAL-RAM management with limited memory resources.*

As a result, only this parameter subset will permit manipulation by means of the aforementioned copy function and backup Flash programming, including page toggling and online calibration.

The data version segment can be determined by memory address or on a parameter basis. If the segment definition is memory based, then the parameters of a contiguous Flash memory segment can be copied into CAL-RAM for subsequent calibration, as shown in Fig. 5-98.

The parameter-oriented definition of a data segment provides a larger measure of user comfort because it allows for more flexible procedures. One of the reasons is that the reference page is no longer a contiguous block of Flash memory; instead, it results, as shown in Fig. 5-99, from the memory areas of the selected parameters. The selection of a parameter subset may take place in the calibration tool, with subsequent replication in the microcontroller by means of a pointer table. As a result, the microcontroller program no longer directly accesses the parameters on the reference page—marked ① in Fig. 5-99—but engages in indirect access with the aid of the pointer table labeled ② in Fig. 5-99. In the procedure thus outlined, the calibration tool can toggle between the parameter access to the reference page (via ③) and access to the working page (via ④).

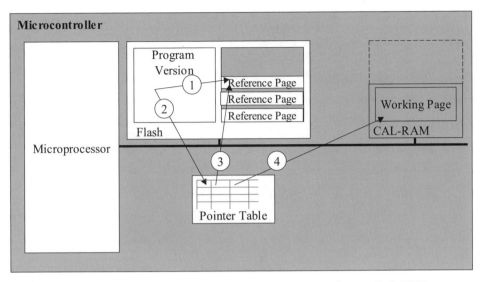

Fig. 5-99. *Pointer table for managing parameter subsets. (Ref. [87])*

If the pointer table is stored in the Flash memory of the microcontroller, then each modification made to the parameter subset will necessitate the respective Flash segment to be newly programmed, and the parameter subset will remain static during the execution of the drive program.

An alternative solution would be to store the pointer table in the CAL-RAM area of the microcontroller. In that case, it also can be dynamically changed while the drive program is in progress.

5.6.9 Parameter and Data Version Management

In addition to the basic measuring and calibration systems functions discussed so far, additional functions must be supported on the tool side. Examples would be those functions that handle parameter-oriented export, import, and merging of data versions, merging of program and data versions, and evaluation of measured data. Other required functions would be the calibration of dependent parameters (Fig. 5-57), the calculation of virtual signals (Fig. 5-58), and interfaces to documentation and configuration management tools.

Figure 5-100 provides an overview of the functions required for the management of parameter values and data versions. With the aid of information from the description file, the data version can be converted inside the tool to the physical display and then stored in a database. These physical parameter values can be edited and are then available for further processing in a variety of applications. Using the specification of the data model of a software component, this facilitates the calibration of the data model of that software component; based on the design of the

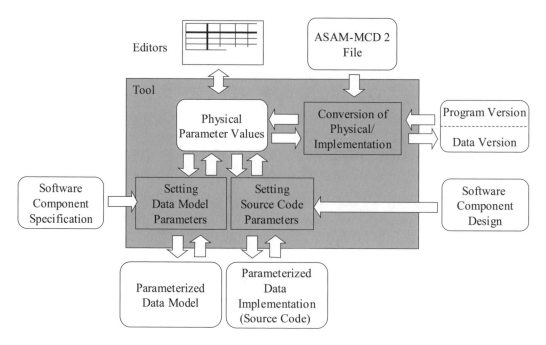

Fig. 5-100. *Parameter value and data version management.*

data model of a software component, it also is possible to calibrate that software component in source code. The reverse procedure is possible, too.

5.6.9.1 Binary Program and Data Version File Calibration

The process concludes with the generation of a final data version and a calibration of the binary file. Both the program version and data version thus are passed on in the binary format required by production and service applications.

The advantage of this procedural approach is that the calibration system can provide the required functionality in its entirety, for the simple reason that it belongs to the standard feature set of the system. It also is possible to split the calibration tasks for distribution across corporate boundaries. In that case, the exchange of program and data versions is unidirectional, that is, restricted to one-way submissions from vendor to automaker.

The disadvantage is that the binary file format tends to restrict the management of data records at the physical level, while constraining their easy utilization across the boundaries of individual projects. Another drawback is seen in the fact that when the calibration procedures have been completed, optimizations concerning the program version can no longer be carried out. The calibration procedure may require certain adaptations of the software structure, which are to some extent already integrated in the production version.

5.6.9.2 Model or Source Code Calibration and Optimization

These drawbacks can be compensated with the use of a procedure where the calibration system exports the final data version and where, with the aid of information about the data model, this version is used for calibration at the source code or model level.

Following this, extensive optimization measures can be carried out. These may range from a file system optimized for runtime or memory capacity, to the adaptation of the number of x-axis points, to the optimization of the quantization, value range, or memory segment of characteristic values, curves, and maps. The model or source code thus optimized is then retranslated—possibly using adapted compiler options—and, subsequent to the required quality checks, is released for use by production and service. Because, after this juncture, parameter values can either no longer be changed or can be modified only to a limited extent, this optimizing step can be carried out only immediately prior to the abovementioned release of the data version to production and service.

5.6.10 *Design and Automation of Experiments*

The use of an automation interface, such as ASAM-MCD 3 [17], provides for the control of a diversity of functions by a high-level automation system. This facilitates not only the automation of offline tasks (e.g., the evaluation of recorded measurement data) but also the automation of online procedures, such as running lengthy tuning procedures on a laboratory vehicle or test bench, as discussed in Section 5.5.4 [29–31].

Many related activities, such as the automation of measured data analysis or the determination of optimized parameter values, are at the core of ongoing research and development efforts.

However, we regret that, despite the tremendous significance of these and related topics, discussing this comprehensive topic in detail would exceed the scope of this book.

CHAPTER SIX

METHODS AND TOOLS FOR PRODUCTION AND SERVICE

In many cases, the various tools used in production and service also support software parameterization and software update functions in addition to the conventional offboard diagnostic functions discussed in Section 2.6.6 of Chapter 2.

However, compared with tool deployment during the development phase, special additional requirements must be fulfilled, particularly with regard to service applications.

Following the dictate of cost considerations, it must be possible to carry out as many tool functions as possible without removing the production ECU from the vehicle. Frequently, the solution entails the standardized routing of communications between the tools in the service facility and the production ECUs onboard the vehicle through the so-called *offboard diagnostic* interface of the vehicle, as shown in Fig. 2-67 of Chapter 2. Another essential prerequisite concerns software updates performed at the service shop; in this case, a high degree of availability must be ensured to dispense with the necessity to physically remove ECUs in response to abnormal behavior or functional aborts.

Increasingly, standardized communications protocols between tools and ECUs (e.g., Keyword Protocol 2000 [25] or Diagnostics on CAN [26]) and standardized databases for the respective tools (ASAM-MCD [17]) are replacing specialized solutions. Figure 6-1 shows an overview of the structure of an offboard diagnostic system according to ASAM-MCD [17]. This standard pursues the objective of defining a uniform (i.e., standardized) software architecture for measuring, calibration, and diagnostic tools deployed in vehicle development, production, and service.

6.1 Offboard Diagnostics

In addition to the basic functions such as downloading hardware and software ID of a given ECU, the offboard diagnostic systems discussed in Section 2.6.6 of Chapter 2 provide the following:

- Diagnostic functions for setpoint generators and sensors

- Diagnostic functions for actuators

- Functions facilitating the downloading and subsequent clearing of fault memory contents

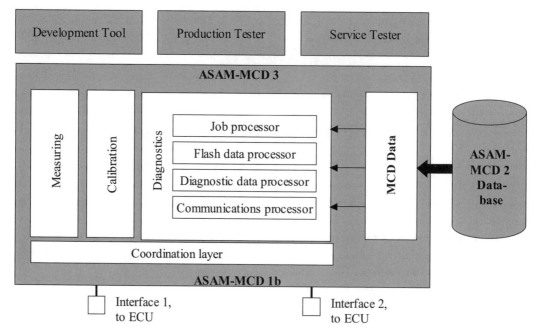

Fig. 6-1. *Structure of a diagnostic system according to ASAM-MCD. (Ref. [17])*

In contrast with the onboard diagnostic functions (OBD), offboard diagnostics are not subject to the same constraints with respect to hardware resources. Therefore, offboard diagnostics can bring to bear troubleshooting algorithms that are at once extensive and comprehensive, even if they come with the prerequisites of considerable runtime and memory capacity requirements. It would exceed the scope of this book to discuss the various diagnostic methods. Thus, reference is made to suggested reading and advanced literature [52].

When designing software for a microcontroller, it must be determined whether or not an offboard diagnostic function may be carried out while the ECU is running the drive program (see Fig. 2-64 in Chapter 2 and Fig. 4-23 in Chapter 4).

Example: Sensor diagnostics concurrent with active drive program

Sensor diagnostics are frequently supported through the acquisition of sensor signals, that is, the variables present at the microcontroller inputs, and by the online transmission of measured values to the offboard diagnostic system. The diagnostic tester is capable of enabling this function onboard the microcontroller while the normal drive program is being executed.

The diagnostic tester often is equipped to accept the connection of additional diagnostic measurement equipment that permits the synchronized recording of additional external signals—the so-called diagnostic instrumentation. As a result, the sensor diagnostics may be performed with the aid of an array of measuring technology not unlike that depicted in Fig. 5-84 of Chapter 5.

Example: Actuator diagnostics with an inactive drive program

By contrast, actuator diagnostics often are supported by the fact that the offboard diagnostic system can directly support the definition of setpoint values for the actuators, that is, the specification and stimulation of desired microprocessor output values.

To this end, at least those functions of the drive program that calculate the setpoint values during normal operation must be disabled. This may be accomplished through the transition to a special operating state dedicated to actuator diagnostics, which is triggered by the diagnostic tester (see Fig. 4-23 in Chapter 4).

As is the case with calibration, the conversion from implementation display to physical display and vice versa, while measuring, or in the presence of predefined internal microcontroller signals, occurs onboard the tool.

6.2 Parameterization of Software Functions

As a general statement with respect to today's manufacture of automobiles, it is safe to say that the overall situation in both production and service is characterized by a large number of vehicle variants. The reasons for this phenomenon are equally manifold. First, on one hand, any automotive customer is able to assemble his customized vehicle by selecting individual equipment options. Second, a variety of regulations and requirements indigenous to the automotive markets of different countries results in vehicle options that are more or less country specific. A third influence factor consists of the option that permits several operators of the same vehicle to store their personal settings—such as mirror positions, favorite radio stations, and/or air conditioner settings—in onboard memory for instant recall. These driver-specific variants are also known as *personal profiles* [96].

Customer and country-specific equipment, as well as personal profiles, result in different vehicle and function variants. In consequence, software variants become a necessity.

In production and service, the aforementioned variants can be controlled by dedicated software configuration parameters. Thus, it is possible to achieve a dramatic reduction in the number of hardware variants to be handled in electronic systems.

All of these logically point to the need to design hardware that is universally deployable. This, in turn, would permit the selection of a given software variant by means of a suitable parameterization procedure almost at the end of the vehicle production timeline, such as shortly before the installation of the ECU in the vehicle. Another alternative would be to defer this selection until it can be performed in the service shop (e.g., on an ECU that is already installed in the vehicle).

With regard to personalizing operator profiles, user-specific software parameters must be set, stored, selected, and enabled. This may be accomplished either in the service shop (by means of a service tester function) or by the user himself or herself (by using a function provided by the user interface).

To prevent the inadvertent specification of faulty or illegal parameter settings, this software parameterization procedure must be taken into account early in the design of the software architecture.

In this context, viewing this task at the level of the logical system architecture of the vehicle, as shown in Fig. 6-2, will result in definite advantages over a view of the technical system architecture.

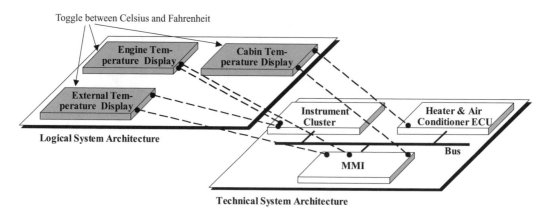

Fig. 6-2. *Functions and ECUs responsible for temperature displays. (Ref. [96])*

Example: Toggling the temperature display unit between degrees Celsius and degrees Fahrenheit

The parameterization option for the unit of measure of the temperature display may serve as a case in point. The intent is that all temperature display functions shall be toggled between degrees Celsius and degrees Fahrenheit by means of a single software parameter. For example, this affects the display functions for engine, cabin interior, and outside temperature. On the ECU side, toggling these display parameters has an effect on the instrument cluster, the heater and air conditioner ECU, and the man/machine interface (MMI), as shown in Fig. 6-2. Because the temperatures are indicated on a variety of display units, such as the display of the engine temperature in the instrument cluster and the MMI, an option to parameterize each individual ECU would allow for different values being set. The resulting inaccuracy can be prevented by setting parameters only at the function level.

As discussed in Section 5.4.4 of Chapter 5, several options are differentiated with respect to the technical implementation. The software parameter values can be stored in Flash memory as shown in Fig. 5-69 of Chapter 5, or they may be written to the EEPROM of the microcontroller, as shown in Fig. 5-70 of Chapter 5. In both cases, a function of the production and service tool can be used to change the values of the software parameters.

In contrast to calibration (see Section 5.6 in Chapter 5), where the intent is to adapt the entire data version wherever possible, the service-based parameterization of software functions affects only selected software parameters that also are stored in a programmable memory segment, such as in EEPROM or Flash memory, onboard the production ECU.

In standard practice, the option of setting these parameters offline (i.e., during an interruption of the drive program) is sufficient. This may be accomplished through the transition to a special operating state dedicated to software parameterization, which is triggered by the parameterization tool (see Fig. 4-23 in Chapter 4). Thus, it has been demonstrated that the parameterization procedure is similar to the procedure used in the offline calibration of selected parameters.

6.3 Software Update Through Flash Programming

The use of Flash memory as a storage technology for program version and data version also is increasing with respect to production ECUs. This opens the door to situations where the software updates for ECUs can be accomplished in the field by newly programming the Flash memory, possible through the central offboard diagnostic interface of the vehicle. This facilitates a software update without the need to remove the ECU from the vehicle. The cost-saving potential over a physical replacement of the ECU is plainly evident.

Subsequent to covering some technical Flash programming prerequisites, this section discusses a basic Flash programming procedure through the offboard diagnostic interface. For the sake of simplicity and clarity, the discussion omits descriptions of some of the optional extensions that would result in higher Flash programming speeds.

6.3.1 Erasing and Programming Flash Memory

It was mentioned in Section 2.3 of Chapter 2 and in Section 5.6 of Chapter 5 that the Flash technologies in current use provide for only the deletion or reprogramming of complete Flash memory segments. The smallest Flash memory unit that is physically contiguous and that can be erased and programmed as a single entity is termed a *segment*, or *Flash segment*. Therefore, Flash programming makes a distinction between the steps of erasing and programming of Flash segments.

Also, note that hindrances of a technical nature prevent the simultaneous execution of a program from within a Flash segment while another Flash segment of the same Flash module is being reprogrammed. For this reason, during actual Flash programming, the program parts needed to control the program flow for a given Flash module must be swapped out or moved to another memory location (e.g., another Flash module or an unused RAM segment onboard the microcontroller).

With the exception of these relevant prerequisites, the following sections shall ignore the details of further microcontroller or memory-specific differentiations.

6.3.2 *Flash Programming Through the Offboard Diagnostic Interface*

In conjunction with large Flash memory segments, the limited transmission speeds and/or performance of the offboard diagnostic interface combine to produce Flash programming intervals of considerable length. Thus, it stands to reason that production and service frequently issue the requirement to reduce Flash programming times. This may be accomplished, for example, by reducing the number of Flash segments requiring reprogramming (i.e., by means of function-oriented Flash programming) or by the separate programming of the respective program version and data version. In actual practice, the program version often is programmed as early as during ECU manufacture, whereas the data version, being vehicle and variant specific, is programmed as the new vehicle is reaching, quite literally, the "end of the line." As a result, software development must store a variety of software functions, as well as the program version and data version, in different Flash segments.

All of the microcontroller program parts handling the communications between the microcontroller and Flash programming tool must be stored in ROM or in a third Flash segment, together with the Flash programming routines and Flash loader (see Fig. 1-22 in Chapter 1). Throughout the discussion to follow, the basic program stored in ROM is termed *startup block*, and its counterpart stored in Flash memory is termed *boot block*. Figure 6-3 depicts the division of the entire program into four parts: startup block, boot block, program version, and data version. The combination of the startup block and boot block makes available the software functionality of the microcontroller required for Flash programming through the offboard diagnostic interface.

The separation into startup block and boot block makes good sense for a number of reasons. First, the boot block—provided that it is stored in Flash memory—can be separately reprogrammed. The procedures for boot block shifting and subsequent Flash programming are discussed in detail in Section 6.3.5. Second, the boot block is the ideal storage venue for the nonvolatile deposit of the current status of a given Flash programming session. This means that a restart is facilitated in the event of a programming interruption or abort. By contrast, the unalterable basic functionality of the startup block can be stored in the more cost-effective ROM.

However, the drive program, being part of the program version and data version, is stored in a different memory segment. The next sections differentiate among the following program parts:

• Startup block
• Boot block
• Program version
• Data version

6.3.3 *Security Requirements*

The Flash programming tool triggers the transition of the microcontroller to the Software Update operating state.

A discussion in Section 5.6 of Chapter 5 highlighted plausibility checks (e.g., the verification of engine standstill in conjunction with engine ECUs) that had to be completed prior to the end of the drive program and to the subsequent transition to the Software Update operating state.

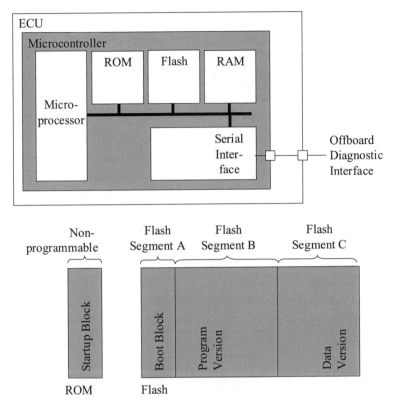

Fig. 6-3. *Memory allocation for startup block, boot block, program version, and data version.*

However, production and service call for additional security measures. Product liability consid-erations require that any unauthorized (i.e., illegal) Flash programming, or Flash programming that conveys, transfers, and/or installs a manipulated program version or data version, must be prevented to the extent possible and, barring this possibility, that the said transfer and/or instal-lation at least may be detected and verified.

For these reasons, Flash programming access normally is protected by two different encryption schemes, termed *authentication* and *signature verification*. Figure 6-4 shows the flow of com-munications procedures between the Flash programming tool and microcontroller.

• Authentication

Following the plausibility check, the actual verification of access rights is carried out. This is the authentication check. The procedure uses a first digital key to ascertain whether or not the respective user of the Flash programming tool is authorized to perform a software update.

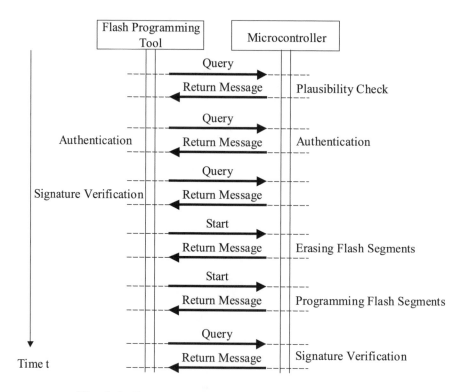

Fig. 6-4. *Security measures protecting Flash programming*
against unauthorized access.

• Signature verification for the new program version or data version to be programmed

Another step checks the data consistency of the new data version or program version to be programmed. This is the signature verification. The procedure uses a second digital key to ascertain whether or not the respective program version and/or data version matches the ECU hardware. The verification also examines whether or not the program version and/or data version to be programmed has been subject to unauthorized modification since the vehicle manufacturer has released it to the production plants or service shops.

• Erasing and programming Flash segments

The boot block will permit the actual erasing and programming actions upon the Flash segments in question to go forward only after both verification steps—authentication and signature verification—have been successfully concluded.

• Signature verification for the newly programmed program version and data version

With the Flash programming session concluded, the microcontroller uses the actual program version and data version just programmed to calculate the signature and to check for possible programming errors. When the signature verification is concluded, the actual result of the signature calculation is deposited in the Flash memory. This is accomplished by storing special memory structures, which are part of the program version and data version, in Flash memory (Fig. 6-5). These are the so-called *program version and data version logistics*. The successful signature verification is the signal for the boot block to enable the activation of the new drive program.

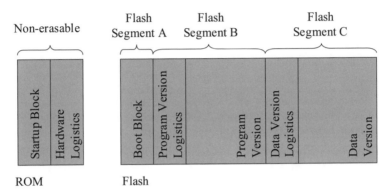

Fig. 6-5. *Hardware, program, and data version logistics for signature calculation, storage, and authentication.*

It would exceed the scope of this book to discuss available encryption schemes. Thus, reference is made to suggested reading and advanced literature [97].

6.3.4 Availability Requirements

Despite the optimization measures discussed in the preceding sections, Flash programming through the offboard interface may take a relatively long time, and interruptions of the programming sequences caused by malfunctions of one kind or another may be expected at any time. Interferences of this kind may come in the guise of power failures in the vehicle electrical system or Flash programming tool, unacceptable responses from other ECUs in the network, or interruptions in the communications connection between the ECU and Flash programming tool, or they may be caused by simple operator error. Failed authentications and signature verifications also cause Flash programming sessions to be aborted.

For all of these reasons, the availability of Flash programming in any possible set of circumstances takes top priority in the design of Flash programming procedures. This requirement may be met, for example, by enabling a restart of the programming sequence after a programming abort. A suitable procedure is presented in the following example.

Example: Flash programming sequence for the program version and data version

Figure 6-6 shows a typical Flash programming procedure of the program version and data version shown in Fig. 6-5.

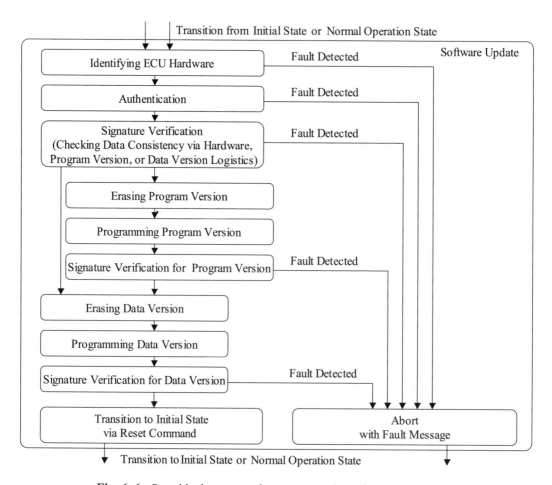

Fig. 6-6. *Boot block states and transitions when Flash programming the program version and data version.*

Upon the successful conclusion of Flash programming, the Flash programming tool issues a Reset command that triggers the transition of the microcontroller to Normal Operation State.

The discussion so far has neglected the swap-out of the boot block into another memory module, which is needed during the actual Flash programming procedure. The following section highlights this boot block shifting, as well as programming of the boot block itself.

6.3.5 Boot Block Shifting and Flash Programming

To complete this area of discussion, one method for Flash programming the boot block shall be examined in detail, taking into account the previously discussed prerequisites of the deployed Flash technology and the availability requirements.

First, and for the duration of the anticipated Flash programming session, the active boot block must be swapped to another memory module onboard the microprocessor. This means that the boot block must be relocatable. This may be accomplished, for example, by copying the boot block into a RAM area that is unoccupied during the Flash programming procedure. The boot block is subsequently run from within the RAM.

A restart of the programming sequence must be possible, even if Flash programming the boot block fails. To retain availability after a programming abort, a fault-free boot block will suffice. This requirement can be met by applying the Recover and Restore commands to the boot block.

Example: Boot block Flash programming sequence

The above-mentioned requirements may be met with the use of the procedural sequence shown in Fig. 6-7. A differentiation is made between the old boot block and its new counterpart.

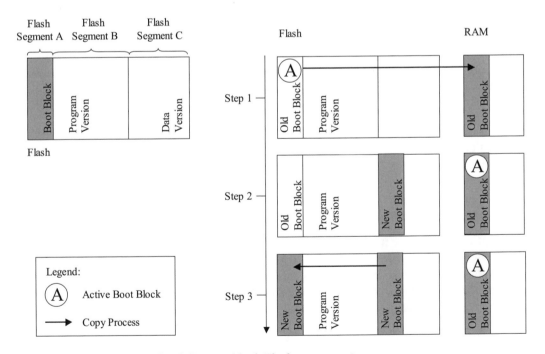

Fig. 6-7. *Boot block Flash programming steps.*

The procedure differentiates three major steps:

Step 1:   Copy the old boot block to free RAM area.

Step 2.1:   Enable the old boot block in RAM, and disable the old boot block in Flash memory.

Step 2.2:   Commit the new boot block to interim storage in Flash segment C.

This step encompasses the procedures "Erase Flash segment C," "Program new boot block in Flash segment C," and "Verify signature for new boot block in Flash segment C."

In the event of a program abort during any one of these operations, the valid old boot block in Flash segment A can be used to restart Flash programming.

Step 3:   Program the new boot block by copying Flash segment C to Flash segment A.

This step encompasses the procedures "Erase Flash segment A," "Program new boot block in Flash segment A by copying Flash segment C to A," and "Verify signature for new boot block in Flash segment A."

In the event of a program abort during any one of these operations, the valid new boot block in Flash segment C can be used to restart Flash programming.

The respective valid boot block in Flash memory must be marked. This validity marker must be committed to nonvolatile storage in Flash memory, making this information the basis for a possible restart.

This is followed by the activation of the new boot block in Flash segment A, and the deactivation of the boot block held in RAM. The final step consists of Flash programming the data version, as described in Fig. 6-6.

6.4 Startup and Testing of Electronic Systems

It may be safe to say that, at the end of the production process, the new vehicle must go to the service shop for the first time. This is the venue for the first startup and testing of the electronic systems of the completely assembled vehicle, which also includes every offboard interface. A similar situation would be occasioned by the replacement of individual electronic vehicle components in a real-life service facility.

All of the methods and tools deployed for the described purpose utilize the functions discussed in Sections 6.1 through 6.3 as a working basis. Application cases in point may be found in the configuration of replaced electronic components taken from a specific vehicle, or in Flash programming of test programs in the production of ECUs.

CHAPTER SEVEN

SUMMARY AND OUTLOOK

Electronic systems and software have become indispensable components of many functions in the modern automobile. There is every reason to believe that the complement of software-supported vehicle functions will continue to grow.

The implementation of vehicle functions based on electronic systems and software requires the concerted application of the knowledge and skills indigenous to several engineering disciplines.

Chapters 1 and 2 addressed this need by providing a comprehensive introduction to vehicle electronics, followed by the basics of control systems, real-time-systems, and distributed and networked systems, as well as reliable and safety-relevant systems.

The development of electronics and the development of software should be viewed as engineering disciplines within the area of system development.

This requires that the hardware-based perception of vehicle functions, systems, and components be expanded to include the software.

Because the development of vehicle functions is a cooperative effort distributed over several departments and companies, software development is organized according to the principle of the division of labor, where various development partners contribute their share in the form of software components, such as real-time operating systems.

Therefore, system and software engineering call for a consistent process that accounts for every single development step—starting with the analysis of user requirements and progressing through specification, design, implementation, integration, and calibration to final acceptance testing. Another important issue is the observation of the entire life cycle of a given vehicle. This requires the early integration of monitoring and diagnostic functions required by customer service at a much later juncture.

The established interdependence of hardware and software is in the process of being loosened. As a basis for defining hardware-independent interfaces between application software and platform software, standards such as ISO, OSEK, ASAM, and future AUTOSAR are gaining importance in the automotive industry.

The processes discussed in Chapters 3 and 4 may be employed to support the development and long-term maintenance of automotive electronic systems and software.

The model-based specification of electronic systems, and of software functions and the environment, fosters an easier understanding of complex interactions while providing a host of benefits throughout the various phases of development.

The use of graphical function models during analysis and specification facilitates the evaluation of alternatives for the technical implementation of the functions. Simulation and rapid prototyping methods likewise are based on function models. With the aid of appropriate tools for code generation, function models also can be mapped to software components for production ECUs.

Models of the vehicle functions and of its environment are needed in laboratory vehicles and on test benches during the integration and test phases of development.

The use of both kinds of models thus clearly supports the testing and integration tasks particular to development projects in which various departments and companies are involved.

In production and service, function models facilitate the implementation of powerful techniques and methods for diagnostics, parameterization, and software updates.

Quality and cost optimization in concert with a reduction of development risk become tangible options through simulation, automation of development tasks, and shifting development steps from the vehicle to the test bench and laboratory. Compared with conventional road testing, all of these benefits add up to a greater scope for freedom of experimentation and a higher degree of test reproducibility.

The foregoing notwithstanding, it is safe to say that the most sophisticated simulation techniques provide answers only to those questions that were actually asked. By contrast, road testing also answers questions that had not even been thought of in advance. Therefore, it stands to reason that road trials will remain indispensable because the final validation of vehicle functions can be obtained only through acceptance testing in the vehicle. Also, note that road testing imposes special demands with respect to the tools employed. Three major items in the "must have" category are the support for a vehicle-compatible offboard interface to the ECUs, mobile measurement equipment suitable for deployment in harsh environments, and, last but not least, user interfaces and displays that are suitable for and easy to use in an in-vehicle environment.

Chapters 5 and 6 examined methods and tools that support the core development processes and the core production and service processes.

In vehicle function development, the trend toward functions that affect several subsystems and that cannot be assigned to one single subsystem is gaining momentum. The capability to network the vehicle and the environment by means of wireless transmission systems created the option of implementing a large set of new functions. In this context, the spectrum goes from pre-crash detection to predictive diagnostic functions. Thus, it appears that the networking paradigm must be expanded to become more encompassing.

This means that environmental systems must be integrated in addition to the in-vehicle systems, making high demands on suitable analysis, specification, and integration methodologies as they apply to the distributed and networked systems thus created.

The fulfillment of numerous requirements and the consideration of many interdependencies make the development of vehicle functions a highly demanding endeavor. The complexity of this endeavor can be managed only by using a small number of simplified design patterns. This approach must be supported by integrated processes, methods, tools, and standards for the entire vehicle life cycle. The established close cooperation among vehicle manufacturers, suppliers, and tool manufacturers will continue to be essential in fostering the further evolution of these processes, methods, tools, and standards.

Given these trends and forecasts of the industry, the discipline of automotive software engineering will continue to provide many exciting challenges.

REFERENCES

[1] Robert Bosch GmbH (Ed.), *Konventionelle und Elektronische Bremssysteme*, Robert Bosch GmbH, Stuttgart, Germany, 2002.

[2] ISO International Organization for Standardization, ISO 11898: Austausch digitaler Informationen; Controller Area Network (CAN) für schnellen Datenaustausch, 1994.

[3] Lapp, A., Torre Flores, P., Schirmer, J., Kraft, D., Hermsen, W., Bertram, T., and Petersen, J., "Software-Entwicklung für Steuergeräte im Systemverbund—Von der CARTRONIC-Domänenstruktur zum Steuergerätecode" ("Software Development for Networked Electronic Control Units—From the CARTRONIC Domain Structure to Code for Electronic Control Units"; original German), in Proceedings of the 10th International Congress "Electronic Systems for Vehicles," Baden-Baden, Germany, September 27–28, 2001, ed. by VDI Society Vehicle and Transportation Technology, VDI-Berichte 1646, VDI-Verlag, Düsseldorf, Germany, 2001, pp. 249–276.

[4] Robert Bosch GmbH (Ed.), *Kraftfahrtechnisches Taschenbuch*, 24th Edition, Vieweg-Verlag, Wiesbaden, Germany, 2002.

[5] International Organization for Standardization, ISO 9141: Straßenfahrzeuge; Diagnosesysteme; Anforderungen für den Austausch digitaler Informationen, 1992.

[6] Robert Bosch GmbH (Ed.), *Motormanagement ME-Motronic*, Robert Bosch GmbH, Stuttgart, Germany, 1999.

[7] Robert Bosch GmbH (Ed.), *Otto-Motormanagement: Grundlagen und Komponenten*, Robert Bosch GmbH, Stuttgart, Germany, 2002.

[8] Robert Bosch GmbH (Ed.), *Elektronische Dieselregelung EDC*, Robert Bosch GmbH, Stuttgart, Germany, 2001.

[9] Frischkorn, Hans-Georg, Negele, Herbert, and Meisenzahl, Johannes, "The Need for Systems Engineering. An Automotive Project Perspective," in Proceedings of the 2nd European Systems Engineering Conference (EuSEC), Munich, Germany, September 13–14, 2000 (keynote, on CD ROM), Herbert Uth Verlag, Munich, Germany, 2000, ISBN 3-89675-935-3.

[10] Fuchs, M., Lersch, F., and Pollehn, D., "Neues Rollenverständnis für die Entwicklung verteilter Systemverbunde in der Karosserie- und Sicherheitselektronik ("New Way to Handle the Development of Distributed Systems in Body and Safety Electronics"; original German), in Proceedings of the 10th International Congress "Electronic Systems for Vehicles," Baden-Baden, Germany, September 27–28, 2001, ed. by VDI Society Vehicle and Transportation Technology, VDI-Berichte 1646, VDI-Verlag, Düsseldorf, Germany, 2001, pp. 135–147.

[11] Eppinger, Andreas, Dieterle, Werner, and Bürger, Klaus Georg, "Mechatronik—Mit ganzheitlichem Ansatz zu erhöhter Funktionalität und Kundennutzen," ATZ/MTZ special issue *Automotive Electronics*, September 2001, pp. 10–18.

[12] Stevens, Richard, Brook, Peter, Jackson, Ken, and Arnold, Stuart, *Systems Engineering. Coping with Complexity*, Prentice-Hall, Upper Saddle River, NJ, 1998.

[13] CMMI® Capability Maturity Model Integration®, http://www.sei.cmu.edu/cmmi.

[14] International Organization for Standardization/International Electrotechnical Commission, ISO/IEC 15504-1: Information Technology—Software Process Assessment—Concepts and Introductory Guide, 1998.

[15] V-Modell—Entwicklungsstandard für IT-Systeme des Bundes. Vorgehensmodell Kurzbeschreibung, 1997, http://www.v-modell.iabg.de/vm97.htm.

[16] OSEK Open Systems and the Corresponding Interfaces for Automotive Electronics, http://www.osek-vdx.org.

[17] ASAM Association for Standardisation of Automation- and Measuring Systems, http://www.asam.de.

[18] Deutsches Institut für Normung e.V., DIN 19250—Grundlegende Sicherheitsbetrachtungen für MSR-Schutzeinrichtungen, 1989.

[19] International Electrotechnical Commission, IEC 61508: Functional Safety of Electrical/Electronic/Programmable Electronic Safety-Related Systems, 1998.

[20] Bundesgesetzblatt, "Verordnung über die Inkraftsetzung der ECE-Regelung Nr. 79 über einheitliche Bedingungen für die Genehmigung der Fahrzeuge hinsichtlich der Lenkanlage" (Verordnung zur ECE-Regelung Nr. 79), Part 2, 1995.

[21] DaimlerChrysler AG, "Übereinkommen über die Annahme einheitlicher technischer Vorschriften für Radfahrzeuge, Ausrüstungsgegenstände und Teile, die in Radfahrzeuge(n) eingebaut und/oder verwendet werden können, und die Bedingungen für die gegenseitige Anerkennung von Genehmigungen, die nach diesen Vorschriften erteilt wurden, ECE-Regelung Nr. 13, Einheitliche Vorschriften für die Genehmigung von Fahrzeugen der Klassen M, N und O hinsichtlich der Bremsen," DaimlerChrysler AG, Stuttgart, Germany, issue 2000-08-31.

[22]   Eckrich, Michael, and Baumgartner, Werner, "By-Wire überlagert Mechanik," *Automobilentwicklung*, September 2001, pp. 24–25.

[23]   IBM International Technical Support Organization, Redbook "Business Process Reengineering and Beyond," September 28, 2001, http://www.ibm.com/support.

[24]   Bertram, Torsten, Opgen-Rhein, Peter, "Modellbildung und Simulation mechatro-nischer Systeme—Virtueller Fahrversuch als Schlüsseltechnologie der Zukunft," ATZ/MTZ special issue *Automotive Electronics*, September 2001, pp. 20–26.

[25]   International Organization for Standardization, ISO 14230: Road Vehicles—Diagnostic Systems—Keyword Protocol 2000, 1999.

[26]   International Organization for Standardization, ISO 15765: Road Vehicles—Diagnostic Systems—Diagnostics on CAN, 2000.

[27]   Lange, K., Bortolazzi, J., Brangs, P., Marx, D., and Wagner, G., "Herstellerinitiative Software" ("Manufacturer Initiative Software"; original German), in Proceedings of the 10th International Congress "Electronic Systems for Vehicles," Baden-Baden, Germany, September 27-28, 2001, ed. by VDI Society Vehicle and Transportation Technology, VDI-Berichte 1646, VDI-Verlag, Düsseldorf, Germany, 2001, pp. 183–199.

[28]   Erben, Meinhard, Fetzer, Joachim, and Schelling, Helmut, "Software-Komponenten—Ein neuer Trend in der Automobilelektronik," ATZ/MTZ special issue *Automotive Electronics*, September 2001, pp. 74–78.

[29]   Gschweitl, Kurt, Pfluegl, Horst, Fortuna, Tiziana, and Leithgoeb, Rainer, "Steigerung der Effizienz in der modellbasierten Motorenapplikation durch die neue CAMEO-Online-DoE-Toolbox," ATZ *Automobiltechnische Zeitschrift*, July/August 2001, pp. 636–643.

[30]   Roy, Ranjit K., *Design of Experiments Using the Taguchi Approach. Steps to Product and Process Improvement*, John Wiley & Sons, New York, 2001.

[31]   Montgomery, Douglas, *Design and Analysis of Experiments*, John Wiley & Sons, New York, 2001.

[32]   Deutsches Institut für Normung e.V., DIN 19226-1—Leittechnik; *Regelungstechnik und Steuerungstechnik,* Allgemeine Grundbegriffe, February 1994.

[33]   Föllinger, Otto, *Regelungstechnik. Einführung in die Methoden und ihre Anwendung,* Hüthig-Verlag, Heidelberg, Germany, 1994.

[34]   Unbehauen, Heinz, *Regelungstechnik*, Vols. 1–3, Vieweg-Verlag, Wiesbaden, Germany, 2000.

[35]   Kiencke, Uwe, and Nielsen, Lars, *Automotive Control Systems. For Engine, Driveline, and Vehicle*, Springer-Verlag, Berlin, Heidelberg, New York, 2000.

[36] Mayr, Robert, *Regelungsstrategien für die automatische Fahrzeugführung. Längs- und Querregelung, Spurwechsel- und Überholmanöver*, Springer-Verlag, Berlin, Heidelberg, New York, 2001.

[37] Kiencke, Uwe, *Signale und Systeme*, R. Oldenbourg Verlag, Munich, Vienna, 1998.

[38] Kiencke, Uwe, *Ereignisdiskrete Systeme. Modellierung und Steuerung verteilter Systeme*, R. Oldenbourg Verlag, Munich, Vienna, 1997.

[39] Robert Bosch GmbH (Ed.), *Mikroelektronik im Kraftfahrzeug*, Robert Bosch GmbH, Stuttgart, Germany, 2001.

[40] Robert Bosch GmbH (Ed.), *Sensoren im Kraftfahrzeug*, Robert Bosch GmbH, Stuttgart, Germany, 2001.

[41] Robert Bosch GmbH (Ed.), *Autoelektrik/Autoelektronik, Systeme und Komponenten*, 4th Edition, Vieweg-Verlag, Wiesbaden, Germany, 2002.

[42] Liu, Jane W.S., *Real-Time Systems*, Prentice-Hall, Upper Saddle River, NJ, 2000.

[43] Wettstein, H., *Architektur von Betriebssystemen*, 3rd Edition, Carl Hanser Verlag, Munich, Germany, 1987.

[44] International Telecommunication Union, Message Sequence Charts, ITU-T Recommendation Z. 120, Geneva, Switzerland, 1994.

[45] Kopetz, Hermann, *Real-Time Systems. Design Principles for Distributed Embedded Applications*, Kluwer Academic Publishers, Norwell, MA, 2002.

[46] International Organization for Standardization/International Electrotechnical Commission, ISO/IEC 7498: Informationstechnik—Kommunikation Offener Systeme—Basis-Referenzmodell, 1994.

[47] International Organization for Standardization/International Electrotechnical Commission, ISO/IEC 10731: Informationstechnik—Kommunikation Offener Systeme—Basis-Referenzmodell—Konventionen für Definition von OSI-Diensten, 1995.

[48] Etschberger, Konrad, *Controller Area Network. Grundlagen, Protokolle, Bausteine, Anwendungen*, 3rd Edition, Carl Hanser Verlag, Munich, Vienna, 2002.

[49] FlexRay, www.flexray.com.

[50] TTP Time Triggered Protocol, www.tttech.com.

[51] International Organization for Standardization, ISO 11898-4: Time Triggered CAN, 2002.

[52] Isermann, Rolf (Ed.), *Überwachung und Fehlerdiagnose. Moderne Methoden und ihre Anwendungen bei technischen Systemen*, VDI-Verlag, Düsseldorf, Germany, 1994.

[53] Birolini, Alessandro, *Reliability Engineering. Theory and Practice*, Springer-Verlag, Berlin, Heidelberg, New York, 1999.

[54] Birolini, Alessandro, *Zuverlässigkeit von Geräten und Systemen*, Springer-Verlag, Berlin, Heidelberg, New York, 1997.

[55] Ehrenberger, Wolfgang, *Software-Verifikation: Verfahren für den Zuverlässigkeitsnachweis von Software*, Carl Hanser Verlag, Munich, Vienna, 2002.

[56] U.S. Environmental Protection Agency, Control of Air Pollution from Motor Vehicles and New Motor Vehicles; Modification of Federal On-Board Diagnostic Regulations for Light-Duty Vehicles and Light-Duty Trucks; Extension of Acceptance of California OBD II Requirements, December 1998.

[57] Halang, W.A., and Konakovsky, R., *Sicherheitsgerichtete Echtzeitsysteme*, R. Oldenbourg Verlag, Munich, Vienna, 1999.

[58] Lin, Shu, and Costello, Daniel J., *Error Control Coding*, Prentice-Hall, Englewood Cliffs, NJ, 1983.

[59] Leveson, Nancy G., *Safeware. System Safety and Computers. A Guide to Preventing Accidents and Losses Caused by Technology*, Addison-Wesley, New York, 1995.

[60] Storey, Neil, *Safety-Critical Computer Systems*, Prentice-Hall, Harlow, England, 1996.

[61] Deutsches Institut für Normung e.V., DIN 25448—Ausfalleffektanalyse (Fehler-Möglichkeits- und Einfluss-Analyse), May 1990.

[62] "Der neue BMW 7er," *Automobiltechnische Zeitschrift/Motortechnische Zeitschrift*, ATZ/MTZ Extra (special issue), November 2001.

[63] International Organization for Standardization, ISO 11519: Straßenfahrzeuge—Serielle Datenübertragung mit niedriger Übertragungsrate, 1994.

[64] Byteflight, www.byteflight.de.

[65] MOST Media Orientated System Transport, www.mostcooperation.com.

[66] "Die neue Mercedes-Benz-E-Klasse," *Automobiltechnische Zeitschrift/Motortechnische Zeitschrift*, ATZ/MTZ Extra (special issue), May 2002.

[67] Bluetooth, www.bluetooth.com.

[68] LIN Local Interconnect Network, www.lin-subbus.de.

[69] Boy, J., Dudek, C., and Kuschel, S., *Projektmanagement. Grundlagen, Methoden und Techniken, Zusammenhänge*, Gabal-Verlag, Offenbach, Germany, 1998.

[70] The Motor Industry Software Reliability Association, Development Guidelines for Vehicle Based Software, 1994, http://www.misra.org.uk.

[71]   International Council on Systems Engineering, http://www.incose.org.

[72]   Balzert, Helmut, *Lehrbuch der Software-Technik*, 2nd Edition, Spektrum Akademischer Verlag, Heidelberg—Berlin, Germany, 2000.

[73]   ETAS GmbH (Ed.), ASCET V5.0 User's Guide. ETAS GmbH, Stuttgart, Germany, 2004.

[74]   Selic, B., Gullekson, G., and Ward, P.T., *Real-Time Object-Oriented Modeling*, John Wiley & Sons, New York, 1994.

[75]   Stoer, Josef, *Numerische Mathematik 1*, 8th Edition, Springer-Verlag, Berlin, Heidelberg, New York, 1999.

[76]   Kernighan, B.W., and Ritchie, D.M., *Programmieren in C*, 2nd Edition, Carl Hanser Verlag, Munich, Germany, 1990.

[77]   Broy, Manfred, *Informatik. Eine grundlegende Einführung, Vols. 1/2*, Springer-Verlag, Berlin, Heidelberg, New York, 1998.

[78]   Wirth, N., *Grundlagen und Techniken des Compilerbaus*, Addison-Wesley, Bonn, Germany, and Paris, France, 1996.

[79]   Manufacturer Supplier Relationship, Working Groups MEGMA and MEDOC, http://www.msr-wg.de.

[80]   The Motor Industry Software Reliability Association, Guidelines for the Use of the C Language in Vehicle-Based Software, 1998.

[81]   van Basshuysen, Richard, and Schäfer, Fred (Eds.), *Handbuch Verbrennungsmotor. Grundlagen, Komponenten, Systeme, Perspektiven*, 1st Edition, Vieweg-Verlag, Wiesbaden, Germany, 2002; also published as van Basshuysen, Richard, and Schäfer, Fred (Eds.), *Internal Combustion Engine Reference Handbook*, SAE International, Warrendale, PA, 2004.

[82]   Pauli, B., and Meyna, A., "Zuverlässigkeitsprognosen für elektronische Steuergeräte im Kraftfahrzeug" ("Reliability of Electronic Control Units in Motor Vehicles"; orginal German), in Proceedings of the 7th International Congress "Electronic Systems for Vehicles," Baden-Baden, Germany, September 13, 1996, ed. by VDI Society Vehicle and Transportation Technology, VDI-Berichte 1287, VDI-Verlag, Düsseldorf, Germany, 1996, pp. 87–105.

[83]   Beer, A., and Schmidt, M., "Funktionale Sicherheit Sicherheitsrelevanter Systeme im Kraftfahrzeug" ("Functional Safety of Safety Relevant Systems in Vehicles"; original German), in Proceedings of the 9th International Congress "Electronic Systems for Vehicles," Baden-Baden, Germany, October 5–6, 2000, ed. by VDI Society Vehicle and Transportation Technology, VDI-Berichte 1547, VDI-Verlag, Düsseldorf, Germany, 2000, pp. 391–409.

[84]   UML Unified Modeling Language™, www.uml.org.

[85]   Harel, D., *Statecharts. A Visual Formalism for Complex Systems, Science of Computer Programming, Vol. 8*, Elsevier Science Publishers, North Holland, 1987.

[86]   ETAS GmbH (Ed.), ERCOS^{EK} V4.2 User's Guide, ETAS GmbH, Stuttgart, Germany, 2002.

[87]   ETAS GmbH (Ed.), INCA V5.0 User's Guide, ETAS GmbH, Stuttgart, Germany, 2004.

[88]   Grams, T., *Denkfallen und Programmierfehler*, Springer-Verlag, Berlin, Heidelberg, New York, 1990.

[89]   ETAS GmbH (Ed.), Data Declaration System V2.3 User's Guide, ETAS GmbH, Stuttgart, Germany, 2001.

[90]   ETAS GmbH (Ed.), LABCAR-OPERATOR V2.0 User's Guide, ETAS GmbH, Stuttgart, Germany, 2003.

[91]   Kühner, T., Seefried, V., Litschel, M., and Schelling, H., "Realisierung Virtueller Fahrzeugfunktionen für Vernetzte Systeme auf Basis Standardisierter Software-Bausteine" ("Implementation of Virtual Vehicle Functions for Networked Systems Using Standardized Software Modules"; original German), in Proceedings of the 7th International Congress "Electronic Systems for Vehicles," Baden-Baden, Germany, September 12–13, 1996, ed. by VDI Society Vehicle and Transportation Technology, VDI-Berichte 1287, VDI-Verlag, Düsseldorf, Germany, 1996, pp. 691–708.

[92]   Institute of Electrical and Electronics Engineers: NEXUS, www.ieee-isto.org/Nexus5001.

[93]   Institute of Electrical and Electronics Engineers: JTAG IEEE 1149.1, www.ieee.org.

[94]   ETAS GmbH (Ed.), ETK S2.0 Emulator Probe for Serial Debug Interfaces, Data Sheet, ETAS GmbH, Stuttgart, Germany, 2002.

[95]   ETAS GmbH (Ed.), ETK 7.1 16-Bit Emulator Probe, Data Sheet, ETAS GmbH, Stuttgart, Germany, 2001.

[96]   Gumpinger, F., Huber, F.-M., and Siefermann, O., "BMW Car & Key Memory: Der Kunde bekommt sein individuelles Fahrzeug" ("BMW Car & Key Memory—The Customer Will Receive His Individual Vehicle"; original German), in Proceedings of the 8th International Congress "Electronic Systems for Vehicles," Baden-Baden, Germany, October 8–9, 1998, ed. by VDI Society Vehicle and Transportation Technology, VDI-Berichte 1415, VDI-Verlag, Düsseldorf, Germany, 1998, pp. 995–1007.

[97]   Singh, S., *Geheime Botschaften. Die Kunst der Verschlüsselung von der Antike bis in die Zeiten des Internet*, Deutscher Taschenbuch Verlag, Munich, Germany, 2001; also published as Singh, S., *The Code Book, Fourth Estate*, ISBN 1857028899, 2000.

ILLUSTRATION CREDITS

Fig. No.	Ref.
Robert Bosch GmbH, Stuttgart, Germany:	
1-1	[1]
1-5	[6]
1-6	[1]
2-3	[4]
2-11	[39]
2-12	[39]
2-14	[39]
2-15	[39]
2-62	[6]
ETAS GmbH, Stuttgart, Germany:	
4-27	[73]
4-29	[73]
5-26	[73]
5-27	[73]
5-28	[73]
5-29	[73]
5-30	[73]
5-43	[73]
5-54	[86]
5-55	[86]
5-56	[86]
5-57	[73, 87]
5-58	[87]
5-71	[89]
5-72	[73]
5-78	[90]
5-79	[90]
5-80	[90]
5-81	[90]
5-82	[90, 91]
5-84	[87]

ETAS GmbH, Stuttgart, Germany:

5-85	[87]
5-88	[87]
5-89	[87]
5-99	[87]

Others (outside copyright):

1-9	[9]	Uth
1-10	[10]	VDI
1-17	[23]	IBM
1-21	[17]	ASAM
1-22	[16]	OSEK
2-18	[42]	Prentice-Hall
2-20	[16]	OSEK
2-21	[16]	OSEK
2-22	[16]	OSEK
2-23	[43]	Hanser
2-24	[16]	OSEK
2-50	[16]	OSEK
2-51	[16]	OSEK
2-52	[48]	Hanser
2-58	[18, 19]	DIN, IEC
2-66	[52]	VDI
2-67	[62]	ATZ
3-21	[23]	IBM
3-22	[23]	IBM
3-24	[9]	Uth
3-26	[12]	Prentice-Hall
3-27	[12]	Prentice-Hall
3-28	[70]	MISRA
4-3	[23]	IBM
4-18	[70]	MISRA
4-28	[72]	Spektrum
5-17	[54]	Springer
5-18	[81]	Vieweg
5-21	[84]	UML
5-22	[84]	UML
5-42	[76]	Hanser
6-1	[17]	ASAM
6-2	[96]	VDI

LIST OF ACRONYMS

ABS	Antilock braking system
ACC	Adaptive cruise control
AFS	Active front steering
API	Application programming interface
ALU	Arithmetic and logic unit
CAL-RAM	Calibration RAM
CAN	Controller area network
CCP	CAN calibration protocol
CMMI®	Capability Maturity Model Integration®
CPU	Central processing unit
CSMA	Carrier sense multiple access
CSMA/CA	CSMA/collision avoidance
CSMA/CD	CSMA/collision detection
D/A	Digital-analog conversion
DMA	Direct-memory I/O access
DRAM	Dynamic RAM
DTC	Diagnostic trouble code
ECU	Electronic control unit
EEPROM	Electrical EPROM
EMC	Electromagnetic compatibility

EPROM	Erasable PROM
ESP	Electronic stability program
ETC	Electronic throttle control
FIFO	First in, first out
FMEA	Failure mode and effects analysis
FO	Fail-operational (system)
FR	Fail-reduced (system)
FS	Fail-safe (system)
FTA	Fault-tree analysis
HAL	Hardware abstraction layer
HiL	Hardware-in-the-loop (simulation)
I/O	Input/output
LOV	Line of visibility (diagrams)
MIL	Malfunction indicator light
MMI	Man/machine interface
MTTF	Mean time to failure
MTTR	Mean time to repair
NV-RAM	Nonvolatile RAM
OBD	Onboard diagnostics
OS	Operating system

PI	Proportional-plus-integral (control)
PPM	Parts per million
PROM	Programmable ROM
RAM	Random access memory
ROM	Read-only memory
SBC	Sensotronic Brake Control (by Bosch)
SiL	Software-in-the-loop (simulation)
SPICE	Software Process Improvement and Capability Determination
SRAM	Static RAM
TCS	Traction control system
TDMA	Time division multiple access
TTF	Time to failure
UML™	Unified Modeling Language™
UV	Ultraviolet
VDA	German Association of the Automotive Industry
WCET	Worst-case execution time
WCRT	Worst-case response time
XCP	Extended calibration protocol

INDEX

Page numbers followed by *f* indicate a figure.

ABOUT THE AUTHORS

Dipl.-Ing. **Jörg Schäuffele** studied Mechanical Engineering at the University of Stuttgart with a focus on control engineering. He started his professional career in 1993 with the firm of ISG GmbH, a spinoff of the Institute of Control Engineering at the University of Stuttgart. In 1995, he joined ETAS GmbH and supported the introduction of ETAS tools in numerous engineering and consulting projects with various customers in the automotive industry worldwide. From 1999 to 2001, he worked in the Systems Engineering Methods, Software Process, Tools department of the Electronics Development section at BMW Headquarters in Munich. Since 2003, he has coordinated the various product divisions at ETAS GmbH.

Dr.-Ing. **Thomas Zurawka** studied electrical engineering at the University of Stuttgart and wrote a detailed doctorate thesis on digital signal processing. He started his professional career in 1992 with ZF Friedrichshafen AG before joining Advanced Development at Robert Bosch GmbH in 1993, where he worked on real-time operating systems. Having joined ETAS in its early days, Dr. Zurawka initially developed code generators. He subsequently headed the development of the ASCET engineering tool for software development. Since 1997, he has been responsible for the overall development at ETAS. Dr. Zurawka is the CEO of ETAS GmbH.